Urban Guerrilla Warfare in Latin America

Latin America

Urban Guerrilla Warfare in Latin America

James Kohl and John Litt

The MIT Press
Cambridge, Massachusetts, and London, England

This book was set in Linotype Baskerville,
printed on Finch Title 93,
and bound in G.S.B. S/535/30 "Granite"
by The Colonial Press, Inc.
in the United States of America

Library of Congress Cataloging in Publication Data

Kohl, James.
    Urban guerrilla warfare in Latin America.

    Bibliography: p.
    1. Latin America—Politics—1948–
2. Guerrillas—Latin America.   I. Litt, John,
joint author.   II. Title.
F1414.2.K58   355.02′184′098   74–5485
ISBN 0–262–11054–7

To the Second War of Independence

Contents

4

Urban Guerrilla Warfare: Argentina 311

Acknowledgments

We have accumulated a number of debts, personal and professional, during the course of this work and would like to express our thanks to: Jaime Calderón, friend and occasional roommate, for his encouragement and criticism; Ernst Halperin, Carlos Waisman, and David Ralston for a critical reading of portions of the manuscript at various phases of completion; Fabio Guzmán for a month's research assistance; Michelle Huggins and Geri Younggren for typing a number of chapters; and our friends in Winchester, Massachusetts for their hospitality during a difficult month. An evening with Jean Marc von der Weid added insight to our understanding of the Brazilian struggle. Finally, to Marjorie Rekant for her love, understanding, and varied assistance during the past two years.

November 1973
JK
JL

1
Introduction

Nixon, Frei, and Pinochet
up to this day this bitter
month of September 1973,
with Bordaberry, Garrastazú, and Banzer,
hyenas ravening
our history, rodents gnawing
at flags that were raised
with so much blood and fire,
hellish predators
wallowing in haciendas,
satraps bribed a thousand times over
and sellouts, scared
by the wolves of Wall Street,
machines starving for pain,
stained by the sacrifice
of a martyred people,
prostitute merchants
of bread and American air,
deadly seneschals, a herd
of whorish bosses
with no other law but torture
and the lashing hunger of the people.*

Urban guerrilla warfare in Latin America first came to the attention of the North American public during the late 1960s. Portrayed as "terrorists," rather than as revolutionaries, urban guerrillas have been presented in the media largely through their actions, with no sense of their history, direction, or social context. Diplomatic kidnappings and occasional assassinations are newsworthy events; but their newsworthiness derives from spectacle and drama and thus obscures the underlying relationship of the urban guerrilla to the revolutionary process. News is a commodity, and as such it is subject to the social forces which dictate its production and distribution. Hence it should occasion no surprise that sensationalist journalism remains pervasive.

* Anonymous 1973 revision of Pablo Neruda's *Las Satrapias*, written in 1948 during another repression of the Chilean Left. For the original see Neruda, *Obras Completas*, vol. I (Buenos Aires: Losada, 1957), p. 472.

It is the purpose of this book to attempt to redress this distortion and to explore the origins, development, strategy, and tactics of urban guerrilla warfare in Latin America.

Urban guerrilla warfare is simply the latest stage in the struggle for <u>social reform</u> in this hemisphere, where for the last seventy years the United States has exercised unchallenged hegemony and has consistently placed itself in opposition to all forces of social change. The Cold War polarization of issues into a simple communist-anticommunist formula has served to mask what can only be seen as obstruction, penetration, and interference. Since World War II, this formula has served as the official rationale for the engagement of American power in three extraordinary efforts to prevent popular structural reform: Guatemala (1954), Cuba (1961), and the Dominican Republic (1965).[1] These incidents provide important background for an understanding of the continental framework in which urban guerrilla warfare is waged.

Cold War and Counterrevolution

In both Cuba and Guatemala, American-supported mercenaries staged invasions with the intent of overthrowing governments bent on serious reform. The 1954 attack on Guatemala, hatched by the Central Intelligence Agency, was launched after the government of Jacobo Arbenz Guzmán initiated expropriation of lands owned by the United Fruit Company.[2] The coup was classic and provided a model for the later attempt against Fidel Castro. Arbenz Guzmán was branded a communist, nominally due to the presence of communists in his government, and United States aid to the country was suspended. At the same time, military aid to neighboring Honduras and Nicaragua was increased, an act which had the effect of frightening and alienating the Guatemalan military establishment. John Peurifoy, a veteran of counterinsurgency operations in Greece, was appointed U.S. ambassador, and a mercenary force under Colonel Carlos Cas-

[1] The Cuban Missile Crisis is omitted here because the confrontation involved big power rivalry, with the hostility between the United States and Cuba as a secondary issue.

[2] For a brief discussion of the coup and the role of United Fruit see David Horowitz, *The Free World Colossus,* rev. ed. (New York: Hill and Wang, 1971), pp. 166–181; and Richard Barnet, *Intervention and Revolution* (New York: World, 1968), pp. 229–236.

tillo Armas was recruited and trained by the CIA in Honduras. When Arbenz Guzmán managed to obtain arms from Czechoslovakia, this was cited as proof of his subservience to Moscow. Guatemalan recourse to international arbitration was frustrated by Secretary of State John Foster Dulles at the Tenth Inter-American Conference. As Guatemalan Foreign Minister Toriello vainly tried to plead his case, the Castillo Armas force, backed by American air support, toppled the government. The new regime headed by Castillo Armas revoked reform legislation, returning more land to United Fruit than had been lost, and was rewarded with massive American aid ($90 million for the period 1954–1965, as compared to $600 thousand for the ten years before 1954).[3]

The struggle for social change continued after Arbenz Guzmán's downfall. In 1960, CIA preparations for the Bay of Pigs invasion of Cuba outraged nationalist military men and led to the November 13 revolt. The rebellion was crushed and the invasion of Cuba staged, but the rebel officers took up arms and began guerrilla warfare in rural Guatemala. By 1965, the guerrillas had succeeded in gaining some support among peasants who remembered Arbenz Guzmán, and as the specter of revolutionary change again hovered over the nation the United States once more stepped into the breach, assisting the Guatemalan government in a campaign of civil terror that was in many respects similar to the later Phoenix Program in Vietnam. In 1966–1967, thousands of peasants and revolutionaries were arrested, tortured, and murdered. The rural movement floundered under the murderous onslaught of the military. The guerrillas then retreated into the cities only to find that violence had followed them. Death squadrons (government-sponsored terrorists) were formed to conduct the urban repression, thus allowing the government to make official disavowals of all forms of violence. The reign of terror continues to this day, as thousands of liberals and leftists, including judges, senators, workers, writers, and students, have been tortured and murdered.[4]

---

3 Horowitz, *Free World Colossus*, p. 180.
4 Guatemala's "pacification" is detailed in Eduardo Galeano, *Guatemala: Occupied Country* (New York: Monthly Review, 1969), pp. 59–82 and Norman Gall, "Slaughter in Guatemala," *New York Review of Books*, 20 May 1971, pp. 13–17.

America's second postwar confrontation with structural reform in Latin America occurred in Cuba, where the successful 1959 Revolution threatened to create an irreparable breach in United States dominance in the region. Although the communist character of the Castro regime was cited as a threat to hemispheric security and thus as reason for its overthrow, plans for intervention had, in fact, been seriously entertained even before Castro seized power. However, the opposition to the Cuban Revolution, both on the island and in the United States, crystallized when Castro undertook to meet his commitment to social reform. A strident anti-Americanism, the product of reciprocal American hostility (i.e., against agrarian and social reform), growing Soviet economic involvement, and the increasing importance of the Communist Party (*Partido Socialista Popular;* People's Socialist Party) in the Cuban government, finally led President Kennedy to activate interventionist plans that had been concocted by the CIA during the Eisenhower years.

The result was the Bay of Pigs operation, which was based on a formula similar to that used in Guatemala seven years earlier. By early 1961, a force of some 1,400 Cuban exiles had been trained and equipped; on April 17, they landed at Playa Girón, fully expecting American airpower to destroy communication facilities and distribute anti-Castro propaganda. At the last moment, however, Kennedy balked at supplying air support. Whatever the reasons for his decision, it was apparent that the plan was defective.[5] The decisive difference between Arbenz Guzmán and Castro was that while Fidel controlled the entire state apparatus, including the army and the popular militias, Arbenz Guzmán did not. American air superiority might have protected the beachhead and disrupted the country, but it could not destroy the Revolutionary Armed Forces: little short of American combat troops could have attempted this. The Guatemalan model for counterrevolution thus met a stunning defeat, and Presi-

---

For a brief discussion of United States involvement in the origins of Guatemalan death squads see José M. Fortuny, "Guatemala: The Political Situation and Revolutionary Politics," *World Marxist Review,* February 1967, pp. 57–58.

[5] This judgment is in terms of the overthrow of the Castro government, not the internal growth of the CIA, a development which is examined in a provocative essay by Andrew St. George, "Watergate: The Cold War Comes Home," *Harpers,* November 1973, pp. 68–82.

dent Kennedy was faced with his first international reverse.

Four years later, the Dominican Republic exploded in the Latin American equivalent of the Paris Commune, again putting the intentions of the United States to the test. After the assassination of dictator Rafael Trujillo in May 1961, latent social and political tensions surfaced; and when reformer Juan Bosch was elected president in December 1962, it seemed that the country was going to begin the social reconstruction which was so much in order. However, Bosch's tenure was abbreviated through a bloodless military coup in September 1963, and Donald Reid Cabral assumed power at the head of a triumvirate. Reid Cabral's temporizing succeeded only in antagonizing almost everyone. On April 24, 1965, a planned military coup was discovered, and attempts by loyalist officers to remove the conspirators from their commands forced the rebels to begin prematurely. Due to the change in timing the coup could not proceed smoothly, and its leaders called the people into the streets to support Bosch's return.

The situation became insurrectionary as military units and civilian commandos fought to restore a progressive government. The police crumbled rapidly—indeed, the elite American-trained *cascos blancos* ("white helmets": riot police) fled the streets for fear of attack—and the rightist military bordered on collapse. At this point the United States intervened; 23,000 American troops were landed in Santo Domingo and the revolution died stillborn. Under the guise of preventing another Cuba, the United States created another Guatemala. The legacy of the invasion includes re-Trujilloization of the country under some of the late tyrant's flunkeys, continued misery for most of the population, death squads, and police terror.[6]

Foquismo and the Continental Revolution

The Cuban experience in the seizure and defense of revolutionary power served as an inspiration and a model to the generation of the 1960s. Its effect on traditional reformist parties was immense. Chal-

[6] Official violence since 1965 has claimed at least 2,000 lives and over 150,000 people have fled the terror: Carlos María Gutiérrez, *The Dominican Republic: Rebellion and Repression* (New York: Monthly Review, 1972), p. 92; and Norman Gall, "Santo Domingo: The Politics of Terror," *New York Review of Books,* 22 July 1971, pp. 15–19.

lenges to the older leaders soon arose as a new generation turned to the left and the Cuban example. Structural reform through parliamentary maneuvering has always been problematic, and the example of Cuba showed younger militants how they might avoid the dilemmas of stalemate and coup. In Venezuela and Peru, two of the continent's most publicized reformist parties, *Acción Democratica* (Democratic Action) and APRA (*Alianza Popular Revolucionario Americano;* American Popular Revolutionary Alliance), encountered serious doctrinal divisions in the early 1960s. In both countries, the left wings bolted the party, regrouped under the name MIR (*Movimiento de la Izquierda Revolucionario;* Movement of the Revolutionary Left), and took up Cuban-style rural guerrilla war. By 1965, guerrillas were operating in Venezuela, Peru, and a number of other countries.

The Cuban doctrine of guerrilla warfare, codified in the writings of Che Guevara and Régis Debray, stressed the electric effect produced by a small band of guerrillas (the *foco:* nucleus) in the countryside.[7] The guerrillas would be "the small motor which moves the large motor of revolution." Certain theoretical viewpoints that downgraded the role of mass organizing and urban militance became sanctified in the course of the Cubans' struggle to obtain the support of Latin American Communist Parties for rural guerrilla struggle. In their attempt to show that the Cuban Revolution was in no way "exceptional," the formulators of the *foco* theory unfortunately overlooked certain crucial features of the Cuban experience, notably the rural support that Fidel had received from the established parties and the importance of the urban underground in hastening Batista's defeat. Moreover, when it actually came time to take to the mountains, most *foquistas* did not pay sufficient attention to security and careful recruitment.[8] A few organizations were able to assure their survival (in Venezuela and Colombia), but none was able to mount a sustained revolutionary challenge. The *foco* period is a chronicle of failure: *focos* were defeated in Argentina (1959, 1964, 1968), Brazil (1962,

[7] Régis Debray, *Revolution in the Revolution?* (New York: Grove Press, 1967). Criticism of *foquismo* is collected in Leo Huberman and Paul Sweezy, eds., *Régis Debray and the Latin American Revolution* (New York: Monthly Review, 1968).
[8] Héctor Béjar, a veteran of the Peruvian ELN, perceptively analyzes the difficulties of *foquismo* in *Peru 1965: Notes on a Guerrilla Experience* (New York: Monthly Review, 1970).

1967, 1969, 1970), Bolivia (1967, 1970), Colombia (1961), the Dominican Republic (1960, 1973), Ecuador (1962), Paraguay (1959, 1962), and Peru (1963, 1965). The list of revolutionary leaders lost in the rural struggle is extensive: Camilo Torres, Luis de la Puente, Guillermo Lobatón, Marco Antonio Yon Sosa, Luis Turcios Lima, Fabricio Ojeda, J. R. Masetti, Inti and Coco Peredo, Francisco Caamaño Deño, and Che Guevara. The death of Guevara, strategist and advocate of guerrilla warfare, symbolizes the failure of *foquismo*.

If Guevara's rural strategy did not meet with success, other aspects of his doctrine have survived his demise. Most important is the notion of Continental Revolution, "two, three, many Vietnams." For a time, the idea seems to have been a part of Cuban national security planning. Because they knew that a social revolution would inevitably attract Washington's hostility, the Cubans at first sought cover under the Soviet nuclear umbrella. However, the missile crisis of October 1962 demonstrated that the Russians did not consider Cuba essential to the security of the Soviet bloc, and the bombing of North Vietnam, beginning in 1965, only reinforced Cuban fears. Guevara had apparently begun to think in terms of a continental revolution as early as 1960, but it was not until the Bay of Pigs invasion in 1961 that the idea received much attention. The first attempt at continental guerrilla warfare came in 1963 when Javier Heraud landed at Puerto Maldonado, Peru. The strategic plan called for Jorge Masetti, an Argentine journalist who had been the first director of the Cuban news agency *Prensa Latina,* to establish a *foco* in northern Argentina and eventually link up with his Peruvian counterparts. Heraud's Peruvian group was quickly defeated, however, and Masetti's group fell in early 1964.[9]

By 1966, plans were underway for a grand strategy involving *focos* in Peru, Argentina, Brazil, and Bolivia (the latter to be personally led by Che). While daring in conception and grandiose in scope, the plan was fraught with difficulty, and its progress would be dogged by ill-

[9] The Bolivian go-betweens, Roberto "Coco" Peredo, Guido "Inti" Peredo, and Rodolfo Saldana, escaped the authorities' attention and were later involved in Guevara's Bolivian *foco*. For their connections here see: the biography of Coco Peredo in *Granma,* 26 September 1968, p. 2, and Ricardo Rojo, *My Friend Che* (New York: Dial, 1968), Chapter 7. A reply from Masetti's lieutenants, Evaristo Mendez and Juan Héctor Jouve, to Rojo appears in *Granma,* 3 October 1968, p. 8.

luck. *Focos* were not established in the first three countries, and Che's Bolivian group ran into serious trouble soon after its inception. The obstructionism of the Bolivian Communist Party proved a serious matter, for although the communists were nominally involved in the venture, they did not support it. The early 1967 Cuban polemics against the Venezuelan Communist Party might just as well have been directed against the Bolivians. By the time of the OLAS (Organization of Latin American Solidarity) conference in July 1967, the situation was desperate. Compounding the problems was the fact that Che found himself operating without an urban infrastructure and in an isolated region, among a sparse and inhospitable peasantry.

A month after the *foco,* now calling itself the **ELN** (*Ejercito de Liberación Nacional*; Army of National Liberation), initiated hostilities, North American military advisors and CIA agents were on the scene. Alarmed by the guerrillas' combativeness and style of operation, the decision was made to train 600 select Bolivian troops in counterinsurgency. Six months later, the *foco* was isolated and its area of operations was sealed by government troops. On October 7, 1967, a company of Bolivian Rangers made contact, and after a brief battle the wounded Guevara was taken prisoner. On the next day, October 8, the guerrilla leader was executed in the village of Vallegrande; Eduardo González, a Cuban exile and CIA agent, was there to confirm the kill. What then was the apparatus behind the death of Che? [10]

Subversion and Intervention

The Green Berets involved in the Bolivian counterinsurgency operation were members of the Eighth Special Forces unit based at Fort Gulick, Panama Canal Zone. While the action culminating in Guevara's death was the most publicized of the unit's mercenary forays, it was but one of over 400 such actions during the period 1962–1968.[11] The elite Special Forces were conceived during the Kennedy Administration in response to the challenge of the 1960s—national

---

[10] Richard Gott traces the role of the CIA in Guevara's death in *Guerrilla Movements in Latin America* (Garden City, New York: Doubleday, 1971), pp. 474–481. An exposé of the uses of American counterinsurgency appears in Andrew St. George, "How the U.S. Got Che," *True,* April 1969, pp. 29–31, 90–100.

[11] Michael Klare, *War Without End* (New York: Vintage, 1972), p. 306.

liberation movements within the radius of American hegemony. Kennedy's policy of flexible response broke fundamentally with those strategic assumptions of the postwar period which had been based on the idea of collective security against an external threat. Security was now seen to be, in large part, a matter of suppressing indigenous revolutionary forces. Cuba and Vietnam demonstrated the necessity of versatile, resolute, and informed counterinsurgency techniques.[12] The result was an apparatus extending from the halls of academia (sparked by an avalanche of foundation support for "relevant" research) to military forces abroad.

The strategy which developed was twofold: a preventative program aimed at winning the allegiance of the population through loans, technical assistance, and propaganda—the Alliance for Progress; and, beneath the velvet glove, the mailed fist of repression—military advisors, the Central Intelligence Agency, and USAID's Office of Public Safety, all supported by a sophisticated technological and logistical apparatus. Since the revolutionary thrust of the early 1960s sprang from attempts to replicate the Cuban *foco* experience, counterinsurgency focused on the development of methods for the domination of the countryside: American Air Force planes mapped the rural terrain; social scientists studied the particularities and history of peasant society;[13] Peace Corps volunteers dispensed tidbits of "modernization" and American goodwill; USAID loans provided bridges and roads linking town and country; and, under the impetus of American advisors, Latin American armed forces began civic action programs to endear themselves to the peasantry by the construction of public works projects. When these well-publicized tokens to alleviate social unrest failed, the response was force, applied with ever greater sophistication and effect.

[12] Klare, *War Without End,* pp. 31–68.
[13] A bungled attempt on the part of United States social scientists to infiltrate the Chilean intellectual community and gather intelligence data, the famous Project Camelot, is discussed in a series of essays edited by Irving Louis Horowitz, *The Rise and Fall of Project Camelot* (Cambridge, Mass.: M.I.T. Press, 1967); similar, but more successful projects, are analyzed in Eric Wolf and Joseph Jorgenson, "Anthropology on the Warpath in Thailand," *New York Review of Books,* 19 November 1970, pp. 26–35; and David Ransom, "The Berkeley Mafia and the Indonesian Massacre," *Ramparts,* October 1970, p. 27.

Behind the Latin American military and their North American advisors (administered by the Pentagon's Military Assistance Program) lies a sophisticated repressive infrastructure developed by modern technology. If the rural guerrilla held the advantage of secrecy, seclusion, and initiative in the early 1960s, the situation had reversed by the latter years of the decade. Reconnaissance aircraft, infrared photography, magnetic, acoustic, olfactory, and seismic detectors, portable radar units, and computer data banks gathered and collated by an invisible corps of mandarins stripped the guerrilla of his earlier edge. *Foquismo* was to become a chronicle of heroic, but tragic resistance against the Yankee behemoth until subsistence itself would become an achievement for the rural guerrilla.

No less a failure was the Alliance for Progress. Washington's widely publicized hemispheric program for socioeconomic development soon proved ineffectual in terms of meeting the real needs of Latin America. President Johnson virtually abandoned the Alliance: the recognition of the Brazilian military regime in March 1964 shattered its underlying democratic-constitutional tenets, and the invasion of the Dominican Republic a year later underscored this shift in policy. The Johnson and Nixon administrations abandoned any remnant of concern for democracy and stressed instead the need for internal order, even if this could be accomplished only through dictatorial regimes. Indeed, the two administrations enjoyed the closest of relationships with the most tyrannical governments in the hemisphere.

In this climate of increased repression, a new form of revolutionary warfare emerged in response to the realities of the late 1960s. Stalemated in the isolated and often inhospitable countryside, guerrilla warfare was reconceived in an urban milieu. Here again the advantages of surprise and initiative, clandestinity and mobility could be reasserted. The strategy was best applied to the highly urbanized areas of the South Atlantic—Montevideo in Uruguay; Buenos Aires, Córdoba, and Rosario in Argentina; and the urban-industrial triangle of Rio-São Paulo-Belo Horizonte in Brazil—where the guerrilla could move undetected among the dense population. The urban guerrilla also enjoyed an initial advantage owing to the fact that counterinsurgency techniques evolved to meet the revolutionary challenge in the countryside were largely inapplicable in the city.

The first line of defense against the urban guerrillas came to be the policeman, with his feel for the city, his natural ties to the population, and his network of contacts. Since 1962, when agents from USAID's Office of Public Safety secretly advised the Venezuelan police in counterguerrilla techniques during the FALN (*Fuerzas Armadas de Liberación Nacional*; Armed Forces of National Liberation) offensive, that department's role in Latin America has steadily increased. In 1972, Public Safety programs involving the training, assisting, and equipping of police in 15 Latin American countries cost the United States nearly $3 million. Over 2,000 Latin American policemen have been trained in the United States and the total figure, including those taught at home, is far greater (e.g., over 100,000 Brazilian police have been instructed through the Office of Public Safety).[14]

Thus, in the city as in the countryside, North American expertise has been directed toward maintenance of the status quo. Ostensibly, aid of this nature is a counterpoise to internal subversion. The trend of increased American support to dictatorial regimes, however, suggests a commitment to stability and "security" in a region desperately in need of rapid and drastic change.

All this, of course, is no departure from historic American diplomatic objectives. Early hegemonic designs are visible as far back as 1823, when the Monroe Doctrine, with its no-colonization and non-intervention clauses, proscribed the Old World from meddling in the affairs of the New. The growth of North American power is reflected in the transformation of the Doctrine from rhetoric to reality. An examination of the record reveals the consistency of this process. During the early years of the nation, United States military forces intervened a dozen times in the Spanish colonies of Florida, Cuba, and Mexico. After the purchase of Florida (1821) and the conquest of the Mexican southwest (1848), continental expansion halted; but as the economic penetration of Latin America increased, intervention took the form of commitment of military forces to protect American interests.

During the years 1830–1945, United States troops were dispatched

---

[14] *North American Congress on Latin America* (NACLA), "AID Police Programs for Latin America, 1971–1972," July–August 1971, p. 3, and "Document: AID Police Plan for 1971–1972," pp. 13–14; Klare, *War Without End,* pp. 241–269.

to Latin America on some 70 occasions.[15] These incidents were most frequent in the Dollar Diplomacy period (1898–1932) when American strategy, influenced by Captain Alfred Thayer Mahan's arguments for an imperial navy, sought to transform the Caribbean into an American lake. This policy is directly responsible for Panamanian "independence" in 1903, an event which is well worth reviewing as illustrative of the conjuncture of economic and strategic interests underlying American diplomacy in the twentieth century.

Impressed by the need for a canal across the Isthmus after the Spanish-American War and frustrated in negotiations with Colombia over purchase of the area, President Theodore Roosevelt turned to subversion. The Roosevelt government supported a successionist clique and the New Panama Canal Company contributed financially to the conspirators. On November 3, 1903, the coup began, and United States warships appeared off the Isthmus to prevent the landing of Colombian troops. The formula was successful: four days later a sovereign Panama was recognized by the Roosevelt administration, with Philippe Bunau-Varilla, Chief Engineer for the New Panama Canal Company, as the government's Ambassador in Washington. Bunau-Varilla proceeded to sign a treaty that gave the United States control of the canal and the right to intervene in Panamanian affairs. Acquisition of the Canal Zone provided the United States with a strategic foothold in Central America which has since been transformed into a formidable military outpost and a staging ground for subversion in the region.

The most direct result of Dollar Diplomacy was the establishment of a series of American "protectorates" (Cuba, Panama, Nicaragua, Haiti, Dominican Republic, Puerto Rico) whose alleged purpose was to tutor the inhabitants in the fundamentals of democratic rule. The result has been quite the opposite: the legacy of American intervention has been the destruction of all indigenous attempts at reform and the establishment of the most durable and vicious dictatorships in Latin America (Batista, Trujillo, the Duvalliers, the Somozas). Although intervention is generally associated with the marine constabu-

15 A list of the "Use of U.S. Armed Forces in Foreign Countries 1789–1945," is provided by Senator Everett Dirksen in the *Congressional Record* 23 June 1969, pp. 16840–16843.

laries and customs receiverships of Dollar Diplomacy, and schoolbooks invariably follow with a chapter on the Good Neighbor Policy, the fact is that the pattern still continues under a variety of forms.

There are clearly a variety of options available to implement the American policy of subversion. Most obvious are overt military intrusions, whether with American or native troops. Dramatic and revealing as these incidents may be, however, they are exceptional in that they represent an extreme response to a "hopeless" situation in which policy is "overtaken by events," and then often entail considerable loss of prestige. Less visible is an entire spectrum of instruments with which it is possible to co-opt or disable reforms. Economic options include aid cutoffs, credit squeezes, and, in most cases, significant market control over a developing nation's exports. An economic blockade will invariably create short-run bottlenecks and deprivations, and offers the advantages of unobtrusiveness and legality. However crippling an economic blockade may be, though, its effects are usually insufficient in themselves to topple a government, as the examples of Cuba, Chile, and Rhodesia demonstrate. Economic pressure, in such forms as the International Monetary Fund's notorious stabilization program, may succeed in moderating and redirecting a wavering reformist government (e.g., the Bolivian MNR in 1956), but such action is merely corrective.

In situations where the government is either relatively secure or seriously committed to reform, covert support of domestic oppositionists can be utilized. This is a multiform process which can involve infiltration of unions, economic sabotage, organized right-wing terror, psychological warfare to arouse the middle classes, and incitement of the military. An economic blockade can be effective in exacerbating economic chaos; for example, in Chile (1972–1973) and Guyana (1963) the decisive erosion of the government's authority began with crippling, foreign-sponsored transport strikes. The final blow usually takes the form of a military coup, as in Brazil (1964), Bolivia (1971), and Chile (1973). The advantages of this approach to the restoration of the status quo ante include flexibility and invisibility, since nationals rather than Americans are directly involved in its implementation.

United States policy has remained remarkably consistent under the last four administrations. Presidents Eisenhower, Kennedy, Johnson, and Nixon have pursued policies divergent in style and emphasis, but with a continuous underlying aversion to serious reform. The Alliance for Progress notwithstanding, the United States has shown a preference for nominal over structural reform. Thus, when a government seriously begins to overhaul the social order, as Allende did in Chile, the United States opts for sedition, subversion, and often turns to conservative charlatans like Eduardo Frei.[16] Serious reform involves issues of economic independence and development, redistribution of wealth, socialization of production, agrarian reform, alteration of social relations, and genuine popular participation. Effective reform necessarily provokes confrontation and class conflict. Thus, for the structural reformer the crux of the matter is how to obtain the power with which to confront the dominant classes. The electoral road may lead to the presidency and a few seats in parliament, but the legislature, courts, provincial governments, and military will remain under the control of the ruling classes.

Complete control of the state thus appears a necessity for any significant structural change in Latin America. Much of the impact of the Cuban Revolution devolves from its solution to the problem of power; Fidel Castro survived and was able to implement basic reforms because he first destroyed Batista's state and disbanded its army. Castro's triumph seemed to many leftists to confirm that the road to social change was through revolutionary warfare. The menacing presence of the United States added the postulate that further advance would necessarily be of continental dimensions to offset the continental scope of its opponents. Urban guerrilla warfare is one result of the widespread diffusion of these views. It is a continuation of the project begun by Che Guevara, who had personally learned the lessons of Guatemala and Cuba. Continental revolution did not die in Bolivia with Che; urban guerrila warfare is an attempt to bring it to fruition.

16 For United States complicity in the coup against the Allende government see Betty and James Petras, "Ballots into Bullets: Epitaph for a Peaceful Revolution," *Ramparts*, November 1973, p. 28; *NACLA*, "Chile: The Story Behind the Coup," October 1973. The scenario for the coup, per the Pentagon's POLITICA simulation project, is revealed by one of its designers, Daniel del Solar, in "Allende's Death: A Pentagon Checkmate," *New Times*, 3 October 1973, pp. 1–2.

Urban Guerrilla Warfare. I. Strategy

Urban guerrilla warfare can be best understood in contrast to earlier strategies of revolutionary struggle, namely, urban insurrection, Maoism, and *foquismo*. This comparison involves two axes: urban–rural, and mass line–armed line. The first axis is a question of strategic terrain: Where can the regime be most expeditiously attacked? Where are its contradictions most acute and explosive? The second axis concerns method and, in particular, the relationship between political and military forces: How much emphasis should be placed on programs to organize workers, peasants, and students en masse for the overthrow of the regime? How much on implementing a military program, that is, the formula for employing violence in the revolutionary process?

The relationship between mass line and armed line is complicated by the fact that the strategic objective of revolution is conditioned by political considerations. Conventional military usage distinguishes tactics, strategy, and policy as distinct levels of analysis: policy defines the overall political objectives; strategy, the role of force in attaining them; and tactics, the use of force in specific situations. For both social and political revolution, the strategic objective is the seizure of state power; however, the respective strategies necessarily differ. The seizure of state power is itself the policy objective of political revolution, whereas it is but a means to social transformation in the case of social revolution. Hence, because the actual struggle for power will lay the foundation for the new regime, the strategy (and tactics) of social revolution must encourage greater and qualitatively different mass participation than is the case otherwise. Herein lies the significance of the mass line and the necessity for its coordination with the armed line: the people must be aroused and organized during the struggle in order to prepare them for the revolutionary transformation to come.

It is important to recognize that neither axis constitutes a set of exhaustive, exclusive categories. It is not a question, for example, of revolution in the city versus revolution in the countryside, but of the relative role of each, the dynamic balance between them over time. The movements examined in this book are armed and urban, but on no account should this suggest the insignificance of either rural or mass struggle.

Each of the three classic strategic models of modern revolution is based on the retrospective, and often dogmatic, formulation of a particular historical experience by the group that employed the model successfully. All of them focus on the establishment of dual power and its transformation into a single, revolutionary power. Removal of the government and the army is the sine qua non of social revolution; and, since neither will simply disappear, they must be destroyed. The revolutionary challenge must represent an alternative in terms of ideas, organization, and institutions, but most essentially it must represent a political alternative, leading to dual power.

The classic strategy is urban insurrection, based on the Russian Revolution and later attempted unsuccessfully in Germany, Estonia, and China. Insurrection begins when the masses will not, and the ruling classes cannot, continue the old regime. Taking advantage of this stalemate, the revolutionary Party seizes the urban centers of communication, transport, and administration. The insurrection is followed by a general strike and, if necessary, civil war, to eliminate the vestiges of the army and government throughout the smaller cities and countryside. The insurrection begins in the capital with the assault of a clandestine group, but it must rally the workers as well as the peasants if it is to consolidate its power. Indeed, the very conjuncture at which insurrection is possible depends on mass participation to create the necessary stalemate. In this, the revolutionary Party has a pivotal role as the agent whereby antagonisms between mass and armed lines are reconciled.

The second paradigm, Chinese-style guerrilla war, is based on peasant mobilization through land reform, peasant soviets, and the Red Army. This strategy aims at seizing land, building counterinstitutions, and militarily defending these liberated areas. Counterinstitutions are the ultimate in armed propaganda because they show the peasant the possibility and meaning of revolution. The Chinese model was repeated throughout South Asia following World War II, with varying success. Its experience is summarized in Mao's three phase formula: terrorism–guerrilla war–conventional war. The political and military bases of the theory are completely harmonious. Counterinstitutions (the political base) are possible only because the liberated territory can be defended by an army with conventional military capabilities (the military base). Maoist dual power, in stage III, is closer to a confrontation between two nation-states than to a conflict between government and insurgent. Throughout the process, it is the Party that rallies mass support and channels it into a coherent military campaign.

The third model, *foquismo*, is like Maoism insofar as both are methods of rural guerrilla warfare. However, *foquismo* differs from Maoism on the issue of liberated territory. Whereas the Yenan region could be militarily detached and defended, there is no comparable opportunity in contemporary Latin America. The army can occupy any particular patch of ground it chooses, and hence the guerrillas are forced into a war of mobility, clandestinity, and attrition. This introduces the problem of security on a greater scale than in China: neither the guerrillas nor their supporters can rely on impenetrability of terrain. Indeed, this was precisely the point at which most *focos* in Latin America fell. Security considerations can hamper mass organization and render full-scale counterinstitutions, such as peasant soviets, impossible. As embodied in the *foco* theory, these security-related problems led to a de-emphasis on mass-line work.

The important difference between *foquismo* and earlier revolutionary scenarios concerns the role of the Communist Party. In Russia, China, and Vietnam the Communist Party was a major force in both the armed-struggle and the consolidation phases; but in Cuba it only came to the fore after Castro had taken power. Subsequent rural guerrillas, notably in Guatemala, Venezuela, and especially in Bolivia, would discover that relations with the Party could prove difficult and at times treacherous. The *foco* doctrine expresses a near-complete disregard for the limited urban electoral struggles of the traditional Moscow-oriented Parties. Urban guerrillas retain this heritage from *foquismo* insofar as they believe that the armed nucleus, not the Party, is the decisive component of the revolutionary process, and that "revolutionary action creates revolutionary organization, consciousness, and conditions."

Urban guerrilla warfare is not unlike *foquismo*. Silence is the guerrilla's shield, mass militance his sword—regardless of terrain. The regime has vast resources including firepower, infrastructure, and the myth of a monolithic, omnipotent government. With resources far less developed, the insurgents must take the initiative to unravel the sinews and tendons of state power. The first target is the regime's mythic basis, its legitimacy: the notions that the government can rule, and that it should rule, must be undermined. As a preliminary to destroying its power, the government's authority must be eroded.

Two factors of extreme importance to the strategy of urban guerrilla warfare are population density and proximity to the enemy. Population density gains the guerrilla two advantages: access to supplies and relative anonymity. Weapons, autos, money, and other materials are much more accessible in cities than in rural areas. Similarly, the guerrilla can move much more freely among the "faceless masses" of the city than he could in the countryside where strangers and disturbances are readily noticed. Balancing these advantages is the fact that the city is the locus of the regime's military might. In terms of space and time, the strategic terrain of the city exacts a toll from the guerrillas. In the countryside, the authorities are more distant and require greater time to respond. Control of rural areas involves hours and tens or hundreds of miles, whereas in the urban setting these parameters are a matter of minutes and miles.

Of the strategic problems inherent in guerrilla warfare, none is so intensified in the urban terrain as the problem of controlling the level of violence. The government has the capacity for almost unlimited violence, whereas the guerrillas do not, and consequently the insurgents must exercise great caution in engaging it. Conventional wisdom has it that guerrilla war is simply a matter of creating a climate of terror which somehow leads to the collapse of the government; however, it is rare that a government find itself so politically debilitated that it can be toppled by the bold action of a few revolutionaries. In fact, terrorism has proved more effective as a means for disrupting leftist governments (e.g., Salvadore Allende) in order to provoke a military coup. Indiscriminate terror is also often the last resort of a regime which finds itself unable to control its subjects otherwise; unable to capture the guerrilla "fish," the government tries to vaporize the "water," the people, through sheer terror. In contrast, the violence of the revolutionaries must be measured, clear, and precise.

In the city, proximity to the mass media raises the visibility of guerrilla action, and may lead to an overestimation of the movement's strength. A premature action can intensify the struggle too soon and draw the guerrillas into an untimely showdown. An ill-conceived action can outrage the public, including the lower classes, and legitimize increased repression. Theoretically, there is a difference in target between the official violence against the guerrillas and that against the masses, but in fact the distinction is never clearly made as the government cannot always discriminate between the two. Indeed, the terror employed in counterinsurgency serves as a deterrent to further recruitment, and if this violence is not always targeted correctly, so much the better for the deterrence. Mass organizations (clandestine or not) are more vulnerable to repression than is the armed underground, but they potentially constitute the greater threat to the regime. While any action, whether armed or not, opens the door to repression, it is much easier for the guerrillas to provoke a holocaust in the city, leading to their isolation from the urban masses terrorized by the government.

In addition to normal law-enforcement and military procedures, two instruments of government policy deserve special attention: torture and death squads. Neither is acknowledged by the regime; both are disavowed as individual excesses by the officers involved. Torture is employed for several reasons: to obtain information, to dissuade guerrillas and their supporters, and sometimes to indulge sadism in the police-military apparatus. Although psychopathology may be an important explanation for the behavior of individual officers, on balance torture must be judged an instrument of policy. Few governments lack the power to prevent the use of torture, yet torturers are rarely pursued with much vigor. The following graphic example from Brazil is illustrative:

He had been held for six months and looked like a rag. Only the eyes on his face were intact. His cheeks, his head, his hands, were covered with welts; his broken jaw was reset crookedly; his body was a mass of scars.

Monotonously, he told how he had to walk all day with a weight of about 20 pounds on his head, always walking, never sleeping. Then he was taken into "the room" and beaten, kicked, burned, knocked unconscious, then awakened and the whole thing started again. They tortured him for a solid week without asking a single question. Ribs broken, nose broken, jaw broken, fingers broken, face smashed. A doctor brought him around and the interrogation began: electricity, water torture, limbs broken with iron bars. Yes, he talked: he denounced two of his friends who had disappeared three months earlier. Then, after he talked, they castrated him. He told me that to celebrate Christmas Eve some of the torturers spent the night tormenting prisoners without ever even questioning them.[17]

Death squadrons are a parody of guerrillas insofar as they enable the authorities to act out their vision of revolutionary war—bombings, kidnapping, and murder, along with some "mass mobilization" of civilian thugs, criminals, and military rightists. What distinguishes death squads from other right-wing attack groups, is their organic connection to the official repressive apparatus. Undoubtedly, nonofficial counterguerrilla groups exist, but alone they lack the organization, intelligence, and firepower to be much of a threat to the guerrillas.

Extraofficial violence presents a formidable problem for the urban guerrilla because it promotes confusion and war weariness; the guerrilla's response should be in a form that will clarify and redefine. Some respite can be obtained by direct assaults on the responsible authorities, ranging from letters to nocturnal visits to assassination. It is not necessary that the guerrilla be able to counter every torturer or death squad member; it is sufficient that each comes to understand that the guerrilla can deal with him in particular. Some successes against clandestine repression can undoubtedly be scored; however, whatever forces are used against the covert police-military apparatus are withdrawn from other fronts. To be drawn into an exclusively military confrontation too early is to court isolation and subsequent disaster.

Urban Guerrilla Warfare. II. Organization

Urban guerrilla warfare is organized through an underground network of the sort used by partisans, resistance fighters, and, to some extent, the underworld. Clandestinity and secrecy are much more im-

[17] Lionel Rotcage, "Going for a Ride with Brazil's Guerrilleros," *Atlas*, August 1970, p. 51.

portant in the city than in a liberated territory defended by a people's army, or even in a contested area. The basic principle is compartmentalization: militants are grouped into cells which are independent in the sense that a member of one ideally knows very little about the operation of the others. Regardless of their function, whether it be propaganda, intelligence action, or support, an attempt is made to keep the cells clearly separate. As the movement grows, various operational capabilities are distributed throughout the organization, thus limiting the damage caused by the loss of any particular cell. Compartmentalization is essentially a matter of information: each member knows only what is essential to his or her activities. Thus, the details of any particular action are known only to the individuals who plan, orchestrate, and execute it, while the specifics of strategic planning are known only to the central executive. Nevertheless, the movement's politics, overall organization, orientation, and strategy must be understood by everyone.

The government's principal sources of information are infiltrators, defectors, informers (whether deliberate or accidental), and tortured revolutionaries. Infiltration and defection can usually, but not always, be handled by careful recruitment. Informers pose a more difficult problem; essential to its solution is the development of a counterintelligence network to provide information on the authorities. It is the torture of prisoners, though, that provides the most important source of information for the authorities, a process described by the Brazilian João Quartim:

Brutally tortured, the four militants who were caught ended by confessing everything; the police and the army were able to make dozens of arrests. The vicious circle, arrests—torture—confession—new arrests, rapidly threatened the very survival of the organization.[18]

The cycle of arrest and torture is the foundation of counterguerrilla operations. To combat it, insurgent groups have several resources, none totally effective. Most basic is to shelter their members in the first place. If all members observe security precautions, know only

18 João Quartim, "Régis Debray and the Brazilian Revolution," *New Left Review*, January–February 1970, p. 62.

what they must, and maintain low profiles, the chances of exposure are reduced for each individual, and the value of any individual to the authorities, in event of capture, is lessened. Needless actions entail needless exposure and must be avoided. Supporters and sympathizers should be protected as much as the guerrillas themselves: they are the roots of the movement. Security must be understood and practiced by sympathizers as well as by militants. Direct action can ease security problems, but in the long run the only security lies in victory.

Within the organization, information is closely related to the issue of centralization. Extreme centralization is typified by hierarchy, a multileveled arrangement of different structural units. In contrast, decentralized control is exemplified by what might be called tissue, the replication of similar units at the same level. A hierarchy can easily mobilize all units for action, but is vulnerable to decapitation. A tissue can resist effectively, since total elimination would require the destruction of each unit individually, but it cannot mobilize. Each type has its strengths and its weaknesses, and the real issue, of course, is what proportion of each to employ. The formula most commonly used is "tactical autonomy, strategic centralism," meaning that base units operate on their own initiative, but within guidelines established at the top and with special regard to priority decisions of the central command.

Behind much of the discussion of centralization lurks the experience of Latin American Communist Parties. To revolutionary ex-Party members, centralization is often synonomous with bureaucratic control and inaction. As a result of their stifling Party life, these militants are often inclined toward radical decentralization and action for the sake of action. The Brazilian Carlos Marighella sums up this point of view when he states that "coordination must cease when it obstructs action."

However, the problem cannot be solved through such simple correctives. Overreaction to Communist Party centralism can lead to such a concern with action that the actions themselves lose coherence. The problem is acute when it comes to recruitment. Just after the initiation of action there is usually an opportunity to incorporate large numbers of recruits attracted by the headlines. However, there is no guarantee that any given individual will bear up under the strains of the struggle, especially if torture is introduced. Whether through betrayal, desertion, or bungling, the results of wholesale integration of unknown individuals can be devastating. The Leninist maxim "better fewer, but better" is appropriate.

Central direction is also at issue when there are numerous guerrilla formations. Separate organizations can provide an additional level of compartmentalization, but the likely difficulties probably swamp this gain in security.[19] Divergent goals (e.g., Peronism versus socialism) or divergent methods (e.g., Leninism versus Guevaraism) can lead to hostility and, in the extreme, factional violence. Also, an organization may attempt a foolish and destructive action merely to get on the scoreboard.

Urban Guerrilla Warfare. III. Action

Armed actions must be viewed in terms of their target, their audience, and their context. A coherent military line selects the target (what is to be attacked) and the audience (who will be affected) based on an analysis of the context (the total social conjuncture at any moment). This is one reason why similar actions at different times or in different countries often lead to vastly different outcomes. In the abstract, it may be simple to identify certain individuals or institutions as exploiters or agents of repression, but this does not insure that an attack on them will promote awareness of that fact. The government and the media will portray an assassinated torturer as the poor father of ten children murdered by the lunatic fringe, a version which will stand unless clarified by the guerrilla through the action itself, rather than through ad hoc statements. To reach the desired audience, the choice of target and context must be appropriate. Consider the Venezuelan FALN urban guerrilla of 1962–1963. The campaign marked the opening move by a vigorous new organization and ended in a rout by the government. The FALN isolated itself by escalating beyond its capacity. Increasingly, their military program lost coherence as they attempted to outgun the regime in Caracas. Politically, their actions failed either to expose the Betancourt government or to

---

[19] Moreover, there is a tendency for collaboration between organizations to lead to fraternization; a useful process perhaps, but one which does away with extra separation.

promote autonomous centers of power. Public understanding was minimal because the FALN's targets were not readily seen as deserving attack, and the organization's final drive to prevent the 1963 elections through military action led to a complete disaster for the same reason.

In contrast, there is the example of the kidnapping of Stanley Sylvester by the Argentine ERP in 1971. Sylvester, an executive of Swift Inc., was abducted following a massive layoff of workers at Swift's meat packing plant in Rosario. Although Sylvester was honorary British consul, the act was not a diplomatic kidnapping. No contact was made with either the British or the Argentine governments. The company, however, was asked, among other things, to rehire the discharged workers and distribute $50,000 in commodities to designated working-class neighborhoods. The demands were met despite objections by the Lanusse administration, and Sylvester was freed unharmed. Several facets of the action stand out: the demands were feasible, and were in fact met; few workers misinterpretated the guerrillas' intent or the outcome, due to the layoffs; the guerrillas avoided assertions of selfish motives by having the ransom distributed to needy sectors of the population.

There are many possible kinds of armed action—seizures, abductions, assassinations, and expropriations are the most common—with countless variations upon them. What is significant is the application of violence as a political instrument in a particular situation. The Tupamaros have used spectacular robberies to great effect in exposing the corruption of the Uruguayan government. They have also occupied the homes of prominent supporters and agents of the government to remind these people of their personal vulnerability. In a nation disintegrating under a corrupt and benighted government, these actions fostered an already strong current of dissent and resistance.

The central problem of guerrilla actions concerns qualitative leaps, or, in the language of the Tupamaros, *saltos*. No revolution progresses uniformly from start to conclusion; rather, the process moves through phases of varying intensity and scope. Certain actions and campaigns bring about a redefinition of the political scene and an escalation and polarization of the struggle. Correct assessment of such actions is crucial to the guerrilla's strategic planning. The problem arises that it is possible to intensify a situation militarily to a point far beyond what can be sustained politically. Premature *saltos* can expose the guerrillas and prove their undoing, especially as the conflict becomes more violent. It is thus important for the guerrillas to be able to distinguish those strategic actions, whatever their drama or magnitude, that remain within previously established confines.

This illuminates why the impact of a particular type of action can vary so greatly as conflict unfolds. For example, a diplomatic kidnapping in 1969 represented a *salto* for the Brazilian guerrillas, albeit one for which they paid dearly. Three subsequent diplomatic kidnappings altered the political balance very little. Today's strategic actions may well become tactical tomorrow, or even constitute a regression. In Uruguay following the June 1973 coup, sensational bank robberies offer little promise of opening new avenues of advancement.

It is imperative that the guerrilla leadership effectively control the intensity of the struggle and the timing of *saltos*. Of course, an action can have unexpected consequences which greatly change the political climate, and mistakes and pure chance can intervene despite the best planning. Nevertheless, a good deal of control remains in the hands of the insurgents.

Prospects

The question of *saltos* naturally leads to the problem of stage III, the final, decisive phase of the struggle which will culminate in the downfall of the regime. Urban guerrilla warfare can contribute to the fall of a government (e.g., Levingston or, in a more subtle way, Lanusse, both in Argentina) and it can transform a conjuncture from crisis to breaking point (e.g., the Tupamaros in Uruguay), but urban guerrilla warfare has yet to win. Moreover, serious doubts have been expressed as to whether it can consummate the seizure of revolutionary power. Indeed, the recent history of Latin America demonstrates the difficulties of any individual strategy when set upon by the continental apparatus of repression.

Rural armed struggle, the most prevalent strategy in the last decade, can threaten an export economy, harass a government, and force an army to emerge from the cities and disperse its force. In Latin America, rural armed struggle has taken a variety of forms (e.g., *focos,* armed self defense, and peasant uprisings) but the result has always been defeat. Peasant organizing (i.e., mass rural struggle) can call into question the rural class structure which has endured for four centuries and can thus threaten the basis of traditional social order. However, militant peasant movements are generally isolated and have suffered devastating repression, the most recent examples being the movements led by Hugo Blanco in Peru and Francisco Julião in Brazil.

In the city, mass militance can be expressed through factory seizures, demonstrations, neighborhood organizations, and the revolutionary general strike. Characteristic of each of these, however, is the inability to deliver the crushing blow to the state. The military can smash popular organizations as it did in Allende's Chile, and foreign support can sustain a government until a general strike can be broken, as in Uruguay in 1973. The prospects for urban insurrection or intensified guerrilla action are similarly problematic. The virtue of an urban uprising is the urgency with which it colors the situation, since it endangers the nerve centers of the state. The 1965 uprising in Santo Domingo, though, illustrates the vulnerability of insurrection to imperialist intervention, a problem which will only be compounded with the rise of Brazilian subimperialism.

What, then, is required to seize power and institute social revolution in Latin America? It seems likely that no individual movement can win alone; hence, victory may well require a combined struggle. Urban guerrillas should thus be seen as but one wing of a movement encompassing militant unionists, peasant organizations, unemployed workers, radical students and middle-class elements, and, perhaps, leftist officeholders. Combined struggle is the synthesis unifying the contradictions between city and countryside, mass line and armed line, and a vital step toward achieving "the people in arms." A government simultaneously beset by demonstrations, strikes, peasant unions, seizures, and guerrillas is less able to deal with any component than it would be if facing one of them alone. At such a conjuncture, an insurrection and general strike could well deliver the coup de grace, depending on the international climate. Combined struggle within a nation finds its international parallel in the notion of a continental revolution. Just as a government can strangle any particular domestic movement, the United States and Brazil have considerable power to apply against any particular nation.

Past challenges to United States domination have been localized and hence easily isolated, contained, and crushed. Only after the Cuban Revolution and the Vietnam War has the United States encountered any serious limitation on its power and been forced to deal with the first continental revolutionary movement since the Wars of Independence. Urban guerrilla warfare is one part of this hemispheric panorama of repression and revolution. Urban guerrillas are not the "party of the revolution," but they have provided an experience which may some day culminate in the liberation of all of the Americas.

Manaus

Belém

Fortaleza

Recife

Brazil

Salvador

Brasília

Goiás

Goiânia

Uberlândia

Belo Horizonte

Serra do Caparão

Niterói

Angra dos Reis

Rio de Janeiro

São Paulo

Sete Quedas

Rio Paraná

Itaipu

Vale de Ribeira

Pôrto Alegre

Lake Mirim

Brazil: Demographic Background

Population: 95 million (1970); 54% urban
Size: 3,286,000 sq. miles
Gross National Product: $32 billion (1969)
Per Capita Income: $350 (1969)
Literacy: 60–70%
Exports: coffee, cotton, minerals
Life Expectancy: 57 years

2

**Urban Guerrilla
Warfare:
Brazil**

"Whoever is dancing can stay; whoever is not
dancing has to go. . . . Take the initiative,
assume the responsibility, do something. It is
better to make mistakes doing something, even
if it results in death."

Carlos Marighella

Introductory Essay
Backdrop: Regionalism and Uneven Development
Brazilian history reveals several themes crucial to understanding the
nation's present situation. "Regionalism" is the phrase commonly used
to describe both the political squabbles between local elites and the
tensions between these elites and the central government. It often
expresses itself by violence, as the government reasserts control over
rebellious or separatist movements. The Republic of Palmares,
founded by runaway slaves in 1630, was only subdued after an eight-
year campaign ending in 1697. During the 1830s and 1840s, numerous
regional rebellions flared, including a ten-year republican revolt in
Rio Grande do Sul, and the 1890s witnessed the extermination of a
millenarian movement centered at Canudos. Parochial civil wars and
insurrections are merely the more extreme manifestations of regional
cleavages which also permeate day-to-day political life.

The origins of regionalism lie in the colonial heritage of Brazil and
the country's resultant uneven development. Unlike Spanish America,
where gold and silver were discovered at the outset of colonization,
Brazil's economy was from the first oriented toward agricultural production for the Portuguese and European markets. The economy of
any given region thus depended on its products, which were in turn
conditioned by the state of the European market. A product such as
brazilwood, for example, might enjoy an immense temporary demand
and create an economic "spurt" in regions where it was available; but
inevitably the demand would lapse due to exhaustion of supply, technological substitution, or competition from foreign producers, and

the producing regions would suffer for a time a serious economic decline. Three export cycles have dominated Brazilian economic history: sugar production in the Northeast (1530–1650); gold and diamond mining in Minas Gerais (1700–1780); and coffee production in São Paulo (1840–1930). Numerous secondary products have enjoyed lesser prominence, although often for longer periods.

Wide regional differences in class structure and racial balance are due in large part to this asynchronous regional economic development. The Northeastern sugar industry utilized slave labor, and for centuries the majority of Brazilians were black or mulatto. Following the abolition of slavery in 1888, rural labor in the Northeast continued on a semifeudal pattern. Slave labor had also been common outside the sugar-growing Northeast, but it was seldom dominant; in fact, part of the reason for the ease with which emancipation came in 1888 was the prior shift of Center-South enterprises toward white immigrant labor.

Urban-rural divisions are another result of uneven development. The growth of industry in the cities has offered the possibility of relatively well-paying employment to both migrant and immigrant. The cities, however, grew faster than industry, forcing newcomers into marginal service jobs. Nevertheless, the cities continue to attract rural migrants driven from the countryside by poverty, disease, and the traditional monopoly of violence wielded by landlords.

The Brazilian state has passed through five distinct phases: Colony (1500–1822); Empire (1822–1889); First Republic (1889–1930); Second Republic (1930–1964); and the present military dictatorship. The transition has been effected in each case by a political (as opposed to a social) revolution, and each can be best analyzed in terms of the groups which were overthrown and those whose dominance was formalized. The transition from colony to empire, for example, freed the plantation lords from the encumbrance of Portuguese rule. The fateful erosion of Portuguese authority began in 1807 when the crown fled to Rio de Janeiro to escape the Napoleonic invasion. Nationalism in Brazil was fostered by the Wars of Independence against Spain and by the irritating presence of the Portuguese crown in Brazil. The struggle was, however, less violent and protracted than elsewhere in the New World; and, in fact, the first Emperor, Pedro I, was heir to the Portuguese throne. He had been encouraged by his father, João IV, to seek independence under his own aegis rather than offer unknown elements the chance to undermine the social order, as had happened in Spanish America. Pedro's links to Portugal remained an issue, however, and in 1831 he abdicated in favor of his infant son, who assumed power in 1841 after a ten-year regency.

The Empire lasted until 1889; during this period the *fazendeiros* (landed oligarchs) retained the social and political prominence they had enjoyed during the colonial period, but not without challenges. During the regency period, assorted regional revolts occurred in Pará, Minas Gerais, Mato Grosso, Maranhão, Paraná, Santa Catarina, and Rio Grande do Sul, often under the banner of republicanism. Immigration, the changing export cycle, and the beginnings of industrial development finally eroded the dominance of the sugar barons. Following the Paraguayan War of 1865–1870, the authority of the emperor began to wane; first the army and then the Church came into conflict with Pedro II. Finally, the abolition of slavery in 1888 alienated the *fazendeiros*, and a year later the monarchy fell.

The proclamation of the Republic represented the political ascendancy of new interests. Slavery had never been the dominant mode of production in the mines of Minas Gerais or the cattlelands of the South. Although coffee plantations initially employed slave labor, the influx of immigrants prompted a shift to contractual labor. Under the First Republic the political center of the nation shifted to the Minas Gerais–São Paulo axis, with the two states alternating their control of the presidency. This period saw the boom and bust of rubber exports from the Amazon, followed by the decline of coffee sales during the depression. Coupled with political scandals, this turn of the export cycle brought about the end of the First Republic.

Populism and The People

The Second Republic was ushered in by the "Revolution of 1930" which led first to a corporatist dictatorship, the *Estado Novo* (New State), and then to a curious arrangement known as populism. Uniting the two phases is the historic figure of Getulio Vargas, a Rio Grande do Sul rancher and a politician par excellence. Vargas twice occupied the nation's highest office, once as dictator, once as president. During his first regime (1930–1945), new political forces were set in motion, and cleavages were established that lasted until the military dictatorship of 1964. When Vargas was ousted in 1945, basic contradictions had already been established, and his dictatorship laid the foundations for both the evolution and the collapse of the parliamentary period.

The 1930 Revolution originated in opposition to the Minas Gerais-São Paulo alliance and the government's coffee support policy. Worldwide depression a year earlier had undermined demand for Brazil's leading export, and the government's policy of buying and burning excess coffee annoyed provincial interests outside the alliance. Getulio Vargas' defeat in a fraudulent presidential election, coupled with the assassination of his running mate João Pessoa, prompted him to assume leadership of a successful conspiracy. The first years of the new regime witnessed two important rebellions, which established lasting hatreds. In 1932, a coalition of middle-class democrats and coffee barons revolted in São Paulo and, despite the fact that the rebellion was crushed, an enduring residue of opposition remained. Similarly, a communist uprising in 1935 earned the Party the military's undying animosity.

If the opposition to Vargas came from middle-class liberals and certain sectors of the upper classes, his support was more broadly based. Vargas' economic policies were designed to give a little to everyone, except the peasant. Inflationary deficit spending was one result of this policy, and this greatly assisted in Brazil's economic recovery from the depression. Inflation and import substitution proved a boon to industry, and the centralized bureaucratic state Vargas founded created jobs for the middle classes. A state-sponsored labor movement and social security program assisted the workers. Even coffee was granted some recognition through price supports. The one class still excluded from political participation was the peasantry. As Goulart would discover, the exclusion of the peasantry was no accident since the landlords considered the rural class structure nonnegotiable. But in the cities, swollen with immigrants from Europe and migrants from the countryside, new social relations were already replacing the traditional mechanisms of control.

Vargas' most important achievement was the creation of the populist labor movement. The Ministry of Labor came to exercise immense power over unions through a system of worker taxation and union subsidization. The Ministry intervened in unions to install or replace leaders, and only recognized unions were eligible for state subsidies. Thanks to a social security program and Ministry-sponsored fringe benefits, the labor movement remained passive and loyal to the government, and socialist inroads were limited. This passivity became ingrained, and, despite the fact that Vargas, and later Goulart, appealed to the workers and talked of popular government, in 1964 the entire apparatus for the control of labor passed intact into the hands of the military dictatorship.

The downfall of Vargas came in 1945 over the issue of democracy, as the clamor for a parliamentary republic increased. Vargas had promised a return to democracy, but he remained vague as to the timing of the return. Finally, the officer corps joined the opposition, deposed the dictator, and held elections. The transition to democracy was notable for several reasons. First, it deprived the opposition to Vargas of the central issue of democracy. The opposition remained in opposition but thereafter sank to a nebulous anticorruption, anticommunism, anti-Vargas posture. Second, the military was shown to be the ultimate arbiter of politics, having inherited the emperor's *poder moderador* (moderating power). Finally, electoral democracy allowed social contradictions to overflow into overt political expression. The urban masses formed the bulk of the electorate and thus had the potential to install a government of their own choosing. The institution of democracy was important insofar as it allowed the articulation of popular demands in a framework in which they could never be fully achieved.

Three of the four major political parties were established in conjunction with the 1945 ouster of Vargas. The PSD (*Partido Social Democratico;* Social Democratic Party) represented a mélange of landowners and industrialists, while the PTB (*Partido Trabalhista Brasileiro*; Brazilian Labor Party) was formed to represent the workers. Neither party was remotely what it implied. Both were vehicles for maintaining paternalistic relations: the PTB, those of industrialists with urban workers; and the PSD, those of rural landowners and their local petty-bourgeois coteries. Both were organized by Vargas and used by him in the 1950 elections.

The UDN (*União Democratica Nacional*; National Democratic

Union) was perhaps the most coherent party in that, while neither democratic nor national, it found itself a haven for right-wing and middle-class elements opposed to Vargas. Originally the nucleus of middle-class, liberal opposition, in 1945 the UDN lost the issue of democracy as a stick to beat Vargas and thereafter represented those center-right groupings eager to beat Vargas and his successors (e.g., Goulart) with whatever stick seemed available.

The PCB (*Partido Communista Brasileiro*; Brazilian Communist Party) was the fourth principal party. Headed by Luis Carlos Prestes, a famous military radical turned communist, the PCB was outlawed between the 1935 uprising and the 1945 elections, in which it ran a modest fourth place behind the PSD, UDN, and PTB. The Party was again outlawed in 1947, although its influence continued to grow until the coup of March 1964. Numerous other parties ranging from socialist to fascist to Adhemar de Barros' personal vehicle, the PSP, added to the confusion.

The essential feature of the party system was the struggle for election by politicians eager for access to the power and patronage of office. Given this vision of politics, it is not surprising that every bizarre form of campaigning imaginable emerged and that strange alliances and double-dealing permeated this atmosphere of political scheming, plotting, and self-aggrandizement. The basic alignment involved the Vargas coalition (PTB-PSD) on the center-left against the anti-Vargas UDN on the right. However, as often as not, alliances would be concluded between a national party and rebellious state organizations of an "opposing" party. In this corruption-laden electoral arena, major social issues nevertheless began to appear, albeit refracted through the haze of party-politicking. On the one hand, the politician promised the lower classes concessions in exchange for votes; on the other, he promised the upper classes the ability to control the lower classes. As the issues of social reform and national development emerged during the 1950s and early 1960s, the balance between upper-class and lower-class demands began to break down. The nationalist left wing of populism articulated a reform program that would seriously encroach on the domain of the propertied classes. With the decline of the coffee cycle after 1955, the economic downturn only made matters worse.

The possibilities of democracy were revealed in 1950, when Getulio

Vargas returned to power as president-elect. At this time Vargas was moving toward a nationalist, proworker stance, symbolized by the creation of the state petroleum monopoly, Petrobrás. The right, having once rid themselves of Vargas, undertook to do it again. An assassination attempt against opposition newspaper editor Carlos Lacerda by a member of the Presidential Guard was the catalyst, and the military demanded Vargas' resignation. Rather than be overthrown, however, Vargas killed himself on August 24, 1954. A caretaker government presided over elections in which Juscelino Kubitschek (PSD) and João Goulart (PTB) were elected as president and vice president. Goulart's background as Vargas' minister of labor made him anathema to the *antigetulistas,* and, amid rumors of a conspiracy to annul the election results, Marshall Lott staged a coup to ensure the accession of Kubitschek and Goulart. The new government's policy was archetypical populism: a contradictory mixture of national development, inflation, encouragement of foreign investment, corruption, and pyramid building (e.g., the construction of Brasília).

It should be apparent that the populist state was none too stable, one result of which was that its critical element was neither party apparatus nor government, but the military. Brazil for a long time enjoyed the undeserved reputation as a nation free from the scourge of military intervention. However, close attention to facts reveals that every decisive transition has been engineered by the officer corps: 1930, 1937, 1945, 1954, 1955, 1961, and 1964. Vargas' heritage included a coterie of right-wing politicians always willing to clamor at the barracks door for the army to throw out the "Vargas gang." The success of these appeals was, of course, dependent on the army, whose intervention came to be central to the resolution of every crisis.

The instability of populism resulted from its attempt to express politically the rise of domestic industry on the model of advanced industrial nations—with one vital insufficiency, namely, the low level of economic development. An electoral alliance between industry and labor is not viable without the appropriate level of economic development to temper working class demands. Inflation as an agent of capital accumulation had long since ceased to benefit the workers, and industrial conflict was a result. Moreover, the urban masses who formed the vital voting bloc were not homogeneous, but were divided into at least three groups with distinct political tendencies: the middle class; the working class; and the lumpen proletariat. With the disintegration of populism, the middle class moved to the right, the workers to the left, and the lumpen elements remained passive.

The paradox of populism rests in the contradiction between giving the masses favors to get votes, thereby fostering the illusion that the populist state will handle everything, and relying on maintaining this same level of political activity when the right decides that it has had enough. In his role as self-appointed mediator between the upper and lower classes, the populist politician uses the symbolic power of the latter, expressed in votes, to wheedle resources from the former to improve the situation of the latter. For the populist left, reformist and revolutionary alike, the major difficulty comes when the upper classes start to view each compromise/concession not as part of the normal workings of pluralist democracy but merely as another step toward their expropriation. In such a case, the symbolic, electoral power of the populist politician proves no match for the real power of the upper classes, as expressed by the army. When approaching such a juncture the populist typically comes to employ the most revolutionary rhetoric available to try to compensate for the mass mobilization that was never organized. Such rhetoric, naturally, only hastens the end.

In more specific terms, the Brazilian crisis of 1960–1961 revealed the limitations of populism. Janio Quadros, a charismatic independent, accepted the UDN presidential nomination, with the proviso that he would not be bound to the party's dictates. Quadros was elected and only one month into his term initiated an "independent foreign policy" which included neutrality toward both Cuba and the socialist bloc. This act alienated conservatives and prompted Carlos Lacerda to flail publicly Quadros' alleged defection to communism. Lacerda's campaign and Quadros' erratic personal and political style ended in the latter's dramatic resignation in August 1961. The reasons behind Quadros' resignation remain clouded: many observers detect in it a ploy to rally public opinion toward the end of installing himself as dictator with a public mandate. This scenario would presumably have entailed mass demonstrations demanding Quadros' return to office. Overlooked was the crucial fact that such a demonstration was highly unlikely and, lacking mass spontaneity, contingent upon organization.

Quadros neglected to prepare the public for his action, and the result was a dismal failure.

The crisis precipitated by Quadros' resignation intensified over the issue of succession. Vice President João Goulart, who had been re-elected in 1960, was unacceptable to both civilian rightists and important sectors of the military, who feared his connections to the late dictator and the labor movement. Dire warnings of Goulart's dictatorial designs based on working-class support (referred to as "Peronist" tendencies) were publicized extensively by Lacerda and others. Sentiment in the ruling classes was divided over the succession issue, but the resolve of the armed forces to prevent Goulart's ascendancy was broken when the commander of the Third Army declared his adherence to the constitution. This defection by one of the highest-ranking line officers thwarted the opposition and assured Goulart's confirmation as president.

The tensions attendant to Goulart's succession were intensified during his administration, and the growing unrest became focused on several issues and personalities. A key figure was Leonel Brizola, governor of Rio Grande do Sul, who was moving toward a strong leftist-nationalist position and much of whose militancy was attributed to his more moderate brother-in-law, Goulart. At the same time, the activities of the Communist Party and its association with Goulart also came under close scrutiny in the conservative media. Another increasingly important political factor was the Church, which was becoming more involved in secular affairs through its organizations of students and peasants and through the Brazilian Education Movement (*Movimento Educação Brasileiro*) that had been created in 1958 by a group of progressive bishops.

Popular mobilization was most explosive in the Northeast where Peasant Leagues (*Ligas Camponesas*), begun in 1955, had by 1960 established land reform as a national issue. The election of left-leaning Miguel Arraes as governor of Pernambuco, the most populous state in the region, deprived landowners of recourse to official violence to suppress peasant organization. Federal initiatives constituted a further threat to the traditional order: the Superintendency of Northeastern Development (*Superintendência do Desenvolvimento do Nordeste*; SUDENE) was created in 1959 to promote regional development; and rural workers were brought under the jurisdiction of the Labor Ministry and granted minimum wages through the Rural Workers Law passed in 1963.[1] In sum, the process underway in the Northeast was far from satisfactory to the estate owners whose centuries-old privileges seemed destined to suffer.

The Coup of 1964

The drift of populism during the first years of the 1960s was alarming to the nation's elite. Inflation, which approached 100 percent by 1964, was only the most visible aspect of the crisis. Particularly disturbed was a clique of influential businessmen, industrialists, and publishers in São Paulo and, to a lesser extent, Rio de Janeiro, who were centered around the Institute of Social Research and Studies (*Instituto de Pesquisas e Estudos Sociais*; IPES).[2] Proponents of economic integration with foreign multinational corporations, the IPES group first directed its energies toward propaganda. Frustrated by indifference and nationalist opposition to its efforts and concerned with the increasing militancy of labor and peasant demands, the group shifted its focus to the preparation of a coup. The pattern which emerged would be repeated elsewhere in Latin America, with Chile the most recent example.

First came a propaganda barrage from the media and the pulpit. The organization, training, and arming of paramilitary groups followed; explosives factories were set up, tactical and logistical questions were pursued, and the residents of suburban neighborhoods in São Paulo were readied for mobilization. Women from these and other suburbs in Rio de Janeiro would, in the weeks before the coup, take to the streets in a number of public demonstrations against the Goulart government; the last, organized by the Catholic right in March 1964 and called "The Family's March with God for Freedom," drew 500,000 demonstrators in São Paulo. The marches accomplished their objective by suggesting to sympathetic but cautious military officers the extent of bourgeois opposition to the government.

1 This gave the Ministry the power to recognize and control unions, which stimulated competition between peasant organizers and may have moderated the struggle somewhat.
2 An account of the coup is provided by Philip Siekman, "When Executives Turned Revolutionaries," *Fortune*, September 1964, p. 147.

Resistance to populism had been a mainstay of the military's Superior War College (*Escola Superior de Guerra*; ESG) since its inception as focus and fountainhead for the nation's military elite in 1949. After fifteen years of proselytization, some 1500 alumni, military and civilian, had left the College influenced by the ESG doctrine of economic development through capitalism, technocratic approaches to socioeconomic problems, formal democracy, and alignment with the West against communism.[3] By the late 1950s, the ESG curriculum reflected a perceptive analysis of developing social tensions within Brazilian society, interpreted militarily as subversion. The victory of revolutionary warfare in Cuba confirmed these estimates, focusing greater attention on the developing reformist and revolutionary currents within the country. When reform reached the military, in the form of an enlisted mens' strike (the "Soldiers and Sailors Revolt" of March 26, 1964), it became clear to the military that, in their terms, the time for action was near.

The possibility of a coup, afoot for some time, now assumed a more immediate character. Lieutenant Colonel Rubens Resstel, a veteran of the World War II Brazilian Expeditionary Force (*Força Expedicionaria Brasileira*; FEB) served as liaison between a conspiring FEB-ESG faction and the civilian IPES group.[4] The events of mid-March—the "Soldiers and Sailors Revolt" and the "Family's March with God for Freedom"—and the militant rhetoric of Goulart and Leonel Brizola added to the crisis atmosphere.

Whatever lingering reservations the conspirators may have held regarding the efficacy of a coup were erased by a timely set of cues from United States diplomats. On March 19, Assistant Secretary of State for Inter-American Affairs Thomas Mann publicly announced an end to sanctions against dictatorial regimes established through the overthrow of democratically elected governments. Mann's statement terminated the Kennedy administration's proscription against dictatorships, enshrined multilaterally in the Punta del Este Charter of 1961.[5] Somewhat earlier, U.S. Ambassador Lincoln Gordon had in-

---

[3] For an analysis of the ESG, see Alfred Stepan, *The Military in Politics* (Princeton: Princeton University Press, 1971), pp. 174–183.
[4] Siekman, "When Executives Turned Revolutionaries," p. 214.
[5] Tad Szulc, *New York Times*, 19 March 1964, p. 1.

formed the conspirators that diplomatic recognition would be forthcoming within 48 hours after the coup's inception. Prepared for the contingency of a longer confrontation (even to the extent of stockpiling U.S. Food for Peace provisions),[6] the plotters were heartened. Lieutenant Colonel Vernon Walters, the U.S. military attaché (a longtime friend of General Castelo Branco and presently a deputy director of the CIA) coordinated activity between military and civilian conspirators, eventually wiring full details of the coup to Washington a week before its onset.[7]

Behind the impetus to revolt provided by United States diplomatic and military personnel was an elaborate infrastructure extending throughout Brazil. Operatives within the USAID (United States Agency for International Development) and AIFLD (American Institute for Free Labor Development) openly engaged in sabotaging the Goulart regime. Thus, for example, USAID frustrated SUDENE in the Northeast through obstruction and selective support of anti-Goulart governors. According to William Doherty, Jr., the director of AIFLD's Social Projects Department, trained personnel from AIFLD "were involved in the revolution, and in the overthrow of the Goulart regime." [8] While the role of the CIA in the coup remains generally obscure, the activities of one agent in the Northeast have come to light. This agent, working under the cover of CLUSA (Cooperative League of the United States of America) co-opted indigenous efforts at peasant organization and gathered valuable intelligence data for the Pernambuco region.[9]

The coup began when General Mourão Filho mobilized his troops in Minas Gerais and marched on Rio de Janeiro. After some hesitation, other generals followed suit and Governors José de Magalhaes Pinto (Minas Gerais), Adhemar de Barros (São Paulo), and Carlos Lacerda (Guanabara) declared their support, backed by their respective state militias. Contrary to the apocalyptic rhetoric on both sides, the coup proved to be little more than a military exercise as Goulart's sup-

6 Siekman, "When Executives Turned Revolutionaries," p. 216.
7 *Newsweek*, 14 November 1966, p. 56.
8 United States Senate, Committee on Foreign Relations, Subcommittee on American Republic Affairs, *Survey of the Alliance for Progress* (April 29, 1969), p. 586.
9 Joseph Page discusses the agent in *The Revolution That Never Was* (New York: Grossman, 1972), p. 155.

port failed to materialize. The president fled to the interior and then to Uruguay while a military junta assumed power. Foremost among the new military rulers were graduates of the ESG and veterans of the FEB: some 60 percent of the ESG's military graduates were among the plotters; six of the ten generals constituting the "inner circle" of the new Castelo Branco government were FEB veterans and nine of the ten had attended the ESG.[10]

The Dictatorship: Castelo Branco and the Technocrats

Overt American support for the coup was immediately forthcoming. Within twelve hours Acting President Manelli received a message of "warmest good wishes" from President Lyndon Johnson. Somewhat later, and equally impolitic, the "revolutionaries" received diplomatic recognition while President Goulart was still in the country, and Ambassador Lincoln Gordon found the coup "one of the century's turning points for democracy."

Now in power, the conspirators soon fell into bickering over issues of position and influence. The bulk of the officer corps was divided into the ESG–FEB clique and a rival *linha dura* (hard-line) group of virulent nationalists, composed primarily of line officers. Nonetheless, personal opportunism was an underlying factor in early postcoup maneuvering, and here General Humberto Castelo Branco, strongly supported by both the ESG and American lobbyists, prevailed. His main rival, General Artur da Costa e Silva, was forced to settle for the position of minister of war. Civilian schemers such as Governors Carlos Lacerda, Adhemar de Barros, and José de Magalhaes Pinto quickly found their presidential aspirations frustrated.

The first indication of the new regime's direction was formally presented in an Institutional Act of April 9, 1964 which set elections for a president and vice president in two days, allowed military personnel to run, and, among other provisions, provided for both revocation (*cassão*: cassation) of individual political rights for ten years and formalized purges of elected politicians and government bureaucrats. A foregone conclusion, General Castelo Branco was "elected" president, and within two months the government had cassated 378 persons including 2 ex-presidents (Quadros and Goulart), 6 governors, and 55

10 Stepan, *The Military in Politics*, pp. 184, 240, 245.

congressmen. Thousands of civil servants lost their jobs because of suspected lack of fealty to the new regime, and, on April 11, 1964, 77 military officers were placed on reserve in an effort to purify the services.

Political repression was a self-proclaimed liability of the new regime, but was held to be essential for the stability upon which the government's economic programs rested. Aside from the purges and cassations of important intellectuals, politicians, and military officers, strong political control was also exercised over the working class. Technocrats Roberto Campos (Planning Ministry) and Octávio Gouvéia Bulhóes (Finance Ministry) undertook an economic program involving anti-inflationary policies, serious tax collection, and rationalization of the industrial sector. Working-class resistance to stabilization was anticipated, and unions were intervened following the coup. Declining real wages (down 14 percent in 1965; 22 percent in 1966), stemming from this policy combined with an end to wage readjustments based on cost of living increases (Decree Law 15), alienated the working class, although direct opposition in the form of strikes would be long in coming.

A more basic change in economic policy was the denationalization of Brazilian minerals and industry. The Castelo Branco government zealously courted foreign investment by terminating, in February 1965, a stringent profit remittance law that had restricted the repatriation of capital. At the same time, it instituted a new mining code and an investment guarantee agreement. The results of this policy were nothing short of spectacular. Within four years highly favored foreign capital had seized control of the private sector: 100 percent of automobile and tire production; 90 percent of cement; 80 percent of the pharmaceutical industry and marine transport; 77 percent of overseas airlines; 62 percent of auto parts factories; and over 50 percent of chemical and machine production.[11] The regime provided a haven for foreign investors to whom it accorded unrestricted outflow of profits. Meanwhile the national bourgeoisie struggled in an unequal contest, paying as much as six times the interest as multinational competitors (a process which was viewed in Social Darwinian terms by Planning Minister Campos). Foreign multinational investors, unsated with legal earnings

---

[11] Eduardo Galeano, "The De-Nationalization of Brazilian Industry," *Monthly Review*, December 1969, p. 13.

($102 million in 1965; $127 million in 1966) quickly resorted to illegal profiteering—slipping $180 million from the country in 1966 alone.[12]

A similar process began the transformation of the rural sector into into a satrapy of foreign interest. *Time* magazine noted in 1967 that foreigners had purchased an area of land in Brazil greater than that of the states of Connecticut, Rhode Island, Delaware, Massachusetts, and New Hampshire combined. The holdings of the nine largest investors totaled over nine billion acres.[13] This land boom, of disastrous consequences to the rural population, was engineered largely by North American agribusiness firms. The military government not only surrendered subsoil rights but also allowed the United States Air Force to undertake a systematic mapping of the country—including its mineral wealth. The North American Congress on Latin America has charged that the maps were circulated to influential American mining conglomerates who spearheaded foreign conquest of subsoil resources. Minerals presently total only 10 percent of Brazilian exports, a figure which is expected to increase greatly by 1980, supplanting coffee as the primary export commodity.[14]

Linha dura nationalists within the military observed the accelerating pace of economic denationalization with alarm. Particularly disturbing to this faction were the foreign inroads into the strategically important state sector. Hanna Mining Company, which had been faced with an impending judicial decision on the eve of the 1964 coup, was rescued by a presidential decree ending the state monopoly on iron reserves. Even more important, Petrobrás, the state oil monopoly and sacrosanct to the nationalists, was opened to foreign penetration: the combined investment of Union Carbide and Phillips Petroleum in Brazilian petrochemicals soon totaled over $120 million. Nationalist suspicions were also aroused by the mapping of the interior by a foreign power and the surrender of national resources, but the *linha dura's* increasing disaffection with Castelo Branco's policies came to a head over another issue.

Fearful of a return of the civilian favorite Juscelino Kubitschek in

12 Ibid., pp. 16–17.
13 *Time*, 22 December 1967, p. 34.
14 *North American Congress on Latin America*, "Brazil: Let Them Eat Minerals," April 1973, p. 3.

THE DICTATORSHIP

the presidential elections which had been set for October 1965, the military successfully pressed for an extension of Castelo Branco's term until March 15, 1967. The postponed elections would be held in November 1966, and to guarantee their outcome Kubitschek was cassated. Nevertheless, two of Kubitschek's supporters, Negrão de Lima (Guanabara) and Israel Pinheiro (Minas Gerais), won the gubernatorial elections of October 3, 1965. More incensed than chagrined at this resurgence of civilian opposition in a highly controlled election, the *linha dura* faction mobilized. General Alfonso Albuquerque Lima together with army line officers in Rio and naval officers in the First Naval District threatened a coup within the coup. Hard pressed to maintain his position, Castelo Branco conceded not only his succession to General Costa e Silva, who posed as a "mediator" between the factions, but also a Second Institutional Act which further undermined serious civilian challenges to the military's democratic facade. This Act dissolved political parties, provided for the indirect election of the president and vice president, increased the Supreme Court from eleven to sixteen members, extended the cassation practice, and explicitly granted to the military the right to intervene in state government. To guarantee control over the electoral charade, two political parties were created on the ruins of the earlier multiparty system: ARENA (*Aliança Nacional Renovadora;* National Renovating Alliance), the government party, and the MDB (*Movimento Democratico Brasileiro;* Brazilian Democratic Movement), organ of the loyal opposition. The way was now clear for an institutionalized transfer of power within the military's constraints, and General Artur da Costa e Silva, ARENA's candidate, was "elected" president on October 3, 1966.

Urban Guerrilla Warfare

Resistance to the dictatorship, once nebulous, had by 1967 coalesced around a number of groups: the Broad Front (*Frente Ampla*); the Church; the student movement; and nationalist ex-military men. The Broad Front was an effort to regroup the old civilian political elite under the aegis of Carlos Lacerda, who had reverted to his familiar role of disloyal oppositionist. The Front was to have united Kubitschek, Quadros, Goulart, and Brizola, thereby spanning the populist spectrum, but Brizola would not hear of the idea and the others soon lost interest. Even the MDB, the official opposition party, was uninterested. Notwithstanding the distrust everyone felt toward Lacerda, the failure is revealing. The military had saved the upper classes from Goulart, but the price of that salvation was political control. The Broad Front represented a last stand by the politicians against the military onslaught; and a late realization that the maintenance of a civilian government would require the aid of precisely those leaders who were ousted in 1964. The civilian faction of the "revolutionary" coalition was obviously in great disarray.

As the defeat of mainstream politicians became evident, other currents of opposition came into prominence. The students were on the move, organizing demonstrations and a student strike in September 1966. The outlawed National Student Union (*União Nacional dos Estudantes*; UNE) remained at the forefront of the student movement, together with Popular Action (*Ação Popular*; AP), a Catholic youth group turned Marxist. One result of the student movement at this time was to facilitate the growing involvement of the clergy. In both 1966 and 1967, the Church began officially to come off the fence on behalf of social activism and thus, implicitly, against the government.

Incidents of armed resistance had occurred before 1967, such as the attempted assassination of War Minister Costa e Silva at Guirapes Airport in Recife, but a *foco* in the Serra do Caparão in early 1967 marked the beginning of serious armed struggle. Behind the *foco* was the MNR (*Movimento Nacionalista Revolucionario*; National Revolutionary Movement), a group composed of ex-military men and other revolutionary nationalists, including Leonel Brizola. Together with the AP and the Chinese-line Communist Party (*Partido Communista do Brasil*; PC do B), the MNR became involved in several rural *focos*.

The rural guerrilla experience, abortive though it was, introduced the notion of picking up the gun, and thereby brought home to Brazil the peaceful road–violent road controversy raging throughout Latin American communism. The effect on the "old left," particularly the Russian-line Communist Party, was devastating. Already in December 1966, an armed-line faction was forming around the figure of Carlos

Marighella. Although he superficially appeared the typical middle-aged, bourgeois communist, Marighella was, in fact, a man whose stature approached that of Che Guevara and Camilo Torres. He had fought his way through the ranks of the Party to the executive committee, at the cost of considerable personal grief visited on him by rivals. Following the coup, he led a mob assault on an officers' club in São Paulo, was later shot and arrested, but escaped from the hospital. Symbolically, it was his attendance at the OLAS (Organization of Latin American Solidarity) conference in August 1967 that indicated his final break with the PCB.

The split convulsed the Party, and numerous groups left, including those which became the MR-8, the PCBR (*Partido Communista Brasileiro Revolucionario*; Revolutionary Brazilian Communist Party), and Marighella's organization, the ALN (*Ação Libertadora Nacional*; National Liberation Action). In a similar fashion, the Marxist intellectual cluster POLOP (*Politica Operaria*; Workers' Politics) fractured into COLINA (*Comando da Liberação Nacional*; National Liberation Command), the VPR (*Vanguarda Popular Revolucionaria*; Popular Revolutionary Vanguard), and the POC (*Partido Operaria Communista*; Communist Workers' Party). In early 1968, several of these organizations were preparing for and engaging in urban guerrilla action. However, the regime's attention was directed elsewhere, toward the revitalized student and labor movements.

The first strike since the coup took place among the metalworkers of Osasco, a São Paulo suburb, in May and June. Originating in a nationwide protest against declining real wages, the strike was met with the full force of the regime. The students opened the year with demonstrations, but the death of one, Edson Luis Soto, in March, galvanized the situation and led to months of demonstrations and street fighting. Radical clergy now stood by the student protesters, as did a growing percentage of the middle class.

A speech in Congress by Deputy Marcio Moreira Alves in August provided the final frustration for the military. The generals demanded the repeal of Alves' congressional immunity following his suggestion that women not date soldiers and that military wives sexually abstain in protest of the dictatorship. Congress deliberated until December 12, whereupon it rejected the demand. As Alves describes it:

. . . a hand-picked Congress, elected by fraud in the countryside and under every kind of intimidation in the cities had rebelled. The military's two-thirds majority had vanished when a hundred of its members crossed party lines to support the right of an unpopular congressman to speak his mind from the floor.[15]

The military responded with Institutional Act V of December 13, 1968, whereby executive-congressional relations were rectified through sweeping powers granted to the president. Even as the ink was drying on the 1967 Constitution, the document was set aside to join the last vestiges of republican democracy. All representative bodies throughout the country were henceforth to meet and recess on demand of the president. Intervention in states, cancellation of electoral mandates, and elimination of habeas corpus in suspected subversion cases went into effect. President Costa e Silva lost no time in applying his new dictatorial powers to suppress the opposition, from workers to congressmen. Carlos Lacerda's scheming was laid to rest by his cassation. Repression became the watchword as the government took the final steps in affirming itself a dictatorship. "Redemocratization" was over.

Following the dispersal of legal and semilegal opposition forces, it was natural that the lead should fall to the illegal forces—the guerrillas. Throughout 1968 the underground prepared itself by means of expropriations, bombings, and training, culminating in the assassination of U.S. Army Captain Charles Chandler on October 12, 1968. The officials had been aware of the guerrilla-Party dispute, and they were not long in recognizing and reacting to the outbreak of revolutionary warfare in the cities.

The first successes in urban counterinsurgency were scored in January 1969. The VPR was discovered through an aborted action and nearly destroyed.[16] Fallout from the investigation led to the desertion of Captain Carlos Lamarca, who left the Army on January 25 with 3 sergeants and 70 automatic weapons. A prizewinning rifleman, Lamarca had achieved notoriety through posters showing him teaching marksmanship to bank clerks as a defense against guerrilla assaults.

15 Marcio Moreira Alves, *A Grain of Mustard Seed* (Garden City, New York: Doubleday, 1973), p. 11.
16 See João Quartim, "Leninism or Militarism?" reprinted below, for a political analysis of these events.

The VPR set about regrouping, a process which led to its merger with COLINA to form the VAR-Palmares (*Vanguarda Armada Revolucionario*; Armed Revolutionary Vanguard). The fusion of these groups was, however, unstable; strategic differences soon emerged and the VAR split into a new VAR-Palmares and a new VPR. Essentially, proponents of the armed line regrouped in the VPR, and proponents of the mass line into the VAR. In the interim, however, the organization had executed the largest robbery in Brazilian history, making off with $2.4 million from the estate of Adhemar ("he steals, but he gets things done") de Barros.

The basic guerrilla strategy was formulated by Marighella. It envisioned the overthrow of the dictatorship through an armed alliance of workers and peasants, aided by middle-class groups such as students, the clergy, and white-collar employees. The result was to be a three-stage revolutionary war: in stage one the urban guerrilla prepares the way through appropriations of matériel, training, and the building of an infrastructure; in stage two the rural guerrilla takes the struggle to the countryside, which is to be the decisive theatre of operations; finally, in stage three, the rural guerrilla lays the foundation for the growth of a people's army and the final defeat of the regime. Marighella was clear as to the primacy of the countryside, insofar as it would be the scene of the critical confrontation. The role of the cities was to provide logistical preparation for opening the vital rural front.

Marighella's strategic line was generally accepted among the urban guerrillas, while his organizational doctrine was not. Perhaps in response to the stultifying centralism of the Communist Party, Marighella stressed initiative from below almost to the point of obsession. At times this concern for producing action became a matter of action for its own sake, and, when there were several collaborating organizations with the same general stance, ALN control became a tenuous affair. Other groups, such as the VPR, favored a "tactical autonomy–strategic centralism" approach, but found it difficult to implement under the rigorous conditions of repression.

The spontaneity associated with Marighella's brand of urban guerrilla warfare was rather ill-suited to the political situation in Brazil during 1969. First, the mass movement experience of 1968 left the impression of a much deeper popular mobilization than had in fact taken place. Second, the political lacuna following Institutional Act V created a strong temptation for those students and workers who wished to continue to leave their respective movements and turn to urban guerrilla action, to the detriment of popular organizing. The result was, of course, a further lapse in the mass movement. Third, the haphazard organization of the guerrillas led to a premature confrontation with the military, as the guerrillas brought the struggle to a level much higher than they could sustain.

The kidnapping of U.S. Ambassador Burke Elbrick on September 4, 1969 illustrates the problem. Its immediate effect was stunning. The kidnapping put the guerrillas on the front page of the world press, secured the release of fifteen prisoners, and gave the guerrillas a moment's access to the Brazilian media. Psychologically, the action was also an immense success, as many sectors of Brazilian society regarded it as something of a national achievement. Yet for all the resonances struck by the abduction, it vastly overplayed the strength of the revolutionaries.[17] The MR-8 (*Movimento Revolucionario do Outubro 8*; Revolutionary Movement of October 8) first approached Marighella with the plan to seize the ambassador and requested armed support. This in itself suggests the gap between capacity and goals. More revealing was the appalling disregard for security: the house at which Elbrick was kept had been rented under the real name of one of the militants. The police quickly identified the building and surrounded it, but allowed the guerrillas safe conduct in exchange for the ambassador's release. Then, after a narrow escape from the building, one student returned to his parents' home for a change of clothes and was apprehended.

The gains produced by the release of fifteen revolutionaries were quickly undone by the nearly 2,000 arrests that followed Elbrick's release. These arrests, and the torture of prisoners which followed, brought about the military's first success: the fall of Carlos Marighella. Interrogations had led to a pair of Dominican monks working with the ALN. A telephone number, revealed under torture, was tapped, and on November 4, 1969 Marighella was shot to death in a police trap. On balance, the Elbrick kidnapping had provoked brutal

17 See Alves, *A Grain of Mustard Seed,* pp. 135–138, for an account of the action.

repression against a movement insufficiently developed to withstand it; the revolutionaries lost control over the level of violence as the regime escalated to a level they were unable to match.

Three more diplomatic kidnappings were carried out, against the Japanese consul in São Paulo, and the German and Swiss ambassadors. (The diplomats were abducted in the order their countries ranked in investment in Brazil, a fact lost on most Brazilians.) But although greater numbers of prisoners were freed, the political impact diminished each time. For one thing, on each occasion the regime released prisoners, a concession other Latin American governments (Guatemala, Uruguay, Argentina) were often unwilling to make. Through these prisoner exchanges the Brazilian government recouped some of the prestige that it had lost because of its use of torture, and thus increased the confidence of foreigners. Also, the massive roundups that followed each diplomat's release more than offset the effect of the release of the prisoners. Kidnappings maintained the guerrillas' visibility during 1970 and early 1971, but obscured the growing toll exacted by the repression and the isolation of the guerrillas from the oppressed classes. Attempts at initiating a rural front were frustrated in the Angra dos Reis in 1969, and in the Vale de Ribeira in 1970.

Operation Bandeirantes[18] was launched by the regime in São Paulo in mid-1969 as the pilot urban counterinsurgency program. Its success led to replication in other cities, with no less deadly results. The guerrillas moved toward a united front in August and September 1970, but the regime was slowly squeezing them out of existence. In October, Operation Birdcage was launched in order to preempt assaults commemorating Marighella's death. Among the casualties was Joaquim Câmara Ferreira, Marighella's successor as head of the ALN.

The November 1970 gubernatorial and congressional elections offered an interesting datum: better than half of the electorate refused to take the elections seriously. Despite mandatory voting requirements, some 30 percent of the electorate abstained and, of those who did vote, 55 percent cast null ballots.[19] But this impressive vote of

[18] Named for the original settlers of the São Paulo area, whose principal activities seemed to be exploring, capturing Indian slaves, and aiding in the suppression of revolts.
[19] *Nation*, 14 December 1970, p. 613.

no-confidence in the government came to naught, as the guerrillas proved unequal to the challenge of channeling public discontent into revolutionary action.

The unequal exchange of blows between the guerrillas and the dictatorship continued in 1971. Individuals connected with the repressive apparatus, both inside and outside the military, were assassinated; however, for each such person eliminated, a hundred revolutionaries fell. Systematic torture served to break guerrillas and deter would-be guerrillas. Two incidents illustrate the political ambience in which torture was (and is) employed. It is reported that in late 1970 a grandson of Marshall Lott, the man who had saved the republic in 1956, was tortured by the army. Lott proceeded to kill the officer in command at the time and then demand a public trial; he was, instead, quietly retired. In early 1971, Rubens Paiva, a socially well-connected MDB deputy with links to the guerrillas, was arrested and never seen again, presumably the victim of torture. Through these actions, the government revealed with chilling clarity its willingness to strike down both members of the upper-class political elite and relatives of high-ranking officers. The message was not lost on the masses, who were reduced to spectators of the guerrilla struggle. The death of Carlos Lamarca in September 1971, a result of information obtained under torture, symbolized the end of the urban guerrilla struggle in Brazil.

Although the urban guerrilla is now in eclipse, resistance nevertheless continues. In April 1972, rural guerrillas began operations along the Araguaia River, bordering the states of Goiás, Mato Grosso, and Pará. The guerrillas, called the Command of the Partisan Forces of Araguaia, appear to have organized popular resistance to the land grabbing of the powerful landlords in the region. The regime became concerned about the situation because of the Trans-Amazon road project which, given the terrain, is particularly vulnerable to guerrilla harassment, and by September over 5,000 troops had initiated a counterinsurgency campaign.

Perhaps more important is the growing opposition of the Church to the dictatorship. Until recently, clerical resistance was sporadic, local, and unorganized. A statement issued after the Thirteenth General Assembly of Bishops in February 1973, however, indicated the beginning of concerted, high-level criticism of the regime's policies, and this was followed in March by a denunciation of land tenure practices, racial and sexual discrimination, genocide of the Indian population, and the lack of legal rights. Even more significant was the declaration of May 6, 1973, issued by the hierarchy of the Northeast, including Archbishops Dom Helder Câmara and Avelar Brandão, which attacked the regime's repression and torture as well as the policies responsible for poverty, illiteracy, and unemployment. This declaration was followed by a call for action against the dictatorship, and this call, combined with the more generalized growth of Church militancy, may well produce the most tenacious opposition yet faced by the military and provide the spark for a resurgence of other forms of resistance.

The Economic "Miracle"

No introduction to Brazil in the 1970s would be complete without mention of the "miracle," the unique program of economic development which emerged under the Médici regime (1969–1974). Because of the country's size and population, the projected economic development of Brazil will lead to its becoming a world power; indeed, this has already led to a growing assertion of Brazilian influence within South America. The Brazilian economic "miracle" is known abroad through its highly publicized achievements: a growth rate of 9–10 percent per annum; industrial growth several points higher; a reduction of yearly inflation to under 20 percent per annum; booming exports and a "crawling peg" devaluation (whereby periodic small devaluations replace a few large ones to discourage currency speculation). Despite its successes, however, there is nothing supernatural about the "miracle," whose performance can be attributed to low wages, prohibition of strikes, and ready access to foreign capital.

Postcoup inflation has decreased wages to the point where Brazilian labor is competitive with that of South Korea and Taiwan. A cautious estimate suggests that between 1958 and 1969 real wages dropped 40 percent while production increased 70 percent. Under Decree Law 1236 of September 1972, the government is encouraging manufacturers to import complete factories into Brazil by offering them preferential treatment. Employers are further guaranteed a passive labor force prohibited from striking. Unemployment, ranging from 8 percent in the Center-South to 30 percent in the Northeast, is an additional deterrent to working-class militancy. Brazil offers the investor the security of military dictatorship, and foreign capital in various forms (loans, investments, and outright gifts) continues to be attracted to the most favorable investment climate in the Americas. The foreign debt is now over $10 billion, an astronomical sum resulting from investment opportunities created by the state's obsession with industrial growth.

Underdevelopment implies the inability to produce industrial goods, which must be purchased abroad in foreign currency. The typical underdeveloped country obtains foreign exchange by exporting agricultural or mineral products. The uniqueness of the "miracle" is its attempt to bootstrap Brazil into industrial development through massive foreign investment and the export of manufactured goods. Low wages attract foreign capital into the industrial export sector, thereby generating the resources with which to repay the investors during the creation of an industrial establishment. Although the composition of Brazilian exports is changing, the market forces behind this process are analogous to those which determined the colonial economy: economic activity is controlled by a foreign market rather than by indigenous factors.

Manufactured goods, whatever their long-range prospects, cannot overnight displace agriculture as the nation's leading export. In the short run, coffee, sugar, and cotton will retain their traditional importance as exchange earners, supplemented by other agricultural products. Despite a proportional decline in their share of exports (e.g., coffee dropped from 50 percent of total export value in 1960 to 25 percent in 1970), these products will continue in importance in the immediate future. The Brazilian government is promoting minerals as a primary export commodity, a strategy which may prove lucrative should Brazil actually hold the largest mineral reserves in the West, as is widely assumed.

The difficulty with the "miracle" involves the difference between the rate at which foreign indebtedness is acquired through loans and investments and the rate at which it can be liquidated through the growth of exports. Although Brazilian exports have been steadily expanding, to the $5 billion level projected for 1974, imports have recently been several hundred million dollars higher per year. The structure of imports shows a preponderance of capital and intermediate goods, machinery, fuels, and chemicals. While these imports contribute to industrial growth, constant trade deficits necessitate good relations with creditors. It is therefore essential that Brazil maintain export growth at a level sufficient both to retain investor confidence and meet prior obligations. Much of the foreign debt is now coming due: some $2 billion will be payable in 1974. Debts must be renegotiated or paid, either of which is dependent on growth.

The regime's economic policy, based as it is on exports and foreign capital, is not without its domestic consequences. For example, the rationalization of agriculture through agrarian reform has become a reality for the landed oligarchy. Even the mildest reform is anathema to most landlords, particularly those in the highly traditional Northeast, but resistance to the government's policy should be minimal given the high prices paid for expropriated land. In industry, the national bourgeoisie faces competition from foreign-financed multinationals, the result of which has been bankruptcy and denationalization. The greatest sacrifices have been borne, however, by the working classes. Unlike other forms of Western capitalism, the current development scheme is unrelated to the home market, and the producing classes have little role as consumers. During the 1960s, the share of national income received by the poorest 80 percent of the population fell from 35 percent to 28 percent, and the share of the richest 5 percent increased from 44 percent to 50 percent.[20] The mass consumption market is estimated at about one-sixth of the population (100 million). Presently, only one of every four Brazilians can afford a pair of shoes per year. For the worker there is no "miracle," but a lifetime of labor unrelieved by such tangible benefits as consumer goods, education, or health care.

At the time of the coup, the upper classes and the military were generally united by their opposition to Goulart. This unity was a fragile construction and fractured soon after the coup. The dictatorship is not monolithic and any further developments will be conditioned by present cleavages. There are important divisions among

[20] *Latin America,* 31 March 1972, pp. 97–98; *Washington Post,* 6 December 1971, reprinted in *Brazilian Information Bulletin,* no. 6 (February 1972), p .4.

both military and civilian supporters of the regime. The upper classes fall into two blocs: the now-dominant industrial sector and the traditional landed oligarchy. However, industry is in the ascendancy and the contradictions therein outweigh those within agriculture or between industry and agriculture.

Democracy and nationalism are the two issues which invoke the deepest divisions. What is called "democracy," or "redemocratization" is in fact a euphemism for civilian participation in government, as it is highly questionable whether the military seriously intends to return to open elections. The ten-year loss of political rights will soon expire for those cassated in the wake of the coup, and the incoming Geisel regime's policy will then become more evident. Whatever the extent of civilian participation, even to the point of a civilian president, the military is unlikely to return to the barracks. Both the military and the upper classes are doing well under the present arrangement and are loath to endanger it. Nevertheless, significant sections of both the military and the upper classes favor a less barbaric image abroad.

Nationalism is the issue most likely to precipitate serious conflict in the near future. Essential to a closer analysis of this factor is the recognition of the role of the Brazilian state in the current economic expansion. Of the 30 largest enterprises in Brazil, 24 are state-controlled. While allowance must be made for private participation in the state sector, it is clear that the government plays a major role in the economy, particularly since state enterprises are oriented toward such infrastructure industries as petroleum, steel, and electric power. Thus, in addition to foreign and domestic capital, there is a third component to industry, the state sector. Foreign and domestic capital are basically antagonistic to each other, and the state has a pivotal role in determining which will prevail. Presently, the state sector has opted for foreign capital, to the detriment of Brazilian industrialists; but nationalist pressure in the military could force a realignment along Brazilian versus foreign lines. Curiously enough, nationalism is the main cleavage in the military because important groups within it are distressed about foreign penetration and debt.

For the armed forces, the opportunity to re-equip with modern hardware has been one of the more alluring attractions of the "miracle." Military governments are usually partial to arms expenditures, a tendency accentuated in the Brazilian case by the drive to regional hegemony. As the development program proceeds, Brazil will acquire the infrastructure for a military-industrial complex, and develop the military capacity of a serious power—tanks, aircraft, submarines, missiles, and possibily nuclear weapons.[21] The origins of this development may be traced to the founding, in 1964, of the São Paulo Industrial Federation, whose purpose has been to stimulate industrial production of military hardware. At present, Brazilian firms manufacture a light armored vehicle, light and heavy military trucks, the Brocoto riot control vehicle, and the amphibious "Urutu" which is also being marketed in other Latin American nations. A number of foreign small arms manufacturers are producing weapons in Brazil (e.g., the Belgian FN-FAL rifle and Italian Beretta machine gun).[22]

Since 1967, the navy has undertaken a program of modernization which will supposedly give Brazil parity with Italy by 1976, at a cost of over $250 million.[23] The navy is also directing the expansion and upgrading of the nation's merchant marine, partly to reduce the shipping costs which contribute heavily to the balance-of-payments deficit. The navy is also crucial to enforcing Brazil's claim to a 200-mile offshore territorial limit, and is important to opening the Amazon basin. More suggestive, though, is the military's vision of Brazil's growing strategic role in the South Atlantic as the guardian of shipping lanes vital to the Western world. There has even been discussion of a Pacific fleet. However, on either ocean, the basic issue is whether the real purpose of the expansion is to facilitate intervention in case of a threat to Brazilian or United States interests.

The air force is likewise acquiring an impressive arsenal.[24] The air defense–air traffic control complex at Anapolis (near Brasília) is to include sixteen Mirage III fighter-bombers and an elaborate radar system to defend the industrial heartland from attack. A less technological, but equally formidable installation at Santa Maria, Rio

[21] Brazil's objection to nuclear nonproliferation may be seen in this light.
[22] *Brazilian Information Bulletin*, no. 9 (January 1973), p. 2.
[23] *Latin America*, 3 November 1972, p. 351.
[24] It is worth mention that an autonomous air force with modern firepower will radically alter the interservice balance of power; see *Latin America*, 13 October 1972, p. 325.

Grande do Sul, provides reconnaissance/attack capacity in the southern cone region.[25]

The state-controlled mixed corporation EMBRAER illustrates the fusion of military and high technology, capital-intensive industrial interests. The company produces the Italian Aermacchi fighter in Brazil under the name Xavante. In this as in other military enterprises, the Brazilians import not only the physical plant but also the technology. Beyond satisfying domestic military needs, an effort is being made to export the Xavante within Latin America, and Bolivia has already purchased eighteen of the jets.[26]

Subimperialism

Brazil has now emerged as a formidable hemispheric power, a goal which has been pursued by successive military governments since 1964. The potential for imperial ambition has long existed: the country is the largest in South America, both geographically and demographically, and it has both vast natural resources and boundaries that touch all but two of the South American republics. This geographic reality has resulted in the accretion of neighboring territory through war and treaty. Contemporary Hispanic American governments fear a continuation of this process arising from the dictatorship's chauvinism, antireformism, and the dictates of a rapidly developing military-industrial complex. While Brazilian influence continues to grow and Uruguay, Paraguay, and Bolivia slip into the status of client states, opposition has been developing under the leadership of Argentina in the Rio de la Plata region and Venezuela in the Caribbean.

A virulent anticommunism has formed a major component of Brazilian military thinking since the Second World War. Internally, severe censorship and political repression, including the systematic use of torture and the deprivation of legal rights, has made for stability and security from even the most illusory threats. However, fears of this nature are not easily assuaged, and thus the concept of an "ideological frontier," which stresses that the forces of subversion (i.e., reform or revolution) know no boundaries and must be universally checked, has become a dominant component of the dictatorship's

---

[25] *Latin America,* 13 October 1972, pp. 324–325.
[26] *Brazilian Information Bulletin,* no. 9 (January 1973), p. 2.

foreign policy. Brazil has therefore supported United States policy against Cuba and Vietnam and even sent troops to the Dominican Republic in 1965. In August 1971, Brazil supported a rightist coup in Bolivia with arms, ammunition, and a troop presence on the Santa Cruz border when the left-leaning government of Juan José Torres violated Brazil's perceived ideological frontiers. Also in 1971, on the eve of Uruguayan elections, "Plan Thirty Hours" was concocted involving a potential Brazilian invasion of that country in the event of an election victory by the leftist Broad Front (*Frente Amplio*) coalition. The defeat of the Broad Front at the polls obviated the need for Brazilian intervention. Two years later, in June 1973, a general strike against the government of Uruguayan President Juan María Bordaberry was defeated, in part, through a timely Brazilian loan of $30 million.[27]

Political interference is only the most dramatic manifestation of Brazil's presence in the buffer states of Uruguay, Paraguay, and Bolivia. Territorial and economic intrusion is a more mundane affair. In Uruguay, cattle smuggling to Brazil from the Northern ranch lands is commonplace, and Brazilian nationals are among the chief beneficiaries. Brazilian land holdings are extensive, and some 20 percent of the Uruguayan Departments of Cerro Largo, Treinta y Tres, and Rocha are owned by Brazilians, and possibly as much as 40 percent of Artigas Department, on the Brazilian border, is Brazilian owned.[28] Eastern Bolivia, conservative, white racist, and separatist, is under Brazilian cultural and ideological influence. Economic penetration is under way, with natural gas and the fabled Mutún iron ore deposits as the prime targets. An estimated 30,000 Brazilian squatters now reside on Bolivian soil.[29] Similarly, in Paraguay the Sete Quedas area is overrun by Brazilians, who outnumber Paraguayans five to one.[30]

To facilitate trade and internal development, the Brazilian government has launched its most grandiose project: the opening of the Amazon. An elaborate road network linking Brazil with its Amazon

[27] *Newsweek*, 20 August 1973, p. 44
[28] *Latin America*, 21 July 1972, p. 226.
[29] *Prensa Libre* (Cochabamba, Bolivia), 23 November 1968, p. 3.
[30] *Latin America*, 10 March 1972, p. 76; also Eduardo Galeano, "The New Frontiers," *Monthly Review*, December 1968, pp. 19–29.

neighbors and, ultimately, connecting the Atlantic with the Pacific and the Caribbean is underway. The effects of the Trans-Amazon project will doubtless be far-reaching. Already involved are genocide of indigenous tribes, forced relocation of dirt poor Northeasterners to alleviate demographic and political pressures, and rapacious exploitation by foreign mineral and agribusiness interests. Ecologists fear permanent devastation of the Amazon basin resulting from hasty and ill-planned exploitation. This is of little concern to the Brazilian government, whose interests are at once economic and strategic. Besides cheaper transport of Brazilian goods, the road network assures rapid intervention in bordering nations and thus facilitates Brazilian hegemonic designs in South America. The diplomatic consequences of the Trans-Amazon project are already manifest. The road link with Guyana (a non-Hispanic nation), cuts through territory disputed by Guyana and Venezuela, and this has led Brazil to support Guyana's territorial claims. The military potential was recently highlighted by the revelation of alleged plans for the invasion of Brazil's northern neighbors (in particular, Venezuela).[31]

Energy sources, especially oil and hydroelectric, are of prime concern to the Brazilian government for insuring the nation's continued industrial growth. A breakdown of Brazil's current sources is revealing: oil provides 45 percent of Brazil's energy requirements, wood contributes 33 percent, hydroelectric 18.4 percent, and coal 3.6 percent.[32] The contribution of wood is almost certain to diminish over the coming years, in part due to the depletion of timber. Hence, oil and hydroelectric power will be called upon to assume an increasing role simply to maintain the current levels of energy consumption.

This increasing demand has led Brazil to pursue hydroelectric and other power projects in Latin America and to seek out oil in Latin America and Africa. The government is likely to proceed with a joint hydroelectric project with Uruguay, either on Lake Merín between the two countries, or on the Rio Negro in central Uruguay. Another project, along the Paraná River in Paraguay, would harness one of the continent's great energy resources. The original proposal involves territory disputed by the two nations and occupied by Brazilian

31 See *Tricontinental News Service*, 16 January 1974, p. 13.
32 *Latin America*, 11 January 1974, pp. 14–15.

troops since 1966. An alternate site, 70 miles downstream at Itaipú, would reduce tensions with Paraguay but is unacceptable to Argentina, which claims the project would lower the level of the river and render it unnavigable. At present Itaipú is the chosen location, and construction is imminent. In Bolivia, Brazil plans to invest $400 million toward building a natural gas pipeline to supply the São Paulo industrial complex.

The quest for oil, however, has brought in its wake a major dilemma for Brazil. Following the October (1973) War in the Mideast, the "oil weapon" was brought to bear not only against Israel's supporters but also against supporters of Portugal, Rhodesia, and South Africa. Brazil obtains 50 percent of its oil from the Arabs and a good part of the remainder from Nigeria, and is thus extremely vulnerable to cutbacks and price increases. Secondary interests in Africa are also present, notably markets for Brazilian manufactured goods and an organization of coffee-exporting nations. Yet equally compelling interests bind Brazil to the colonialist powers in Africa. Brazilian trade with South Africa is at the $100 million mark, which exceeds Brazil's combined trade with the rest of Africa. Brazilian affinities to Portugal are even stronger, and they have been codified in a treaty signed in September 1971 that grants reciprocal political and economic rights to citizens of the two nations, including the rights of voting and holding office. Through this unique arrangement, Brazil gains entry into Portugal, "Portuguese" Africa, and Europe in the event that Portugal joins the Common Market. Moreover, Brazil shares with the Lisbon-Johannesburg-Pretoria axis a common strategic and ideological position.

Portugal's military situation in Guinea-Bissau, Mozambique, and Angola is deteriorating, and pressure for outside aid is being exerted. At the same time, Arabs and Africans are also mounting pressure on Brazil for a repudiation of "racism and colonialism" in Africa and the Middle East. The immediate problem is thus whether Brazil wishes to mortgage its economic future in Africa to defend Portugal's empire. The same problem arises in connection with Brazil's ties to the settler states of South Africa, Rhodesia, and Israel. The recent drift of Brazilian diplomacy indicates an effort to placate the Arab and Black African states, without damaging relations with the colonial powers. In the long run, though, Brazil will face a difficult choice between its natural allies on the South Atlantic and its potential markets and suppliers.

Brazil's ambitions now span two continents. Paraguay, Uruguay, and Bolivia are on the road to becoming client states. Expanding trade, hydroelectric and other power projects, and the Trans-Amazon highway network provide the incentive and potential for a subimperial role in South America, backed by Brazil's considerable military might relative to its neighbors. Yet obstacles to unlimited expansion are already in sight. Most basic is the fact that Brazil must operate in an international context whose parameters are outside Brazilian control. A general crisis in Western capitalism could undermine the "miracle" overnight by terminating both the influx of foreign capital and the level of exports. Similarly, Brazil's African policy is fraught with dangers, particularly those of the "oil weapon." Argentina, meanwhile, has launched a diplomatic offensive that challenges Brazil both in Africa and Latin America. Hence, despite Brazil's considerable power and presence throughout South America, the economic "miracle" and the global imperial designs that have been based upon it are rather delicate operations. Brazil will continue as a formidable subimperial power in Latin America, but it may have to abandon some of its more grandiose schemes.

Chronology

1964

March 31–April 2   Revolution of March 31; military coup over-throws populist regime of João Goulart.

April 9   Institutional Act I institutes "revolutionary government."

April–July   Wholesale purges throughout military, unions, Congress, judiciary, civil service, state and local governments.

April 16   General Castelo Branco elected president by Congress.

May 9   Carlos Marighella injured in shootout with police.

July   Purges decline as regime consolidates; Carlos Lacerda, one of the initiators of the coup, goes into opposition.

October   Leadership of Brazilian Communist Party arrested; purge reinstituted.

November 26   Goiás Governor Borges ousted for subversion.

November 27   Two hundred jailed in Rio Grande do Sul for allegedly plotting leftist insurrection in conjunction with Borges and ex-deputy Leonel Brizola.

1965

March 17   *New York Times* reports 2,000 people in jail without charges.

March 27   Guerrilla raid on barracks in Rio Grande do Sul.

May 18   Bomb found in United States Embassy.

October 27   Institutional Act II; Castelo Branco dissolves political parties, increases executive powers, decrees appointment of judges and indirect election of future presidents.

1966

February 5	Bombing of home of United States consul in Pôrto Alegre.
June 24	U.S.I.S. building in Brasília bombed.
July	Bomb at Recife airport kills 3; assassination attempt on General Costa e Silva; hundreds arrested.
September 15–23	Students demonstrate and clash with police in Rio.
October 4	Bombings of war, finance, and foreign ministers' homes.
December 1	A. P. Pimentel sentenced to 5 years in prison for attempted assassination of Castelo Branco in 1965.
December 10	Carlos Marighella and others resign from Communist Party Executive Committee.

1967

Early 1967	Mario Alves and others found Revolutionary Brazilian Communist Party.
March 15	Costa e Silva becomes president; new Constitution inaugurated.
Early April	Rural *foco* in Serra do Caparão aborted; MNR and (allegedly) Leonel Brizola involved.
August	First OLAS (Organization of Latin American Solidarity) Conference held in Havana; Carlos Marighella is one of the Brazilian delegates.
August 1	Peace Corps office in Rio bombed.

August 20	One hundred seventy suspected guerrillas seized in Mato Grosso; led by Tarzan de Castro.
September 27	United States air attaché's residence in Rio bombed.
October 15	Five persons arrested for attempting to form guerrilla band in Amazonas.
December 30	Ten boxes of dynamite and 200 detonators taken from Cajamar cement company.
Late 1967	Marighella returns to Brazil and begins mobilizing ALN.

1968

January	Beginnings of several guerrilla groups: VPR in São Paulo and MR-8 in Niteroi.
March 19	United States Consulate in São Paulo bombed.
March 28	Edson Luis Soto, 16-year-old student, killed by police in Rio de Janeiro.
March 30	Student demonstration in Rio protests killing of students by administration.
April 15	French and Italian Bank armored car attacked; 100,000 NCr (New Cruzeiros) expropriated.
April 20	Conservative newspaper *O Estado do São Paulo* bombed by VPR.
April 23	Commerce and Industry Bank in São Paulo robbed of 110,000 NCr by guerrillas.
May 1	Governor Abreu Sodre stoned by mob in São Paulo.
June 20–21	Students clash with police in Rio and demonstrate in São Paulo and Brasília; 1,500 arrested.
June 22	São Paulo Army Hospital raided for weapons in first direct attack on army by the VPR.

June 26	One hundred thousand students demonstrate in protest against repression.
June 26	Second Army headquarters in Ibirapuera bombed by VPR.
June 28	Nineteen boxes of dynamite and blasting caps stolen from Fortaleza stone quarry by VPR.
July	Students occupy University of São Paulo Philosophy Faculty; first death-squad attacks initiate backlash to 1968 turmoil.
July	Osasco metal workers strike, led by union head and VPR leader José Ibrahim; increased repression follows.
July 13	Peasant leader Manoel Conceição shot by police; he eventually loses a leg from gangrene.
August 10	Payroll train attacked; 110,000 NCr expropriated.
October	MR-8 *foco* in Paraná begun; first support action executed.
October 12	*United States Captain Charles Chandler assassinated by VPR in São Paulo.*
	Eight hundred students arrested for holding congress of outlawed National Student Union.
October 14	Seizure of 180,000 NCr from Bank of São Paulo.
October 27	Sears, Roebuck & Company store bombed.
November	Bank assault linked to Marighella and the ALN; realization by police of "subversive threat."
December 12	Congress balks at government demand for trial of Deputy Marcio Moreira Alves for insulting military honor; climax of a long "constitutional crisis."

December 13	*Costa e Silva closes Congress; Institutional Act V promulgated, giving president dictatorial powers.*
December 14–18	Hundreds arrested including 94 government party deputies, ex-President Juscelino Kubitschek and Carlos Lacerda.
1969	
January 22	Planned action against IV Army Quitauna barracks uncovered, exposing VPR.
January 25	Captain Carlos Lamarca, with three noncommissioned officers and 70 automatic weapons, defects to VPR.
February 25	Expropriation of 120,000 NCr from Auxiliary Bank of São Paulo.
March	Residence of General Ademar de Rocha Santos bombed.
April	Monguagua Conference held to reorganize VPR and attempt merger with COLINA: initially there is little success, but soon after the two groups join to form VAR-Palmares.
May 1	Guerrillas seize São Bernardo radio station and broadcast message.
May 5	Seizure of 248,000 NCr from National Credit Bank.
May 27	Six guerrillas escape Lemos de Brito prison and become involved in MAR *foco*.
June	Operation Bandeirante launched nationwide to combat subversion.
June 22	Military police barracks attacked; weapons and ammunition expropriated.

July	Political parties reorganized by government decree.
July	Over 30 MR-8 members arrested.
July 8	Two theaters showing "The Green Berets" bombed.
July 18	$2.4 million taken from estate of politician Adhemar de Barros.
August	MAR guerrillas driven out of forests of Angra dos Reis, 200 miles south of Rio de Janeiro.
	Over 200 revolutionaries arrested during mid-1969.
August 15	Marighella speech read over Radio São Paulo during occupation by guerrillas.
September 4	*United States Ambassador Burke Elbrick kidnapped by ALN and MR-8; 15 prisoners exchanged for Elbrick.*
September 10	Institutional Act XIV decrees death penalty for subversion; first time death penalty has been decreed since 1891; some 1,800 persons arrested following Elbrick kidnapping.
September	Tarresopolis Conference results in split within VAR-Palmares; armed-struggle wing leaves and calls itself VPR again.
Late September	Thirteen ALN factories raided by authorities.
November 4	*Carlos Marighella trapped and shot to death.*
December 17	Shooting incident leads to discovery of PCBR urban guerrilla activity; campaign against PCBR begins.
1970	
January	João Domingues Palmares command (VAR) hijacks airplane to Cuba.

January	VAR hit hard by repression.
January 13	PCBR continues to face repression, culminating in arrests of Mario Alves (who dies under torture) and Apolonio de Carvalho.
February 20	Death of Antonio Raimundo de Lucena, VPR leader, during police raid.
March 11	Japanese consul Nobuo Okuchi abducted by VPR; 5 prisoners exchanged for Okuchi.
April 5	Curtis Cutter, United States consul in Pôrto Alegre, thwarts kidnap attempt.
April 21	ALN leader Juarez Guimarez de Brito killed in attempted kidnapping of West German Ambassador von Holleben.
April 21–May 31	Operation Vale de Ribeira mobilizes thousands of troops to eliminate VPR training camp headed by Lamarca.
June 11	West German ambassador kidnapped by Juarez Guimarez de Brito command of ALN and VPR; 40 prisoners released in exchange for him.
July 12	Eduardo Leites (VPR) arrested in attempted skyjacking to free prisoners.
July	ALN, MR-8, VPR, MRT begin merger into United Front.
August 12	Carlos Franklin Peiyao de Araujy (VAR) arrested.
September	PCBR joins United Front effort.
September	VAR suffers another split, led by Adilson Ferreira da Silva.
October 1–3	Operation São Paulo; police campaign against São Paulo guerrillas; 500 arrested, including most of VAR-Palmares, São Paulo branch.

October 23	*Joaquim Camara Ferreira, successor to Marighella as head of ALN, arrested and dies of "heart attack" in prison.*
November	Grandson of Marshall Lott savagely tortured; Lott kills army captain in revenge, and demands public trial; military quietly retires him.
November	Arms cache in São Paulo tombs discovered.
November 4–5	Operation Cage launched to preempt guerrilla actions commemorating Marighella's death; 5–10,000 people detained.
November 15	Elections: 30 percent of electorate abstain despite illegality of abstention; 55 percent cast blank ballots.
December 3	Education Minister Jarbas Passarinho admits to occasional use of torture in jails.
December 7	*Swiss Ambassador Giovanni Bucher kidnapped by Juarez Guimarez de Brito command of ALN; 70 prisoners released.*
December 8	Police announce deaths of 3 guerrillas, including Eduardo Leite (VPR).
December 10	Expropriation of 64,000 NCr from Itau-America Bank; police claim 9 of 14 commandos captured within 2 days.
1971	
January 12	VAR-Palmares distributes food to slum dwellers.
January 20	Rubens Paiva (labor party ex-deputy linked to guerrillas) and family arrested; Paiva dies under torture.
February 6	Raids in Recife lead to captured documents and whereabouts of guerrillas, including Tarzan de Castro.

March 11	$35,000 expropriated from 3 private firms.
March 12	Five VAR-Palmares members arrested.
March 14	$13,800 seized from supermarket.
March 23	Marcio Leite Toledo (VPR) killed in São Paulo; links leading to Carlos Lamarca allegedly discovered.
April 5	MRT leader Devanir José de Carvalho arrested and killed.
April 14	Major Toja Martinez assassinated in Rio.
April 15	*Conservative industrialist Henning Albert Boilesen assassinated by MRT in retribution for death of Carvalho.*
April 18	Dimas Antonio Cassemiro of MRT killed.
April 23	MR-8 student cell at Rio de Janeiro Federal University broken.
May 1	Zilda Xavier Periera (ALN) escapes Pinel Hospital in Rio.
May 16	Two presses seized by guerrillas from printing press factory.
May 28	Five guerrillas from VAR-Palmares arrested.
	MR-8 cell broken up.
June 23	José Anselmo dos Santos, ex-navy corporal and leader of naval insurrection of March 26, 1964, allegedly dies in prison.
July 22	Guerrillas seize 350,000 NCr from bank.
July 24	João Carlos dos Santos, leader of group which kidnapped von Holleben, captured.
August 5	José Raimundo Costa (VPR) shot to death resisting arrest.
September 18	*Carlos Lamarca killed in Salvador, Bahia.*

1972

January 19	Alex de Paula Xavier-Pereira (ALN) killed.
January 23	Peasant leaders Manoel de Conceição and Luis Campos arrested.
April	Armed resistance begins in Amazonia State.
April 11	Antonio Caros Noguiera Cabral (ALN) killed in Rio de Janeiro.
April 29	Eighteen AP members sentenced to prison.
	Garage of Myers Craig (director of Brazilian Johnson & Johnson) bombed.
June 14	Luri de Paula Xaxier Pereira (ALN) killed, and two students arrested.
July 18	Trial of 55 VPR members in São Paulo.
August 2	Aloisio dos Santos Filhos (PCB foreign affairs committee) taken.
August 12	Fuad Saad (head of PCB foreign affairs) arrested.
September 22	Manoel de Conceição brought to trial.
September 25	Five thousand troops sent to Xambia, Amazonia in counterinsurgency action.
September 28	Police station in Garibaldi, Rio Grande do Sul, raided for weapons.
October 3	Seventeen AP and PRT cadres put on trial.
October 21	Nineteen urban guerrillas (MLN) arrested.
November 2	Two guerrillas (MOLIPO) killed in São Paulo shootout.
November 22	Twenty-two PCB members arrested in São Paulo.
December 3	João Felipe de Sampiao Lacerda (PCB) arrested; 6 other foreign affairs cadre taken soon after.
December 6	Six PCB members arrested in Campo Grande district of Rio de Janeiro.

December 8	PCB sections hit in Goiás and Rio de Janeiro.
December 11	Four Trotskyites arrested in São Paulo.
December 29	Six PCBR members killed and one captured including two National Command members.

1973

January 5	Six bombings in Fortaleza, Ceara.
January 10	Sixth VPR member (including one Paraguayan) shot in one week near Recife.
January 11	Government announces arrests of 32 members of ALN splinter group MOLIPO in São Paulo.
	VPR denounces José Anselmo for defection; his information allegedly set up recent assassinations in Recife, plus others.
January 17	Nine leftists killed in Rio de Janeiro.
January 24	Ex-PCB deputy José María Crispim and daughter sentenced in absentia for association with VPR.
	Anatalia de Melo Alves (PCB) tortured to death in Pernambuco.
February 7	Rubens Berado, deputy and former vice-governor of Guanabara, killed by unknown assailants.
	British naval officer David Cuthberg assassinated in Rio.
February 21	Manuel Henrique de Olivera, Portuguese national and alleged police informer, executed by Aurora Maria Nacimiento Furtado command.
March 1	São Paulo police agent Octavio Gonzalves Moreira killed in Guanabara.

Questions of Organization
by Carlos Marighella

The classic organizational statement by the founder of the National Liberation Action, stressing the need for initiative, mobility, secrecy, and intransigence in the face of the dictatorship. Written during the crescendo of urban guerrilla activity in December 1968, the statement is highly critical of the traditional Left and emphasizes the need for armed struggle.

Our organization was formed to apply a practical revolutionary policy with guerrilla warfare as its strategy. The principles of the organization should not be confused with those of the traditional political organizations of the Brazilian Left whose functions seem to include only establishing a meeting place for elaborating documents and occasionally conducting more or less bureaucratic tasks, dictated by the leadership and never put into practice.

The functioning of our organization, on the contrary, is based on freeing action in the revolutionary struggle, thus emphasizing the initiative taken by the groups that constitute our base. The small initial group of combatants is oriented toward construction of an infrastructure that will permit action, instead of worrying about building a hierarchical structure through meetings of delegates or the calling together of leaders of the old conventional parties.

The Initial Structure of Our Organization

Given these premises, our organization emerged, based upon a strategic and tactical sector which was dedicated to conducting secret work in the strategic area of guerrilla operations and initiating the clandestine formation of a guerrilla training center. This branch of our organization is mobile in character, since it functions in accord with the strategic interests and immediate tactics of the guerrilla and is subject to dismantling operations.

Our organization consists of this sector and of local revolutionary groups of two types:

1. groups derived from the transformation of old conventional organizations into revolutionary groups;

Carlos Marighella, *Teoría y Acción Revolucionarias* (Cuernavaca, Mexico: Editorial Diogenes, 1971), pp. 17–25. Translation by the authors.

2. nonconventional groups, freed of party bonds, which have opted for our principles and reinforced our ranks.

Uniting the existing groups is the urban organization, broadened by other groups which have appeared with the advance of the movement. At the same time, in various parts of the country, small autonomous organizations and some sectors of revolutionary activists, including clerics and independent revolutionaries, have integrated into our organization.

Changes Produced by the Formation of Special Groups and the Importance of Perfecting these Groups

Our organizational concept is neither static nor dogmatic, in accordance with Marxist-Leninist theory which holds that no organization exists in the abstract, but that, rather, organization always serves a political purpose. In our judgment, qualitative changes in the revolutionary movement must induce qualitative changes in the revolutionary organization. As the revolutionary movement advances, changes are introduced into the revolutionary organization. In turn, certain changes in the organization's staff will influence the movement's progress. In our organization a change occurred when the guerrilla training center began to produce results, so that we were able to provide some groups for strategic and tactical tasks and to reinforce local activity. Our primary preoccupation with the training center and with better selecting personnel should produce results. This may bring about a change in the quality of our revolutionary organization and in the form and content of guerrilla operations and tactics, as well as in local activities.

The Emergence of Mobile Units

Another change in our organization resulted in the appearance of two mobile units: the strategic task force and armed tactical group. The task force and the armed tactical group have developed essential activities, independent of each other and with scarcely a link between them. The armed tactical group was a great support for the strategic group. It considerably increased the latter's firepower, effected important operations against enemy positions, and with its notable experience and capacity for action will permit in the immediate future the launching of an open struggle against the dictatorship in the strategic area—the countryside.

The armed tactical group represents with special relevance in our organization the shift from a situation where we had nothing and no firepower to a situation in which we have reasonable firepower: a most important qualitative change. This alone is evidence that we have progressed in revolutionary terms. The armed tactical group is a special instrument to be used in the most complex operations which need the greatest firepower. The management of this firepower requires more specialized and technical knowledge, which will condition and mold the armed tactical group into a special instrument. For this reason, the armed tactical group should not be confused with less technically prepared revolutionary groups, which lack firepower and thus the means to carry out operations. The sources of recruitment for the armed tactical group are the most decisive and determined independent revolutionaries and those experienced militants who opt for transfer to the armed tactical group and accept the demands of that change in their situation.

The Emergence of the Three Fronts

As far as the activity of the local revolutionary groups is concerned, the new factor whose emergence caused the most decisive change in our organization was the appearance in 1968 of three fronts of activity against the dictatorship: the guerrilla front; the mass front; and the support network. These three fronts are typical of local activity throughout the country. Nevertheless, the characteristic of the revolutionary movement is that it develops unevenly, with the result that in some parts of the country one of these fronts disappears or develops more than the others. The next objective, with reference to local activity, is to ensure that the three fronts develop in all parts of the country and that their effects are as forceful as possible. The combination of the three fronts should result in the intensification of urban guerrilla warfare.

The Guerrilla Front

The guerrilla front is characterized by: the capture of arms and explosives; terrorist revolutionary acts, sabotage, and armed anti-imperialist actions of all types; agitation produced by armed groups who paint walls, distribute leaflets, hold flash meetings, and operate the clandestine antidictatorial press. The guerrilla front results from the formation of an infrastructure based on the production of the arms and matériel necessary for war. This infrastructure, together with captured arms and explosives, is one of the decisive factors in changing both the nature of the revolutionary movement and its organization. A guerrilla front which is constantly growing should go as far as a scorched-earth policy in order to assail the dictatorship and divert a good part of the forces of repression, thus preventing them from pursuing the guerrilla. In whatever part of the country, local activity should count on the existence of the guerrilla front and direct its efforts to forming local revolutionary organizations.

The Mass Front

The mass front, led by the student movement, has played an unprecedented role in the struggle against the dictatorships. Occupations, demonstrations, protests, strikes, the fight against censorship, the capture of police and their exchange for political prisoners, all constitute elevated forms of mass struggle. Continued activity by local revolutionary groups among workers, peasants, and exploited sectors of the population will signify a great advance in the antidictatorial struggle. The role of students and priests has been important in terms of showing that the Brazilian middle class repudiates the dictatorship and constitutes one of the most combative forces in the present revolutionary process.

The mass front requires the organization of revolutionary groups both in places of work and study in the city and in rural areas. Besides this, it is necessary to give the mass front reasonable firepower. Mass movement activities should be armed activities, and an infrastructure identical to that of the guerrilla front should be mounted in the mass front. Above all, we should construct an infrastructure among the peasantry, given the pressing need for radicalizing the rural struggle. However, we should not confuse "mass front" with "mass work." The mass front is the edge of the struggle, an action front on an elevated level leading to armed struggle. Mass work involves the infiltration of the masses and the creation of consciousness and demands through the cultural media. Revolutionaries should neither deprecate these means nor confuse them with the mass front.

The Support Network

The support network is the great logistics front behind the Brazilian revolution and guerrilla warfare. Here too, revolutionary support groups are necessary as centers of individual and collective support in the city and, especially, in the countryside. Houses, addresses, hiding places, financial resources, supplies, and information: such are the needs of the support network whose formation merits the special attention of revolutionaries.

Characteristics of Our Organization

Due to changes and new developments, the structure of our organization has evolved to its present form, with the following fundamental features:

1. We have a strategic command in which the problems of rural guerrilla warfare are related to secret strategic affairs and to the control of combat training centers.
2. We have mobile units, such as the strategic task force and tactical armed group. These units are subordinate to the strategic command concerned with the rural guerrilla and they have no fixed place of operation, working wherever the strategic command decides.
3. In each large important urban area we have regional coordinators. Regional coordinators maintain the infrastructure for armed struggle and are responsible for the urban guerrilla. They create the firepower necessary for the urban guerrilla and promote the functioning of the three fronts of activity: the guerrilla front; the mass front; and the support network. Regional commands, if necessary, should be able to complement the infrastructure of the armed struggle and intensify the urban guerrilla warfare. The regional command does not establish permanent contact with any mobile unit subordinate to the strategic command, in order to avoid everyone knowing everyone and everything. The strategic command is tied to the regional command through the communications network.
4. Small autonomous organizations and individual revolutionary militants, or free shooters, may enter our organization with entire

freedom of action and tactical liberty if they accept, defend, and fulfill without reservation our strategic and tactical principles.

5. The backbone of our organization is formed by the revolutionary groups, which are characterized by their initiative and combativeness. The revolutionary groups have the right to reject anyone who, in the name of the command, impedes the revolutionary initiative of the groups based on the principles and tactics of our organization.

6. In our organization there is no complex chain of command, in order to allow simplicity of functioning, rapidity of action, mobility, and the group's capacity for initiative. Neither do we have any type of official as in traditional organizations; everything is based on the application of our principles and on the revolutionaries' capacity for initiative.

7. Leadership in our organization, and in the coordination and command groups in particular, is very simple and is always based upon a small number of comrades who, in order to merit confidence, distinguish themselves in the most hazardous and responsible actions by their capacity for initiative and their intransigence in the defense and application of the revolutionary principles to which we are committed.

A New Experiment in Revolutionary Organization and Leadership

This form of revolutionary organization is a new experience for the Brazilian revolutionary movement. Thus, there exist new problems concerning the national and global functioning of our organization which will only be resolved after we advance further in the execution of guerrilla tactics and operations. Autonomy and freedom of political and revolutionary action are necessary and even indispensable to the functioning of the local organization, although revolutionary leadership should never be spontaneous. Leadership is the direct result of mobile strategic and tactical actions of a broad kind, together with the greatest volume of efficient and technically capable firepower.

Our Principles of Organization

1. The basic principle of our revolutionary organization is to wage guerrilla warfare and to make the organization an instrument of the political policy which follows from this strategy.

2. For an organization to be revolutionary it should permanently exercise the practice of revolution, it should never relinquish its strategic conception, its ideological and organizational principles, or its discipline.

3. A revolutionary organization is not converted into the vanguard by the act of calling itself such. To be the vanguard it is necessary to act and accumulate a convincing revolutionary practice, since action alone makes the vanguard.

4. Our principal activity is not to construct a party, but to initiate revolutionary action.

5. What is fundamental in a revolutionary organization is not to hold unproductive meetings about general and bureaucratic themes, but rather to dedicate oneself systematically to planning and executing even the smallest revolutionary activity.

6. The decisive propelling element in the functioning of a revolutionary organization is the capacity for initiative of the revolutionary groups. No command has the authority to impede any initiative of the revolutionary groups.

7. We do not have a separate political and military policy with the military policy subordinate to the political policy. Our policy is a unique revolutionary policy which contains both military and political aspects.

8. The guerrilla is not the armed wing of a party or political organization. The guerrilla is both the political and military command of the revolution.

9. What determines the emergence and growth of political leadership is the practice of revolutionary action, its success and consequence, and the definitive, constant, direct, and personal participation of leaders in the execution of these actions.

10. There is no political leadership without sacrifice and direct participation in revolutionary action. Political leaders have neither merit nor recognition because of their office or position in the hierarchy. Office has no value. In a revolutionary organization there are only missions and tasks to complete.

11. The duty of every revolutionary is to make the revolution.

12. We ask license of no one to perform revolutionary actions.

13. We have a commitment only to the revolution.

14. The limits of our revolutionary organization are those of our influence and revolutionary capacity.

15. The most fundamental obligation of our revolutionary organization is to maintain the strictest vigilance against the class enemy and in particular against the police. Informers, spies, and traitors within the revolutionary organization should be punished exemplarily.

16. Our basic principle in matters of security is that everyone should only know that which relates to his own work. Without this, it is impossible to guarantee the clandestine functioning of the revolutionary organization.

Problems and Principles of Strategy by Carlos Marighella

A companion piece to the earlier "Questions of Organization," this statement argues the primacy of the countryside within a revolutionary struggle involving an armed alliance of workers, peasants, and students. It is dated January 1969.

The most important problem of the Brazilian revolution is that of strategy, and regarding this—the sense in which it should be directed —there exists no complete accord among revolutionaries. Our organization has adopted a determined strategic concept through which it has been oriented, but it is evident that other organizations have different viewpoints.

The concepts and principles expressed here refer, therefore, to those questions about which our organization can give an opinion acquired from experience. For us the strategy of the Brazilian revolution is guerrilla warfare. Guerrilla warfare forms part of revolutionary people's warfare. In "Some Questions About the Brazilian Guerrillas" we have already established the principles that orient our strategy, and for those who wish to know them it is sufficient to refer to the mentioned work. To the principles already enumerated there, we would like to add some others which will help form an idea of our strategic concepts regarding the Brazilian revolution.

Study and application of these principles by revolutionary groups combined with the personal experience of militants will contribute to a better comprehension not only of the desired objectives of our struggle, but also of the fundamental means to reach them. The following are the strategic principles to which we refer:

The Strategy of the National Liberation Action

1. In a country like Brazil, where a permanent political crisis exists resulting from a deepening of the chronic structural crisis together with the general crisis of capitalism and where, as a consequence, military power has been established, our strategic principle is to transform the political crisis into an armed struggle of the people against military rule.

Carlos Marighella, *Teoría y Acción Revolucionarias* (Cuernavaca, Mexico: Editorial Diogenes, 1971), pp. 9–15. Translation by the authors.

2. The basic principle of revolutionary strategy under the conditions of a permanent political crisis is to release, in the city as well as in the countryside, such a volume of revolutionary action that the enemy will be obliged to transform the political situation into a military one. Then dissatisfaction will reach all the strata of society, and the military will be held absolutely responsible for all failures.

3. The main aim of revolutionary strategy in the transformation of the permanent political crisis into an armed struggle and of the political situation into a military solution, is to destroy the bureaucratic-military machine of the state and replace it with the people in arms.

4. To destroy the bureaucratic-military apparatus of the Brazilian state, revolutionary strategy starts from the premise that that apparatus, within the conditions of the permanent political crisis that characterizes the national situation, entails ever closer relations with the interests of North American imperialism. This machine cannot be destroyed unless the main blow is aimed against North American imperialism, which is the common enemy of humanity and primarily of the Latin American, Asian, and African peoples.

5. Our conception of revolutionary strategy is global both in the sense that its main function consists in countering the global strategies of North American imperialism and in the sense that the political and military strategies exist and act as one, rather than as two separate entities. At the same time, tactical functions are subordinate to strategy, and there exists no possibility of their employment outside of this subordination.

6. Given the global character of our strategy, in undertaking the struggle for the overthrow of the military, we must take into account as a strategic principle the radical transformation of the class structure of Brazilian society toward the goal of socialism. North American imperialism is our principal enemy and we must transform the struggle against it into a national liberation and antioligarchic action.

Thus, in the face of revolutionary attacks, the military will be compelled to come to the defense of North American imperialism and of the Brazilian oligarchy and will become publicly discredited. On the other hand, with the overthrow of military power and the annihilation of its armed forces, we shall expel the North Americans and destroy the Brazilian oligarchy, eliminating the obstacles in the road to socialism.

Strategies of Urban and Rural Struggle

1. The urban struggle acts as a complement to the rural struggle, and thus all urban warfare, whether from the guerrilla front or from the mass front (with the support of the respective supply network), always assumes a tactical character.

2. The decisive struggle is the one in the strategic area (i.e., the rural area) and not the one that evolves in the tactical area (i.e., the city).

3. If by some mistake, urban guerrilla warfare were to be conducted as the decisive struggle, the strategic conflict in the rural area of the peasantry would become relegated to a secondary level. Noting the weak or nonexistent participation of the peasantry in the struggle, the bourgeoisie would take advantage of such circumstances to suborn and isolate the revolution; it will try to maneuver the proletariat which, lacking the support of its fundamental ally, the peasantry, will try to preserve untouched the bureaucratic-military apparatus of the state.

4. Only when the reactionary armed forces have already been destroyed and the military-bourgeois state cannot continue to act against the masses, can a general strike in the city be called which, in combination with guerrilla struggle, will lead to victory. This principle, derived from that which affirms that the primary end of revolutionary struggle is the destruction of the military-bureaucratic apparatus and its substitution with the people in arms, is employed to prevent the bourgeoisie from subverting the general strike and resorting to a coup d'etat in order to seize the initiative from the revolutionaries and cut their road to power.

Strategy of the Urban Guerrilla

1. Because the city is the complementary area of struggle, the urban guerrilla must play a tactical role in support of the rural guerrilla. We must make of the urban guerrilla therefore an instrument for the destruction, diversion, and containment of the armed forces of the dictatorship in order to avoid their concentration of repressive operations against the rural guerrilla.

2. In the process of unleashing the urban guerrilla, the forms of struggle that we employ are not those of mass struggle, but those of small armed groups supplied with firepower and dedicated to the battle aganist the dictatorship. Seeing that the firepower of the revolutionaries is directed against their enemies, the masses, who until then were powerless before the dictatorship, will look upon the urban guerrillas with sympathy and lend them their support.

3. The forms of struggle that characterize the urban guerrilla are guerrilla tactics and armed actions of all types, actions of surprise and ambush, expropriations, seizure of arms and explosives, revolutionary terrorist acts, sabotage, occupations, raids, punishment of North American agents or police torturers, in addition to flash meetings, distribution of leaflets, painting of murals by armed groups, etc.

4. The infrastructure of the urban and rural guerrillas have common points: the training and specialization of the guerrilla; physical conditioning; self-defense; the utilization of professional skills; the technical preparation of homemade weapons; the development of firepower and training for its handling; information networks; means of transportation and communication; medical resources and first aid. Our aim is to rely on both infrastructures, in order not to be reduced to one or the other guerrilla forms, and to combine the two correctly.

5. Revolutionaries engaged in guerrilla warfare give enormous importance to the mass movement in the urban area and to its forms of struggle, such as acts of restitution, strikes, marches, protests, boycotts, etc. Our strategic principle with respect to the urban mass movement is to participate in it with the objective of creating an infrastructure for armed struggle by the working class, students, and other forces: to employ urban guerrillas and to unleash their operations through the use of armed mass groups.

Strategy of the Rural Guerrilla

1. Peasant struggles resulting from demands against landlords, or from the organization of rural syndicates, will develop into armed clashes and in this sense are positive. However, without firepower the peasants will be crushed by the forces of reaction. It is unlikely

that rural guerrillas will emerge, in a strategic sense, out of peasant conflicts. The Brazilian peasantry has a very limited political consciousness and its tradition of struggle does not reach farther than mysticism or banditry; its experience of class struggle under the direction of the proletariat is recent and limited.

Under the present conditions of the country, dominated by the dictatorship, the strategic struggle in the rural area will develop from a guerrilla infrastructure emerging among the peasantry. Seeing in their midst the emergence of a firepower that combats the landlords and does not violate their interests, the peasants will support and participate in guerrilla warfare.

2. The main strategic principle of guerrilla struggle is that it can neither have any consequence nor any decisive character in revolutionary warfare unless it is structured and consolidated in an armed alliance of workers and peasants united with students. Such an alliance, supplied with growing firepower, will give the guerrillas firm foundations and advance their cause. The armed alliance of the proletariat, peasantry, and the middle class is the key to victory.

3. Rural guerrilla warfare is decisive because, in addition to the extreme mobility possible in the interior of the country, it leads to the formation of the revolutionary army of national liberation which can be built from an embryo constituted by the armed alliance of workers and peasants with students. The peasants, without whom the revolution cannot reach its ultimate consequences, are impossible to incorporate into the urban guerrilla.

4. In no event should the Brazilian guerrilla defend areas, territories, regions, or any base or fixed position. If we were to do such, we would permit the enemy to concentrate its forces in campaigns of annihilation against known and vulnerable targets.

5. The Brazilian rural guerrilla should always be mobile. Similarly, the urban guerrilla ought to be extremely mobile and never stage an occupation without meticulously organizing a retreat. Revolutionary warfare in Brazil is a war of movement, whatever the circumstances.

6. The guerrilla plays the principal strategic role in revolutionary warfare, and its political objective is the formation of a revolutionary army of national liberation and the seizure of power. In the

revolutionary struggle we must avoid the distortion of this political objective and prevent the guerrilla, urban or rural, from transforming itself into an instrument of banditry, or unifying with bandits or employing their methods.

Organizational Strategy

1. The continental size of the country, the varying strategic importance of its areas, and the principle of diversity of revolutionary action combine with other factors to determine the existence or emergence of multiple revolutionary centers with regional coordination. Such revolutionary centers will dedicate themselves to implementing a guerrilla infrastructure to unleash the revolutionary struggle and dispose freely of political and tactical action at the regional level.

2. The strategic direction and global tactics of our organization—i.e., the unified political and military direction—will not emerge at once. Such leadership is formed through a permanent process in which armed struggle assumes the fundamental form of guerrilla warfare, going from the strategic field to the tactical and vice versa, until affirming itself in a group of men and women identified with revolutionary action and capable of carrying it to its ultimate consequences.

3. The revolutionary unity of our organization exists in terms of the strategic, tactical, and organic principles that we have adopted and not in terms of names or personalities. It is this identity of ideology, theory, and practice which will ensure that unconnected revolutionaries in various parts of the country will perform acts that will identify them as belonging to the same organization.

Minimanual of the Urban Guerrilla by Carlos Marighella

Written in June 1969 as a training manual for the ALN and other guerrilla groups, the "Minimanual" is the most famous document to emerge from the urban struggle in Brazil.

would like to make a twofold dedication of this work: first to the memories of Edson Souto, Marco Antônio Brás de Carvalho, Nelson José de Almeida ("Escoteiro"), and so many other heroic fighters and urban guerrillas who fell at the hands of the assassins of the Military Police, the Army, the Navy, the Air Force, and the DOPS, [Department of Public and Social Order] hated instruments of the repressive military dictatorship.

Second, to the brave comrades—men and women—imprisoned in the medieval dungeons of the Brazilian Government and subjected to tortures that even surpass the horrendous crimes practiced by the Nazis.

Like those comrades whose memory we revere, as well as those taken prisoner in battle, what we must do is fight.

Each comrade who opposes the military dictatorship and wants to fight it can do something, however insignificant the task may seem.

I urge all who read this minimanual and reach the conclusion that they cannot remain inactive, to follow its instructions and join the fight now. I do so because, under whatever hypothesis and in whatever circumstances, the duty of every revolutionary is to make the revolution.

Another important problem is not merely to read the minimanual here and now, but to circulate its contents. This circulation will be possible if those who agree with its ideas make mimeographed copies or print it in a pamphlet, though in this latter case, armed struggle itself will be necessary.

Finally, the reason that the present minimanual bears my signature, is that the ideas expressed or systematized here reflect the personal experience of a group of men engaged in armed struggle in Brazil,

Tricontinental Bulletin (Havana, Cuba), no. 56 (November 1970) pp. 1–56.

among whom I have the honor to be included. So that certain individ
uals will have no doubt about what this minimanual proclaims and
can no longer deny the facts or continue to state that the conditions
for the struggle do not exist, it is necessary to assume responsibility for
what is said and done. Hence anonymity becomes a problem in a
work such as this. The important fact is that there are patriots prepared to fight like ordinary soldiers, and the more there are the better

The accusation of assault or terrorism no longer has the pejorative
meaning it used to have. It has acquired new clothing, a new colora-
tion. It does not factionalize, it does not discredit; on the contrary it
represents a focal point of attraction.

Today to be an assailant or a terrorist is a quality that ennobles any
honorable man because it is an act worthy of a revolutionary engaged
in armed struggle against the shameful military dictatorship and its
monstrosities.

A Definition of the Urban Guerrilla

The chronic structural crisis characteristic of Brazil today, and its
resultant political instability, are what have brought about the upsurge of revolutionary war in the country. The revolutionary war
manifests itself in the form of urban guerrilla warfare, psychological
warfare, or rural guerrilla warfare. Urban guerrilla warfare or psycho
logical warfare in the city depends on the urban guerrilla.

The urban guerrilla is a man who fights the military dictatorship
with arms, using unconventional methods. A political revolutionary
and an ardent patriot, he is a fighter for his country's liberation, a
friend of the people and of freedom. The area in which the urban
guerrilla acts is in the large Brazilian cities. There are also bandits,
commonly known as outlaws, who work in the big cities. Many times
assaults by outlaws are taken as actions by urban guerrillas.

The urban guerrilla, however, differs radically from the outlaw. The
outlaw benefits personally from the action, and attacks indiscrimi-
nately without distinguishing between the exploited and the exploiters, which is why there are so many ordinary men and women
among his victims. The urban guerrilla follows a political goal and
only attacks the government, the big capitalists, and the foreign imperialists, particularly North Americans.

Another element just as prejudicial as the outlaw and also operating n the urban area is the right-wing counterrevolutionary who creates confusion, assaults banks, hurls bombs, kidnaps, assassinates, and commits the worst imaginable crimes against urban guerrillas, revolutionary priests, students, and citizens who oppose fascism and seek liberty.

The urban guerrilla is an implacable enemy of the government and systematically inflicts damage on the authorities and on the men who dominate the country and exercise power. The prinicpal task of the urban guerrilla is to distract, to wear out, to demoralize the militarists, the military dictatorship and its repressive forces, and also to attack and destroy the wealth and property of the North Americans, the foreign managers, and the Brazilian upper class.

The urban guerrilla is not afraid of dismantling and destroying the present Brazilian economic, political, and social system, for his aim is to help the rural guerrilla and to collaborate in the creation of a totally new and revolutionary social and political structure, with the armed people in power.

The urban guerrilla must have a certain minimal political understanding. To gain that he must read certain printed or mimeographed works such as:

"Guerrilla Warfare" by Che Guevara
"Memories of a Terrorist"
"Some Questions about the Brazilian Guerrillas"
"Guerrilla Operations and Tactics"
"Problems and Principles of Strategy"
"Certain Tactical Principles of Comrades Undertaking Guerrilla Operations"
"Questions of Organization"
O Guerrilheiro, newspaper of the Brazilian revolutionary groups.

Personal Qualities of the Urban Guerrilla

The urban guerrilla is characterized by his bravery and his decisive nature. He must be a good tactician and a good shot. The urban guerrilla must be a person of great astuteness to compensate for the fact that he is not sufficiently strong in arms, ammunition, and equipment.

The career militarists or the government police have modern arms and transport, and can go about anywhere freely, using the force of their power. The urban guerrilla does not have such resources at his disposal and leads a clandestine existence. Sometimes he is a convicted person or is out on parole, and is obliged to use false documents.

Nevertheless, the urban guerrilla has a certain advantage over the conventional military or the police. It is that, while the military and the police act on behalf of the enemy, whom the people hate, the urban guerrilla defends a just cause, which is the people's cause.

The urban guerrilla's arms are inferior to the enemy's, but from a moral point of view, the urban guerrilla has an undeniable superiority.

This moral superiority is what sustains the urban guerrilla. Thanks to it, the urban guerrilla can accomplish his principal duty, which is to attack and to survive.

The urban guerrilla has to capture or divert arms from the enemy to be able to fight. Because his arms are not uniform, since what he has are expropriated or have fallen into his hands in different ways, the urban guerrilla faces the problem of a variety of arms and a shortage of ammunition. Moreover, he has no place to practice shooting and marksmanship.

These difficulties have to be surmounted, forcing the urban guerrilla to be imaginative and creative, qualities without which it would be impossible for him to carry out his role as a revolutionary.

The urban guerrilla must possess initiative, mobility, and flexibility, as well as versatility and a command of any situation. Initiative especially is an indispensable quality. It is not always possible to foresee everything, and the urban guerrilla cannot let himself become confused, or wait for orders. His duty is to act, to find adequate solutions for each problem he faces, and to retreat. It is better to err acting than to do nothing for fear of erring. Without initiative there is no urban guerrilla warfare.

Other important qualities in the urban guerrilla are the following: to be a good walker, to be able to stand up against fatigue, hunger, rain, heat. To know how to hide and to be vigilant. To conquer the art of dissembling. Never to fear danger. To behave the same by day as by night. Not to act impetuously. To have unlimited patience. To remain calm and cool in the worst conditions and situations. Never to leave a track or trail. Not to get discouraged.

In the face of the almost insurmountable difficulties of urban warfare, sometimes comrades weaken, leave, give up the work.

The urban guerrilla is not a businessman in a commercial firm nor is he a character in a play. Urban guerrilla warfare, like rural guerrilla warfare, is a pledge the guerrilla makes to himself. When he cannot face the difficulties, or knows that he lacks the patience to wait, then it is better to relinquish his role before he betrays his pledge, for he clearly lacks the basic qualities necessary to be a guerrilla.

How the Urban Guerrilla Lives and Subsists

The urban guerrilla must know how to live among the people and must be careful not to appear strange and separated from ordinary city life.

He should not wear clothes that are different from those that other people wear. Elaborate and high fashion clothing for men or women may often be a handicap if the urban guerrilla's mission takes him into working class neighborhoods or sections where such dress is uncommon. The same care has to be taken if the urban guerrilla moves from the South to the North or vice versa.

The urban guerrilla must live by his work or professional activity. If he is known and sought by the police, if he is convicted or is on parole, he must go underground and sometimes must live hidden. Under such circumstances, the urban guerrilla cannot reveal his activity to anyone, since that is always and only the responsibility of the revolutionary organization in which he is participating.

The urban guerrilla must have a great capacity for observation, must be well informed about everything, principally about the enemy's movements, and must be very searching and knowledgeable about the area in which he lives, operates, or through which he moves.

But the fundamental and decisive characteristic of the urban guerrilla is that he is a man who fights with arms; given this condition, there is very little likelihood that he will be able to follow his normal profession for long without being identified. The role of expropriation thus looms as clear as high noon. It is impossible for the urban guerrilla to exist and survive without fighting to expropriate.

Thus, within the framework of the class struggle, as it inevitably and necessarily sharpens, the armed struggle of the urban guerrilla points toward two essential objectives:

1. the physical liquidation of the chiefs and assistants of the armed forces and of the police;
2. the expropriation of government resources and those belonging to the big capitalists, latifundists, and imperialists, with small expropriations used for the maintenance of individual urban guerrillas and large ones for the sustenance of the revolution itself.

It is clear that the armed struggle of the urban guerrilla also has other objectives. But here we are referring to the two basic objectives, above all expropriation. It is necessary for every urban guerrilla to keep in mind always that he can only maintain his existence if he is disposed to kill the police and those dedicated to repression, and if he is determined—truly determined—to expropriate the wealth of the big capitalists, the latifundists, and the imperialists.

One of the fundamental characteristics of the Brazilian revolution is that from the beginning it developed around the expropriation of the wealth of the major bourgeois, imperialist, and latifundist interests, without excluding the richest and most powerful commercial elements engaged in the import-export business.

And by expropriating the wealth of the principal enemies of the people, the Brazilian revolution was able to hit them at their vital center, with preferential and systematic attacks on the banking network—that is to say, the most telling blows were leveled against capitalism's nerve system.

The bank robberies carried out by the Brazilian urban guerrillas hurt such big capitalists as Moreira Salles and others, the foreign firms which insure and reinsure the banking capital, the imperialist companies, the federal and state governments—all of them systematically expropriated as of now.

The fruit of these expropriations has been devoted to the work of learning and perfecting urban guerrilla techniques, the purchase, the production, and the transportation of arms and ammunition for the rural areas, the security apparatus of the revolutionaries, the daily maintenance of the fighters, of those who have been liberated from prison by armed force, and of those who are wounded or persecuted by the police, or to any kind of problem concerning comrades liberated from jail or assassinated by the police and the military dictatorship.

The tremendous costs of the revolutionary war must fall on the big capitalists, on imperialism, on the latifundists, and on the government too, both federal and state, since they are all exploiters and oppressors of the people.

Men of the government, agents of the dictatorship and of North American imperialism principally, must pay with their lives for the crimes committed against the Brazilian people.

In Brazil, the number of violent actions carried out by urban guerrillas, including deaths, explosions, seizures of arms, ammunition, and explosives, assaults on banks and prisons, etc., is significant enough to leave no room for doubt as to the actual aims of the revolutionaries. The execution of the CIA spy Charles Chandler, a member of the U.S. Army who came from the war in Vietnam to infiltrate the Brazilian student movement, the military henchmen killed in bloody encounters with urban guerrillas, all are witness to the fact that we are in full revolutionary war and that the war can be waged only by violent means.

This is the reason why the urban guerrilla uses armed struggle and why he continues to concentrate his activity on the physical extermination of the agents of repression, and to dedicate twenty-four hours a day to expropriations from the people's exploiters.

Technical Preparation of the Urban Guerrilla

No one can become an urban guerrilla without paying special attention to technical preparation.

The technical preparation of the urban guerrilla runs from a concern for his physical preparedness to a knowledge of and apprenticeship in professions and skills of all kinds, particularly manual skills.

The urban guerrilla can have strong physical resistance only if he trains systematically. He cannot be a good fighter if he has not learned the art of fighting. For that reason the urban guerrilla must learn and practice various kinds of fighting, of attack, and of personal defense.

Other useful forms of physical preparation are hiking, camping, the practice in survival in the woods, mountain climbing, rowing, swimming, skin diving, training as a frogman, fishing, harpooning, and the hunting of birds and of small and big game.

It is very important to learn how to drive, pilot a plane, handle a motor boat and a sail boat, understand mechanics, radio, telephone, electricity, and have some knowledge of electronic techniques.

It is also important to have a knowledge of topographical information, to be able to locate one's position by instruments or other available resources, to calculate distances, make maps and plans, draw to scale, make timings, work with an angle protractor, a compass, etc.

A knowledge of chemistry, of color combination, and of stamp-making, the domination of the techniques of calligraphy and the copying of letters, and other skills are part of the technical preparation of the urban guerrilla, who is obliged to falsify documents in order to live within a society that he seeks to destroy.

In the area of auxiliary medicine he has the special role of being a doctor or understanding medicine, nursing, pharmacology, drugs, elemental surgery, and emergency first aid.

The basic question in the technical preparation of the urban guerrilla is nevertheless to know how to handle arms such as the machine gun, revolver, automatic, FAL, various types of shotguns, carbines, mortars, bazookas, etc.

A knowledge of various types of ammunition and explosives is another aspect to consider. Among the explosives, dynamite must be well understood. The use of incendiary bombs, smoke bombs, and other types are also indispensable prior knowledge.

To know how to make and repair arms, prepare Molotov cocktails, grenades, mines, homemade destructive devices, how to blow up bridges, tear up and put out of service rails and sleepers, these are requisites in the technical preparation of the urban guerrilla that can never be considered unimportant.

The highest level of preparation for the urban guerrilla is the center for technical training. But only the guerrilla who has already passed the preliminary examination can go on to this school—that is to say, one who has passed the proof of fire in revolutionary action, in actual combat against the enemy.

The Urban Guerrilla's Arms

The urban guerrilla's arms are light arms, easily exchanged, usually captured from the enemy, purchased, or made on the spot.

Light arms have the advantage of fast handling and easy transport. In general, light arms are characterized as short-barrelled. This includes many automatic arms.

Automatic and semiautomatic arms considerably increase the fighting power of the urban guerrilla. The disadvantage of this type of arm for us is the difficulty in controlling it, resulting in wasted rounds or in a prodigious use of ammunition, compensated for only by optimal aim and firing precision. Men who are poorly trained convert automatic weapons into an ammunition drain.

Experience has shown that the basic arm of the urban guerrilla is the light machine gun. This arm, in addition to being efficient and easy to shoot in an urban area, has the advantage of being greatly respected by the enemy. The guerrilla must know thoroughly how to handle the machine gun, now so popular and indispensable to the Brazilian urban guerrilla.

The ideal machine gun for the urban guerrilla is the Ina .45 calibre. Other types of machine guns of different calibres can be used—understanding, of course, the problem of ammunition. Thus it is preferable that the industrial potential of the urban guerrilla permit the production of a single machine gun so that the ammunition used can be standardized.

Each firing group of urban guerrillas must have a machine gun managed by a good marksman. The other components of the group must be armed with .38 revolvers, our standard arm. The .32 is also useful for those who want to participate. But the .38 is preferable since its impact usually puts the enemy out of action.

Hand grenades and conventional smoke bombs can be considered light arms, with defensive power for cover and withdrawal.

Long-barrelled arms are more difficult for the urban guerrilla to transport and they attract much attention because of their size. Among the long-barrelled arms are the FAL, the Mauser guns or rifles, hunting guns such as the Winchester, and others.

Shotguns can be useful if used at close range and point blank. They are useful even for a poor shot, especially at night when precision isn't much help. A pressure airgun can be useful for training in marksmanship. Bazookas and mortars can also be used in action, but the conditions for using them have to be prepared and the people who use them must be trained.

The urban guerrilla should not try to base his actions on the use of heavy arms, which have major drawbacks in a type of fighting that demands lightweight weapons to insure mobility and speed.

Homemade weapons are often as efficient as the best arms produced in conventional factories, and even a cut-off shotgun is a good arm for the urban guerrilla.

The urban guerrilla's role as gunsmith has a fundamental importance. As gunsmith he takes care of the arms, knows how to repair them, and in many cases can set up a small shop for improvising and producing efficient small arms.

Work in metallurgy and on the mechanical lathe are basic skills the urban guerrilla should incorporate into his industrial planning for the construction of homemade weapons.

This construction and courses in explosives and sabotage must be organized. The primary materials for practice in these courses must be obtained ahead of time to prevent an incomplete apprenticeship—that is to say, so as to leave no room for experimentation.

Molotov cocktails, gasoline, homemade contrivances such as catapults and mortars for firing explosives, grenades made of tubes and cans, smoke bombs, mines, conventional explosives such as dynamite and potassium chloride, plastic explosives, gelatine capsules, and ammunition of every kind are indispensable to the success of the urban guerrilla's mission.

The method of obtaining the necessary materials and munitions will be to buy them or to take them by force in expropriation actions especially planned and carried out.

The urban guerrilla will be careful not to keep explosives and materials that can cause accidents around for very long, but will try always to use them immediately on their destined targets.

The urban guerrilla's arms and his ability to maintain them constitute his firepower. By taking advantage of modern arms and introducing innovations in his firepower and in the use of certains arms, the urban guerrilla can change many of the tactics of city warfare. An example of this was the innovation made by the urban guerrillas in Brazil when they introduced the machine gun in their attacks on banks.

When the massive use of uniform machine guns becomes possible, there will be new changes in urban guerrilla warfare tactics. The firing group that utilizes uniform weapons and corresponding ammunition, with reasonable support for their maintenance, will reach a considerable level of efficiency. The urban guerrilla increases his efficiency as he improves his firing potential.

The Shot: The Urban Guerrilla's Reason for Existence

The urban guerrilla's reason for existence, the basic condition in which he acts and survives, is to shoot. The urban guerrilla must know how to shoot well because it is required by his type of combat.

In conventional warfare, combat is generally at a distance with long-range arms. In unconventional warfare, in which urban guerrilla warfare is included, the combat is at close range, often very close. To prevent his own extinction, the urban guerrilla has to shoot first and he cannot err in his shot. He cannot waste his ammunition because he doesn't have large amounts, so he must save it. Nor can he replace his ammunition quickly, since he is part of a small group in which each guerrilla has to take care of himself. The urban guerrilla can lose no time and must be able to shoot at once.

One fundamental fact, which we want to emphasize fully and whose particular importance cannot be overestimated, is that the urban guerrilla must not fire continuously, using up his ammunition. It may be that the enemy is not responding to the fire precisely because he is waiting until the guerrilla's ammunition is used up. At such a moment, without having time to replace his ammunition, the urban guerrilla faces a rain of enemy fire and can be taken prisoner or be killed.

In spite of the value of the surprise factor which many times makes it unnecessary for the urban guerrilla to use his arms, he cannot be allowed the luxury of entering combat without knowing how to shoot. And face to face with the enemy, he must always be moving from one position to another, because to stay in one position makes him a fixed target and, as such, very vulnerable.

The urban guerrilla's life depends on shooting, on his ability to handle his arms well and to avoid being hit. When we speak of shooting, we speak of marksmanship as well. Shooting must be learned until it becomes a reflex action on the part of the urban guerrilla.

To learn how to shoot and to have good aim, the urban guerrilla must train himself systematically, utilizing every apprenticeship method, shooting at targets, even in amusement parks and at home.

Shooting and marksmanship are the urban guerrilla's water and air. His perfection of the art of shooting makes him a special type of urban guerrilla—that is, a sniper, a category of solitary combatant indispensable in isolated actions. The sniper knows how to shoot, at close range and at long range, and his arms are appropriate for either type of shooting.

The Firing Group

In order to function, the urban guerrillas must be organized in small groups. A group of no more than four or five is called the *firing group*.

A minimum of two firing groups, separated and sealed off from other firing groups, directed and coordinated by one or two persons, this is what makes a *firing team*.

Within the firing group there must be complete confidence among the comrades. The best shot and the one who best knows how to manage the machine gun is the person in charge of operations.

The firing group plans and executes urban guerrilla actions, obtains and guards arms, studies and corrects its own tactics.

When there are tasks planned by the strategic command, these tasks take preference. But there is no such thing as a firing group without its own initiative. For this reason it is essential to avoid any rigidity in the organization in order to permit the greatest possible initiative on the part of the firing group. The old-type hierarchy, the style of the traditional left, doesn't exist in our organization.

This means that, except for the priority of objectives set by the strategic command, any firing group can decide to assault a bank, to kidnap or to execute an agent of the dictatorship, a figure identified with the reaction, or a North American spy, and can carry out any kind of propaganda or war of nerves against the enemy without the need to consult the general command.

No firing group can remain inactive waiting for orders from above. Its obligation is to act. Any single urban guerrilla who wants to establish a firing group and begin action can do so and thus becomes a part of the organization.

This method of action eliminates the need for knowing who is carrying out which actions, since there is free initiative and the only important point is to increase substantially the volume of urban guerrilla activity in order to wear out the government and force it onto the defensive.

The firing group is the instrument of organized action. Within it, guerrilla operations and tactics are planned, launched, and carried through to success.

The general command counts on the firing groups to carry out objectives of a strategic nature, and to do so in any part of the country. For its part, it helps the firing groups with their difficulties and their needs.

The organization is an indestructible network of firing groups, and of coordinations among them, that functions simply and practically with a general command that also participates in the attacks; an organization which exists for no purpose other than pure and simple revolutionary action.

The Logistics of the Urban Guerrilla

Conventional logistics can be expressed by the formula CCEM:

C—food (*comida*)
C—fuel (*combustível*)
E—equipment
M—ammunition (*munições*)

Conventional logistics refer to the maintenance problems for an army or a regular armed force, transported in vehicles, with fixed bases and supply lines.

Urban guerrillas, on the contrary, are not an army but small armed groups, intentionally fragmented. They have neither vehicles nor fixed bases. Their supply lines are precarious and insufficient, and have no established base except in the rudimentary sense of an arms factory within a house.

While the goal of conventional logistics is to supply the war needs of the gorillas to be used to repress urban and rural rebellion, urban guerrilla logistics aim at sustaining operations and tactics which have nothing in common with a conventional war and are directed against the military dictatorship and North American domination of the country.

For the urban guerrilla, who starts from nothing and has no support at the beginning, logistics are expressed by the formula MDAME, which is:

M—mechanization
D—money (*dinheiro*)
A—arms
M—ammunition (*munições*)
E—explosives

Revolutionary logistics takes mechanization as one of its bases. Nevertheless, mechanization is inseparable from the driver. The urban guerrilla driver is as important as the urban guerrilla machine gunner. Without either, the machines do not work, and as such the automobile like the machine gun becomes a dead thing. An experienced driver is not made in one day and the apprenticeship must begin early. Every good urban guerrilla must be a driver. As to the vehicle, the urban guerrilla must expropriate what he needs.

When he already has resources, the urban guerrilla can combine the expropriation of vehicles with other methods of acquisition.

Money, arms, ammunition and explosives, and automobiles as well, must be expropriated. And the urban guerrilla must rob banks and armories and seize explosives and ammunition wherever he finds them.

None of these operations is undertaken for just one purpose. Even when the assault is for money, the arms that the guards bear must also be taken.

Expropriation is the first step in the organization of our logistics, which itself assumes an armed and permanently mobile character.

The second step is to reinforce and extend logistics, resorting to ambushes and traps in which the enemy will be surprised and his arms, ammunition, vehicles, and other resources can be captured.

Once he has the arms, ammunition, and explosives, one of the most serious logistics problems the urban guerrilla faces at any time and in any situation, is a hiding place in which to leave the material and appropriate means for transporting it and assembling it where it is needed. This has to be accomplished even when the enemy is on the lookout and has the roads blocked.

The knowledge that the urban guerrilla has of the terrain, and the devices he uses or is capable of using, such as guides especially prepared and recruited for this mission, are the basic elements in the solution of the eternal logistics problem the revolutionary faces.

Characteristics of the Urban Guerrilla's Technique

The technique of the urban guerrilla has the following characteristics:

1. it is an aggressive technique, or in other words, it has an offensive character. As is well known, defensive action means death for us. Since we are inferior to the enemy in firepower and have neither his resources nor his power base, we cannot defend ourselves against an offensive or a concentrated attack by the gorillas. And that is the reason why our urban technique can never be permanent, can never defend a fixed base nor remain in any one spot waiting to repel the circle of reaction;

2. it is a technique of attack and retreat by which we preserve our forces;

3. it is a technique that aims at the development of urban guerrilla warfare, whose function will be to wear out, demoralize, and distract the enemy forces, permitting the emergence and survival of rural guerrilla warfare which is destined to play the decisive role in the revolutionary war.

The Initial Advantages of the Urban Guerrilla

The dynamics of urban guerrilla warfare lie in the urban guerrilla's violent clash with the military and police forces of the dictatorship. In this clash, the police have the superiority. The urban guerrilla has inferior forces. The paradox is that the urban guerrilla . . is nevertheless the attacker.

The military and police forces, for their part, respond to the attack by mobilizing and concentrating infinitely superior forces in the persecution and destruction of the urban guerrilla. He can only avoid defeat if he counts on the initial advantages he has and knows how to exploit them to the end to compensate for his weaknesses and lack of matériel.

The initial advantages are:

1. he must take the enemy by surprise;
2. he must know the terrain of the encounter better than the enemy;
3. he must have greater mobility and speed than the police and other repressive forces;
4. his information service must be better than the enemy's;
5. he must be in command of the situation and demonstrate a decisiveness so great that everyone on our side is inspired and never thinks of hesitating, while on the other side the enemy is stunned and incapable of responding.

Surprise

To compensate for his general weakness and shortage of arms compared to the enemy, the urban guerrilla uses surprise. The enemy has no way to fight surprise and becomes confused or is destroyed.

When urban guerrilla warfare broke out in Brazil, experience proved that surprise was essential to the success of any urban guerrilla operation.

The technique of surprise is based on four essential requisites:

1. we know the situation of the enemy we are going to attack, usually by means of precise information and meticulous observation, while the enemy does not know he is going to be attacked and knows nothing about the attacker;
2. we know the force of the enemy that is going to be attacked and the enemy knows nothing about our force;
3. attacking by surprise, we save and conserve our forces, while the enemy is unable to do the same and is left at the mercy of events;
4. we determine the hour and the place of the attack, fix its duration, and establish its objective. The enemy remains ignorant of all this.

Knowledge of the Terrain

The urban guerrilla's best ally is the terrain and because this is so he must know it like the palm of his hand.

To have the terrain as an ally means to know how to use with intelligence its unevenness, its high and low points, its turns, its irregularities, its regular and secret passages, its abandoned areas, its thickets, etc., taking maximum advantage of all this for the success of armed actions, escapes, retreats, covers, and hiding places.

Impasses and narrow spots, gorges, streets under repair, police control points, military zones and closed off streets, the entrances and exits of tunnels and those that the enemy can close off, viaducts to be crossed, corners controlled by the police or watched, its lights and signals, all this must be thoroughly known and studied in order to avoid fatal errors.

Our problem is to get through and to know where and how to hide, leaving the enemy bewildered in areas he doesn't know.

Familiar with the avenues, streets, alleys, ins and outs, and corners of the urban centers, its paths and shortcuts, its empty lots, its underground passages, its pipes and sewer system, the urban guerrilla safely crosses through the irregular and difficult terrain unfamiliar to the police, where they can be surprised in a fatal ambush or trap at any moment.

Because he knows the terrain the guerrilla can go through it on foot, on bicycle, in automobile, jeep, or truck and never be trapped. Acting in small groups with only a few people, the guerrillas can reunite at an hour and place determined beforehand, following up the attack with new guerrilla operations, or evading the police circle and disorienting the enemy with their unprecedented audacity.

It is an insoluble problem for the police in the labyrinthian terrain of the urban guerrilla, to get someone they can't see, to repress someone they can't catch, to close in on someone they can't find.

Our experience is that the ideal urban guerrilla is one who operates in his own city and knows thoroughly its streets, its neighborhoods, its transit problems, and other peculiarities.

The guerrilla outsider, who comes to a city whose corners are unfamiliar to him, is a weak spot and if he is assigned certain operations, can endanger them. To avoid grave errors, it is necessary for him to get to know well the layout of the streets.

Mobility and Speed

To insure a mobility and speed that the police cannot match, the urban guerrilla needs the following prerequisites:

1. mechanization;

2. knowledge of the terrain;
3. a rupture or suspension of enemy communications and transport;
4. light arms.

By carefully carrying through operations that last only a few moments, and leaving the site in mechanized vehicles, the urban guerrilla beats a rapid retreat, escaping persecution.

The urban guerrilla must know the way in detail and, in this sense, must go through the schedule ahead of time as a training to avoid entering alleyways that have no exit, or running into traffic jams, or becoming paralyzed by the Transit Department's traffic signals.

The police pursue the urban guerrilla blindly without knowing which road he is using for his escape.

While the urban guerrilla quickly flees because he knows the terrain, the police lose the trail and give up the chase.

The urban guerrilla must launch his operations far from the logistics base of the police. An initial advantage of this method of operation is that it places us at a reasonable distance from the possibility of persecution, which facilitates the evasion.

In addition to this necessary precaution, the urban guerrilla must be concerned with the enemy's communication system. The telephone is the primary target in preventing the enemy from access to information by knocking out his communication system.

Even if he knows about the guerrilla operation, the enemy depends on modern transport for his logistics support, and his vehicles necessarily lose time carrying him through the heavy traffic of the large cities.

It is clear that the tangled and treacherous traffic is a disadvantage for the enemy, as it would be for us if we were not ahead of him.

If we want to have a safe margin of security and be certain to leave no tracks for the future, we can adopt the following methods:
1. purposely intercept the police with other vehicles or by apparently casual inconveniences and damages; but in this case the vehicles in question should neither be legal nor have real license numbers;
2. obstruct the road with fallen trees, rocks, ditches, false traffic signs, dead ends or detours, and other ingenious methods;
3. place homemade mines in the way of the police, use gasoline, or throw Molotov cocktails to set their vehicles on fire;
4. set off a burst of machine-gun fire or arms such as the FAL aimed

at the motor and the tires of the cars engaged in pursuit.

With the arrogance typical of the police and the military fascist authorities, the enemy will come to fight us with heavy guns and equipment and with elaborate maneuvers by men armed to the teeth. The urban guerrilla must respond to this with light weapons easily transported, so he can always escape with maximum speed, without ever accepting open fighting. The urban guerrilla has no mission other than to attack and retreat.

We would leave ourselves open to the most stunning defeats if we burdened ourselves with heavy arms and with the tremendous weight of the ammunition necessary to fire them, at the same time losing our precious gift of mobility.

When the enemy fights against us with the cavalry we are at no disadvantage as long as we are mechanized. The automobile goes faster than the horse. From within the car we also have the target of the mounted police, knocking him down with machine gun and revolver fire or with Molotov cocktails and grenades.

On the other hand, it is not so difficult for an urban guerrilla on foot to make a target of a policeman on horseback. Moreover, ropes across the streets, marbles, cork stoppers are very efficient methods of making them both fall. The great disadvantage of a mounted policeman is that he presents the urban guerrilla with two excellent targets: the horse and its rider.

Apart from being faster than the horseman, the helicopter has no better chance in persecution. If the horse is too slow compared to the urban guerrilla's automobile, the helicopter is too fast. Moving at 200 kilometers an hour, it will never succeed in hitting from above a target lost among the crowds and the street vehicles, nor can it land in public streets in order to catch someone. At the same time, whenever it tries to fly low, it will be excessively vulnerable to the fire of the urban guerrilla.

Information

The possibilities that the government has for discovering and destroying the urban guerrillas lessen as the potential of the dictatorship's enemies becomes greater and more concentrated among the popular masses.

This concentration of opponents of the dictatorship plays a very important role in providing information as to moves on the part of the police and men in government, as well as in hiding our activities. The enemy can also be thrown off by false information, which is worse for him because it is a tremendous waste.

By whatever means, the sources of information at the disposal of the urban guerrilla are potentially better than those of the police. The enemy is observed by the people, but he does not know who among the people transmits information to the urban guerrilla. The military and the police are hated for the injustices and violence they commit against the people, and this facilitates obtaining information prejudicial to the activities of government agents.

The information, which is only a small area of popular support, represents an extraordinary potential in the hands of the urban guerrilla. The creation of an intelligence service with an organized structure is a basic need for us. The urban guerrilla has to have essential information about the plans and movements of the enemy, where they are, how they move, the resources of their banking network, their means of communication, and the secret moves they make.

The trustworthy information passed along to the urban guerrilla represents a well-aimed blow at the dictatorship. It has no way to defend itself in the face of an important leak that jeopardizes its interests and facilitates our destructive attack.

The enemy also wants to know what steps we are taking so he can destroy us or prevent us from acting. In this sense the danger of betrayal is present and the enemy encourages betrayal or infiltrates spies into the organization. The urban guerrilla's technique against this enemy tactic is to denounce publicly the traitors, spies, informers, and provocateurs.

Since our struggle takes place among the masses and depends on their sympathy—while the government has a bad reputation because of its brutality, corruption, and incompetence—the informers, spies, traitors, and the police come to be enemies of the people, without supporters, denounced to the urban guerrillas and, in many cases, properly punished.

For his part the urban guerrilla must not evade the duty—once he knows who the spy or informer is—of wiping him out physically. This is the correct method, approved by the people, and it minimizes considerably the incidence of infiltration or enemy spying.

For the complete success of the battle against spies and informers, it is essential to organize a counterespionage or counterintelligence service. Nevertheless, as far as information is concerned, it cannot all be reduced to a question of knowing the enemy's moves and avoiding the infiltration of spies. Information must be broad, it must embrace everything, including the most insignificant matters. There is a technique of obtaining information and the urban guerrilla must master it. Following this technique, information is obtained naturally, as a part of the life of the people.

The urban guerrilla, living in the midst of the people and moving about among them, must be attentive to all types of conversations and human relations, learning how to disguise his interest with great skill and judgment.

In places where people work, study, and live, it is easy to collect all kinds of information on payments, business, plans of all kinds, points of view, opinions, people's state of mind, trips, interiors of buildings, offices, and rooms, operation centers, etc.

Observation, investigation, reconnaissance, and exploration of the terrain are also excellent sources of information. The urban guerrilla never goes anywhere absentmindedly and without revolutionary precaution, always on the alert lest something occur. Eyes and ears open, senses alert, his memory engraved with everything necessary, now or in the future, to the uninterrupted activity of the fighter.

Careful reading of the press with particular attention to the organs of mass communication, the investigation of accumulated data, the transmission of news and everything of note, a persistence in being informed and in informing others, all this makes up the intricate and immensely complicated question of information which gives the urban guerrilla a decisive advantage.

Decision

It is not enough for the urban guerrilla to have in his favor surprise, speed, knowledge of the terrain, and information. He must also demonstrate his command of any situation and a capacity for decision without which all other advantages will prove useless.

It is impossible to carry out any action, however well planned, if the urban guerrilla turns out to be indecisive, uncertain, irresolute.

Even an action successfully begun can end in defeat if the command of the situation and the capacity for decision falter in the middle of the actual execution of the plan. When this command of the situation and a capacity for decision are absent, the void is filled with caviling and terror. The enemy takes advantage of this failure and is able to liquidate us.

The secret for the success of any operation, simple or complicated, easy or difficult, is to rely on determined men. Strictly speaking, there are no easy operations. All must be carried out with the same care exercised in the case of the most difficult, beginning with the choice of the human elements, which means relying on leadership and capacity for decision in every test.

One can see ahead of time whether an action will be successful or not by the way its participants act during the preparatory period. Those who are behind, who fail to make designated contacts, are easily confused, forget things, fail to complete the basic elements of the work, possibly are indecisive men and can be a danger. It is better not to include them.

Decision means to put into practice the plan that has been devised with determination, with audacity, and with an absolute firmness. It takes only one person who vacillates to lose all.

Objectives of the Guerrilla's Actions
With his technique developed and established, the urban guerrilla molds himself on models of action leading to attack and, in Brazil, has the following objectives:

1. to threaten the triangle in which the Brazilian state system and North American domination are maintained in Brazil, a triangle whose points are Rio, São Paulo and Belo Horizonte and whose base is the axle Rio-São Paulo, where the giant industrial-financial-economic-political-cultural-military-police complex that holds the entire decisive power of the country is located;

2. to weaken the local guards or the security system of the dictatorship, given the fact that we are attacking and the gorillas defending, which means catching the government in a defensive position with

its troops immobilized in defense of the entire complex of national maintenance, with its ever-present fears of an attack on its strategic nerve centers, and without ever knowing where, how, and when that will come;

3. to attack on every side with many different armed groups, few in number, each self-contained and operating separately, to disperse the government forces in their pursuit of a thoroughly fragmented organization instead of offering the dictatorship the opportunity to concentrate its forces of repression on the destruction of one tightly organized system operating throughout the country;

4. to give proof of its combativeness, decision, firmness, determination, and persistence in the attack on the military dictatorship in order to permit all malcontents to follow our example and fight with urban guerrilla tactics. Meanwhile, the government, with all its problems, incapable of halting guerrilla operations in the city, will lose time and suffer endless attrition and will finally be forced to pull back its repressive troops in order to mount guard over the banks, industries, armories, military barracks, prisons, public offices, radio and television stations, North American firms, gas storage tanks, oil refineries, ships, airplanes, ports, airports, hospitals, health centers, blood banks, stores, garages, embassies, residences of outstanding members of the regime, such as ministers and generals, police stations, and official organizations, etc.;

5. to increase urban guerrilla disturbances gradually in an endless ascendancy of unforeseen actions such that the government troops cannot leave the urban area to pursue the guerrillas in the interior without running the risk of abandoning the cities and permitting rebellion to increase on the coast as well as in the interior of the country;

6. to oblige the army and the police, with the commanders and their assistants, to change the relative comfort and tranquillity of their barracks and their usual rest, for a state of alarm and growing tension in the expectation of attack or in a search for tracks that vanish without a trace;

7. to avoid open battle and decisive combat with the government, limiting the struggle to brief and rapid attacks with lightning results;

8. to assure for the urban guerrilla a maximum freedom of maneuvers

and of action without ever relinquishing the use of armed violence, remaining firmly oriented toward helping the beginning of rural guerrilla warfare and supporting the construction of the revolutionary army for national liberation.

On the Types and Nature of Action Models for the Urban Guerrilla

In order to achieve the objectives previously enumerated, the urban guerrilla is obliged, in his technique, to follow an action model whose nature is as different and as diversified as possible. The urban guerrilla does not arbitrarily choose this or that action model. Some actions are simple, others are complicated. The urban guerrilla without experience must be incorporated gradually into actions and operations that run from the simple to the complex. He begins with small missions and tasks until he becomes a completely experienced urban guerrilla.

Before any action, the urban guerrilla must think of the methods and the personnel at his disposal to carry out the action. Operations and actions that demand the urban guerrilla's technical preparation cannot be carried out by someone who lacks the technical skill. With these cautions, the action models which the urban guerrilla can carry out are the following:

1. assaults;
2. raids and penetration;
3. occupations;
4. ambush;
5. street tactics;
6. strikes and work interruptions;
7. desertions, diversions, seizures, expropriations of arms, ammunition, explosives;
8. liberation of prisoners;
9. executions;
10. kidnappings;
11. sabotage;
12. terrorism;
13. armed propaganda;
14. war of nerves.

Assaults

Assault is the armed attack which we make to expropriate funds, liberate prisoners, capture explosives, machine guns, and other types of arms and ammunition.

Assaults can take place in broad daylight or at night.

Daytime assaults are made when the objective cannot be achieved at any other hour, as for example, the transport of money by the banks, which is not done at night.

Night assault is usually the most advantageous to the urban guerrilla. The ideal is for all assaults to take place at night when conditions for a surprise attack are most favorable and the darkness facilitates flight and hides the identity of the participants. The urban guerrilla must prepare himself, nevertheless, to act under all conditions, daytime as well as nighttime.

The most vulnerable targets for assault are the following:

1. credit establishments;
2. commercial and industrial enterprises, including the production of arms and explosives;
3. military establishments;
4. commissaries and police stations;
5. jails;
6. government property;
7. mass communications media;
8. North American firms and properties;
9. government vehicles, including military and police vehicles, trucks, armored vehicles, money carriers, trains, ships, and planes.

The assaults on establishments are of the same nature because in every case the property and building represent a fixed target.

Assaults on buildings are conceived as guerrilla operations, varied according to whether they are against banks, a commerical enterprise, industries, military camps, commissaries, prisons, radio stations, warehouses for imperialist firms, etc.

The assault on vehicles—money-carriers, armored cars, trains, ships, airplanes—are of another nature since they are moving targets. The nature of the operations varies according to the situation and the possibility—that is, whether the target is stationary or moving.

Armoured cars, including military cars, are not immune to mines. Obstructed roads, traps, ruses, interception of other vehicles, Molotov cocktails, shooting with heavy arms, are efficient methods of assaulting vehicles.

Heavy vehicles, grounded planes, and anchored ships can be seized and their crews and guards overcome. Airplanes in flight can be diverted from their course by guerrilla action or by one person.

Ships and trains in movement can be assaulted or taken by guerrilla operations in order to capture the arms and munitions or to prevent troop displacement.

The Bank Assault as Popular Model

The most popular assault model is the bank assault. In Brazil, the urban guerrilla has begun a type of organized assault on the banks as a guerrilla operation. Today this type of assault is widely used and has served as a sort of preliminary examination for the urban guerrilla in his apprenticeship for the techniques of revolutionary warfare.

Important innovations in the technique of assaulting banks have developed, guaranteeing flight, the withdrawal of money, and the anonymity of those involved. Among these innovations we cite shooting the tires of cars to prevent pursuit; locking people in the bank bathroom, making them sit on the floor; immobilizing the bank guards and removing their arms, forcing someone to open the coffer or the strong box; using disguises.

Attempts to install bank alarms, to use guards or electronic detection devices of US origin, prove fruitless when the assault is political and is carried out according to urban guerrilla warfare technique. This technique tries to utilize new resources to meet the enemy's tactical changes, has access to a firepower that is growing every day, becomes increasingly astute and audacious, and uses a larger number of revolutionaries every time; all to guarantee the success of operations planned down to the last detail.

The bank assault is a typical expropriation. But, as is true in any kind of armed expropriatory action, the revolutionary is handicapped by a two-fold competition:

1. competition from the outlaw;
2. competition from the right-wing counterrevolutionary.

This competition produces confusion, which is reflected in the people's uncertainty. It is up to the urban guerrilla to prevent this from happening, and to accomplish this he must use two methods:

1. he must avoid the outlaw's technique, which is one of unnecessary violence and appropriation of goods and possessions belonging to the people;

2. he must use the assault for propaganda purposes, at the very moment it is taking place, and later distribute material, leaflets, every possible means of explaining the objectives and the principles of the urban guerrilla as expropriator of the government, the ruling classes, and imperialism.

Raids and Penetrations

Raids and penetrations are quick attacks on establishments located in neighborhoods or even in the center of the city, such as small military units, commissaries, hospitals, to cause trouble, seize arms, punish and terrorize the enemy, take reprisal, or rescue wounded prisoners, or those hospitalized under police vigilance.

Raids and penetrations are also made on garages and depots to destroy vehicles and damage installations, especially if they are North American firms and property.

When they take place on certain stretches of the highway or in certain distant neighborhoods, the raids can serve to force the enemy to move great numbers of troops, a totally useless effort since he will find nobody there to fight.

When they are carried out in certain houses, offices, archives, or public offices, their purpose is to capture or search for secret papers and documents with which to denounce involvements, compromises and the corruption of men in government, their dirty deals and criminal transactions with the North Americans.

Raids and penetrations are most effective if they are carried out at night.

Occupations

Occupations are a type of attack carried out when the urban guerrilla stations himself in specific establishments and locations for a temporary resistance against the enemy or for some propaganda purpose.

The occupation of factories and schools during strikes or at other times is a method of protest or of distracting the enemy's attention.

The occupation of radio stations is for propaganda purposes.

Occupation is a highly effective model for action but, in order to prevent losses and material damage to our ranks, it is always a good idea to count on the possibility of withdrawal. It must always be meticulously planned and carried out at the opportune moment.

Occupation always has a time limit and the faster it is completed, the better.

Ambush

Ambushes are attacks typified by surprise when the enemy is trapped across a road or when he makes a police net surrounding a house or an estate. A false message can bring the enemy to the spot where he falls into the trap.

The principal object of the ambush tactic is to capture enemy arms and punish him with death.

Ambushes to halt passenger trains are for propaganda purposes and, when they are troop trains, the object is to annihilate the enemy and seize his arms.

The urban guerrilla sniper is the kind of fighter especially suited for ambush because he can hide easily in the irregularities of the terrain, on the roofs and the tops of buildings and apartments under construction. From windows and dark places, he can take careful aim at his chosen target.

Ambush has devastating effects on the enemy, leaving him unnerved, insecure, and fearful.

Street Tactics

Street tactics are used to fight the enemy in the streets, utilizing the participation of the masses against him.

In 1968, the Brazilian students used excellent street tactics against police troops, such as marching down streets against traffic and utilizing slings and marbles as arms against the mounted police.

Other street tactics consist in constructing barricades; pulling up paving blocks and hurling them at the police; throwing bottles, bricks, paperweights, and other projectiles from the top of apartment and office buildings against the police; using buildings under construction for flight, for hiding, and for supporting surprise attacks.

It is equally necessary to know how to respond to enemy tactics. When the police troops come protected with helmets to defend themselves against flying objects, we have to divide ourselves into two teams: one to attack the enemy from the front, the other to attack him in the rear, withdrawing one as the other goes into action to prevent the first from becoming a target for projectiles hurled by the second.

By the same token it is important to know how to respond to the police net. When the police designate certain of their men to go into the masses to arrest a demonstrator, a larger group of urban guerrillas must surround the police group, disarming and beating them and at the same time letting the prisoner escape. This urban guerrilla operation is called the *net within the net*.

When the police net is formed at a school building, a factory, a place where the masses assemble, or some other point, the urban guerrilla must not give up or allow himself to be taken by surprise. To make his net work, the enemy is obliged to transport the police in vehicles and special cars to occupy strategic points in the streets in order to invade the building or chosen locale. The urban guerrilla, for his part, must never clear a building or an area and meet in it without first knowing its exits, the way to break the circle, the strategic points that the police might occupy, and the roads that inevitably lead into the net, and he must hold other strategic points from which to strike at the enemy.

The roads followed by the police vehicles must be mined at key points along the way and at forced stopping points. When the mines explode the vehicles will fly into the air. The police will be caught in the trap and will suffer losses or will be victims of ambush. The net must be broken by escape routes unknown to the police. The rigorous planning of the retreat is the best way of frustrating any encircling effort on the part of the enemy.

When there is no possibility of a flight plan, the urban guerrilla must not hold meetings, assemblies, or do anything else since to do so will prevent him from breaking through the net the enemy will surely try to throw around him.

Street tactics have revealed a new type of urban guerrilla, the urban guerrilla who participates in mass demonstrations. This is the type we designate as the urban guerrilla demonstrator, who joins the ranks and participates in popular marches with specific and definite aims.

These aims consist in hurling stones and projectiles of every type, using gasoline to start fires, using the police as a target for their fire arms, capturing police arms, kidnapping agents of the enemy and provocateurs, shooting with careful aim at the henchmen torturers and the police chiefs who come in special cars with false plates in order not to attract attention.

The urban guerrilla demonstrator shows groups in the mass demonstration the flight route if that is necessary. He plants mines, throws Molotov cocktails, prepares ambushes and explosions.

The urban guerrilla demonstrator must also initiate the net within the net, going through government vehicles, official cars, and police vehicles before turning them over or setting them on fire, to see if any of them have money and arms.

Snipers are very good for mass demonstrations and along with the urban guerrilla demonstrator, can play a valuable role.

Hidden at strategic points, the snipers have complete success, using shotguns, machine guns, etc., whose firing can easily cause losses among the enemy.

Strikes and Work Interruptions

The strike is a model of action employed by the urban guerrilla in work centers and schools to damage the enemy by stopping work and study actvities. Because it is one of the weapons most feared by the exploiters and oppressors, the enemy uses tremendous fighting power and incredible violence against it. The strikers are taken to prison, suffer beatings, and many of them wind up assassinated.

The urban guerrilla must prepare the strike in such a way as to leave no tracks or clues that identify the leaders of the action. A strike is successful when it is organized through the action of a small group, if it is carefully prepared in secret and by the most clandestine methods.

Arms, ammunition, Molotovs, homemade weapons of destruction and attack, all this must be supplied beforehand in order to meet the enemy. So that it can do the greatest possible damage, it is a good idea to study and put into effect a sabotage plan.

Work and study interruptions, although they are of brief duration, cause severe damage to the enemy. It is enough for them to crop up at different points and in different sections of the same area, disrupting daily life, occurring endlessly one after the other in authentic guerrilla fashion.

In strikes or simple work interruptions, the urban guerrilla has recourse to occupation or penetration of the locale, or he can simply make a raid. In that case, his objective is to take hostages, to capture prisoners, or to kidnap enemy agents and propose an exchange for the arrested strikers.

In certain cases, strikes and brief work interruptions can offer an excellent opportunity for preparing ambushes or traps whose aim is the physical liquidation of the cruel, bloody police.

The basic fact is that the enemy suffers losses and material and moral damage, and is weakened by the action.

Desertions, Diversions, Seizures, Expropriations of Arms, Ammunition, Explosives

Desertion and the diversion of arms are actions effected in military camps, ships, military hospitals, etc. The urban guerrilla soldier, chief sergeant, subofficial, and official must desert at the most opportune moment with modern arms and ammunition to hand them over for the use of the Brazilian revolution.

One of the opportune moments is when the military urban guerrilla is called upon to pursue and to fight his guerrilla comrades outside the military quarters. Instead of following the orders of the gorillas, the military urban guerrilla must join the revolutionaries by handing over the arms and ammunition he carries, or the military plane he pilots.

The advantage of this method is that the revolutionaries receive arms and ammunition from the army, the navy, the air force, the military police, the civilian guard, or the firemen without any great work, since it reaches their hands by government transport.

Other opportunities may occur in the barracks, and the military urban guerrilla must always be alert to this. In case of carelessness on the part of the commanders or in other favorable conditions, such as bureaucratic attitudes and behavior or relaxation of discipline on the part of sublieutenants and other internal personnel, the military urban guerrilla must no longer wait but must try to advise the organizations and desert alone or accompanied, but with as large a supply of arms as possible.

With information from and participation of the military, urban guerrilla raids on barracks and other military establishments for the purpose of capturing arms can be organized.

When there is no possibility of deserting and taking arms and ammunition, the military urban guerrilla must engage in sabotage, starting explosions and fires in munitions and gunpowder.

This technique of deserting with arms and ammunition, of raiding and sabotaging the military centers, is the best way of wearing out and demoralizing the gorillas and of leaving them confused.

The urban guerrilla's purpose in disarming an individual enemy is to capture his arms. These arms are usually in the hands of sentinels or others whose task is guard duty or repression.

The capture of arms may be accomplished by violent means or by astuteness and by tricks or traps. When the enemy is disarmed, he must be searched for arms other than those already taken from him. If we are careless, he can use the arms that were not seized to shoot the urban guerrilla.

The seizure of arms is an efficient method of acquiring machine guns, the urban guerrilla's most important arms.

When we carry out small operations or actions to seize arms and ammunitions, the material captured may be for personal use or for armaments and supplies for the firing groups.

The necessity to provide firing power for the urban guerrilla is so great that, in order to take off from zero point we often have to purchase one weapon, divert or capture a single arm. The basic point is to begin, and to begin with a great spirit of decisiveness and of boldness. The possession of a single arm multiplies our forces.

In a bank assault, we must be careful to seize the arm or arms of the bank guard. The remainder of the arms we find with the treasurer, the bank teller or the manager must also be seized ahead of time.

The other method we can use to capture arms is the preparation of ambushes against the police and the cars they use to move around in.

Quite often we succeed in capturing arms in the police commissaries as a result of raids from outside.

The expropriation of arms, ammunition, and explosives is the urban guerrilla's goal in assaulting commercial houses, industries, and quarries.

Liberation of Prisoners

The liberation of prisoners is an armed operation designed to free the jailed urban guerrilla. In daily struggle against the enemy, the urban guerrilla is subject to arrest and can be sentenced to unlimited years in jail. This does not mean that the revolutionary battle stops here. For the guerrilla, his experience is deepened by prison and continues even in the dungeons where he is held.

The imprisoned urban guerrilla views jail as a terrain he must dominate and understand in order to free himself by a guerrilla operation. There is no prison, either on an island, in a city penitentiary, or on a farm, that is impregnable to the slyness, the cleverness, and the firing potential of the revolutionaries.

The urban guerrilla who is free views the penal establishments of the enemy as the inevitable site of guerrilla action designed to liberate his ideological brothers from prison.

It is this combination of the urban guerrilla in freedom and the urban guerrilla in jail that results in the armed operations we refer to as the liberation of prisoners.

The guerrilla operations that can be used in liberating prisoners are the following:

1. riots in penal establishments, in correctional colonies and islands, or on transport or prison ships;
2. assault on urban or rural penitentiaries, houses of detention, commissaries, prisoner depots, or any other permanent, occasional, or temporary place where prisoners are held;
3. assaults on prisoner transport trains and cars;
4. raids and penetrations of prisons;
5. ambushing of guards who are moving prisoners.

Execution

Execution is the killing of a North American spy, of an agent of the dictatorship, of a police torturer, of a fascist personality in the government involved in crimes and persecutions against patriots, of a stool pigeon, informer, police agent, or police provocateur.

Those who go to the police of their own free will to make denunciations and accusations, who supply clues and information and finger people, must also be executed when they are caught by the urban guerrilla.

Execution is a secret action in which the least possible number of urban guerrillas are involved. In many cases, the execution can be carried out by one sniper, patiently, alone and unknown, and operating in absolute secrecy and in cold blood.

Kidnapping

Kidnapping is capturing and holding in a secret spot a police agent, a North American spy, a political personality, or a notorious and dangerous enemy of the revolutionary movement.

Kidnapping is used to exchange or liberate imprisoned revolutionary comrades, or to force the suspension of torture in the jail cells of the military dictatorship.

The kidnapping of personalities who are known artists, sports figures, or are outstanding in some other field, but who have evidenced no political interest, can be a useful form of propaganda for the revolutionary and patriotic principles of the urban guerrilla, provided it occurs under special circumstances, and is handled so that the public sympathizes with it and accepts it.

The kidnapping of North American residents or visitors in Brazil constitutes a form of protest against the penetration and domination of United States imperialism in our country.

Sabotage

Sabotage is a highly destructive type of attack using very few persons and sometimes requiring only one to accomplish the desired result. When the urban guerrilla uses sabotage, the first phase is isolated sabotage. Then comes the phase of dispersed and generalized sabotage, carried out by the people.

Well-executed sabotage demands study, planning, and careful execution. A characteristic form of sabotage is explosion using dynamite, fire, and the placing of mines.

A little sand, a trickle of any kind of combustible, a poor lubrication, a screw removed, a short circuit, pieces of wood or of iron, can cause irreparable damage.

The objective of sabotage is to hurt, to damage, to make useless, and to destroy vital enemy points such as the following:

1. the economy of the country;
2. agricultural or industrial production;
3. transport and communication systems;
4. the military and police systems and their establishments and deposits;
5. the repressive military-police system;
6. the firms and properties of North Americans in the country.

The urban guerrilla should endanger the economy of the country, particularly its economic and financial aspects, such as its domestic and foreign commercial network, its exchange and banking systems, its tax collection system, etc.

Public offices, centers of government services, and government warehouses are easy targets for sabotage.

Nor will it be easy to prevent the sabotage of agricultural and industrial production by the urban guerrilla, with his thorough knowledge of the local situation.

Industrial workers acting as urban guerrillas are excellent industrial saboteurs since they, better than anyone, understand the industry, the factory, the machine or the part most likely to destroy an entire operation, doing far more damage than a poorly informed layman could do.

With respect to the enemy's transport and communication systems, beginning with railway traffic, it is necessary to attack them systematically with sabotage arms.

The only caution is against causing death and fatal injury to passengers, especially regular commuters on suburban and long-distance trains.

Attacks on freight trains, rolling or stationary stock, stoppage of military transport and communications systems, these are the major sabotage objectives in this area.

Sleepers can be damaged and pulled up, as can rails. A tunnel blocked by a barrier after an explosion, an obstruction by a derailed car, causes enormous harm.

The derailment of a cargo train carrying fuel is of major damage to the enemy. So is dynamiting railway bridges. In a system where the weight and the size of the rolling equipment is enormous, it takes months for workers to repair or rebulid the destruction and damage.

As for highways, they can be obstructed by trees, stationary vehicles, ditches, dislocations of barriers by dynamite, and bridges blown up by explosion.

Ships can be damaged at anchor in seaports and river ports or in the shipyards. Airplanes can be destroyed or sabotaged on the ground.

Telephonic and telegraphic lines can be systematically damaged, their towers blown up, and their lines made useless.

Transport and communications must be sabotaged at once because the revolutionary war has already begun in Brazil and it is essential to impede the enemy's movement of troops and munitions.

Oil lines, fuel plants, depots for bombs and ammunition, powder magazines and arsenals, military camps, commissaries must become targets par excellence in sabotage operations, while vehicles, army trucks, and other military and police cars must be destroyed wherever they are found.

The military and police repression centers and their specific and specialized organs, must also claim the attention of the urban guerrilla saboteur.

North American firms and properties in the country, for their part, must become such frequent targets of sabotage that the volume of actions directed against them surpasses the total of all other actions against vital enemy points.

Terrorism

Terrorism is an action, usually involving the placement of a bomb or fire explosion of great destructive power, which is capable of effecting irreparable loss against the enemy.

Terrorism requires that the urban guerrilla should have an adequate theoretical and practical knowledge of how to make explosives.

The terroristic act, apart from the apparent facility with which it can be carried out, is no different from other urban guerrilla acts and actions whose success depends on the planning and determination of the revolutionary organization. It is an action the urban guerrilla must execute with the greatest cold bloodedness, calmness, and decision.

Although terrorism generally involves an explosion, there are cases in which it may also be carried out by execution and the systematic burning of installations, properties, and North American depots, plantations, etc. It is essential to point out the importance of fires and the construction of incendiary bombs such as gasoline bombs in the technique of revolutionary terrorism. Another thing is the importance of the material the urban guerrilla can persuade the people to expropriate in moments of hunger and scarcity resulting from the greed of the big commercial interests.

Terrorism is an arm the revolutionary can never relinquish.

Armed Propaganda

The coordination of urban guerrilla actions, including each armed action, is the principal way of making armed propaganda.

These actions, carried out with specific and determined objectives, inevitably become propaganda material for the mass communications system.

Banks assaults, ambushes, desertion and diverting of arms, the rescue of prisoners, executions, kidnappings, sabotage, terrorism, and the war of nerves, are cases in point.

Airplanes diverted in flight by revolutionary action, moving ships and trains assaulted and seized by guerrillas, can also be solely for propaganda effects.

But the urban guerrilla must never fail to install a clandestine press and must be able to turn out mimeographed copies using alcohol or electric plates and other duplicating apparatus, expropriating what he cannot buy in order to produce small clandestine newspapers, pamphlets, flyers, and stamps for propaganda and agitation against the dictatorship.

The urban guerrilla engaged in clandestine printing facilitates enormously the incorporation of large numbers of people into the revolutionary struggle, by opening a permanent work front for those willing to carry on revolutionary propaganda, even when to do so means acting alone and risking their lives as revolutionaries.

With the existence of clandestine propaganda and agitational material, the inventive spirit of the urban guerrilla expands and creates catapults, artifacts, mortars and other instruments with which to distribute the antigovernment pamphlets at a distance.

Tape recordings, the occupation of radio stations, and the use of loudspeakers, drawings on walls and in other inaccessible places are other forms of propaganda.

In using them, the urban guerrilla should give them the charatcer of armed operations.

A consistent propaganda by letters sent to specific addresses, explaining the meaning of the urban guerrilla's armed actions, produces considerable results and is one method of influencing certain segments of the population.

Even this influence exercised in the heart of the people by every possible propaganda device revolving around the activity of the urban guerrilla does not indicate that our forces have everyone's support.

It is enough to win the support of a part of the people and this can be done by popularizing the following slogan: "Let he who does not wish to do anything for the revolutionaries do nothing against them."

The War of Nerves

The war of nerves or psychological war is an aggressive technique, based on the direct or indirect use of mass means of communication and news transmitted orally in order to demoralize the government.

In psychological warfare, the government is always at a disadvantage since it imposes censorship on the mass media and winds up in a defensive position by not allowing anything against it to filter through.

At this point it becomes desperate, is involved in greater contradictions and loss of prestige, and loses time and energy in an exhausting effort at control which is subject to being broken at any moment.

The object of the war of nerves is to misinform, spreading lies among the authorities, in which everyone can participate, thus creating an air of nervousness, discredit, insecurity, uncertainty, and concern on the part of the government.

The best methods used by the urban guerrilla in the war of nerves are the following:

1. using the telephone and the mail to announce false clues to the police and the government, including information on the planting

of bombs and any other act of terrorism in public offices and other places, kidnapping and assassination plans, etc., to oblige the authorities to wear themselves out, following up the information fed them;

2. letting false plans fall into the hands of the police to divert their attention;

3. planting rumors to make the government uneasy;

4. exploiting by every means possible the corruption, the errors, and the failures of the government and its representatives, forcing them into demoralizing explanations and justifications in the very mass communication media they maintain under censorship;

5. presenting denunciations to foreign embassies, the United Nations, the papal nunciature and the international judicial commissions defending human rights or freedom of the press, exposing each concrete violation and use of violence by the military dictatorship and making it known that the revolutionary war will continue its course with serious danger for the enemies of the people.

How to Carry Out the Action

The urban guerrilla who correctly carries through his apprenticeship and training must give the greatest importance to his method of carrying out action, for in this he cannot commit the slightest error.

Any carelessness in the assimilation of the method and its use invites certain disaster, as experience teaches every day.

The outlaws commit errors frequently because of their methods, and this is one of the reasons why the urban guerrilla must be so insistently preoccupied with following the revolutionary technique and not the technique of the bandits.

And not only for that reason. There is no urban guerrilla worthy of the name who ignores the revolutionary method of action and fails to practice it rigorously in the planning and execution of his activity.

The giant is known by his toe. The same can be said of the urban guerrilla who is known from afar for his correct methods and his absolute fidelity to principles.

The revolutionary method of carrying out action is strongly and forcefully based on the knowledge and use of the following elements:

1. investigation of information;

2. observation or *paquera* [vigilance];
3. reconnaissance or exploration of the terrain;
4. study and timing of routes;
5. mapping;
6. mechanization;
7. selection of personnel and relief;
8. selection of firing capacity;
9. study and practice in completion;
10. completion;
11. cover;
12. retreat;
13. dispersal;
14. liberation or transfer of prisoners;
15. elimination of clues;
16. rescue of wounded.

Some Observations on the Method

When there is no information, the point of departure for the planning of the action must be investigation, observation, or *paquera*. This method also has good results.

In any event, including when there is information, it is essential to take observations or *paquera*, to see that the information is not at odds with observation or vice versa.

Reconnaissance or exploration of the terrain, study and timing of routes are so important that to omit them is to make a stab in the dark.

Mechanization, in general, is an underestimated factor in the method of conducting the action. Frequently mechanization is left to the end, to the eve of the action, before anything is done about it.

This is an error. Mechanization must be considered seriously, must be undertaken with considerable foresight and according to careful planning, also based on information, observation, or *paquera*, and must be carried out with rigorous care and precision. The care, conservation, maintenance, and camouflaging of the vehicles expropriated are very important details of mechanization.

When transport fails, the principal action fails with serious moral and material consequences for the urban guerrilla activity.

The selection of personnel requires great care to avoid the inclusion of indecisive or vacillating personnel with the danger of contaminating the other participants, a difficulty that must be avoided.

The withdrawal is equally or more important than the operation itself, to the point that it must be rigorously planned, including the possibility of failure.

One must avoid rescue or transfer of prisoners with children present, or anything to attract the attention of people in casual transit through the area. The best thing is to make the rescue as natural as possible, always winding through, or using different routes or narrow streets that scarcely permit passage on foot, to avoid an encounter of two cars. The elimination of tracks is obligatory and demands the greatest caution in hiding fingerprints and any other sign that could give the enemy information. Lack of care in the elimination of tracks and clues is a factor that increases nervousness in our ranks and which the enemy often exploits.

Rescue of the Wounded

The problem of the wounded in urban guerrilla warfare merits special attention. During guerrilla operations in the urban area, it may happen that some comrade is accidentally wounded or shot by the police. When a guerrilla in the firing group has a knowledge of first aid he can do something for the wounded comrade on the spot. In no circumstances can the wounded urban guerrilla be abandoned at the site of the battle or left to the enemy's hands.

One of the precautions we must take is to set up nursing courses for men and women, courses in which the urban guerrilla can matriculate and learn the elementary techniques of first aid.

The urban guerrilla doctor, student of medicine, nurse, pharmacologist, or simply the person trained in first aid, is a necessity in modern revolutionary struggle.

A small manual of first aid for the urban guerrilla, printed on mimeographed sheets, can also be undertaken by anyone who has enough knowledge.

In planning and completing an armed action, the urban guerrilla cannot forget the organization of medical logistics. This will be accomplished by means of a mobile or motorized clinic. You can also set up a mobile first aid station. Another solution is to utilize the skills of a nursing comrade who waits with his bag of equipment in a designated house to which the wounded are brought.

The ideal would be to have our own well equipped clinic, but this is very costly unless we use expropriated materials.

When all else fails, it is often necessary to resort to legal clinics, using armed forces if necessary to force the doctors to attend to our wounded.

In the eventuality that we fall back on blood banks to buy blood or whole plasma, we must not use legal addresses and certainly not addresses where the wounded can really be found, since they are under our care and protection. Nor should we supply addresses of those involved in the organization's clandestine work to the hospitals and health centers where we take them. Such concerns are indispensable to cover any track or clue.

The houses in which the wounded stay cannot be known to anybody with the unique and exclusive exception of the small group of comrades responsible for their treatment and transport.

Sheets, bloody clothing, medicine, and any other indications of treatment of the comrades wounded in combat with the police, must be completely eliminated from any place they visit to receive medical treatment.

Guerrilla Security

The urban guerrilla lives in constant danger of the possibility of being discovered or denounced. The chief security problem is to make certain that we are well hidden and well guarded, and that there are secure methods to keep the police from locating us or our whereabouts.

The worst enemy of the urban guerrilla and the major danger we run is infiltration into our organization by a spy or an informer.

The spy trapped within the organization will be punished with death. The same goes for those who desert and inform to the police.

A good security is the certainty that the enemy has no spies and agents infiltrated in our midst and can receive no information about us even by indirect or distant means. The fundamental way to insure this is to be cautious and strict in recruiting.

Nor is it permissible for everyone to know everyone and everything else. Each person should know only what relates to his work. This rule is a fundamental point in the ABC's of urban guerrilla security.

The battle that we are waging against the enemy is arduous and difficult because it is a class struggle. Every class struggle is a battle of life or death when the classes are antagonistic.

The enemy wants to annihilate us and fights relentlessly to find us and destroy us, so that our great weapon consists in hiding form him and attacking him by surprise.

The danger to the urban guerrilla is that he may reveal himself through imprudence or allow himself to be discovered through lack of class vigilance. It is inadmissible for the urban guerrilla to give out his own or any other clandestine address to the enemy or to talk too much. Annotations in the margins of newspapers, lost documents, calling cards, letters or notes, all these are clues that the police never underestimate.

Address and telephone books must be destroyed, and one must not write or hold papers; it is necessary to avoid keeping archives of legal or illegal names, biographical information, maps, and plans. The points of contact should not be written down but simply committed to memory.

The urban guerrilla who violates these rules must be warned by the first one who notes his infraction and, if he repeats it, we must avoid working with him.

The need of the urban guerrilla to move about constantly and the relative proximity of the police, given the circumstances of the strategic police net which surrounds the city, force him to adopt variable security methods depending on the enemy's movements.

For this reason it is necessary to maintain a service of daily news about what the enemy appears to be doing, where his police net is operating and what gorges and points of strangulation are being watched. The daily reading of police news in the newspapers is a great fountain of information in these cases.

The most important lesson for guerrilla security is never, under any circumstances, to permit the slightest sign of laxity in the maintenance of security measures and regulations within the organization.

Guerrilla security must be maintained also and principally in cases of arrest. The arrested guerrilla can reveal nothing to the police that will jeopardize the organization. He can say nothing that may lead, as a consequence, to the arrest of other comrades, the discovery of addresses and hiding places, the loss of arms and ammunition.

The Seven Sins of the Urban Guerrilla

Even when the urban guerrilla applies his revolutionary technique with precision and rigorously abides by security rules, he can still be vulnerable to errors. There is no perfect urban guerrilla. The most he can do is to make every effort to diminish the margin of error since he cannot be perfect.

One of the methods we should use to diminish the margin of error is to know thoroughly the seven sins of the urban guerrilla and try to fight them.

The first sin of the urban guerrilla is inexperience. The urban guerrilla blinded by this sin, thinks the enemy is stupid, underestimates his intelligence, believes everything is easy and, as a result, leaves clues that can lead to disaster.

Because of his inexperience, the urban guerrilla can also overestimate the forces of the enemy, believing them to be stronger than they really are. Allowing himself to be fooled by this presumption, the urban guerrilla becomes intimidated, and remains insecure and indecisive, paralyzed and lacking in audacity.

The second sin of the urban guerrilla is to boast about the actions he has completed and broadcast them to the four winds.

The third sin of the urban guerrilla is vanity. The urban guerrilla who suffers from this sin tries to solve the problems of the revolution by actions erupting in the city, but without bothering about the beginnings and the survival of the guerrilla in rural areas. Blinded by success, he winds up organizing an action that he considers decisive and that puts into play all the forces and resources of the organization. Since the city is the area of the strategic circle which we cannot avoid or break while rural guerrilla warfare has not yet erupted and is not at the point of triumph, we always run the fatal error of permitting the enemy to attack us with decisive blows.

The fourth sin of the urban guerrilla is to exaggerate his strength and to undertake projects for which he lacks forces and, as yet, does not have the required infrastructure.

The fifth sin of the urban guerrilla is precipitous action. The urban guerrilla who commits this sin loses patience, suffers an attack of nerves, does not wait for anything, and impetuously throws himself into action, suffering untold reverses.

The sixth sin of the urban guerrilla is to attack the enemy when they are most angry.

The seventh sin of the urban guerrilla is to fail to plan things, and to act out of improvisation.

Popular Support

One of the permanent concerns of the urban guerrilla is his identification with popular causes to win public support.

Where government actions become inept and corrupt, the urban guerrilla should not hesitate to step in to show that he opposes the government and to gain mass sympathy. The present government, for example, imposes heavy finanical burdens and excessively high taxes on the people. It is up to the urban guerrilla to attack the dictatorship's tax collection system and to obstruct its financial activity, throwing all the weight of violent revolutionary action against it.

The urban guerrilla fights not only to upset the tax and collection system; the arm of revolutionary violence must also be directed against those government organs that raise prices and those who direct them, as well as against the wealthiest of the national and foreign profiteers and the important property owners; in short, against all those who accumulate huge fortunes out of the high cost of living, the wages of hunger, excessive prices and rents.

Foreign trusts, such as refrigeration and other North American plants that monopolize the market and the manufacture of general food supplies, must be systematically attacked by the urban guerrilla.

The rebellion of the urban guerrilla and his persistence in intervening in public questions is the best way of insuring public support of the cause we defend. We repeat and insist on repeating: *it is the way of insuring public support.* As soon as a reasonable section of the population begins to take seriously the action of the urban guerrilla, his success is guaranteed.

The government has no alternative except to intensify repression. The police networks, house searches, arrests of innocent people and of suspects, closing off streets, make life in the city unbearable. The military dictatorship embarks on massive political persecution. Political assassinations and police terror become routine.

In spite of all this, the police systematically fail. The armed forces, the navy, and the air force are mobilized and undertake routine police functions. Even so they find no way to halt guerrilla operations or to wipe out the revolutionary organization with its fragmented groups that move around and operate throughout the national territory persistently and contagiously.

The people refuse to collaborate with the authorities, and the general sentiment is that the government is unjust, incapable of solving problems, and resorts purely and simply to the physical liquidation of its opponents.

The political situation in the country is transformed into a military situation in which the gorillas appear more and more to be the ones responsible for errors and violence, while the problems in the lives of the people become truly catastrophic.

When they see the militarists and the dictatorship on the brink of the abyss, and fearing the consequences of a revolutionary war which is already at a fairly advanced and irreversible level, the pacifiers, always to be found within the ruling classes, and the right-wing opportunists, partisans of nonviolent struggle, join hands and circulate rumors behind the scenes, begging the hangmen for elections, "redemocratization," constitutional reforms, and other tripe designed to fool the masses and make them stop the revolutionary rebellion in the cities and the rural areas of the country.

But, watching the revolutionaries, the people now understand that it is a farce to vote in elections which have as their sole objective, guaranteeing the continuation of the military dictatorship and covering up its crimes.

Attacking wholeheartedly this election farce and the so-called "political solution" so appealing to the opportunists, the urban guerrilla must become more aggressive and violent, resorting without letup to sabotage, terrorism, expropriations, assaults, kidnappings, executions, etc.

This answers any attempt to fool the masses with the opening of Congress and the reorganization of political parties—parties of the government and of the oppositions it allows—when all the time parliament and the so-called parties function thanks to the license of the military dictatorship in a true spectacle of marionettes and dogs on a leash.

The role of the urban guerrilla, in order to win the support of the people, is to continue fighting, keeping in mind the interests of the masses and heightening the disastrous situation in which the government must act. These are the circumstances, disastrous for the dictatorship, which permit the revolutionaries to open rural guerrilla warfare in the midst of the uncontrollable expansion of urban rebellion.

The urban guerrilla is engaged in revolutionary action in favor of the people and with it seeks the participation of the masses in the struggle against the military dictatorship and for the liberation of the country from the yoke of the United States. Beginning with the city and with the support of the people, the rural guerrilla war develops rapidly, establishing its infrastructure carefully while the urban area continues the rebellion.

Urban Guerrilla Warfare, School for Selecting the Guerrilla

Revolution is a social phenomenon that depends on men, arms, and resources. Arms and resources exist in the country and can be taken and used, but to do this it is necessary to count on men. Without them, the arms and the resources have no use and no value. For their part, the men must have two basic and indispensable obligatory qualities:
1. they must have a politico-revolutionary motivation;
2. they must have the necessary technical-revolutionary preparation.

Men with a politico-revolutionary motivation are found among the vast and clearheaded contingents of enemies of the military dictatorship and of the domination of U.S. imperialism.

Almost daily such men gravitate to urban guerrilla warfare, and it is for this reason that the reaction no longer announces that it has thwarted the revolutionaries and goes through the unpleasantness of seeing them rise up again out of their own ashes.

The men who are best trained, most experienced, and dedicated to urban guerrilla warfare and at the same time to rural guerrilla warfare, constitute the backbone of the revolutionary war and, therefore, of the Brazilian revolution. From this backbone will come the marrow of the revolutionary army of national liberation, rising out of guerrilla warfare.

This is the central nucleus, not the bureaucrats and opportunists hidden in the organizational structure, not the empty conferees, the clichéd writers of resolutions that remain on paper, but rather the men who fight. The men who from the very first have been determined and ready for anything, who personally participate in revolutionary actions, who do not waver or deceive.

This is the nucleus indoctrinated and disciplined with a long-range strategic and tactical vision consistent with the application of Marxist theory, of Leninism and of its Castro-Guevara developments, applied to the specific conditions of the Brazilian situation. This is the nucleus that will lead the rebellion through its guerrilla phase.

From it will come men and women with politico-military development, one and indivisible, whose task will be that of future leaders after the triumph of the revolution in the construction of the new Brazilian society.

As of now, the men and women chosen for urban guerrilla warfare are workers; peasants whom the city has attracted as a market for manpower and who return to the countryside indoctrinated and politically and technically prepared; students, intellectuals, priests. This is the material with which we are building—starting with urban guerrilla warfare—the armed alliance of workers and peasants, with students, intellectuals, priests.

Workers have infinite knowledge in the industrial sphere and are best for urban revolutionary tasks. The urban guerrilla worker participates in the struggle by constructing arms, sabotaging and preparing saboteurs and dynamiters, and personally participating in actions involving hand arms, or organizing strikes and partial paralysis with the characteristics of mass violence in factories, workshops, and other work centers.

The peasants have an extraordinary intuition for knowledge of the land, judgment in confronting the enemy, and the indispensable ability to communicate with the humble masses. The peasant guerrilla is already participating in our struggle and it is he who reaches the guerrilla core, establishes support points in the countryside, finds hiding places for individuals, arms, munitions, supplies, organizes the sowing and harvesting of grain for use in the guerrilla war, chooses the points of transport, cattle raising posts, and sources of meat supplies, trains the guides that show the rural guerrillas the road and creates an information service in the countryside.

Students are noted for being politically crude and coarse and thus they break all the taboos. When they are integrated into urban guerrilla warfare, as is now occurring on a wide scale, they show a special talent for revolutionary violence and soon acquire a high level of political-technical-military skill. Students have plenty of free time on their hands because they are systematically separated, suspended, and expelled from school by the dictatorship and so they begin to spend their time advantageously, in behalf of the revolution.

The intellectuals constitute the vanguard of resistance to arbitrary acts, social injustice, and the terrible inhumanity of the dictatorship of the gorillas. They spread the revolutionary flame and they have great power in communication and great influence on people. The urban guerrilla intellectual or artist is the most modern of the Brazilian revolution's adherents.

Churchmen—that is to say, those ministers or priests and religious men of various hierarchies and persuasions—represent a sector that has special ability to communicate with the people, particularly with workers, peasants, and the Brazilian woman. The priest who is an urban guerrilla is an active ingredient in the ongoing Brazilian revolutionary war, and constitutes a powerful arm in the struggle against military power and North American imperialism.

As for the Brazilian woman, her participation in the revolutionary war, and particularly in urban guerrilla warfare, has been marked by an unmatched fighting spirit and tenacity, and it is not by chance that so many women have been accused of participation in guerrilla actions against banks, quarries, military centers, etc., and that so many are in prison while others are sought by the police.

As a school for choosing the guerrilla, urban guerrilla warfare prepares and places at the same level of responsibility and efficiency the men and women who share the same dangers fighting, rounding up supplies, serving as messengers or runners, as drivers, sailors or airplane pilots, obtaining secret information, and helping with propaganda and the task of indoctrination.

The Politics of Violence: The Urban Guerrilla in Brazil by Andy Truskier

This interview was conducted in Algeria following the release of 44 guerrillas in exchange for the kidnapped West German ambassador. The four freed revolutionaries interviewed are: Ladislaw Dobor (VPR); Carlos Eduardo Fleury (ALN); Fernando Nagle Gabeira (MR-8); and Angelo Pezzutti.

There has been a great deal of publicity in the United States about the kidnapping of diplomats who are then traded for political prisoners. Can you describe how one of these kidnappings was accomplished?

Dobor: The kidnapping of the Japanese consul was really rather funny. On one side of the place where we seized him is the federal police headquarters; on the other side, less than 100 yards away, is the headquarters of the civil police; on the third side is the district police station; and only 50 yards away is the state security agency! Militarily this type of action is usually very simple. He was in his car with a chauffeur. One person in a Volkswagen began to swerve about the road as if his car were out of control, and he motioned to the ambassador's chauffeur to stop, which of course he did because he didn't want to ram into the VW. Six of our people stepped in at this point. I was on the corner and explained to the ambassador's chauffeur that he should remain calm. Two people then took the consul and put him into a car and drove away.

There was also a second car. We always have one main car and one security car. Both cars have firing teams and if there is any police intervention we try to get the police car in the middle between the two. That's what happened in this case. A few kilometers away, the police managed to find us, seemingly by coincidence. They took a look at our car. The car behind blocked them; we turned to the left and the police just went straight. They didn't want any trouble.

Why did you choose kidnapping as a tactic?

Gabeira: In Brazil the only way to get a person out of jail is through kidnapping. We have about 500 revolutionaries in jail. The judicial

Ramparts, October 1970, pp. 31–33. Copyright 1970 by Noah's Ark, Inc. (for *Ramparts Magazine*), reprinted by permission of the editors.

system is very closely linked to those responsible for the repression. When we go before the judges, we know they will condemn us to about 20 years in jail. It is not possible to contact a lawyer or to make a defense. So the only way to get people out is to kidnap an important personality. We see nothing "unfair" in kidnapping "an innocent person," since the authorities arrest not only revolutionaries but many ordinary people as well. Besides, as Carlos Lamarca, the head of the VPR, has said, "A diplomat who can live with a dictatorship can live with us for three days."

We have found that large numbers of people relate very positively to the kidnappings. When the American ambassador, Elbrick, was kidnapped, the police received hundreds of anonymous phone calls saying he is here, he is there. And when the government, as one of the conditions of the release, was forced to broadcast our message on the official radio station, many small groups of people with transistor radios appeared on the street—it was a form of demonstration.

You have been able to capture many of your weapons from the government. How are you able to do this?
Dobor: I can tell you about a raid on a military police barracks in which I participated. We had 12 people and we staged the raid at ten o'clock at night. We put out people as sentinels; they pretended they had come to find some girls to bring into the barracks for the soldiers. Our people went inside. I was directing the outside part. I had a walkie-talkie. They had a second one inside, so that if they had problems we could give them help. We usually take no chances; we have a lot of arms.

On this raid we had two cars and a small truck that we sent. There was no resistance. We caught everybody sleeping. We didn't even have to take their arms. They were very scared since they were victims of the government propaganda which says that we like to kill and slaughter the poor soldiers. They were so happy that we were not killing them that they actually helped us gather up the rifles and machine guns and hand grenades and load them in the truck. It took 20 minutes. A lot of people watched the action, but nobody called the police. From the car where I was sitting, I saw some MPs coming. I signalled the others with the walkie-talkie, and they took the MPs prisoner the minute they came in. They had no chance to run and they didn't try any heroics. They knew that when a police headquarters is attacked it is the revolutionaries, and they were afraid.

In fact, during several actions we have had a police car pass right by. They don't stop because they know if they do they may be killed. They know it is a political action, and they don't understand what it is about. They usually don't even radio in for help, because if they did they would later have to explain why they didn't stop.

This barracks raid was one of the longest actions we have done. Usually our actions in banks last three or four minutes. Grabbing the Japanese consul took about 40 seconds.

How is an action planned?
Dobor: The actions are usually very simple. We prepare them very carefully, usually for two or three weeks. Everyone is perfectly acquainted with the terrain and the habits of the police in the vicinity. We plan everything well because we don't want to fire a shot. In the VPR we have never fired a shot, except when I was captured.

How did that happen?
Dobor: The police had tortured a young girl very badly and she had told them where I could be found. Some 20 plainclothes police jumped me from behind. I managed to get off one shot at a policeman as I was being thrown down. I missed. I had a Luger and there are many problems with automatic pistols. The second shot didn't go off and they managed to take me alive.

How did you come to choose the urban battleground?
Pezzutti: In the beginning our objective in the cities was to get money and arms—resources necessary to initiate rural guerrilla warfare. We didn't intend to begin the fight in the big cities yet. But in 1968 to 1969 we realized that the urban actions themselves had a very good impact. They were very well received by the workers and the students.

So we started to engage in acts more directly linked to the immediate needs of the workers. In the industrial city of Belo Horizonte in October 1968, workers in the metal industries and the banks were on strike. The police were arresting and attacking strikers who went back to the factory to agitate, and they were forcing the workers at the banks to continue work. So we decided to rob a government bank in Belo to symbolize the oppression of the workers and to show the power a small number of people could have by using the tactics of the guerrilla—surprise, organization, and a concentration of force.

Nine of us went into the bank. In three minutes we had peacefully subdued the 40 people inside, taken all the money, and distributed pamphlets explaining the reason for the action. There were troops near the bank and police cars passing in front every five minutes. But they never saw a thing.

How do you choose your actions?
Dobor: We try to pick actions which speak for themselves. We have attacked supermarkets—especially American supermarkets—and distributed the food, inviting the people from the *favelas* [shantytowns] to help themselves. And they do. Or we seize a truck with American canned food, such as Armour or Swift, take it to a slum, leave it there and write on it the American slogan, "What is good for America is good for Brazil?" Many people in the slums understand the joke.

We follow one basic rule: We do not use violence that is not understood by the people. If the people don't understand it, the government can use it against us. This is why we must be gradual. For example, we kidnap a company owner who does not pay his wages, and force him to pay. What can the government say? We are forcing the owner to abide by the law. This kind of action will never turn the people against us. After we leave food in the slums, the people don't give a damn for propaganda that says we are bandits and murderers. On the other hand, the army always reacts against us in such a situation. By firing on workers, the army makes the people angry and brings them to the point of understanding action on yet another level—that is, action directed against the military.

And the people, especially poor people, often do support us. Sometimes when militants have gotten into armed fights with the police, they have escaped into the *favelas*, often holding their guns. When the police question the people there, they say they saw nothing. Sometimes, due to inexperience, we get into a situation where hundreds of people are observing an action and laughing. In the first bank action I did, people were watching, but no one called the police. One man wanted to call them and went to a bar and asked to use the telephone. The man there refused to let him use it. "It's not *my* money," he said.

It is very wrong to imagine that we are highly trained agents, able to do things very skillfully. It's not like that. We are simply people who are very determined in what we do. That is why the police and army are afraid of us.

Do you use bombs?
Dobor: No. We do not use forms of violence that can be twisted by the government. If the people heard that we use bombs, the government would do exactly what the United States does in Vietnam, and what the French did here in Algeria. They would put a few bombs in a movie-house on a Saturday afternoon, when it is full of children. And then we would have the entire population running after us in the streets.

We choose very selective targets whose meaning cannot be distorted by the government.

What is the meaning of the bank robberies?
Dobor: We try to show the people that the big capitalists are robbers and that the government uses the army against the workers to stop strikes, even killing people. This helps the capitalists get more money. We go to get the money where they put it: in the banks. Tactically, we always characterize the bank actions as "getting the money back," and we do get a lot of it back. We also rob the generals and politicians who are in the pay of the Americans. They are so tremendously corrupt that they cannot put their money into banks. They keep it at home—so we go there to get it.

In one case we got $2.4 million cash! It was very funny: it was one of the biggest robberies ever made in Latin America, but instead of accusing us, as they always do, the government suppressed the story for six months because so many in the government had their hands in this money. They finally admitted that the robbery had happened, but only because it had become a "scandal"—a fairly large number of people had seen us do it. We had to take out a safe weighing 250 kilos, which required the use of a truck.

Are many people in the organization actually underground?
Gabeira: Yes; those people who are actually sought by the police cannot have a job because they might be recognized. One such person is

the leader of the VPR, Carlos Lamarca, who is the most wanted man in Brazil. But many members do have "cover" identities and lead a seemingly normal life.

How do you guard against infiltration by government spies?
Dobor: First, we accept only people whom several members of the organization have known for at least a few years, or even before 1964. We try to take no chances. Although according to our intelligence section the Brazilian Army has trained 800 infiltrators, we have never had an infiltration. On the other hand, we are taking countermeasures, which means that we ourselves are infiltrating the various intelligence services of the government. We can do this more easily now because many people in the army are disgusted by the dictatorship.

Gabeira: Before a person actually comes into our organization, he is given a series of tests—some small actions to see how he performs. In some cases a person will be functioning for a long time with no contact with the organization.

When the police killed Marighella, the government said the Dominicans had betrayed him. Is that what happened?
Fleury: Marighella was very hard to disguise. He was very tall, quite dark, and very big. The police recognized him in the street; they encircled him. There was an exchange of shots and he was killed. He had nothing to do with the Dominican fathers. The government blamed the priests in order to demoralize the movement, to split the leftist movement in general from the leftist Church.

Brazil is known for having won independence from Portugal, abolished slavery, overthrown the monarchy, and made the revolution of 1930, all with little or no actual violence. What brought you to the point of armed struggle?
Gabeira: We did not choose this way of fighting; it was chosen by the dictatorship and by its ally, the United States. Before 1964, we thought change might come in Brazil through peaceful means, but with the right-wing military coup, the only way left to us was armed struggle.

After the coup, how did the armed struggle get its start?
Dobor: In the first years after the coup, we had many discussions and splits. By 1967 only a few small groups had taken up arms—though

one group even assassinated the CIA agent Norman Chandler [sic].[1]
But then in 1968, very large mass movements among the students and
workers erupted and the government had the police shoot into the
strikers and demonstrators. Many were killed. The mass movements
practically disappeared, but some of the leaders and cadres wanted to
continue to fight. Since the government had closed off the peaceful
forms, they came into the armed organizations. It was then that the
urban guerrilla commandos really began.

Our organizations grew tremendously. We didn't know what to do
with all the people who wanted to join and begin fighting. But it is
not as simple as that. To join an armed organization you have to be
contacted in a secure manner, you have to know how to fight, you have
to know how to shoot, how not to be followed, how to write codes,
how to remember certain kinds of things, and most of all, how to
organize. It's difficult. It's a big investment, and our problem is that
we simply have too many people to train adequately with the resources
available.

We did a lot of actions, and our people were very heroic. But they
were inexperienced so it ended up as a slaughter. Many were killed,
many arrested and put in prison, where they were unprepared to resist
the tortures. Many of the first revolutionaries are still in prison. I was
arrested in November 1968, managed to come out and was arrested
again two months ago. Now, as you see, we are developing better techniques to get people out.

Another problem was that initially the police were not working very
hard against us. As a result, we did not build the type of organizational structure that could withstand the concerted assault by the police which came later. We also did not expect so much violence and
torture. After days of torture and electric shock, many people could
not resist, and gave away information. Thus the police managed, with
a little luck, to take the important sectors of the organization. Most
of the initial structures we had built are now gone.

Now we are building a different kind of movement. We have fewer
people, but they are much better trained. Most have been shooting
and fighting some two years. We can already speak of experienced

[1] The reference is to Captain Charles Chandler; see Chronology, October 12, 1968.

cadres. We have good organization, good arms and a lot of money. Gradually it has become a stable, more intelligent, and more organized movement. A few months ago we even gave orders to one of our sectors in Rio de Janeiro to stop all recruiting because the problem is not to get more people but to give the people we already have the ability to fight. To do this for even one person is a lot of work. We have found that one experienced person can work with and train five or six others at most. This is the way in which our new commando groups are formed, and it is working quite well.

Where are the new recruits coming from? What kind of people are they?
Gabeira: With a few exceptions, the members are under 30, some as young as 16. There are many students from sociology, the letters and arts, and law, fields with few prospects on the job market. We are beginning to recruit a few workers, mainly those who participated in the 1968 strikes. Although there are fewer women than men, the women perform the same functions as the men, and we hope that as the revolutionary process escalates, more women will join.

How do you relate your military and political strategies?
Dobor: At this point our goals are not so much military in the sense of inflicting significant military losses; what is more important is the political tactic of getting the people on our side and isolating the government. When that happens there will be no stopping us because we will have a social base, a base of sympathetic people to support us and hide us and join us. This will also mean that we will have a military effect, and that when we perform purely military actions the people will accept it.

Right now, we are not interested in making a show of strength, because we are very few and very weak. Mostly we want to show the people that we are fighting for them. The fact that the government is torturing us, the fact that dozens of us are prepared to die for our country—all this penetrates to the population. And they will easily come to despise the police because they know that they are corrupt and morally deficient, while the people who are opposing them are very clearly idealistic. . . . While the gun is always a political instrument, in the beginning it is almost wholly that.

Gabeira: Our plans for the coming year also involve working on two other problems. First, we want to continue to unify and centralize the revolutionary organizations. At the moment, groups are planning actions together—the kidnapping of the German ambassador was done by two organizations, VPR and ALN. This sort of action can really lead to integration; you can find out what you have in common. Whereas if you only discuss, you usually find out what you don't have in common.

Our common experience, both in jail and here in exile, will no doubt also contribute to unification.

Second, we want to establish ourselves in the countryside, which many of us feel will ultimately be the more important arena of battle. Right now we are laying the basis for this by beginning to mount isolated incidents in the countryside. For example, sugar plantations in several regions have been burned to the ground.

You are still interested in rural guerrilla warfare?
Pezzutti: We think the most exploited class in Latin America is the peasantry. They are a population living on subsistence. They are a potential revolutionary force that will prove very important. Also, the country is a better place to wage guerrilla warfare.

Gabeira: There are other factors, too. The working class in Brazil is very small. Also, many of the workers have only recently come from the countryside. They are just entering the consumer economy, which seems a step up for them. They are getting some privileges—they have more privileges than their brothers in the countryside. And the agricultural sector of the economy is in stagnation.

Pezzutti: We believe that the machinery of the dominant classes' power is stronger in the cities, so the opportunities for a popular army are better in the country. We think the urban fight is slightly secondary, but the popular army must be built in the revolutionary fight, both urban and rural.

Does the revolution have a platform or program?
Dobor: At the moment our movement is mostly a movement of young people, especially students. We feel it is part of a general youth movement that has sprung up in many parts of the world—in the United

States, in Poland, and tomorrow probably in Russia. Most of all, this is a movement of revolt against the world as it is, and as such it brings something new into politics—a kind of morality.

Since our movement is a popular movement, we cannot have a narrow and precise program. But what we basically want is to bring the initiative in politics back to the people. We are not going to be presidents and prime ministers; we want to start a popular movement which will allow the masses of people to have their say as to what kind of government and society will be constructed in Brazil.

We in the VPR do have a general program, which is the same as that of Marighella's group, the ALN.

First, we are fighting for the freedom of the Brazilian people. We want to abolish the dictatorship; we want freedom of organization, freedom of association, all those rights which allow the people to stand up with a minimum of dignity. When the people are afraid, they don't usually have dignity.

Second, we are fighting for independence. Our development has always before been linked to foreign powers, first to Portugal, then to England, now to the United States. Because of this intolerable dependency, we have, amidst great luxury, people dying of hunger and of simple, controllable diseases. We need development that is linked to the basic need of the people: real independence; to be economically independent of other countries, especially the United States.

Third, Brazil is now a land of gross inequalities. We are fighting for political, economic, and social justice.

Gabeira: We all think that the revolution will be socialist, and at the same time a popular revolution in which all the people will participate.

Dobor: Most important, we believe that we can achieve this program only through arms. We are willing to fight alongside any movement that has taken up arms against the dictatorship and against U.S. imperialism. We are much closer to a priest who is fighting for the freedom of the country than, for example, to a speaker from the Communist Party who likes talking and won't get involved in the fight.

We are a small movement, and we will not take power immediately. But we think that whenever a small group forms and takes up arms, it is very important. One small group is nothing; but we know that people are forming small groups all over the world, and that they will develop into a powerful force which will change the whole situation.

You have all spent a lot of time in the jails. What are they like?
Pezzutti: The regular prisoners are treated much better than the political prisoners, who are kept in small isolated cells 19 hours or more a day. It is very difficult to have visitors, see an attorney, or prepare a defense. You are denied access to writing materials, you cannot prepare petitions, and you can say nothing about the torture, which the government officially does not acknowledge. It is very bad.

Then the torture continues, despite the publicity and protests?
Pezzutti: All of the people who are here were tortured. Torture is now an institution, a systematic, standard form of interrogation. Usually it is "scientifically" administered, for the purpose of obtaining information. Doctors are present to determine the victim's physical capacity for torture. Nevertheless, the interrogators sometimes get carried away and cannot stop. This has resulted in at least 20 deaths. A political prisoner, when first arrested, is almost invariably tortured. This can go on for a long time; for many people it lasted two months. And whenever the police get some new information they start all over again. I myself was a guinea pig for a class of 100 army sergeants who were being taught the techniques of torture.

The methods include: beating; electric shock, often applied to the tongue or genitals; having needles thrust under the fingernails; strangling; and simulated drowning. Women are often stripped and sexually assaulted. Sometimes pincers are applied to their breasts, leaving wounds. Another technique is the "hydraulic" torture, in which water under pressure is inserted in the nose, with the mouth closed, causing choking and ultimately loss of consciousness. The interrogators also make use of "truth serum" drugs during their interrogations.

They have imprisoned families. Do they also torture the children?
Fleury: Among the families freed in exchange for the Japanese consul last March, there was a nine-year-old boy whom they beat savagely in an attempt to get information from his mother. Another case involved a woman with a two-year-old child, whom they dropped from a height while she watched; they would catch him in the nick of time. The

smallest of the four children here was present while his parents were being tortured. This is a great trauma for a small child.

Is the United States government involved in any of this?
Dobor: The American involvement in Brazil has become more "rationalized." Since people like less and less to see Americans around, they now train Brazilian officers mainly in the United States, rather than sending Americans to Brazil. We know that many army and police officers, including the torturers, are being trained in the United States. Some have undergone antiguerrilla training at the U.S. base in Panama. Some have also studied at the FBI academy.

In the interior, another kind of work is done by the Peace Corps. While no doubt many Peace Corps people have much idealism and little comprehension of the situation, the Peace Corps is also infiltrated by agents with other purposes. For example, a university researcher may come "to study social conditions" for the purpose of pinpointing the most politically explosive regions in the interior. U.S. personnel are also busy preparing aerial photography maps of regions of the interior that may become centers of guerrilla activities. We use such American-made maps which we manage to get—they are much better than the Brazilian ones.

Gabeira: Edward Kennedy gave a speech against the Brazilian government, but he did not have the true details of what is going on. The CIA is now sending into Brazil groups to organize small groups of rightists to kill people; they are preparing a military organization among the right wing to fight against us. The CIA agent Chandler was training the right wing. But they have many people. Even U.S. Ambassador Elbrick has said that there are many CIA agents working in Brazil.

What can people in the United States do to help your struggle?
Gabeira: First, you can help isolate the Brazilian dictatorship, expose what they are doing. Second, you can expose and denounce the participation of the U.S. government in the repression in Brazil, in training our torturers. But more important, the fight we are waging will be in many places, even inside the United States. We think that the main contradiction in the world today is not between capitalism and socialism but between the giant monopolies and the people they exploit.

Such organizations as SDS and the organizations of people of color inside the U.S. are part of this struggle because they are oppressed too. Personally, I think that the level of repression in the United States is getting very high, and I am worried about the necessity for the organizations to face this.

What can stop the capacity of the U.S. to intervene is the fight inside the U.S. itself, plus a fight all around the world. I think that one day the force inside the United States will be very important in protecting us. But at the moment, this is not the case.

Leninism or Militarism?
by João Quartim

João Quartim, a member of the VPR who left that organization in the purges of January 1969, was sought by the police in connection with the assassination of Captain Charles Chandler three months earlier, and he subsequently went into exile. Here he critically examines the question of militarism in the Brazilian urban guerrilla movement.

We can summarize the limitations of urban guerrilla: it is cut off from the masses by its clandestinity. The mobile strategic detachment in the country can retreat in space to progress in time, since rural guerrilla warfare is a war of attrition in which mobility gives the guerrilleros choice of terrain on which to fight. The urban guerrilla fighter on the other hand can only repeat indefinitely the same operation. Starting from a clandestine base of support, he attacks some objective only to return immediately to the point of departure. The role of time as a factor in the build-up of strength, which enables the rural guerrilla movement to shift the balance of forces bit by bit, and to become a peoples' army through the constant recruitment of sections of the peasant masses (a process which signals the transition from strategic defence to strategic equilibrium), has not the same effect in the case of the urban guerrilla. For as long as there is no permanent contact between the armed vanguard and the masses, there will be no progressive transformation of the vanguard detachment into a peoples' army. This is what is meant by saying that urban guerrilla action is not a mass struggle. The urban vanguard is thus in no way an 'insurrectional *foco*', that is, a political-military organization of revolutionary cadres that develops into an insurrection via protracted war. Proselytism in the urban guerrilla movement is *individual* proselytism: the urban guerrilla movement recruits *new cadres,* it does not recruit *sections of the masses.*

One can now understand the spontaneist deviations so frequent in the Brazilian armed organizations, especially after two years of urban guerrilla action—a very peculiar spontaneism, since it is backed up by

Excerpted from João Quartim, *Dictatorship and Armed Struggle in Brazil* (London: New Left Review Editions, 1971). Reprinted by permission of *New Left Review.*

a rigorous, even "militarist" conception of "organizational life" and of professional militancy. Just because armed struggle in the city is limited (there is an abyss between urban guerrilla warfare, the vanguard struggle, and popular insurrection, the mass struggle; an abyss that cannot be bridged by the development into protracted war, contrary to what happens in the countryside), it is necessary to combine the military and the political struggle. One must rely right to the end on a "war of interpenetration," sending detachments of the revolutionary army out everywhere. Revolutionary war in the city is a form of struggle on the border between war and politics, especially when military operations are confined to "commando" actions. It is natural in such circumstances for differences to appear between those who consider the decisive factor in overcoming the limitations of urban guerrilla action to be organized political work amongst the mass of the people, and those who rely on the distant perspective of insurrection and on the future inauguation of rural guerrilla warfare, and who reject the "politicization" of armed organizations in order to "prevent the military organization becoming the armed wing of a party."

Behind this attempt at mimicry which completely distorts the theory of the Cuban guerrilla, quite serious deviations are concealed.

Terrorism and Armed Propaganda

The revolutionary organizations' use of terror as a tactic was a new feature of political struggle in Brazil, since apart from isolated cases, this form of violent action was previously unknown in our country. The first terrorist attacks (bombing of the U.S. Consulate-General in São Paulo, of the oligarchy's newspaper *O Estado de São Paulo,* and of the headquarters of the Second Army in the same city) were accompanied by the first bank raids, and coincided with the upsurge of the mass movement (March–June 1968). . . . The armed organizations of the revolutionary left have nevertheless overestimated the "mobilizing" value of terrorist attacks. Their rejection of the methods of the "traditional left" often became, especially for those militants and groups that lacked a minimal Marxist-Leninist training, a sort of cult of action for action's sake, in which the most blind "activism" was passed off as political "theory."

Under these conditions it became extremely difficult to know in what circumstances terrorism was an adequate form of struggle. For certain activists, a week without an attack seemed a week in which the revolution made no progress. Arguments of the kind that "the workers are on the side of those who are throwing bombs" were used by the partisans of unlimited terror. In fact—and here the *class content* of the overestimation of terrorism shows itself—these militants let themselves be tempted by the free publicity they received in the bourgeois press (ever greedy for news that increases the sale of its papers) and mistook the fuss made about their bombs by the class enemy for the support of the masses.

There are criteria however according to which terrorist actions should be evaluated. First of all it must be made clear to the mass of the people that the relation between ruling class violence and terrorist violence is one of cause and effect. Revolutionary violence is a response to specific acts of violence by the state. The attacks mounted by COLINA in Minas for instance which struck at union offices reoccupied by the agents of repression after the 1968 occupation were perfectly correct according to this criterion.

Other attacks did not fulfill the above criterion. One example, among many others, was the "Sears bomb" in São Paulo. At the time of McNamara's visit to Brazil (while he was still Secretary of Defence), the revolutionary organizations decided on violent protest against the presence in our country of one of the men most responsible for the genocide of the Vietnamese people. But what form should this take? If it had been possible to kidnap McNamara (as one year later it was possible to kidnap the American ambassador), or to mobilize the people against the visitor, the armed organizations would no doubt have obtained a major political success. However they were not in a position to do so. The POLOP opposition/MNR nevertheless took the decision to set off a bomb at the entrance of the Sears Roebuck department store in São Paulo.

A few remarks are sufficient to show the major political errors behind this attack—about which the least that can be said is that it did not even attract public attention. Firstly, its subjectivism: no one in Brazil, except the initiated few, knew that McNamara owned shares in Sears Roebuck. A manifesto was admittedly left at the place of the attack, but it was only read by a few policemen. The bourgeois press only makes known *certain aspects* of the revolutionary struggle and these are generally the most sensational and the most ambiguous. One must consider here as well the failure to understand the feelings of the population and its level of consciousness. Sears, like all the big stores, sells its goods cheaper than the small shops. Closing it down for a few days meant upsetting the local housewives, without ever explaining to them the political meaning of the action.

A second criterion for evaluating terrorist actions applies to the character of the attack itself. Terrorism against the civil population, for example, is a characteristic feature of fascist violence, of the despair of the possessing classes, who will use any method of intimidation when they feel that their privileges are threatened. In September 1968, for example, at the time of the destruction of the Philosophy Faculty, the CCC,[1] in the presence of the police, fired on an unarmed crowd. The armed organizations of the Brazilian left have always respected this second criterion. Every attack, without exception, has been directed either against public buildings at times when no one was inside, or against particular individuals marked out as agents of repression responsible for acts of violence against the people or against revolutionary militants. The armed organizations have moreover given advance warning on many occasions that the torturers would be punished.

But the most important criterion for evaluating the role of terrorism is the political one. Before throwing a bomb, one must decide what use it will be to the cause of the liberation of the exploited and oppressed. Here ultraleftist errors are as dangerous as those of the right. The partisans of unlimited terror, for example, try to justify themselves by citing historical examples, such as the national liberation struggle in Algeria, and the methods of urban guerrilla used by the NLF in Saigon. They forget one "small" detail. The NLF is at the stage of strategic counteroffensive. It has already liberated the greater part of the country and is fighting not only against internal reaction but also against a foreign army of occupation. The clandestine organizations of the Brazilian revolutionary left were to begin with almost unknown, even to the most advanced sections of the popular movement. They are now well-known but they have failed to develop a peo-

[1] A right-wing terrorist group, the *Comando Caça Communista:* Communist Hunting Command.

ples' war, because there was no foreign army *directly* and therefore demonstrably present in Brazil.

In fact, fetishist attachments to certain forms of violence, which by their very nature are the acts of small groups cut off from the masses, have encouraged the tendency to measure the progress of a revolutionary organization primarily by its capacity to harass the enemy police and military apparatus, and not by its capacity to enlist the participation of the masses in decisive struggles.

Overestimation of terrorism as a form of struggle only increases the uncertainties and difficulties of the armed organizations. The value of terrorism was indeed so overestimated that some elements on the Brazilian left failed to distinguish the different stages of revolutionary warfare (thus precluding an understanding of the role of each particular form of struggle at each specific stage of the war). It was argued, for example, that terrorism immobilized an important part of the enemy's armed forces in the city. But one small detail was forgotten. During the years 1968–1969 the forces of the revolution were themselves concentrated in the city. . . .

In other words, the present stage of the Brazilian revolutionary war, at which rural guerrilla warfare had not even begun, was confused with a later stage at which it would be widespread enough to attract the main weight of the ruling classes' repressive apparatus. At that stage, it is true, any act of terrorism against the government's military and political centers in the cities, besides encouraging the masses, weakens the enemy's ability to fight the rural guerrilla by forcing him to divide his forces.

The political criterion for assessing terrorist actions—how does an action win the support of the masses?—raises the question of armed propaganda. In 1968 the main effect of terrorism was to concentrate the attention of the state on subversive activities. It was easy to confuse the impact of the publicity which the bombings received with a real building up of strength among the people. Many militants imagined that merely by exploding bombs they were bringing the Brazilian revolution nearer. It became essential however to ask whether throwing bombs in large cities in fact achieved this.

The partisans of unlimited terror had a reply to this question—armed propaganda. This expression is used to mean many things. The first, put into practice by AP (Popular Action), is propaganda *for the necessity of armed struggle.* When the students shouted the slogan "Only the armed people will overthrow the dictatorship," they carried out armed propaganda in this sense. This "ideological" conception of revolutionary propaganda became known as "unarmed armed propaganda." For the armed organizations, armed propaganda meant primarily direct action. In this second sense of the expression, armed propaganda became the form that revolutionary warfare acquired in the city. Through it the clandestine organizations addressed themselves to the whole people. It enabled them to emerge from below ground, where they had been incapable of political work by themselves.

The most important distinction from a political point of view is between generalized armed propaganda and local armed propaganda. Which is the better tactic to adopt has become a major question among the armed organizations. The first kind is intended to have repercussions throughout the country as a whole. Kidnapping an ambassador, carrying out acts of revolutionary justice, or seizing a radio station to broadcast a message to the people are all examples of generalized armed propaganda.

The armed organizations have no way of making their programmes heard at national level except by such means as seizing radio stations. On 1 May 1969 the radio station in São Bernardo was seized by a group of militants who broadcast messages and slogans, and a few weeks later the Radio Nacional was occupied by an ALN commando to broadcast a tape of one of Marighella's speeches. Because the military state has a monopoly on the means of communication, any propaganda of this sort must be accompanied by arms. Acts of "revolutionary justice" such as the execution of the U.S. officer Captain Chandler, who after tours of duty in Vietnam and Bolivia had come to Brazil charged with the organization and training of ultraright terrorist groups, may also serve as propaganda.

But this category "revolutionary justice" must be used with care. The kidnapping of an ambassador may have many tactical justifications, but revolutionary justice is not one of them. It is torturers and not diplomats who deserve to be shot. To the extent that kidnappings succeed in their immediate aims such as freeing prisoners and victims of torture, they deserve unconditional support. However, if there is to be revolutionary justice in kidnappings, only those victims should be chosen whom one would be justified in shooting should the negotiations fail. One does not shoot hostages because they are hostages, but because they are war criminals. If this principle is not scrupulously observed, one runs the risk either of shooting someone without justification (and thereby of vitiating the propaganda effect of the action) or of having to free the hostage before the demands have been met.

1970 saw a return to the tactic of kidnapping, in many cases for the liberation of prisoners. The June kidnapping of the West German ambassador Von Holleben was from this point of view a complete success: forty prisoners were freed. In March the Japanese consul, Okuchi, was kidnapped in São Paulo, and Bucher, the Swiss ambassador, was kidnapped from Rio in December. The former was released unharmed in exchange for five prisoners and the latter for seventy prisoners.

Actions of this kind no doubt demoralize the regime, particularly since it has committed itself so openly to the "crushing of subversion." However, they pose the problem which arises in any debate on tactics: should one's main goal be to crush the enemy or to win the masses? It is essential for the success of kidnappings, bombings or other "generalized" actions that they be carried out by small and highly disciplined groups. The mass of the people cannot participate. They are in many respects the passive recipients of the "propaganda effect."

It is no accident that the more militarist of the armed organizations have favored such actions. They are not of course in themselves any more or less militarist than any other form of struggle. They become, however, a purely militarist tactic if they are practised to the exclusion of any other forms, particularly to the exclusion of propaganda at a local level. They can never be justified as an organization's normal method of struggle.

Localized armed propaganda is not aimed at the people as a whole. News of such actions does not have to be channelled through a press and broadcasting network which is predominantly under government control. Local propaganda is aimed at a particular factory, the people of a particular suburb, the peasants of a particular village. The size of the groups among which local actions are carried out is so small that communication can be direct. In the cities, it most often takes the form of rapidly assembled factory meetings at which speeches are made and pamphlets distributed attacking the regime. Because the police will almost invariably intervene, it is necessary to protect such meetings with arms. Similar meetings can take place in the *favelas* [shanty-towns]. In the country, such propaganda may take the form of reprisals against landlord's agents, burning records, sacking a company store, or slaughtering cattle and distributing the meat to starving peasants. Such actions must be chosen which will evoke a response in a particular factory or village, and slogans must appeal directly to workers' and peasants' most immediate needs and aspirations. . . .

The political error made by the partisans of unlimited terror does not arise from a tactical choice which presents "armed propaganda" as a specific form of struggle, but from believing dogmatically that any action directed "against the system" produces a propaganda effect, and from failing to understand that a struggle isolated from the broad masses is always a limited form of struggle. The danger does not lie in armed propaganda as such. On the contrary, this can be an important moment in the process of formation of the peoples' armed vanguard. The danger lies rather in the tendency to make armed propaganda a substitute for the mass struggle.

In the present phase of the revolutionary struggle therefore, localized armed propaganda should be the principal form and actions with national repercussions should be kept to a minimum and only attempted when certain political conditions have been met. In doing this the armed organizations may win themselves less international fame, but they will forge far stronger links with the masses.

The First Two Years of Urban Warfare

The newspapers made much noise over the bombs at the U.S. Consulate in São Paulo and at the Second Army HQ and over the bank raids and arms thefts. The desire of most activists to participate in these actions was flatly contradictory to their very nature, which required rigorous clandestinity and the smallest possible number of participants. The great majority of revolutionaries had to be left out of these activities, and, given the absence of a clear strategic conception of revolutionary war (in particular the activists' underestimation of the tasks of organization), this great majority remained in practice quite unmobolized and could only stand by admiring in silence the exploits of the small armed groups. To remedy this, small tasks were invented of little or no objective importance simply so as not to demobilize the mass of activists. Despite their lack of importance these tasks often carried serious risks. Slogan-writing or the distribution of leaflets often led to savage beatings, and, because activists caught while engaged in these things were usually interrogated, it became necessary to reduce even this sphere of work.

For the armed organizations in the cities, the slogan that "action builds organization" revealed its one-sidedness in practice. The POLOP opposition/MNR under its new name of VPR started an internal struggle on these questions toward the end of 1968, which was to last for a whole year and which ended in the absolute hegemony of what we have called the "militarist" tendency, characterized by the following positions:

1. rejection of systematic work in the mass movement;
2. rejection of the "traditional" forms of agitation and propaganda;
3. tendency toward reducing organizational structure to armed groups alone;
4. adoption of the *foco* theory as presented in *Revolution in the Revolution?*

The Leninist tendency held quite opposed positions, and was accused of seeking to return to the "theory of the party"—a completely justified charge, if by "party" one understands the fighting vanguard of the popular masses. This accusation really touched the root of the problem of the nature and tasks of the revolutionary vanguard in Brazil: whether or not the generalization of guerrilla warfare presupposes the existence of a national organization able to coordinate the popular struggle as a whole. The militarists replied in the negative and the Leninists in the affirmative. The former believed that guerrilla warfare could be indefinitely extended by the action of urban and rural "small motors" alone; the latter insisted on the dialectical interdependence of the political and the military tasks of the revolution. This internal struggle was interrupted for a time by the police and military offensive that followed Institutional Act V of December 1968, and by the "Fourth Infantry Regiment action" in January 1969. The latter episode deserves a close analysis. Besides providing a concrete example of partisan warfare in São Paulo, it spotlights the practical implications of the political and tactical debate within the armed organizations, and particularly the VPR.

By the time of the Fifth Act, the VPR was no longer a small, isolated grouping. It had made links with important sections of the popular movement, sought to take a public position on all major national problems and took on responsibilities that went far beyond the limited perspectives of a small urban armed nucleus. Institutional Act V signalled both a deepening political crisis within the ruling classes and the regime's decision to move to the counteroffensive. It was obvious to all that this final liquidation of the facade of "redemocratization" would only pay off for the ruling classes if they succeeded in "crushing subversion." In these circumstances, the correct response for the armed organizations would have been tactical withdrawal until the wave of repression had subsided. This tactic would not have been incompatible with carrying out a few rapid and effective armed actions in order to discredit the repressive apparatus and to show the urban masses that "subversion" could not be abolished by decree. The application of such a tactic would have shown a correct understanding of the balance of forces between revolution and counterrevolution, and would have been a practical development of the strategy of protracted war.

But the VPR did exactly the reverse. While mass prison camps were being improvised in almost every city in the country, while all those vaguely suspected of "communism" were being arrested, and torture was being used for the first time as the *principal* means of extracting information from the detainees, the VPR decided to attack the Fourth Infantry Regiment, stationed in the suburbs of São Paulo, near the workers' district of Osasco. The very fact that such a decision could have been taken in this conjuncture shows that the militarists had already prevailed within the organization. In fact, following a stormy conference, the urban military sector seized control of the central VPR command and prepared for the attack on the Fourth Infantry Regiment. The aim of this operation was purely logistic: to secure a few hundred FAL automatic rifles, submachine guns, and grenades, as well as some heavier weapons such as machine guns, flamethrowers, etc. The existence of a VPR cell within the regiment seemed to justify the operation, all the more so as the VPR leadership at this time had an unfortunate tendency to confuse the military possibility of an action with its political correctness. This cell was organized by Captain Lamarca. . . .

The attack on the Fourth Infantry Regiment was prepared in an almost suicidal fashion. Despite the vigorous protests of the Leninists, powerless since the internal crisis of December 1968, the VPR mobilized militants from all sectors of its organization, and particularly those working in the countryside, which on paper was considered the principal field of struggle. Prepared in such an irresponsible way, the project was bound to fail. In fact, it was never even carried out. The militants of one cell were discovered painting a truck in army colors, and the whole of the dictatorship's repressive apparatus was put on the alert. The cell in the Fourth Infantry Regiment had just enough time to take flight, in a truck loaded with automatic weapons—which proves that the operation could have been carried out without committing to it almost the entire VPR strategic potential. The cost of this action was too heavy. The four militants arrested on the eve of the operation were savagely tortured and ended by disclosing everything. (One of them even went beyond the limit that separates weakness in the face of pain—which is always understandable—from collaboration with the enemy.) The vicious circle of capture-torture–confession–further captures, etc. rapidly endangered the very survival of the VPR, which found itself on the very edge of disintegration. The manhunt raged for two months, and enabled the regime to penetrate deep into the organization's clandestine structure. The São Paulo urban network was shattered, and by March the police could boast of having arrested around thirty VPR militants. However, in April the VPR was already reborn from its ashes, if no longer quite the same. Without understanding the profound reasons for the disaster that they themselves had prepared, the militarists took the occasion to purge the most prominent militants among the Leninists, while managing, thanks to their undeniable courage and tenacity, to reconstruct the organization's urban infrastructure. The VPR came out alive from the ordeal of January–March 1969, but it had squandered its strategic resources in operations of a purely tactical significance. It emerged decimated, but "homogeneous." However, the problems brushed under the carpet with the purge of the Leninists were to reappear some months later, with the foundation of the VAR-Palmares.

The VPR disaster happened just when the changing political conjuncture considerably increased the importance of armed propaganda in the city. The violent repression of the student movement and the "democratic" trade-union opposition (i.e., those trade-unionists who, while far removed from an independent working-class position, were not simply the regime's agents) severely limited the possibilities of mass struggle, as did the white terror of the CCC and MAC,[2] which after organizing in 1968 the assassination of students and the punitive expeditions into "left-wing" theaters, in 1969 turned their attentions towards the progressive sectors of the Catholic church. . . . The very weakness of the popular movement, whose most combative sectors were exhausted after the struggles of 1968, also tended to restrict popular resistance to the fighting organizations alone.

In these circumstances, a vanguard was needed that could lead the masses in a tactical withdrawal, while continuing to harass the regime's repressive apparatus in the urban zone and to advance both the political and military preparation of people's war in the countryside. But these very conditions also generated "immediatist" tendencies within the armed organizations. Eager to respond to the dictatorship's crimes, whatever the cost, and wishing to show the masses that struggle was possible and that the criminals were vulnerable, the urban partisans took the risk of giving priority to direct confrontation with the repressive apparatus rather than to the development, necessarily slow, silent, and marked by frequent retreats, of the strategic objectives of the Brazilian revolution. Forgetting that the annihilation of the enemy's armed forces required preserving its own, the revolutionary vanguard lost sight of the particular features of the actual situation, and overexposed itself to the regime's counteroffensive. This was all the more true insofar as the development of armed propaganda and partisan operations in the city was matched by a parallel development of counterrevolutionary warfare.

This is why 1969 was the year of urban "battles." These are still not

[2] *Movimento Anti-Communista;* Anticommunist Movement, another right-wing terrorist group.

at an end, but their outcome so far has not been favourable to the revolutionary forces. In these battles, first in São Paulo, then in Belo Horizonte, Rio, and later in Pôrto Alegre and almost all the major cities, the revolutionary organizations joined battle with the forces of repression in conditions unforeseen by contemporary theorists of revolutionary warfare—including the technicians of counterrevolution. . . .

Regroupment and the Question of a National Organization

In 1969 the two main centres of revolutionary regroupment were the ALN and COLINA. The VPR, decimated by purges and by the disasters of January to March 1969, first had to rebuild its underground infrastructure. In July it fused with COLINA to form the VAR-Palmares. The creation of this new organization could have been a great step forward in the unification of the Brazilian revolution movement, but it turned out to be an ephemeral coexistence between two politically heterogeneous tendencies. One of these, the VPR majority, wanted to confine the revolutionary organization to the armed nuclei alone. The contrary tendency, which formed the majority in COLINA, saw the urban and rural armed detachments as the embryonic form of the proletarian party, which was to be constructed in and through the development of armed struggle. In certain respects this polemic repeated on a larger scale that between militarists and Leninists within the VPR. As always happens, a compromise on overall strategic objectives broke down once it was necessary to draw practical and organizational conclusions from it. The questions that arose were whether it was already necessary to forge links with the urban masses, and whether or not the national unification of the revolutionary movement was a political precondition for generalized guerrilla warfare. The complete disagreement between the two tendencies on these issues led to a new step backwards in September 1969, scarcely two months after the unification: first the militarist tendency from the VPR (led by ex-captain Lamarca,) then the *foquista* tendency from COLINA, broke with the VAR-Palmares, leaving this organization with the Leninist COLINA majority and the Leninist minority from the VPR. The dissident groups joined together in a new organization which once more took the name of VPR, and combined in its ranks both the partisans of an exclusively military urban struggle, and the orthodox Debrayists.

The VAR-Palmares lost the greater part of its military cadres, but it held to its more correct political positions. It also continued to attract those militants who broke with the small Marxist parties, which had failed to stand the test of the events of 1968–1969: some of the "dissidents," a fraction of the PC do B "red wing." The "new VPR" on the other hand became a strictly military organization, which claimed to represent the most "radical" current within the Brazilian left.

On all these questions the ALN stood between the VAR-Palmares, with its stress on the need for a Leninist party, and the VPR. The ALN upheld the necessity of "mass work," though not of a revolutionary party. It benefited more than any other organization from the process of revolutionary regroupment. Before discussing the question of a national organization, and its dialectical relationship with the generalization of revolutionary warfare, the ALN's more rapid rate of growth demands a few words of explanation.

This transformation of "revolutionary group" into "national organization" is not unique to the ALN. But the ALN has been better able than others to combine a correct line on the absorption of small independent revolutionary groups with a correct line on alliances.

The fragmentation of the Brazilian revolutionary movement raises these two different, but mutually dependent, types of task: the construction of a national revolutionary *organization,* and the construction of a *front* against the dictatorship and imperialism. The former is built up by organizing militants around a common maximum programme; the latter by organizing groups or parties around a common minimum programme. In principle a national organization (i.e., a party) organizes a social class, or a socially and ideologically defined sector of a class, while a front organizes several social classes or sectors (e.g., the "workers' united front" organizes different secttions of the working class, and in particular different ideological tendencies— revolutionary and reformist). In Brazil this problem presents special features. It is not that the general laws of political organization and struggle are different in Brazil. In the last instance, the political fate of the Brazilian fighting organizations will be determined by the social classes whose historic interests they claim to represent. But the concrete tasks that confront revolutionary organizations at a particular moment cannot be mechanically deduced from the general objective interests of this or that social class. As we prevously emphasized, the armed resistance and mass struggles of 1968 expressed the undifferentiated aspirations and demands of all sections of the population oppressed by the dictatorship. The urban partisans did not function as the vanguard of the working class as such, nor of the middle classes and still less of the peasantry, but of the most advanced sectors of the popular movement as a whole.

If the Brazilian working class were as organized as the Argentinian, and could therefore play the role of the vanguard in the struggle against the dictatorship and imperialism, the question of the party and the front could be presented in more classical terms. However, the concrete movement of history pays no attention to classicism. The principal task in 1968 was to generalize armed struggle, given the undifferentiated present role of the various popular classes, and the fragmentation of the revolutionary movement. To claim a priori that the *first* task is either to "construct" the proletarian party, or to organize the "masses in their millions" around democratic demands, is to fall into opportunism, either of the "left" (viz., the amateur ideologues of the POC, the "Maoist" spiritualists of Popular Action, etc.), or of the right (the PCB, the so-called Maoist PC do B, etc.). This was the specific situation in which the ALN was able both to build itself into a national organization and to make tactical alliances with other revolutionary groups too heterogeneous to permit organizational integration. The VAR-Palmares, on the other hand, reacting to the experiences of July–September 1969, has since then tended to swing too far in the direction of "classicism," tending to apply Lenin's formulas too mechanically to Brazilian conditions. It failed to understand why the July 1969 unification had been an error, based on a confusion between the sufficient conditions for an alliance and the sufficient conditions for integration. Premature integration may be more damaging to the cause of revolutionary unity than continued fragmentation. The attempt to form a single organization where the conditions only exist for an alliance may lead to internal conflicts which destroy not only the too hastily sought unity but also the possibility of alliance which had been deemed insufficient. The ALN has certainly not found some sort of magic formula able to indicate in every specific instance with whom it is possible to integrate and with whom to limit the relationship to one of alliance. Even a correct method has its limitations, and the ALN's flexible policy on alliances carries certain risks. . . .

Perspectives for the Revolution

The unifying theme of this book has been that armed struggle in Brazil is not the adventure of a handful of radicals. The dangers of adventurism, however, must be repeatedly stressed, for there is a risk that the armed organizations will be wiped out before guerrilla warfare can be generalized. The "surround-and-destroy" mission is at its height, and to underestimate the strength of the government at this stage could lead to disasters like Cuzco, Ñacahuazú, and Caparaó. The army and the police have failed in their declared aim to "crush subversion" but they have scored tactical successes. The government's response to the kidnapping of the Japanese consul should be cited as an example of what such tactical successes can involve. The casualties suffered by the VPR as a result of the massive search by the police and the army were not justified by the political gains of the kidnapping. Moreover, the police learnt from those arrested the existence of an important VPR training camp in the Vale de Ribeira in the southern part of São Paulo State. In this poor region, relatively hilly and wooded, where immigrants of Japanese origin cultivate bananas and a local variety of tea, the VPR had several military cadres working and had built up a clandestine support network. All indications show however that this was not intended as a *foco* but simply as a training zone. It should not need pointing out that given the present military initiative of the enemy it was a mistake to concentrate weapons and valuable cadres in a region less than three hundred kilometres from São Paulo. The region was encircled in mid-April and bombarded with napalm. Some VPR militants were captured though the majority managed to break the encirclement.

The rapidity and ferocity of the armed forces' intervention shows yet again that present conditions in Brazil do not permit the survival of isolated bases of "red power" in the countryside and that consequently the formation of mobile strategic detachments is more than ever dependent on the overall situation of class struggle and revolutionary war. Second the claim that a *foco* will serve as a tactical instrument inspiring the urban masses to struggle has also been disproved. These positive lessons were drawn from the disaster, and the failure of the Vale de Ribeira experiment has thus, paradoxically, strengthened the urban guerrilla. Nevertheless if the guerrillas now solidly entrenched (the ALN, the VPR, the VAR-Palmares and others less prominent) are to survive and broaden the struggle certain conditions must be met.

Unless an upsurge of the mass movement comes to relieve the revolutionary fighters, unless there is considerable progress in the reorganization of the popular forces on a national scale, unless the vanguard organizations understand that the military initiative of the counterrevoluton is not an isolated event but depends on the balance of forces between the dictatorship and the people; in short, unless the revolutionary forces respond tactically in the present situation according to the slogan "retreat in breadth to advance in depth" then there is a real danger that armed struggle begun in 1968 may end with the death of a whole generation of revolutionaries.

Any change in the present situation will depend on three things: first, on whether the regime's increasingly nationalist stance is a sign of a genuine change of policy; second, on whether there will be an upsurge of the mass movement as there was in 1968; and third, on the revolutionary movement itself.

Both military and political work must be developed in the cities. The struggle must be carried on both clandestinely and among the masses, mobilizing them around the tactical slogans against the dictatorship for democracy and socialism. Work in the countryside must aim at the widespread construction of peasant cells and the eventual generalization of guerrilla warfare. The transition to armed actions in the country should only be made when the clandestine infrastructure is secure and support has been won among the peasants.

Finally, the revolutionary left must become united, since it is only its fragmentation which prevents it from posing a real threat to the established order. To accomplish this, the small organizations which have resulted from the numerous splits of the last few years must reorganize around the strongest and most consistent. Next, the different fighting organizations must unite around a minimum antioligarchic and anti-imperialist programme. The extent to which this will be socialist and the extent to which Marxist-Leninists win hegemony will depend on the development of workers' struggles and the concrete role which Marxist-Leninist *fighters* play in this unification. Lastly there must be the formation of a vast anti-imperialist and antioligarchic front, organizing all the democrats and socialists—all those really opposed to the regime—even if they are not fighting for socialism but only against the regime.

The revolutionaries must continue with all these tasks. It is not only the liberation of the Brazilian people that is at stake. The struggle in Brazil is part of a worldwide struggle against imperialism. Victory is not inevitable because it is not inevitable that socialism will triumph.

Urban Guerrilla Organizations

Armed Action Groups ("United Front" of September 1970)

ALN	*Ação Libertadora Nacional*; National Liberation Action Formed around a group of ex-PCB members led by Carlos Marighella and Joaquim Câmara Ferreira; good relations with Cuba, since Marighella headed the Brazilian OLAS delegation; began armed struggle in February 1968, in São Paulo.
VPR	*Vanguarda Popular Revolucionara*; Popular Revolutionary Vanguard Began as a merger of the São Paulo division of POLOP and ex-military survivors of the MNR; devastated by repression at the beginning of 1969, the VPR began to regroup in July 1969 around COLINA, resulting in the VAR-Palmares; shortly thereafter one wing, led by Carlos Lamarca, split and returned to the name VPR.
MRT	*Movimento Revolucionario Tiradentes*; Tiradentes Revolutionary Movement Named for a Brazilian national hero, the MRT was the action team of the Red Wing of the (Maoist) PC do B; became independent in 1969, led by Devanir José de Carvalho and his brothers.
MR-8	*Movimento Revolucionario do Outubro 8*; Revolutionary Movement of October 8 Named in commemoration of Che Guevara's death, the MR-8 began rural guerrilla warfare in October 1968; the *foco* and its support networks were hard hit during March and April 1969; subsequently worked closely with the ALN in cities; formed around dissidents of POLOP and the PCB.

PCBR	*Partido Communista Brasileiro Revolucionario;* Revolutionary Brazilian Communist Party

PCBR   *Partido Communista Brasileiro Revolucionario;* Revolutionary Brazilian Communist Party
Formed by dissidents from the PCB who left with Marighella in 1967 (Mario Alves, Apolonio de Carvalho, and Jacob Gorende); adopted name in early 1968; initially reticent about armed struggle, the PCBR took up the gun in 1969 when its Rio branch coalesced with MR-26 remnants.

Mass-Line Groups

AP   *Ação Popular*; Popular Action
Formed in 1961 around the left wing of the Christian Student Youth; became Marxist-Leninist after the coup; heavily into mass-line organizing as exemplified by its leading role in the 1968 student movement; currently active in peasant/worker organizing, especially in the Northeast.

PC do B   *Partido Communista do Brasil*; Communist Party of Brazil
1962 Maoist splinter of PCB, led by Mauricio Grabois and João Amazonas; lost two splinters itself in 1966—the Red Wing and the PCR (*Partido Communista Revolucionaria*); generally mass-line orientation.

VAR-Palmares   *Vanguarda Armada Revolucionaria*; Armed Revolutionary Vanguard
Named for the slave republic of 1630–1697; initially a merger between the VPR and COLINA, but the VAR split almost immediately; the mass-line faction retained the name, while the armed line faction went back to the name VPR; occasionally used armed struggle, but generally focused on organizing workers, peasants, and secondary school students; very hard hit by the regime.

Precursors and Transitional Groups

MNR   *Movimento Nacionalista Revolucionario*; National Revolutionary Movement

MAR   *Movimento Armada Revolucionario;* Armed Revolutionary Movement

MR-26   *Movimento Revolucionario-26*; Revolutionary Movement, July 26 (commemorating Fidel Castro's 26th of July movement)

The MNR came into being as a coalition of revolutionary nationalists regrouping in the wake of the 1964 coup; group was dominated by ex-military men from the Soldiers and Sailors Associations and elements from Leonel Brizola's Groups of 11; issued manifesto in May 1966; attempted Serra do Caparão *foco* in March 1967; survivors of the group turn up everywhere among armed struggle organizations:

• São Paulo group and a POLOP faction became the VPR;

• Rio group became the MAR and attempted a *foco,* in August 1969, in the Angra dos Reis;

• Survivors of the MAR *foco* joined the Rio PCBR group to influence that group's move into armed action.

POLOP   *Politica Operaria*; Workers' Politics

A Marxist, non-PCB group from the precoup period; university based, although active among workers; suffered a major break-up in September 1967:

• São Paulo group became part of the first VPR;

• Guanabara and Minas groups became COLINA;

• The remainder became the POC (*Partido Operaria Communista*) which was later absorbed into the VAR-Palmares.

COLINA   *Comando da Liberação Nacional*; National Liberation Command

	The Minas group of POLOP, which became the nucleus for the VAR-Palmares.
PCB	*Partido Communista Brasileiro*; Brazilian Communist Party
	Typical Moscow-oriented CP; founded in 1922, it staged an insurrection in 1935; attempted to infiltrate Goulart government, for which it paid dearly; provided numerous guerrilla combatants.

Other Organizations

MLN	*Movimento da Liberação Nacional*; National Liberation Movement
MOLIPO	*Movimento da Liberação Popular*; Popular Liberation Movement
	A group which left the ALN in 1972; badly repressed at the end of 1972.
FALN	*Forças Armadas da Liberação Nacional*; Armed Forces of National Liberation
FLN	*Frente da Liberação Nacional*; National Liberation Front
PRT	*Partido Republicão Trabalhista*; Republican Labor Party
MCR	*Movimento Communista Revolucionario*; Revolutionary Communist Movement

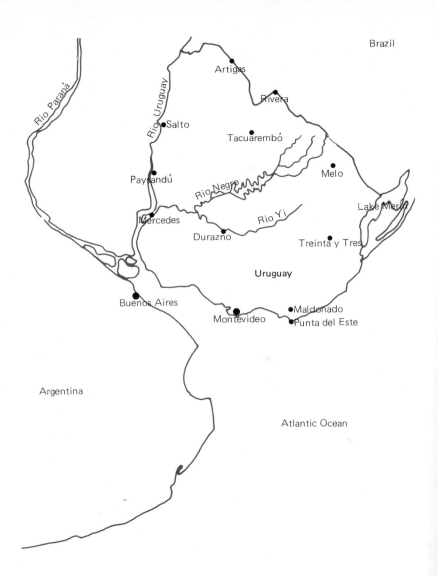

Uruguay: Demographic Background

Population: 3 million (1968); 80% urban
Size: 72,000 sq. miles
Gross National Product: $1.56 billion (1968)
Per Capita Income: $537 (1965)
Literacy : 91%
Exports: wool, beef, hides
Life Expectancy: 71 years

3

Urban Guerrilla Warfare: Uruguay

"It is true that we are operating right in the mouth of the enemy, but it is also true that the enemy is gagging on us."

Urbano

Introductory Essay

Nowhere was the appearance of urban guerrilla warfare more dramatic than in Uruguay. The Tupamaros, or MLN, burst into public view in a series of bold and sensational armed actions. Their example and moral influence has been felt from Tokyo to New York to Berlin, not to mention São Paulo and Buenos Aires. During their formative period, the members of MLN built up a mystique of themselves as archetypical romantic revolutionaries. Their actions were characterized by flawless planning and execution, and, perhaps most important, by style. For example: there was the time when a Tupamaro delivered first aid to a bystander who had fainted during a bank hold-up; or the action where a commando insisted that an old man's desposit be entered in his bank book before expropriating the money; or the sign, found in the tunnel through which over 100 Tupamaros had escaped from Punta Carretas, which proclaimed "Movement for National Liberation Transit Authority—Please Keep to Your Left." Mystique is undoubtedly an important ingredient in the Tupamaros' propaganda effort. Being newsworthy in the eyes of the media brings publicity, and, after censorship was instituted, the world press was a significant factor in breaking the information blockade placed around the guerrillas. Yet propaganda is not revolution, and the Tupamaros did not parlay themselves into a serious revolutionary challenge through publicity alone. It is often overlooked that Uruguay is undergoing a major structural crisis. For this reason, it will be helpful to start with an examination of the social and economic milieu in which the urban guerrilla movement has evolved.

Uruguay: The Switzerland of South America?

Following the First World War, Uruguay became known as the "Switzerland of South America." And indeed, so it might have been. During that period, Uruguay had an almost unblemished record for democracy, the best in Latin America. Stable but not repressive, it was nearly the model republic. There were honest and regular elections, a free press, civil liberties, few coups, and minimal military interference and civil violence. Uruguayans still enjoy one of the continent's highest standards of living. About one-half of the population is middle class, one-third working class, and the remainder divided between the very top and the very bottom strata. Further, Uruguayans are overwhelmingly literate, urban, and white (mainly of Italian and Spanish descent). Paradoxically, while this Switzerland image is still current, it is no less common to speak of the crisis of the 1960s. Following the Korean War, the nation entered into a period of decline, marked by inflation, strikes, violence, and military intervention. By the early 1970s, Uruguay had fallen from the Switzerland to the Greece of Latin America.

One of the basic factors in this change has been economic, and this factor is refracted throughout the society. To take a simple measure, economic growth has been slower than population growth over the last decade—rather surprising given a 1.2 percent annual increase in population. As a result, per capita income was lower in 1971 than in 1961. This deterioration raises two issues: first, what are the forces behind it (i.e., who is responsible?); and second, what are its social implications (i.e., who pays for it?).

These issues highlight the central dilemma of modern Uruguay: the contradiction between a middle-class, urban society and a monoculture, export economy. The nation's wealth derives from animal husbandry, from cattle and sheep, rather than from industry. Between 75 and 90 percent of Uruguay's exports consist of wool, meat, and leather products. With occasional contributions from tourism (the classic nonindustry), animal products provide the bulk of the country's earned foreign exchange. Industry is sparse and of the import-substitution variety, meaning that it is dependent on imported machinery and materials, while producing light consumer goods.

As is well known, a monoculture (single product) export economy

is not conducive to long-term economic diversification and development. Tied to a single product line, the vendor is subjected to the vicissitudes of a single market. The long-run terms of trade will probably
be unfavorable to the supplier (especially the raw material supplier),
since new suppliers can come onto the market and since substitute
products (both natural and technological) can be devised. Uruguay
has experienced both fluctuation (in meat prices) and decline (in wool
prices) in the market performance of its vital exports. On balance, Uruguay's terms of trade did improve somewhat during the 1960s, but not
sufficiently.

More important, though, is the stagnation of the production side of
the market. The export sector, on which economic development is
based, is neither modern nor dynamic. Ranching techniques are essentially those of 50 years ago. Thus, "it has been estimated that if Uruguay could achieve the productivity per animal of Argentine cattle
ranches, meat exports could be increased by about 40 percent without
increasing herds." [1] Herd size is also that of about 50 years ago, and in
1971 was smaller than in 1961.

Aggravating the export situation has been what the military now
likes to call "economic subversion," that is, smuggling, speculation, and
corruption. Smuggling from the northern ranch lands into Brazil is
perhaps the most significant, as some 500,000 head reportedly left il-
legally in 1971.[2] Foreign exchange losses thus incurred are estimated to
be $30–$100 million annually. Another instance involves the ultra-
modern Nueva Palmira airport, most of the traffic through which is
contraband. Oddly enough, President Jorge Pacheco Areco (1967–1972)
initially authorized the airport, and his successor, Juan María Bordaberry, renewed the authorization.

Speculation and corruption are harder to estimate. Notorious inci-
dents abound, although for obvious reasons documentation is sparse.
Bank failures are frequent and often linked to speculative activities.
The multimillion peso failure of the Transatlantic Bank in 1965 put

1 Economist Intelligence Unit, *Uruguay-Paraguay,* annual supplement 1971 (London:
Economist Intelligence Unit, 1972), p. 3.
2 Livestock Minister Benito Medero issued a statement giving an exact figure of
150,000 for the period between September 1971 and March 1972. One might think
that a government with such detailed information would take action.

a dozen highly respectable persons in jail and cost the public a good deal of money. Yet the Tupamaros' Financiera Monty raid in 1969 exposed precisely the same sort of speculation. Corruption and graft appear to be epidemic at all levels of government.

Uruguay's economic problems (compounded by "economic subversion") can be laid at the door of the export sectors. The nation is trapped between faltering income and the continued misuse of income. Added to this is the problem of the government payroll. The labor force consists of about 1 million people out of a population of 3 million. For every two people working, there is one drawing benefits from Uruguay's vast welfare system. In addition, over 25 percent of the labor force is employed by the government, adding a further burden to the economy. It could be argued that welfare and the bureaucracy are equivalent, insofar as both distribute income without generating any. If this is true, the question remains as to why the economy cannot integrate the bureaucrats into more useful employment. In any event, the problem of welfare and bureaucracy does not constitute the structural basis of Uruguay's economic problems.

In social terms, the decline has meant inflation, unemployment, and strikes. Rampant inflation (ranging from 15 percent in 1969 to 136 percent in 1967) has steadily eroded the foundations of Uruguay's social peace.[3] Taking 100 to be the cost-of-living index in 1963, by 1969 it was just over 2,000 and by 1973 the index was pushing 6,000. The corrosive effects of an inflation of this magnitude should not be underestimated. Inflation is socially a matter of income redistribution, and, while the question of who wins during an inflation may be disputed, it is certain that workers, employees, and pensioners lose.

Unemployment also has a redistributive aspect to it: no job, no money. In Uruguay, unemployment is more difficult to gauge than inflation. The standard figure for the early 1960s is 12.5 percent in 1963. For the 1970s, figures are harder to obtain, but it may be around 17–20 percent. Disguised unemployment or underemployment must also be considered. It is estimated that some 20 percent of the men and 40 percent of the women in the labor force work less than 30 hours per week.

---

[3] The government's typical response to wage increases is the issuance of new currency—perpetuating the inflation. Uruguay's money supply grew from 3.4 million pesos in 1961, to 115.78 million in 1971.

The result is that, while important, unemployment is less visible a problem than inflation.

The struggle over who will pay for the nation's economic problems has assumed a major role in Uruguayan politics. The labor movement, while not revolutionary, has been enfranchised since the turn of the century and offers a reasonable defense of labor's economic interest. Uruguay's middle-class unionism is a phenomenon which foreign observers occasionally think curious; yet it is obvious that a clerk suffers the same erosion in purchasing power that a meat packer does. Bank clerks and public employees, for example, took a leading role in the militant, bitter strikes of the 1960s.

Labor unrest hit full stride between 1965 and 1969. On October 7, 1965, constitutional guarantees were suspended following an epidemic of strikes, and by December over 500 unionists were under arrest. A year later, riots, shootings, and strikes culminated in an effective general strike on October 16, 1966. Another year passed and emergency measures were again renewed, against the bank employees and the CNT (*Confederación Nacional de Trabajadores;* National Confederation of Workers). May Day 1968 brought a CNT demonstration which became violent, leaving one dead and 50 injured. Students, already active over issues like university affairs and United States intervention (e.g., Vietnam and Santo Domingo), began to join in. On June 13, 1968, the new government of Jorge Pacheco Areco[4] decreed special security powers to the president. Strikes and demonstrations continued until August 14, when a student, Liber Arce, was killed. A month later, two more students died from police gunfire. Effective general strikes were called after each incident, and Liber Arce's funeral drew several hundred thousand people. However, the government had already instituted censorship of the news in early August. A January 1969 civil servants' riot in Montevideo left one dead and 32 wounded. By March, the government lifted the state of siege, only to reinstate it in June. Strikes waned somewhat in 1970–1971, but in 1972–1973, they were again a visible feature of the nation's life.

By this point, it should be clear that the guerrillas do not account for

4 Vice President Pacheco assumed the presidency following the death of Oscar Gestido in December 1967.

the political, much less the economic, decline. The collapse of Uruguay's democracy was well advanced by the time the guerrillas actually took to the field in 1968–1969. A state of siege (i.e., a period of suspension of constitutional guarantees) was implemented every year from 1965 to 1972, excepting 1966: the first four times against labor and the next three against the Tupamaros. The states of siege were more the result of defective government than of "terrorist intimidation." In a time of growing national crisis, the government came into the hands of men who could not rule by authority, but only by the use of force.

Uruguayan Politics: Batlle and the Parties

Uruguayan politics date from the postindependence period. The *Banda Oriental* (East Bank, as Uruguay was then called) had been a contested border territory between the Spanish and Portuguese empires in America. Following the declaration of independence by the junta of Buenos Aires in 1810, control of the region passed from the junta to José Gervasio Artigas in 1815, and from him to the Portuguese in 1817. Artigas and his gaucho army were forever driven from the area three years later.[5] After Brazil's succession from Portugal in 1822, it exercised hegemony in the *Banda* until April 1825 and the advent of the "Immortal 33 Uruguayans." Under the direction of Juan Lavelleja, 33 patriots crossed the Rio de la Plata and initiated the final round of the independence struggle. Aided by Buenos Aires, Lavalleja scored a number of victories against Brazil. In 1825, British pressure finally brought about an independent buffer state between the two powers.

A constitution was framed in 1830, and General Fructuoso Rivera (an Artigas lieutenant) was elected the nation's first president. Lavalleja soon fell out with Rivera and revolted in 1832. A truce enabled General Manuel Oribe to assume the presidency through elections, but the conflict did not end. The Riveristas revolted in 1836 and two years later decisively defeated Lavalleja and Oribe. This cleavage congealed into a two-party system. The Colorado and Blanco parties draw their names from the Battle of Carpínteria in September 1836, when Rivera's troops wore red (*colorado*) hatbands and Oribe's wore white (*blanco*).

Until the turn of the century, politics was the continuation of Blanco-Colorado faction fighting by every means available: civil war,

[5] Ironically, over one-third of Artigas Department is now owned by Brazilians.

invasion, coup d'etat, and assassination. In 1843, Oribe's Argentine army began the "Guerra Grande," a nine-year siege of Montevideo against Rivera. Continued scheming and intrigue precipitated the Paraguayan War of 1865–1870. A truce was arranged following a civil war in 1872, and another after an uprising in 1897. In 1903, Uruguay's greatest statesman, José Batlle y Ordoñez, was elected president. Symbolically, his first achievement was to suppress an uprising led by Aparicio Saravía. Ending in a truce in 1904, the rebellion was the last of its kind.

Batlle served two terms in office (1903–1907; 1911–1915). During the intervening years he visited Switzerland, an experience which would have an important effect on his policies. Two accomplishments mark Batlle's tenure: the "Pact of the Parties," and the recognition of labor. Through the Pact, party struggles were removed from the battlefield to the more liberal settings of the ballot box, the Senate floor, and the smoke-filled room. And to complement this peace between the factions at the top, it was decided that there should be peace between the top and the bottom. Batlle's initiatives in the fields of labor legislation, social security, and education laid the foundations for Uruguay's middle-class welfare state.

Batlle's political reforms deserve closer attention because they are the basis for the political system which ran aground 50 years later. The Pact of the Parties was premised on the idea that the largest minority party should not be cut off from power and patronage while out of office. The formula, quaintly called proportional representation, decreed that the majority party (at that time, the Colorados) should get two-thirds of the spoils and the leading minority party (the Blancos) should get one-third. As the Blancos were out of office nationally for nearly 100 years (1865–1958), this concern for their prerogatives was not a wholly abstract matter. Batlle transformed the Blanco-Colorado struggle into peaceful competition for power; from competition between rural *caudillos* (chieftains) into that between professional politicians. However, while it may have been the only way to preclude future Blanco rebellions, the Pact of the Parties also precluded the rise of more deserving third parties to prominence.

Batlle's campaign for good government led him to advocate a Swiss-style national council. The collegiate form of government (*collegiado*), based of course on "proportional representation," was established in 1918 to balance the ambitions and aberrations of any given politician by those of other politicians, equally ambitious and aberrant. From the vantage point of 1917, the problem may have been abuse of executive power, but by 1966 it was clear that the solution was not collegiate government. The scheme was adopted in 1918, abandoned in 1923, re-adopted in 1952, and reabandoned in 1966. In its attempt to guarantee a weak executive, the *collegiado* often degenerated into confusion, corruption, and in-fighting.

Another feature of Uruguayan government which originated in the Batlle era was the 1910 *Ley de la Lema* (Law of the Slogan), which stipulates that both primary and general elections are held on the same ballot. As in any election, votes are cast for the candidate of choice; however, parties can enter as many candidates, of whatever ideologies and programs, as they wish. The winner is the leading candidate from the party that has received the most votes.

A good example of the *Ley de la Lema* in action was provided by the November 1971 election, in which the Blancos and Colorados were faced with a serious challenge from the left, in the form of an Allende-style coalition, the FA (*Frente Amplio;* Broad Front). When the final count was in (several months later owing to irregularities and alleged fraud), Blanco Senator Wilson Ferreira Aldunate had received the largest personal vote, followed by General Liber Seregni[6] of the FA and Juan María Bordaberry of the Colorados. However, the Colorado Party had an edge of 10,000 votes over the Blanco Party; and thus Borda-berry became president, despite the fact that he had received some 50,000 votes less than Ferreira Aldunate. Ideologically, the vote made little sense. The victor was a hard-line conservative although the ma-jority of votes had gone to reform candidates. The total vote for the liberal Ferreira plus that of the leftist Seregni plus that of reformist Blancos and Colorados clearly exceeded the vote for Bordaberry and the other rightist candidates. The results of the Lema Law are baroque: ideological and programmatic lines are buried beneath an artificial party unity, and third parties have a very difficult time in elections.

[6] General Seregni resigned his post as commander-in-chief of the Montevideo region in 1968. His departure from one of the nation's most prestigious military posts was a protest against the government's hard line.

Each election since 1951 has revealed a clear undercurrent of discontent. In 1951, the *collegiado* was resurrected. In 1958, the Blancos won their first election in almost 100 years. In 1966, the *collegiado* was again abolished. And in 1971, a nontraditional party mustered 20 percent of the vote. If this undercurrent has indeed been a vote for change, it has yet to be translated into reality.

Uruguayan Politics: Generals and Guerrillas

In the long run, Uruguay must make a choice between structural reform and continued degeneration. The export sector is the obvious candidate for overhaul, since foreign exchange will be needed to finance reforms and since the foreign aid picture is bleak. The need to modernize, diversify, and expand the export sector is evident; the problem, however, lies in the nature of the oligarchy that controls it. The interlocking cliques of financiers and ranchers, the agribusinessmen, who are so influential in the government are the same ones who own the export sector; and they form the nucleus of the upper class, since Uruguay lacks a vigorous industrial sector. While certain varieties of structural reform are no doubt in the interests of the oligarchy as a class, any reform will antagonize certain very powerful individuals. Hence, the problem with Peruvian-style reforms is to muster the power to overcome the resistance of those oligarchs affected by even the mildest reform. Thus far, the politicians have failed to address the issue even at this level, and they are not likely to do so in the future. The military seems the only group within this system that might be able to implement reforms, although their resolve to do so is not clear at this point.

The short-run policy options are somewhat simpler: someone has to pay the bills. The last four governments have opted for a hard line, that is, they have left it to the middle and working classes to do the belt tightening. None of the regimes after 1965 has chosen (if, indeed, any has had the power to choose) to attack such obvious problems as smuggling and corruption. The reason, of course, concerns the identity of the smugglers and grafters, who range from petty bureaucrats to men of influence.

The consequences of the hard-line economic policy are threefold: dissension within the political elite, intensified mass struggle, and government reliance on the military. As the government's policy has unfolded, it has become ever more isolated from both reformist politicians and the unions, and has been increasingly forced to rely on the military as a source of authority. First against strikers, then students, then guerrillas, and finally against Congress, the president has needed the military as an instrument with which to chastise the opposition. Intent on an undemocratic policy, the president could not rely on the usual democratic instruments of compromise and bargaining. But the military does not come cheap; indeed, why should it enforce a bankrupt policy in which it has no voice? An analogy might be made to borrowing from a bank. Just an an entrepreneur will borrow money to meet short-terms debts, so the president can use the power of the military when his own authority wanes. But just as no bank will endlessly finance ridiculous ventures, neither will the military forever underwrite a regime bent on defending its narrow interests against those of the nation.

By February 1973, the president had overdrawn his account, and the military foreclosed. After a final altercation, Bordaberry was forced to sign away most of his power, and a National Security Council (*Consejo de Seguridad Nacional;* COSENA) was established. One might view COSENA as a return to collegiate government, only this time with the military as the majority party. Four months later, Congress and the graft-ridden municipal councils were abolished, burying the last artifacts of Uruguayan democracy.

The crucible of the present dictatorship in Uruguay was the period April 1972 to June 1973. Following multiple assassinations on April 14, 1972, the military was unleashed on the guerrillas. A state of siege was obtained, only now it was a "state of internal war" rather than a mere emergency. For reasons to be discussed later, the military scored a number of highly publicized victories against the MLN, culminating in the shooting and capture of Raúl Sendic on September 1. Also evident during the same period was a growing military disregard for the prerogatives of the president. The military refused to give Bordaberry information; they refused to honor his request for the release of certain prisoners; they refused to shut down a newspaper which chided him to "govern or resign"; and they refused to break a strike because they felt the strikers' demands just.[7] In June 1972, the so-called *peruanista*[8] wing of the army entered into negotiations with the Tupamaros concerning a cease-fire. This defiance, supported more or less by the entire officer corps, outraged the politicians: as one bureaucrat complained, the military would talk to the guerrillas but not to the politicians.

This remark is quite to the point, as the MLN probably had more to offer than the politicians, particularly with regard to the issue of corruption. And as the military congratulated itself on the suppression of the guerrillas, their attention turned toward that very issue. Their campaign attacked state agencies, the Montevideo City Council, and Senator José Batlle y Ibañez (Batlle y Ordoñez's nephew), to mention the most visible instances. The Tupamaros' old friend Ulysses Pereira Reverbel (whom they had twice kidnapped) was recalled from Washington to face charges of maladministration and corruption during his tenure at UTE (*Administración General de las Usinas Electricas y de los Telefones del Estado;* General Administration of State Electric and Telephone Services), the state electric monopoly.

Conservatives, as well as "economic criminals," chose to weather the storm in silent acquiescence, regarding the campaign as a momentary discomfort. The reformists did not; they chose to resist the growing military intervention. Strident attacks by liberal deputies and senators provoked the military to seek their impeachment. A campaign for the removal of Senator Enrique Erro provided a focus for the military's extended campaign against the politicians. Erro was accused of participation in the Tupamaro movement, and it appears that the accusation was true in thrust if not in detail. The impeachment proceedings became a constitutional crisis, as the resistance forces struggled to rally Congress to regain the powers that had been usurped by the president and the military. The Senate surrendered jurisdiction to the Chamber of Deputies which finally voted 49-48 against impeachment. That was too much for the military, and Congress was closed on June 27, 1972.

This last act caused considerable trouble for the president, as he was forced to authorize wage increases which violated a letter of intent with the IMF to abide by the IMF's noninflationary wages policy. As a result, a $20 million temporary credit was cancelled until Bordaberry later managed to get it reinstated.

Named for the reformist, neutralist military government of Peru.

The coup[9] was met by an indefinite general strike, which prompted the executive branch to outlaw strikes and the CNT (which represents 50 percent of the labor force). Labor had earlier shown no sympathy for Bordaberry, but the closing of Congress brought a resurgence of the mass movement, including students and liberals as well. For the future, two questions seem pertinent: Can the military rule? Will the mass resistance effectively link up with the remaining guerrillas? We turn now to the first of these questions.

The problems confronting the military are complex. They face the same fundamental policy decisions as did the politicians and they appear almost as fragmented and factionalized, but they are additionally handicapped by their lack of experience in administering a government. Their easiest course of action would be simply to continue past policy, which would leave the government exposed to a more serious union-guerrilla-student threat than before. Yet an effective reform policy, however mild, does not appear to be in the military's grasp. Should the military be unable to consolidate and rule, and should the prospects for revolution improve dramatically, they may find it necessary to call on Brazil to underwrite their rule, just as they themselves were once called on.

In sum then, Uruguay was a nation in trouble long before the Tupamaros appeared. Moreover, it was this time of troubles which contributed to the growth of the MLN, not vice versa. Batlle's "Swiss-style socialism," however remarkable it might have been 60 years ago, could not sustain itself under the strains of time and its own development. Reforms, and revolutions, need periodic rejuvenation, which was not forthcoming in the case of Uruguay. The collapse of vestigial democracy in Uruguay should not be attributed to results that are mistake for causes.

The MLN: Background and Origins

The date of origin of the MLN is most often given as July 31, 1963, when a group of leftists raided the Swiss Shooting Club in Colonia. O

---

9 Two "coincidental" events should be mentioned here. First, General William R son, chief of the Southern Command in Panama, was in Uruguay in mid-Ma Second, less than two weeks before the coup, Ernest Siracusa became U.S. ambassado to Uruguay. Siracusa was ambassador to Bolivia previously, and is widely credite with a major role in the overthrow of the Torres government in August 1971.

that day, a nucleus of some twenty revolutionaries broke with parliamentary tradition and returned to an earlier insurrectionary one. However, it was five years before the Tupamaros took the offensive with the kidnapping of Dr. Ulysses Pereira Reverbel. The intervening period was crucial to the subsequent development of the movement: militants were recruited and trained, materials acquired, and safe houses established. An infrastructure was thus slowly assembled without provoking crippling levels of repression. The guerrillas did not move from anonymity to the front page of the *New York Times* overnight. In 1965, two years after the first armed action, the guerrillas adopted the name *Movimiento de Liberación Nacional (Tupamaros)*. The year 1966 saw the first deaths in combat, and in 1967 the first communiqué was issued. This preparatory phase should not be underestimated as a factor in the Tupamaros' stunning technical level and organizational durability.

The initial membership of the movement was drawn from diverse sectors of the Left—Socialists, Anarchists, Maoists, and Trotskyites, as well as unaffiliated Nationalists. The best known of these groupings was from the Socialist Party, led by Raúl Sendic Antonaccio. Sendic left law school in the late 1950s to organize for the UTAA (Artigas Sugar Workers Union). The organizing drive culminated in a march on Montevideo in 1962 to dramatize the sugar workers' plight. Sendic was later detained by the police, and upon release published the prophetic editorial "Waiting for the Guerrilla."

The initial ideological diversity of the group had a large bearing on the Tupamaros' basic premise of nonsectarian armed struggle. Moreover, the Cuban Revolution was an important inspiration in the decision to pick up the gun, and Cuban doctrine lays more emphasis on action than polemic. Their early documents (particularly "Thirty Questions to a Tupamaro") stress the difference between a revolutionary guerrilla movement and an organization whose leaders proclaim the founding of the party of the revolution, open a few offices, and hold press conferences. By 1971, the MLN had articulated a program, yet still maintained the attitude that the detail of a socialist transformation is cut-and-dried: what must be addressed, they held, is the question of power.

During 1965 and 1966, there occurred a rather bizarre collaboration between the MLN and Argentine exiles from Tacuara, a rightist Peronist organization. Tacuara had been in the fascist wing of Peronism until 1962 when its left wing split off under the leadership of José ("Joe") Baxter. Following a bank robbery in 1963 in which two guards died, Baxter left Argentina for a world tour which included Spain (to see Perón), Algeria, Egypt, Congo, Angola, North Vietnam, Cuba, and, apparently, China. In 1965, Baxter, together with José Luis Nell Tacci, Jorge Andrés Cataldo, and Daniel Ruben Rodriguez, settled in Montevideo with Violeta Setelich, who introduced them to the MLN. It appears that during this interval certain features of Tupamaro ideology were defined, notably the feasibility of revolutionary war in the cities. Joint Tupamaro-Tacuara actions were conducted, but the fateful days of December 1966 apparently ended the collaboration.

It is ironic that the MLN's first major public exposure should have occurred by chance. On December 22, 1966, a group of Tupamaros in an expropriated car encountered a police patrol, and a shoot-out took place that left the revolutionary Carlos Flores mortally wounded. Soon afterwards, police investigation led to another confrontation in which officer Silviera Regaldo was killed by Mario Robaina, who then shot himself to death with his last bullet. The ensuing police action brought about a crisis for the nascent movement. Premature attention from the police forced about twenty Tupamaros[10] underground. Facilities were uncovered, safe houses lost, and militants arrested. On July 15, 1967, José Nell Tacci was taken. The MLN survived, however, only to encounter a similar accident at the end of 1967. The only casualty of the second incident was the newspaper *Época,* which was closed for printing the Tupamaros' first communiqué explaining the encounter.

By the time of their emergence in 1968, the MLN had begun to develop a strategy. The basic premise, nonsectarian armed struggle, has been mentioned. Uruguay's political geography dictates two added premises: urban struggle and continental revolution. Uruguay is a nation with 50 percent of its population in one city alone, and another

---

[10] In January 1967, the police identified the following people as important figures in the MLN: Edith Moraes Alves de Rodríguez; Maria Elsa Ferriero Martínez; America Garcia Rodríguez; Alicia Rey Morales; Carlos Heber Mejias Collazo; Eleuterio Fernández Huidobro; Héctor Amodio Perez; Tabare Euclides Rivero Cedres; Juan Carlos Pena Moran; Julio Angel Marenales Saenz; Gabino Falero Montes de Oca; Jorge Ámilcar Manera Lluveras; Heraclio Jesús Rodriguez Recald The last four persons were considered the main leaders.

30 percent in lesser urban centers. To ignore urban struggle in such a context would be suicidal. Nor can the implications be ignored of the rival giants on Uruguay's borders. A small dependent country cannot achieve a successful revolution without international support, preferably, in this case, in the form of revolution in Argentina or Brazil. Consequently, international relations, especially the chances of intervention by a foreign power, play a large role in the Tupamaros' strategic planning.

Mention should be made of a Spanish exile named Abraham Guillén, the *eminence grise* of revolutionary politics in the Rio de la Plata basin. A Marxist-anarchist, Guillén lives in Uruguay and writes for José Batlle's newspaper *Acción*. A veteran of the Spanish Civil War, he is a link to some of the better traditions of socialism in Europe. He has been an influential proponent of urban guerrilla warfare throughout Latin America. Guillén was involved with Joe Baxter in 1962, first in Buenos Aires and later in Montevideo following Guillén's emigration to Uruguay. His works, *Teoría de la Violencia* (1965) and *Estrategia de la Guerrilla Urbana* (1966), are said to be based on discussions between him and the Tupamaro-Tacuara group.[11] As applied to urban guerrilla warfare, the highlights of "Guillenismo" include: the feasibility, desirability, and necessity of urban struggle; the integration of rural guerrilla warfare, urban guerrilla warfare, and mass-line organizing (combined struggle); continental revolution; and, of course, the socialism of workers' control. It may be too much to label Guillén the ideological founder of the Tupamaros, but certain points of similarity exist between his views and those of the Tupamaros.

The preparatory years were productive, laying the groundwork for the rapid growth of the movement between 1968 and 1972. During this time, the Tupamaros became an effective, vital force on the left. Several trends were evident: the stalemate between the government and the mass movement; the growing dependence of the government on the military apparatus; and the appearance of torture and death squads. During its early "Robin Hood" phase, the MLN emphasized publicizing itself and exposing the regime, rather than moving against the gov-

11 See Donald C. Hodges, ed. *Philosophy of the Urban Guerrilla* (New York: William Morrow and Co., 1973). Guillén's son was arrested in December 1966 for connections with the MLN.

ernment as such. But following the seizure of the town of Pando on October 8, 1969, the level of violence escalated. Three Tupamaros died and sixteen were captured at Toledo Chico during the withdrawal from Pando. Torture appeared in the prisons. In retaliation, the MLN assassinated Carlos Ruben Zembrano for his role as a police agent at Toledo Chico. Official violence increased; guerrilla violence increased. In April 1970, Police Inspector Héctor Moran Charquero[12] paid with his life for torturing prisoners.

Then came the Mitrione affair. On July 31, 1970, the Tupamaros kidnapped three foreigners: USAID police advisor Dan Mitrione; Brazilian Consul Alyoso Dias Gomide; and U.S. embassy First Secretary Gordon Jones,[13] who escaped. This was the first attempt to bring the war home to the foreign sponsors of the government. For seven days, Pacheco faced the prospects of releasing 150 political prisoners in exchange for the officials. On August 7, when the Tupamaros abducted USAID agronomist Claude Fly, the end seemed to be almost at hand; the movement had just about brought down the government. Then came the windfall capture of nine central persons in the organization. With such serendipity, Pacheco held on, confident that the MLN was decapitated. Negotiations were suspended, and, as a result, on August 9 Dan Mitrione was killed.

The MLN: Organization and Action

The organization survived its "decapitation." Neither recruitment nor technical capacity nor leadership capability was, in fact, seriously impaired. Indeed, one key to the movement's durability has been its nonleadership orientation. At each level, members are prepared under fire to assume the responsibilities of the next higher level; and internal political education and discussion have thus assumed a vital role in maintaining the organization's dynamism.

The organization is structured as much like a tissue as like a hierarchy. At the top is a central executive committee directing a number of

---

[12] Moran's estate was found to be worth some $500,000; an impressive display of saving on an inspector's salary.

[13] The Department of State routinely covers CIA agents with embassy titles. For example, William Colby (now head of the CIA) was station chief in Saigon during the early 1960s, first as a political officer, then as first secretary.

groupings called columns. Within each column are replicated virtually all the facilities of the organization as a whole. The basic organizational principle is, of course, compartmentalization. The organization proper is divided into columns of 30 to 50 people, and the columns are divided into cells of 5 to 10 people. Each column is supposed to effect its own intelligence, logistics, and striking capabilities—safe houses, factories, arsenals, hospitals, presses, action units, etc. Each column organizes its own network of support, technical services, and recruitment. If only one column survives, the possibility exists of regenerating the whole movement.

From a hierarchical standpoint, the organization is not unlike concentric circles. At the very center is the leadership cadre, organized into the central executive. Surrounding the central executive are the columns comprised of active militants, who either are or will soon be underground. These two strata comprise the cutting edge of the guerrilla movement. Surrounding them on the outer layers are the CATs (*Comités de Apoyo Tupamaro;* Tupamaro Support Committees). These groups focus the activities of supporters and collaborators and attract sympathizers. On the one hand, the CATs serve to augment the organization's technical skills without lowering security standards. On the other, they serve to recruit and train new members.

Despite the clear strategic primacy of the city, serious efforts have been made to open a rural front. While victory will not be achieved in the countryside (with only 20 percent of Uruguay's population), a second front would complement and strengthen the urban struggle. Because Uruguay is economically an agrarian nation, the regime cannot cede control of the countryside to the Tupamaros. But can the regime retain control of the rural areas in the face of a sustained assault by the guerrillas? And if the countryside can be subdued, can both the countryside and the cities be simultaneously held? A rural front would certainly strain Uruguay's 18,000 man army (which was only 9,000 men before 1973). Such is the thinking behind the so-called *tatucera*[14] program. The *tatuceras* were to be base camps, quite literally holes in the ground, from which rural columns would operate. The program was

14 A *tatu* is a local species of armadillo; a *tatucera* is the animal's burrow.

in full swing by the end of 1971, although it had been in the works for perhaps as much as two years. Major setbacks were suffered following the April 15, 1972 declaration of a state of internal war.

One other structure deserves mention, the CAI (*Comité de Asuntos Internacionales;* International Affairs Committee). Introduced in 1969, the CAI was formed to consolidate and extend the movement's foreign relations. The Tupumaros pay considerable attention to developments on the international scene, especially in the Rio de la Plata region. They have good relations with the ELN in Bolivia, the MIR in Chile, and the ERP and Montoneros in Argentina, and fraternal feelings are expressed toward revolutionary movements throughout Latin America and the world. As for governments, the MLN is most interested in establishing relations with anti-imperialist Latin American regimes, with Cuba leading the list. Other governments of interest include Algeria, North Korea, Egypt, North Vietnam, the Soviet Union, and China. The question of foreign assistance is rather murky at this time. The CAI may have been created to supplement, or even replace, local sources of supply (especially arms and funds) with foreign sources. The extent to which this has been done is unclear, although there seem to have been fewer expropriations (especially bank robberies) after 1970. On balance, it would appear that the movement both receives aid from foreign governments and extends it to foreign movements.

The Tupamaros rely heavily on the concept of an extensive, fixed-base infrastructure. Over the years, they have acquired an awesome array of skills, technical services, and materials. Notable is their medical capability, which includes apparatus and expertise ranging from first aid to plastic surgery. In addition to their own independent medical services, the movement enjoys, as needed, the collaboration of outside specialists and the use of outside facilities. Indeed, each member brings to the organization his own combination of talent and training, not to mention intelligence information. However, an infrastructure of this extent is not without its price. Rents must be paid, equipment acquired and maintained, and underground militants supported. This creates pressure toward both expropriations and foreign support. Security problems are also involved. A *casa de seguridad* (safe house) is secure only so long as the authorities do not know where it is. Torture, betrayal, and informers pose cumulative security problems. Rural safe houses are particularly vulnerable to informers since strangers and unusual events are more obvious in the countryside.

The movement has recruited adherents from every sector of Uruguayan society: librarians, sugar workers, mechanics, students, engineers, clerks, police, ranchers, industrialists, and military officers. It is often said that the MLN is a middle-class movement, but it should be added that Uruguay is a middle-class country. The number of working-class and lumpen proletarian adherents in the MLN is not so disproportionate, given the social composition of the nation as a whole. Recruitment tends to be among family and friendship groups. Every new or aspiring member must be known to someone already in the organization. In this way, cells can be cohesive and free from infiltration, yet separate from one another.

The criticism is made of the MLN, by Guillén and others, that it too closely resembles a counterstate without counterinstitutions supporting it. At some level, this criticism is valid, as the Tupamaros have not had a particularly strong mass line. The MLN's version of dual power is heavily oriented toward the use of instruments like assassination and the people's prison—the basic repressive instruments of a government. This conception was evident in their strategic line during 1970–1972. By 1971, the movement was considering "the problem of power" and direct assaults on the military, enhanced by a rural front. Perhaps following the 1972 repression a stronger mass line will emerge, as well as another rural front.

The MLN: Elections and Repression

After Mitrione's death in 1970, the movement was quiescent and seemed to be on the decline. This impression was, however, soon undermined by the largest bank robbery in Uruguayan history in November 1970, and the abduction of British Ambassador Geoffrey Jackson in January 1971. About this time, however, the Broad Front made its appearance, and the Tupamaros adopted a defensive posture pending the outcome of the presidential election.

As the election campaign unfolded, so did a campaign of white terror. By mid-1971 the tempo had quickened to the point that assaults by death squadrons were a daily occurrence. Much of the brunt of these assaults was borne by the Broad Front, although the rest of the Left, including the Communist Party and the MLN, was also attacked. Several people were murdered and two persons associated with the Tupamaros were tortured and killed.

The Tupamaros' response to the escalation of death-squad violence was delayed by their unilateral election truce. The mass exodus from Punta Carretas Prison and the subsequent release of Geoffrey Jackson was an event which looked both forward and backward. On the one hand, the escape was in character with the flashy, spectacular actions of the Robin Hood days, as was the release of Geoffrey Jackson. On the other, the communiqué announcing Jackson's release also denounced the recent level of white terror:

We would have preferred to ignore these sordid provocations so as to keep the climate cool at this difficult time and save embarrassment, but there are limits. Murder cannot continue to be done with impunity forever. If they persist, they will feel our retaliation and they know it. We shall strike back with the full power of the people against all those responsible—whose names and addresses are in our possession. . . . We tell you clearly, if you go on in the way you have started our retaliation will be implacable. Bear it in mind. We never speak in vain.[15]

The elections were held and Bordaberry was elected president. The MLN returned to the offensive with the "Proclamation of Paysandú" and a number of armed actions in support of it. Action against the police was not long in coming. Police Inspector José Pedro Macchi, warned in the Jackson communiqué, was critically wounded by an assault in February 1972. Then, on February 24, Nelson Bardesio was abducted. Complementing his official role as a police photographer, Bardesio was a leading figure in the organization and execution of death-squad activities. He had been the chauffeur of USAID public safety advisor William Cantrell, and a nuclear member of the DII (*Dirección de Información e Inteligencia;* Directorate of Information and Intelligence), a modernized police agency set up in 1968. His inter-

---

15 María Esther Gilio, *The Tupamaro Guerrillas* (New York: Saturday Review Press, 1972), pp. 193–194.

rogation by the Tupamaros resulted in four documents which were read into the public record by Senator Enrique Erro on April 15, 1972. Later that month, the president of the Chamber of Deputies was abducted by the MLN for a discussion of the Bardesio affair, which led him to certify the documents' validity. Taken together, these documents, virtually unknown in the United States, constitute a damning indictment of American-sponsored subversion in Latin America. Contrary to the know-nothing public stance of the Uruguayan and United States governments, Bardesio's testimony indicates quite clearly that death squadrons are a matter of official, if covert, policy on the part of both governments.[16]

On the basis of Bardesio's information, the MLN issued a decree condemning eleven officials to death and recommending the abduction of sixteen others for their participation in death squads. The decree concluded: "We wish and urge all revolutionaries to carry out these sentences whenever, wherever, and however possible." Four men named on the list sought asylum in foreign embassies soon thereafter. Then, on April 14, the MLN assassinated three others, and an assistant to one of them. The military was thus given its chance, and moved resolutely. Three months later, the Joint Forces announced that 100 Tupamaros had died, 600 to 700 had been arrested, and 70 safe houses had been uncovered since the declaration of internal war. The toll continued to grow throughout 1972.

The conventional wisdom at the time suggested that, by their latest outrage, the MLN had simply gone too far, and the military finally had to step on them. This statement is somewhat misleading. First, it seems that a major counterinsurgency effort was underway before April 14, and that the raids in Malvín (a Montevideo suburb frequented by the Tupamaros) on that day may have had no connection to the assassinations. Second, the retreat to the *tatuceras* during the height of the repression was perhaps precipitous. The *tatuceras* were, in fact, still in formation when the army moved against them; and security is difficult

---

16 President Bordaberry once remarked that death squadrons and torture are not authorized and that what is not ordered cannot be ordered stopped. (See *Foreign Broadcast Information Service*, 10 January 1973, p. 51.) This line of reasoning does not apply to the MLN, of course.

enough in rural areas without the added burden of supporting refugees from the cities. Many of the losses during 1972 were in these rural areas, as one column after another collapsed.

But the decisive factor in the army's drive was the defection of Héctor Amodio Perez. This incident is shrouded in uncertainty, but its impact was immense. A former printer, Amodio disappeared after the death of Carlos Flores in 1966. He and Eleuterio Fernández Huidobro were said to have been Raúl Sendic's principal lieutenants in the San Rafael Casino, Pando, Pereira Reverbel, and Pellegrini Giampietro actions. He planned the 1970 Women's Prison escape, was arrested later that year, and himself escaped in September 1971. The defection of a major personality, with seven years combat experience, is certain to be damaging: Amodio apparently identified over 30 safe houses, including the people's prison and the field hospital. He also testified against Enrique Erro, at the behest of the military.

In conjunction with Amodio's betrayal, it is interesting to note that he was recaptured in February 1972 and escaped on April 12, just two days before the reciprocal attacks. Two of the men who escaped with Amodio died in Malvín, and Fernández Huidobro was captured there. It was not until more than a month later, however, that the hospital and the people's prison were found. Whenever the defection may have occurred, it is said by the Tupamaros to have been due to a collective move to limit Amodio's ambitions within the organization.

During June 1972, a round of negotiations between the MLN and the military took place. Fernández Huidobro and Mauricio Rosencoff were released to consult the organization. The military position was clemency plus reform, perhaps the platform of Senator Ferreira Aldunate. The MLN appeared to demand at least the program of the Broad Front and amnesty, not clemency. In early July, several Tupamaros were killed and the negotiations were no longer a serious issue. On July 25, Colonel Artigas Alvarez, head of the civil defense corps and brother of the commander-in-chief of the Joint Forces, General Gregorio Alvarez, was assassinated, marking definitively the end of the negotiations.

Various leaders of the MLN were captured, including Julio Marenales, Raúl Sendic, and Lucia Topolanski. But toward the middle of the year, the military turned its attention elsewhere—toward the politicians. Subsequent Tupamaro activity has been subdued.

Conclusion and Prospects

From the viewpoint of mid-1973, final judgment on the Tupamaros should be withheld. Their influence, both moral and material, will be felt again. The unfortunate tendency to identify the MLN with Raúl Sendic has led to the widespread conclusion that the movement no longer exists. Sendic is out of action, but numerous other important individuals are not.[17] Many less prominent individuals are also still at large. Recruitment is variously reported as ranging from brisk to overwhelming. Current activities of the MLN are not highly visible and the organization proper may no longer exist as before, but the revolutionary process of which it was a part continues. The experience of the Tupamaros has not been forgotten—there are many who remember it well. Moreover, the political situation is deteriorating rapidly, since the military wants power but lacks the ability to rule. Given the explosive national situation and the human resources still at the Tupamaros' disposal, premature obituaries are not in order.

17 Raúl Bidegain Greissing, Fernando Garín Laneiri, Efraín Martinez Platero, Heber Mejias Collazo, Heraclio Rodriguez Recalde, and Gabino Falero Montes de Oca, to name six.

Chronology[1]

1959–1962   UTAA (Artigas Sugar Workers Union) organized.

1962

June 5   First UTAA march; 600 workers and families march from Artigas to Montevideo to protest conditions and demand land; marchers are fired upon from headquarters of Uruguayan Trade Union Confederation.

June 11   Raúl Sendic (UTAA) detained in Paysandú; released after several days in jail; he then publishes "Waiting for the Guerrilla" in *Época*.

1963

July 31   *Swiss Rifle Club in Nueva Helvecia, Colonia, robbed of firearms; first armed action by the MLN.*

August 1   Police investigation of traffic accident leads to discovery of bolt from a rifle seized from the Swiss Rifle Club.

August 13   Eduardo Pinella killed in accident at work.

September 6   Police raid on FIDEL (Popular Union and Leftist Front) yields suspects claimed to be Socialist Party (PS) militants responsible for Nueva Helvecia action.

Arms from Nueva Helvecia raid found in cache on bank of Rio Negro; 4 suspects arrested.

September 9   Police report that Sendic is in Brazil, that he planned to seize and distribute land and a sugar mill to the UTAA, and that he directed assault on Swiss Rifle Club without PS sanction.

---

[1] Unless otherwise specified, individuals and actions cited are assumed to be related to the Tupamaros.

	Police detain Eleuterio Fernandez Huidobro, bank employee, for suspected subversive activities.
December 24	"Hunger Commando" seizes contents of food chain truck and distributes turkeys and chickens in Montevideo slums.

1964

January 1	Customs office at Bella Unión, on Brazilian border, attacked; 11 rifles seized.
March 30	Mistaken for a smuggler, Sendic narrowly escapes arrest at Paysandú Airport.
April 25	Expropriation of 540 kilos of gelatenite from National Cement Company, on the outskirts of Pan de Azúcar, Maldonado.
June 11	Atalivia Castillo, Julio Vique, and Nelson Santana (UTAA) caught by police during expropriation of Banco de Cobranzas.
September 9	Government severs relations with Cuba; MLN bombs First National City Bank and offices of Moore-McCormack lines in Montevideo; two cars with diplomatic plates parked in front of U.S. Embassy firebombed.
September 10	Bomb explodes in garden of Brazilian ambassador.
	Houses of four government advisors firebombed.
October 14	Branch of Banco de Cobranzas attacked; 93,000 pesos seized; Julio Marenales Saenz and Oscar Andrade Gimenez arrested for bank robbery.
October 15	Police detain Jorge Maneras Lluveras for arming the commandos involved in Banco de Cobranzas action; suspect's vehicle yields arms cache.

| December 16 | Raúl Sendic, Anacleto Silvera, and Ramón Pedrozo detained at Monte Caseros, Argentina, for evasion of border post and possession of arms; Uruguay requests extradition. |
| December 31 | Argentine police free Sendic and companions. |

1965

May 5	Violent repression of student demonstration against U.S. intervention in Dominican Republic.
May 6	Bombings of All-American Cable and Western Telegraph companies.
July 10	Brazilian Embassy in Montevideo bombed.
August 9	Warehouse of Bayer (West German chemical company) bombed for involvement in U.S. war in Vietnam; commandos identify themselves, for the first time, as Tupamaros.
October 7	National Council of Government adopts Immediate Security Measures to forestall impending demonstration of government employees; 40 people detained.
November 15	National Councillor Amilcar Vasconcellos denounces police repression, claims 250 political detainees being held.
November 18	Residences of Alberto Heber, member of the National Council, and his brother Mario Heber, president of the Chamber of Deputies, bombed.

1966

| January | First national convention of MLN. |
| February 2 | Two armed men occupy Montevideo theater, seize 18 uniforms and 10 rifles used in plays; leaflets distributed signed by Tupamaros. |

May 13	Banco de la Caja Obrera robbed of 301,000 pesos.
November 15	Subsecretary of Interior Dr. Rodolfo Canabal's house bombed.
November 22	Banco Popular in Paso de la Arena robbed of 642,000 pesos.
November 27	El Cazidor armory robbed of 63 weapons and 1,000 rounds of ammunition.
December 22	*Carlos Flores dies in shoot-out with police, becoming first Tupamaro killed in action; the ensuing repression damages the organization severely.*
	MLN training center discovered.
December 23	MLN target range and explosives range discovered by police.
December 26	MLN printing shop discovered by police.
December 27	Mario Robaina (MLN) and Silviera Regalado (Chief of Command, Radio Patrol), killed in shoot-out.
December 29	MLN base in Montevideo discovered in same building as bank previously robbed by Tupamaros; apartment had been rented to Violeta Setelich.

1967

January 1	Argentine national Silvio Halperín Burnstein arrested in Montevideo carrying a pistol, 1,000,000 pesos and incriminating letters; linked to Argentine Tacuara.
January 5	Police discover Tupamaro hideout; complete maps of Montevideo sewer system recovered.
January 6	Arrest orders issued for Tuparamos Heber Mejias Collazo, America Garcia Rodríguez, Eleuterio Fernández Huidobro, and Héctor Amodio Perez.

January 12	MLN safe house discovered, revealing extensive intelligence documentation about Uruguayan armed forces; MLN internal documents also found.
January 23	U.S. Consulate in Montevideo bombed.
February 16	Abraham Guillén and Carlos Caballero Ferreira (Paraguayan exile) arrested for subversion; later released.
March 16	Fernando Bassini Campiglia, ex-medical student, identified as Tupamaro.
April 11	Lyndon Johnson arrives in Montevideo for Punta del Este meeting; anti-U.S. demonstrators clash with police.
April 12	Burroughs building bombed.
July 15	José Luis Nell Tacchi (Argentine exile) arrested for links to MLN.
August 29	President Gestido announces establishment of scholarships for police study in United States.
October 10	Emergency Security Measures enacted to deal with labor unrest.
November 16	Police announce arrest of Gustavo Inzaurralde (FSU and MLN); Inzaurralde linked to Joe Baxter and Tacuara.
November 29	Shoot-out between police and four Tupamaros at Shangrila bathing resort as police mistake Tupamaros for delinquents.
December 6	President Oscar Gestido dies of heart attack; Vice President Jorge Pacheco Areco succeeds him.
December 11	Firebombings of CUTCSA (Uruguayan Bus Company, Inc.) to protest fare increase; 6 buses destroyed.

December 12	One week after assuming office, Pacheco Areco closes down six leftist groups (Socialist Party, Movement of the Revolutionary Left, Uruguayan Anarchist Federation, Eastern Revolutionary Movement, Uruguayan Popular Action Movement, Epoca) following tactical alliance between them; two papers (*El Sol, Época*) closed down for printing MLN explanation of Shangrila confrontation.
1967	Uruguay experiences 700 strikes.

1968

January 3	Five hundred kilos of gelatenite stolen from stone quarry at Pan de Azúcar.
January 18	Branch of Unión de Bancos de Uruguay (UBUR) assaulted; 2,400,000 pesos seized.
March	Second national convention of MLN.
May 1	May Day demonstration becomes violent, leaving one dead and fifty injured.
June 13	Pacheco Areco reinstates Emergency Security Measures to combat student and labor unrest.
July 1	Minutes before President Pacheco Areco is to deliver a radio speech, four MLN commandos bomb Radio Ariel.
July 26	Pedro Dubra involved in motorcycle accident, but manages to escape from hospital.
August 7	*Ulysses Pereira Reverbel, personal friend of President Pacheco Areco and director of UTE (General Administration of State Electric Power and Television) kidnapped by MLN, held for four days.*
August 9	Student Mario Toyos killed by police during search of student areas.

August 14	Student Liber Arce killed by police during demonstration.
September 10	Branch of BOLSA (Bank of London and South America) attacked; 5,000,000 pesos seized.
September 11	Branch of UBUR assaulted; 1,800,000 pesos expropriated.
September 12	Bombs explode in branches of Banco Mercantil, Banco de la Caja Obrera, and Banco Popular del Uruguay; leaflets with CAP insignia are left.
September 21	Students Susana Pintos and Hugo de los Santos killed by police during demonstration.
October 3	Arroyo Seco branch of Banco Commercial attacked; 3,215,600 pesos seized.
October 7	Expropriation of 11,800,000 pesos from branch of BOLSA.
October 8	Julio Marenales Saenz, Leonel Martínez Platero, and Carlos Rodriguez Bucos arrested in interior; four other suspected Tupamaros detained.
October 10	Identity cards and forgery equipment discovered in house of Rodríguez Candan, photographer.
October 13	Tupamaros Marenales Saenz, Martínez Platero, and Rodríguez Bucos denounce electric shock torture in Department of Intelligence and Liaison.
October 18	Minister of Industry and Commerce Jorge Peirano Facio, victim of triple sabotage; his residence, a bank he owns, and the stock exchange where he works are bombed.
	Branch of Sociedad de Bancos loses 5,890,000 pesos through armed expropriation.

October 24	3,427,400 pesos taken from La Paz branch of Banco Commercial.
October 28	Trotskyist Congress raided by police in Montevideo; 17 Uruguayans are arrested, 13 Argentines and 1 French national are deported for violation of internal security laws.
November 1	Branch of UBUR attacked and 3,329,000 pesos expropriated.
November 25	Theft of 255 kilos of gelatenite from construction company in Tacuarembo.
November 29	Armed expropriation of 6,250,000 pesos from Hotel Carrasco Casino in Montevideo.
November 30	Teresa Labroca Rabellino arrested; her apartment had allegedly been used as staging for Carrasco Casino operation.
December 10	Ismael Bassini Campiglia, Gabino Falero Montes de Oca, Pedro Dubra, Corina Devita de Cuadra, Jesus Manuel Rodríguez, Victoriario Aluear Leal, and the brothers Liber and Anibal Delucia Grajales arrested on estate north of Pando.
December 11	Branch of Banco Popular del Uruguay assaulted; 3,416,924 pesos seized.

1969

January 1	Tupamaros 22 December (1966) command recovers from Police Court arms confiscated during last two years.
January 3	Police break into house in Cerro; three machine guns, transmitter, six kilos of gelatenite taken.
January 9	Police raid house in Punta Corda; 28 rifles, 40 kilos of gelatenite seized.

February 7	Tupamaros return 100 kilos of dangerously decomposed gelatenite to army bomb specialist.
February 14	*Tupamaro Liber Arce group occupies Financiera Monty and seizes 17,792,633,250 Argentine pesos, 1,889,600 Brazilian cruzeiros, 324,250 Uruguayan pesos, 3 packets of Focier-Altamira-Monty stocks, and 6 accounting ledgers.*
February 16	MLN releases leaflet explaining financial irregularities of Financiera Monty.
February 18	Casino San Rafael hit for 55,000,000 pesos by Mario Robaina command of MLN.
February 25	MLN releases second leaflet explaining Financiera Monty irregularities.
March 1	Unexplained fire in Financiera Monty offices destroys crucial documents which could either prove or disprove MLN allegations of financial misdealings.
March 4	Tupamaros announce impending return of part of money expropriated from San Rafael Casino; money is said to belong to workers and will be returned to same.
March 9	Honario Alejandro Manuel Grieco Nieves, employee of San Rafael Casino, arrested for collaboration with MLN in Casino action.
March 13	Bank in Fray Bentos loses 15,000,000 pesos from armed expropriation.
March 15	Government dissolves Trotskyist Revolutionary Workers Party and closes its paper *Frente Orbero*.
March 18	Prisoners Gabino Falero Montes de Oca and Corina Devita de Cuadra married in special ceremony in Punta Carretas Prison.

March 21	Jorge Ámilcar Manera Lluveras and eight other Tupamaros arrested.
March 23	Edelmar Ribeiro shot to death by police.
April 12	Three Tupamaros, Vetty Larrosa de Listre, her husband Julio Cesar Listre, and Julio Rocatagliatta, arrested (latter two were bank employees).
April 26	America Garcia Rodríguez and husband Carlos Heber Mejias Collazo, injured in bomb explosion outside Montevideo, manage to get treatment at hospital under assumed names and thus avoid detention.
April 28	Tupamaros seize 80 kilograms of .50 calibre machine-gun ammunition from La Paloma naval dockyard.
April 30	COPRIN (Commission of Prices and Income) building bombed by Tupamaros.
May 2	Three banks robbed; 4,000,000 pesos seized.
May 7	In 20-minute period, three banks are assaulted; 3,000,000 pesos are taken.
May 9	Three banks occupied; 6,000,000 pesos expropriated.
May 10,12,14	Attacks on food warehouses; large quantity of foodstuffs seized.
May 15	Tupamaros occupy Radio Sarandi station during broadcast of soccer game and transmit recorded message.
May 21	Heraclio Jesus Rodríguez Recalde captured.
May 22	Tupamaro commandos seize 66 firearms and 200 rounds of ammunition from armory located 50 meters from Central Police Department.

May 27	Expropriation of 13,900,000 pesos from branch of UBUR located next to Government House.
June 10	Hunger strike by Tupamaros in Punta Carretas Prison, protesting bad treatment.
June 20	Tupamaro commandos burn General Motors plant following Nelson Rockefeller's visit; MLN leaflets left at site.
June 21	MLN occupies downtown Montevideo radio station and broadcasts message protesting Nelson Rockefeller's visit.
June 24	State of siege instituted against strikers.
	Home of Senator and ex-Minister Manuel Flores Mora broken into by MLN; documents seized.
June 25	Acts of sabotage committed against homes of Minister of Foreign Relations Venancio Flores, Minister of Work and Social Welfare Jorge Sapeli, and Prosecutor Francisco Bayardo Bengoa.
June 27	General Motors plant in Penarol attacked; 500,000,000 pesos taken.
July 4	Policeman killed while resisting disarmament.
	Executive decree prohibits circulation of information regarding Tupamaros.
July 7	Tupamaros attack six police officers; policeman Garay Dama killed.
July 8	*Democracia* (previously *Extra*) publishes first issue; issues confiscated by police and offices closed.
July 16	IBM-360 computer and records of Banco Commercial destroyed by bomb.
July 26	Pectro Zabalza, Atalivia Castillo, Cesar Gerardo Longo, Natalio Dergan, and Roberto Emilio Manes are arrested in Montevideo.

July 31	Policeman killed guarding City Bank.
September 9	Publisher and bank president Gaetano Pellegrini Giampietro kidnapped as insurance for striking bank employees; kidnappers later identified as Raúl Bidegain, Nestor Peralta Larrosa, Sergio da Rosa Silveira, and Juan Pablo Schroeder.
September 10	Clandestine radio station begins broadcasting every Wednesday and Sunday, issuing 5-minute statements.
	BOLSA robbed of 5,000,000 pesos.
September 11	UBUR branch assaulted; 1,800,000 pesos expropriated.
September 23	Numerous firearms, pieces of office equipment, and 200,000 pesos are seized from home of a judge.
October 2	Intendant of Salta loses 10,000,000 pesos through armed expropriation.
October 3	6,000,000 pesos expropriated from Banco de la Unión.
October 6	Manuel Antonio Ramos Filipini, a junior official in Ministry of Foreign Relations, placed on trial as Tupamaro.
October 8	*Pando operation: in commemoration of Che Guevara's death, MLN occupies town of Pando; police and fire departments attacked, communications severed, four banks expropriated for 81,000 pesos; during the retreat one column is intercepted by 1000 troops and Tupamaros Jorge Salerno, Ricardo Zabalza, and Alfredo Cultelli are killed; 16 others, including Eleuterio Fernandez and Lionel Martinez, are captured; bystander Carlos Burgueno and policemen Enrique Fer-*

nandez Diaz also die from wounds inflicted during the action.

October 15	Six million pesos expropriated from clandestine money exchange house.
October 21	Garcia Rodriguez, her husband, Mejias Collazo, Jaime Machado Ledesmena, and two others are arrested.
November 1	Assault on police patrol car leads to death of Arturo Cardama Martinez and capture of Fermin Chapitel Bottini.
November 6	In Chamber of Deputies, Héctor Gutierrez Ruiz denounces the government for detaining 5,616 political prisoners since 1968.
November 12	Shoot-out: Indalecio Olivera da Rosa, ex-priest and Tupamaro, killed along with one policeman.
	Aguada branch of Banco de Montevideo suffers armed expropriation of 15,000,000 pesos by 10 FARO guerrillas.
November 15	Carlos Ruben Zambrano becomes first police official assassinated by MLN, in retaliation for his role as informer during Pando action.
November 21	Gaetano Pellegrini Giampietro released after a donation of 7,500,000 pesos is made to the Caja de Auxilo del Frigonal and 7,500,000 pesos to a school.
November 25	7,000,000 pesos expropriated from Banco Popular.
November 26	Policeman Antonio Maria Fernandez killed in El Pinar while trying to detain José Alberto Lopez Mercao and Marcos Suarez Piriz.
December 1	Minister of interior forbids use of words related to Tupamaros.

	Two seminary students, Luis Samandu Sieria and Mario Caceres Martínez, and air cadet Fernando Bossio Guiterrez are arrested for planning a raid on Aeronautics Technical School.
December 4	Seminary student Luis Ernesto Fernandez arrested for planned Aeronautics Technical School raid.
December 7	MLN open letter to police announces forthcoming move toward aggressive policy.
December 11	Air Force Colonel Armando Muter is seriously injured by guerrillas in an assault on his house.
December 13	Expropriation of 26,000 ampules of penicillin from a laboratory.
December 26	380,000 pesos seized from Montevideo branch of Banco Francés e Italiano.

1970

January	Raúl Bidegain and Nestor Peralta Larrosa are arrested in a park; they are promptly freed by the intervention of 10 armed guerrillas.
January 12	Violetta Maria Rogue Setelich is arrested.
February 5	Branch of Banco de Salta y de la Republica loses 20,000,000 pesos in armed expropriations.
March 8	Thirteen Tupamaro women prisoners escape from Women's Jail, including Jesse Arlette Macchi Torres.
March 9	Six Tupamaros seize 6,000,000 pesos from UBUR branch of Montevideo.
March 19	Tupamaros retrieve 10,000,000 pesos and documents from tunnel under police surveillance.
March 31	Guerrillas seize 6,000,000 pesos from UBUR branch.

April 5	Oracio Mailhos, tobacco magnate, robbed of 100,-000,000 pesos in gold ($400,000); documents taken.
April 7	Tupamaro safe house raided by police; six militants captured, together with documents, plans, arms, and explosives.
April 8	MLN releases to press photocopies of compromising documents seized from Mailhos estate; documents are annotated by an ex-employee of estate who helped engineer the action; later, a record fine of 587,000,000 pesos is levied against Mailhos for tax evasion.
April 13	*Police Inspector Héctor Moran Charquero, accused by MLN of torturing prisoners, is assassinated.*
April 14	Juan Almiratti is captured; he had earlier led Mailhos action.
May 29	*Navy training center and garrison occupied by Tupamaros; 421 weapons and 10,000 rounds of ammunition are expropriated; action is led by sailor Fernando Garin Lanieri.*
May 30	Fernan Pucurral Saenz de la Pena dies, Jorge Washington Puig Leivas and Antonio Bandera Lima (Brazilian) are arrested in a police raid; a potential people's prison is discovered.
May–June	Mauricio Cruz Ruiz Diaz arrested in Santiago, Chile carrying training manuals and 880 gold coins from the Mailhos action, presumably as aid to the Chilean MIR.
June	Republican Guard mutinies to demand special duty pay and right to wear civilian clothes for urban counterinsurgency; mutiny comes on heels

of a warning to police to discontinue mistreatment of captured Tupamaros; Republican Guard is subsequently disbanded.

June 16 UBUR branch assaulted; 6,733,340 pesos seized.

June 23 Manager of Banco Palestino del Uruguay kidnapped; 18,000,000 pesos seized.

Branch of Banco de Pan de Azucar robbed of 8,000,000 pesos by MLN unit.

June 30 Sayago branch of BOLSA occupied; 12,000,000 pesos expropriated.

July 1 Héctor Amodio Perez arrested.

July 4 Six incidents in 90 minutes, four police wounded, officer Armando Leses killed, one Tupamaro captured.

July 17 Media receives declaration from MANO (Eastern Armed National Movement) threatening reprisals against Tupamaros.

July 28 Judge Daniel Pereyra Manelli, head of Court of Proceedings of First Session, who had tried many Tupamaros, captured by MLN; freed August 5.

July 31 *Dan Mitrione (USAID public safety officer) and Aloysio Dias Gomide (Brazilian consul) abducted; Gordon Jones (first secretary, U.S. embassy) escapes kidnap attempt; MLN demands release of 150 political prisoners; government institutes state of siege.*

August 6 Branch of Banco Mercantil del Rio de la Plata relieved of 4,800,000 pesos by guerrillas.

August 7 United States agricultural expert Claude Fly kidnapped.

August 7	*Twelve thousand police and troops search Montevideo, sector by sector, for people's prison.*
	Police apprehend Raúl Sendic, Raúl Bidegain Greissing, Jorge Candan Grajales, Alicia Rey Morales, Edith Morales A. de Rodríguez, Nelly Graciela, Jorge Panzera, Luis Efrain Martínez Platero, and Asdrubal Pereira Cabrera; negotiations suspended.
August 9	*Dan Mitrione executed by Tupamaros.*
August 11	General Legislative Assembly votes to suspend personal guarantees for 20 days.
	Andrés Cultelli Chiribao caught by police.
August 14	Alejandro Otero (ex-police commissioner) states in Brazilian daily *Journal do Brasil* that Dan Mitrione "had used violent methods of repression and torture."
October 7	Deputy Ariel Collazo and Senator Zelmar Michelini read, in their respective chambers, an MLN document condemning the government; Tupamaros had demanded publication of same as condition for release of Claude Fly.
October 9	Tupamaro prisoners in Punta Carretas begin hunger strike to protest prison conditions.
October 29	Roberto Ron and Carlos Andrés Lopez killed in explosion at Carrasco Bowling Club.
October	Juan Carlos Larrosa shot and killed by police.
November 12	Tupamaros raid Banco de la Republica; $7,000,000 in jewels and $48,000 seized; action directed from inside by Daniel Ginovart.
December 4	Police claim to have searched 7,168 homes in counterinsurgency raids since beginning of year.

1971

January	*MLN announces support for Broad Front coalition in forthcoming elections.*
January 1	Government ends ban on use of the word "Tupamaros" in media.
January 6	MLN celebrates Day of the Kings by distributing toys and 1,000 litres of milk in Montevideo slums.
	MLN unit holds meeting in wrought-iron shop and reads manifesto; similar actions used over last two months.
January 8	*British Ambassador Geoffrey Jackson abducted.*
January 9	Government refuses to negotiate with MLN over Jackson's release.
January 10	"Armando Leses" Death Squadron bombs residence of ex-Deputy Arturo Dubra, the father of two Tupamaros and a Tupamaro defense attorney.
January 12	Personal liberties suspended for 40 days; extensive police-military search, house by house, of a number of Montevideo zones, for people's prison.
	Maria Teresa Labrocca Rabellino caught; police claim she masterminded attacks on Carrasco and San Rafael Casinos.
January 18	Police sergeant wounded; police captain's house raided by MLN; Lucia Topolanski captured.
January 27	Operation Fan begins, an attempt to search all homes in Montevideo for Geoffrey Jackson.
February 1	Jessie Arlette Macchi Torres caught.
February 6	Extensive search of Punta Carretas Prison for possible escape tunnel.

February 9	Rain washes out tunnel leading to Punta Carretas Prison.
February 10	Tupamaros seize 4,000,000 pesos from money exchange house.
February 21	Dias Gomide released; $250,000 ransom paid.
February 26	Six buildings owned by Pacheco Areco supporters bombed.
March 2	Claude Fly released.
March 4	Police capture MLN dossiers on 500 police officials and families.
March 6	Bombs explode in political clubs supporting Pacheco Areco.
March 10	Attorney General and Public Prosecutor Guido Berro Oribe abducted.
March 11	Guerrillas seize 210 wigs from Montevideo beauty parlor.
March 12	Minister of interior announces creation of special judicial tribunal for Tupamaros.
March 15	Pacheco Areco asks Congress to suspend personal rights once more to facilitate search for people's prison, Jackson, and Berro.
March 23	Berro released by MLN.
	Juan Pablo Miyra Bergeghi (Egyptian) caught by police.
March 26	Montevideo demonstration in support of Broad Front attended by 140,000 people.
March 30	Pereira Reverbel kidnapped again.
	Fifteen Tupamaros occupy plastics factory and lecture workers; unit detected, surrounded, and captured by police.

March 31	Government mobilizes 10,000 police, army, navy, and air force troops in search for Pereira Reverbel; thousands of citizens searched; minister of interior speaks of "virtual state of war."
April 1	General strike by CNT; demands of 400,000 strikers include salary increases and rehiring of discharged employees.
April 4	Government begins census of households to locate Tupamaros; special prison on Isla de Flores, in Rio de la Plata, established for Tupamaro prisoners; these actions follow cabinet shakeup and adoption of new hard line on April 2.
April 5	Government plans to initiate system to register everyone in Montevideo.
April 6	Cabinet shakeup; soft-liners Jorge Peirano Facio (foreign minister) and Cesar Borba (defense minister) replaced.
April 7	Fifteen rifles seized from artist; Police Inspector Washington Carreras' home firebombed; United States Marine billet in Montevideo damaged by bomb.
April 13	Industrialist Ricardo Ferres Terra kidnapped.
April 14	Government reinstates censure of MLN-related information.
April 14–15	Army lieutenant arrested for being Tupamaro; MLN cell in army uncovered.
April 18	Spectacular gunfight leads to death of one Tupamaro (Luis Correa); two captured in chase following attempted assassination of Lieutenant Carlos de los Santos of the Metropolitan Guard.
April 21	Two kidnap attempts foiled; medical supplies stolen; one policeman killed and two wounded by MLN to avenge Luis Correa.

April 22	Forty weapons stolen from gun collector; two Tupamaros captured while hijacking taxicab.
May 2	Pereira Reverbel sentenced to life imprisonment by MLN; Ferres Terra given one year.
May 10	Radio Vanguardia broadcast interrupted by MLN communiqué denouncing Metropolitan Guard.
	Twelve offices of (Pacheco Areco's) Colorado Party bombed.
May 13	Ex-Minister of Agriculture and Cattle Carlos Frick Davies kidnapped.
May 14	Kidnapping attempt on industrialist Alfredo Deambrosis fails.
May 16	Tupamaro and policeman wounded in shooting incident when police discover Tupamaro unit distributing leaflets and propagandizing in movie theater.
May 19	Bomb damages residence of ex-Foreign Minister Jorge Peirano Facio.
	Four Tupamaros destroy movie projector, equipment, and copy of movie *Che*.
May 22	Government offers $50,000 reward for information on location of people's prison.
May 23	Maria Elena Topolanski captured.
May 27	Juan Almiratti Nieto escapes in transit to court from Punta Carretas Prison.
May 29–30	Violent clashes between rightist and leftist high school students in Montevideo.
June 3	Cabinet shakeup; retired General Danilo Sena appointed minister of interior.

	Attempted assassination of the chief of the Metropolitan Guard.
June 5	Bombing attacks by Tupamaros, including an assault on an auto carrying Rear Admiral Hispano Perez Fontana.
June 9	Home of Juan Almiratti's lawyer bombed by rightists.
June 10	Strike by 400,000 CNT workers to protest government's social and economic policies; industry, commerce, banks, transportation, media, universities, and high schools close down for 24 hours.
June 23	Attorney Alfredo Camban kidnapped and held two days for questioning by MLN.
July 10	Daniel Camilo Ginovart Tonelli arrested.
July 11	Homes of four police officials occupied by MLN.
July 12	Argentine industrialist Jorge Berembau kidnapped.
	MLN column (20 guerrillas; 3 bases) captured.
July 14	MLN rejects $1,000,000 ransom for Pereira Reverbel.
	State of siege cancelled by Parliament.
July 15	State of siege reimposed by Pacheco Areco.
	Bank of the Republic in Tacuarembo robbed; 330,000 pesos seized.
July 17	Raúl Bidegain Greissing escapes Punta Carretas Prison by exchanging places with his brother during a visit.
July 22	Ten bombings in Montevideo; MLN declares war on government and imperialists supporting it.

Rightists launch bombing campaign with leaflets signed "Dan" (Mitrione).

July 23   MLN denounces plot to kill General Liber Seregni, presidential candidate of the Broad Front; MLN lists 43 rightist actions and warns it will match them "death for death."

July 27   Metropolitan Guard officer escapes MLN attack.

July 28   Radio Colonia attacked; radio's transmitters had allegedly been taken from MLN leaders in prison.

                Tupamaros demand 100,000,000 pesos be given to three textile unions for release of Jorge Berembau.

July 30   *Thirty-eight Tupamaros escape from Women's Prison.*

July 31   Oscar Burgueno Tupamaro-Hunting Command tortures and kills Manuel Ramos Filipini in its first action.

August 17   Attorney Carlos Maeso held by MLN for three days.

August 18   Industrialist Luis Fernandez Llado kidnapped.

September 1   Student Julio Cesar Sposito killed by police in demonstration.

September 5   Leftist students riot in university district during afternoon and evening.

September 6   *One hundred six Tupamaros, including Sendic, Maneras Lluveras, Marenales Saenz, Martínez Platero, and Amodio Perez, escape Punta Carretas Prison.*

September 9   Geoffrey Jackson released by MLN.

October 8	Two light aircraft skyjacked to distribute leaflets commemorating Pando action and Che Guevara's death; one action team captured.
October 22	Pereura Gonzalez (editor of rightist paper *El Día*) kidnapped by OPR-33; released 2 weeks later.
November 28	National elections; conservative Colorado candidate Juan María Bordaberry wins presidency.
December 5	General Liber Seregni, 55-year-old candidate of the Broad Front, duels General Pedro Ribas, 70-year-old candidate of Colorado Reformist Movement; Ribas had insulted Seregni, and a military court decided the solution.
December 19	Tupamaro command seizes 20 radios and transmitters from taxi company.
	Casino at Parque Hotel assaulted; $68,000 taken.
	CUTSA (Uruguayan Transport Company) occupied; MLN seizes 10,000,000 pesos.
	Police capture Héctor Alfredo Romero, eighteenth of Punta Carretas escapees recaptured.
December 22	Uruguayan Golf Club (located near Punta Carretas Prison) firebombed by December 22 group, a splinter from MLN; 60,000,000 pesos damage.
December 30	*Paysandú proclamation; Tupamaros Leandro Gomez column announces end of election truce and occupies facilities in city of Paysandú (airport, radio station, quarry, police station); other actions in northwestern region of country follow; first column level action.*
1972	
January 28	Ricardo Ferres Terra freed by MLN after nine month's captivity.

February 10	Police Chief José Pedro Macchi wounded by MLN.
February 12	Homero Farina (editor of *Acción*) kidnapped.
February 13	Assault on town of Socci, 60 kilometers from Montevideo.
February 21	Nineteen Tupamaros captured and arms cache discovered in Mercedes.
February 24	Nelson Bardesino, photographer and death squadron agent, kidnapped by MLN.
	Héctor Amodio Perez arrested in Montevideo and found to be carrying plans to the house of the president-elect.
March 1	Juan María Bordaberry takes office as president.
	Legislative Assembly votes to end state of siege.
March 3	MLN safe house uncovered in a cave in Espinillos, near Minas; Ruben Héctor Garcia Bianchimaro and eight others arrested.
March 19	General strike by CNT (National Workers Union) to protest government monetary policy.
March 26	Massive Broad Front demonstration in Montevideo.
April 12	Fifteen Tupamaros and several criminals escape Punta Carretas Prison, including Efrain Martínez Platero, Héctor Amodio Perez, Alberto Candan Grajales, Tabre Rivero Cedres, and Antonio Mas Mas.
April 13	One-day general strike in Montevideo by CNT.
April 14	*Tupamaros execute four persons associated with death squadron: Deputy Commissioner Delega and his secretary Alberto Leites, Navy Captain*

Ernesto Motto Benvenuto, and Armando Acosta y Lara.

Police raid in Malvín leads to deaths of Jorge Alberto Candan Grajales and Tabre Rivero Cedres; Eleuterio Fernández Huidobro, Carlos Campora, and six others captured; another police action leads to deaths of several other Tupamaros and the arrest of several hundred, including Juan Almiratti Nieto; death toll of eight Tupamaros total.

April 15   "State of internal war" proclaimed.

Senator Enrique Erro reads four documents from testimony of Nelson Bardesio into Senate record; Bardesio's revelations to MLN detail official support for death squadrons.

April 16   Twenty attacks by right-wingers and death squads reported.

April 17   Seven members of Paso Molino branch of Communist Party shot to death by police during alleged search of Sectional No. 20 for Tupamaros; one communist later dies from wounds.

April 18   CNT general strike to protest deaths of communists and increased repression.

April 24   Héctor Gutierrez Ruiz (president of Chamber of Deputies) kidnapped by MLN for one-day discussions with Nelson Bardesio on the subject of death squads.

José Alberto López Mercao and one other Tupamaro arrested in Treinta y Tres Department.

Seven Tupamaros arrested in Dolores near Espinillo forest; continued MLN activity reported in this area.

May 3	Nestor Peralta Larrosa and seven other Tupamaros captured in Flores Department.
May 11	Sergio Molaquero, son of an industrialist, abducted.
May 18	Four soldiers gunned down by MLN while guarding home of army commander-in-chief.
May 19	Mauricio Rosencoff arrested.
May 21	Field hospital discovered beneath ESTESU, Inc. (Technical Soil Studies, Inc.); operating room, X-ray machine, and vast quantities of medicine captured.
May 22	Ismael Bassini Campiglia, Conrado Fernandez Cabeles, and seven others arrested in raid on Spartacus ranch.
May 27	People's prison discovered and raided in Montevideo; Pereira Reverbel and Frick Davies freed; six Tupamaros captured.
June 4	Thirty-four Tupamaros captured in Durazno.
June 23	Joint Forces announce 16 arrests in Tacuarembo Department.
June 25	Seventeen Tupamaros captured in Durazno.
July 5	Joint Forces announce 30 arrests in Treinta y Tres Department.
July 7	Fernando Alberto Secco Aparacio, wealthy rancher and land owner, arrested for MLN connections.
July 15	Government announces 600–700 Tupamaros and supporters captured, 100 killed, and 70 safe houses uncovered since April 15, 1972.
July 25	*Colonel Artigas Alvarez (chief of Civil Defense force and brother of commander-in-chief of Join*

	Forces) *assassinated, ending a period of truce and negotiations.*
August 19	Twelve Tupamaros arrested in Montevideo, including Lucia Topolanski Saavedra de Martinez Platero and Alberto Mujica Cordano.
September 1	Raúl Sendic wounded and captured in Montevideo along with Xenia Itte Gonzalez and Jorge Bernardo Ramada Piendibeni.
October 5	Seven December 22 Group members taken; according to police, the group is destroyed.
October 27	Senator Jorge Batlle y Ordoñez arrested for insult to military; held for several days.
November 10	Army post outside Montevideo assaulted.
November 24	Abortive action against Radio Rural.
December 5	Nineteen Tupamaros arrested.
December 7	Hugo Rodolfo Castro Spino dies in custody of police; death called "suicide" by police.
	Socialist Party's 37th Congress bombed.
December 12	Ten CAT (Committee of Tupamaro Support) members arrested.

1973

January 18	Strike by 60,000 public employees.
January 23	MLN unit takes weapons from home of Joint Forces member; first action in several months.
February 8	Army and air force commanders issue statement answering charges by Senator Vasconcellos and sharply attacking him; executive branch considers disciplinary action; military rebellion starts, aimed at removing Minister of Defense Frances.

February 9	Navy supports President Bordaberry against army and air force challenge; censorship of news enforced; sporadic fighting within military cabinet.
February 11	Negotiations lead to truce both between military and president and within military; the commander-in-chief of the navy, Admiral Juan J. Zorrilla, resigns.
February 17	Joint Forces announce capture of eight Tupamaros involved in the assassination of Colonel Artigas Alvarez.
February 23	COSENA (National Security Council) established.
February 24	Four Tupamaros escape Punta Carretas Prison, including Gabino Falero and Asudrubal Pereyra Cabrera.
February 26	Aborted attempt to kidnap ex-Minister of Interior Alejandro Rovira: one guard killed, one wounded, one Tupamaro wounded and captured.
March 29	CNT general strike attempts to topple Bordaberry.
April 24	Military initiates action against Senator Erro for collaboration with MLN.
May 7	Héctor Amodio Perez testifies for military against Erro.
May 14	Three thousand troops brought to Montevideo from interior.
	General William Rosson (commander of U.S. Southern Command in Panama) arrives in Montevideo.

June 18	Ernest Siracusa becomes U.S. ambassador to Uruguay.
June 20	Student demonstration; 230 arrested.
	Nine guards at Punta Carretas Prison indicted and dismissed for role in 1971 escape.
June 21	Chamber of Deputies declines impeachment of Enrique Erro.
June 25	Juan José Carozo and six other members of PCR arrested in Paysandú.
June 27	*Coup d'etat; Bordaberry closes Congress, abolishes Municipal Councils, and adopts military-civilian council of state as executive authority; arrest of opposition senators ordered.*
	CNT calls for revolutionary general strike to answer coup; economy soon paralyzed; military begins negotiations with CNT.
June 29	Strike continues as CNT-military negotiations fail.
June 30	CNT proscribed; 100 arrests at headquarters of bank employees association.
July 4	Two thousand women demonstrators dispersed by tear gas and water.
	Right to strike lifted.
July 6	Two thousand students demonstrate; Ramón Bardier (PS militant) shot to death by police in street fight.
	Agreement signed with Brazilian oil monopoly for short-term oil loans to conpensate for refineries shut down by strikers.
July 8	Student Walter Medina shot to death by police while putting up posters.

July 9	Fifteen thousand demonstrators clash with police; six shot and 100 arrested.
	Reports circulate that 600 persons are held in Cilindrom stadium for lack of other prison facilities.
July 16	Classes at university resume; popular resistance wanes.
July 20	Arrests announced of 25 PCR members in Soriano Department.
July 24	New labor law enacted: no more politics or political strikes; right to strike only on appoval of the government.

Thirty Questions to a Tupamaro

This interview gives the first systematic definition of the Tupamaros' political position. It was circulated internally in late 1967 and first made public in the Chilean journal *Punto Final* in mid-1968.

1. What has been the fundamental principle on which you have based the activity of your organization until now?

The principle that revolutionary action in itself, the very act of arming oneself, preparing, equipping, and pursuing activities that violate bourgeois legality, generates revolutionary consciousness, organization, and conditions.

2. What is the fundamental difference between your organization and other organizations of the left?

The majority of the latter seem to place their faith in making declarations and issuing theoretical statements about revolution in order to prepare militants and revolutionary conditions; they do not realize that fundamentally it is revolutionary action which precipitates revolutionary situations.

3. Could you give me any historical example illustrating the principle that revolutionary action generates revolutionary consciousness, organization, and conditions?

Cuba is an example. In place of the long process of forming a Party of the masses, a guerrilla *foco* of a dozen men was installed, and this deed generated revolutionary consciousness, organization, and conditions. Given the revolutionary fait accompli, authentic revolutionaries saw themselves as obliged to follow in its path.

4. Do you mean to say that once revolutionary action is launched the famous unity of the left can develop in the struggle?

Yes, the forces calling themselves revolutionary will find themselves obliged to choose between support or disappearance. In Cuba, the Popular Socialist Party[1] opted to support the struggle, which it had

Revolución y Cultura (Havana, Cuba), no. 21 (December 1970), pp. 22–27. Translation by the authors.

1 The Moscow-line Communist Party.

neither initiated nor led, and survived. But Prío Socarrás,[2] who called himself the principal opponent of Batista, did not support it and disappeared.

5. This is with respect to the left, but what of the people in general?
For the people—those who truly disagree with the injustices of the regime—the choice is much simpler. They want change, and they must choose between the improbable and remote change which some offer through proclamations, manifestos, or parliamentary action and the direct road embodied by the armed group and its revolutionary action.

6. Do you mean to say that the armed struggle, at the same time that it is destroying bourgeois power, can create the mass movement an insurrectional organization needs to make the revolution?
Yes, without considering as lost that effort used to create a Party or Movement of the masses before beginning the armed struggle, it must be recognized that the armed struggle hastens and precipitates the mass movement. And Cuba is not the only example; in China, too, the mass Party was created in the course of the armed struggle. That is to say that the rigid formula of certain theoreticians "first create the Party, then begin the Revolution," is historically more the exception than the rule. At this stage of history nobody can deny that an armed group, however small, has more possibility of becoming a people's army than does a group limited to issuing revolutionary "positions."

7. Nevertheless, a revolutionary movement needs a platform, documents, etc.
Of course, but one should not be confused. It is not only by polishing platforms and programs that the Revolution is made. The basic principles of socialist revolution are given and tested in countries like Cuba—there is nothing more to discuss. It is sufficient to adhere to those principles and to show in action the insurrectional road to their application.

8. Do you believe that a revolutionary movement should prepare for armed struggle even when conditions for the armed struggle are not present?

---

[2] A former president and leading politician who aided Castro during the early years of the guerrilla movement but went into opposition soon after the seizure of power.

Yes, for at least two reasons. Because an armed movement of the left can be attacked by repression at any point in its development, it should be prepared to defend its existence . . . remember Argentina and Brazil. Also, because if each militant is not instilled with the mentality of a fighter from the very beginning, we shall be building something else—a support movement for a revolution others will make, for example—but not a revolutionary movement in itself.

9. Can this be interpreted as denigration of all other activities except preparing oneself to fight?
No, work among the masses which leads the people to revolutionary positions is also important. What the militant must remember—including those at the head of the masses—is that on the day the armed struggle is launched he is not going to stay at home awaiting the outcome. And he should prepare himself as a result, even though his present militancy may be on other fronts. Moreover, this will give authority, authenticity, sincerity, and seriousness to his present revolutionary message.

10. What are the concrete tasks of a militant in the mass movement who belongs to your organization?
If a militant in a union or a mass movement is involved, his task should consist of creating a circle, whether a group in the union or the entire union, where support can be organized for the activities of the armed apparatus and preparations made to join it. Theoretical and practical training and recruitment will be the concrete tasks within that circle. In addition, there is propaganda for armed struggle. And where possible, the union should be impelled toward more radical struggles and more definite stages of the class struggle.

11. In general, what are the fundamental objectives of the movement at this stage?
To have an armed group, as well prepared and equipped as possible, and tested in action.
    To have good relations with all popular movements which support his type of struggle.
    To create propaganda organs to radicalize the struggle and raise conciousness.

To have an efficient apparatus to absorb militants by offering opportunities for theoretical training, and to absorb groups within the mass movement that fulfill the above-mentioned functions.

12. Does the importance that the movement gives to preparation for armed struggle imply that a combatant cannot improvise?

The armed struggle is a technical act which requires, then, the technical knowledge, practice, equipment, and mentality of a fighter. Improvisation in this area is very costly in terms of lives and failures. The spontaneity promoted by some who speak vaguely of either the "revolution which the people will make" or "the masses" is either mere stalling or else it means leaving to improvisation the culminating phase of the class struggle. Every vanguard movement must, to preserve that vanguard character at the culminating moment of the struggle, intervene in it and know how to give technical guidance to the popular violence against oppression in such a manner that the objective is attained with the least possible sacrifice.

13. Do you believe that parties of the left can achieve that preparation for armed struggle by maintaining a small body of shock troops or a self-defense force?

No Party complies with the revolutionary principles it enunciates if it does not seriously face up to this preparation at every level of the Party. Otherwise it will not achieve the maximum possible efficiency with which to confront reaction at each stage, which can lead to fatal negligence (remember Brazil and Argentina) or to wasting a revolutionary conjuncture.

If they are not prepared for their specific objective, the small armed Party groups can become a sad mess of political maneuverings. A miserable example to recall in this regard is the incident which occurred at the demonstrations of last May Day: some armed groups were reduced to the task of protecting the distribution of a leaflet in which other groups of the left were attacked, and yet other armed groups confined themselves to the task of preventing the handing out of leaflets.

14. What do you think that militants of the armed Party apparatus can demand of their respective leaderships?

That their action be directed solely against the class enemy, against the bourgeois apparatus and its agents. No armed group can fulfill its specific objective if its leadership does not meet these minimum requisites:

a. That it be responsible and demonstrate by deeds its unwavering adherence to the principle of armed struggle, giving it importance and supplying the material means necessary for its preparation.

b. That it offer the necessary conditions of security and discretion to those militants who carry out illegal tasks.

c. That, through its scope and correct line, it should have a chance— as immediate as possible—of becoming the leader of the proletarian masses.

15. Do you not believe that an armed apparatus should depend on a political party?

I believe that every armed group should form part of a political apparatus of the masses at a certain point in the revolutionary process, and that, in case such an apparatus does not exist, it should contribute to creating one. This does not mean that it should be obliged, in the present situation of the left, to adhere to one of the existing political groups or that it should launch a new one. This could serve only to perpetuate the mosaic or to add to it. It is necessary to combat the current meager idea of a party as being identified by a headquarters, meetings, a newspaper, and positions on everything around it. It is necessary to get over the idea that the other parties of the left will dissolve before its verbal broadsides, that all their base units and the people in general will one day come to it. This is what has happened for sixty years in Uruguay and the result is plain to see. It is necessary to start with reality. It is necessary to recognize that there are authentic revolutionaries in all parties of the left, and that there are many more who are not organized. To take these elements and groups wherever they are and to unite them is a task for the left in general, in preparation for the day when sectarianism will be left behind, something which does not depend on us. But the Revolution cannot stop and wait until this happens. Each revolutionary, each revolutionary group has only one duty: to prepare to make the revolution. As Fidel Castro said in one of his recent speeches ". . . with a Party or without a Party." The Revolution cannot wait.

16. Can you give me details of the strategy for seizing power in Uruguay?

No, I cannot give you a detailed strategy. On the other hand, I can give you some general strategic lines, and even these are subject to change with circumstances. That is to say, strategic lines valid for the day, month, and year they were mentioned.

17. Why can you not give me a detailed and definitive strategy?

Because a strategy is elaborated on the premise of basic real facts, and reality changes independent of our will. You understand that a strategy premised on the existence of a strong and organized union movement is not the same as one based on the fact the movement has been scattered, to give an illustrative example.

18. On what basic real facts does your organization premise its general strategic lines at this time?

To cite only the most important ones:

—The conviction that the crisis, far from having been overcome, is becoming worse by the day. The country is established on a capitalist plan of development to increase the production of exportable items, which if applied will yield only very minimal returns and only after several years. This means that we have several years ahead in which the people will have to tighten their belts. And with $500 million in foreign debt it is not foreseeable that sufficient credits will be coming from abroad to allow those sectors of society whose standard of living has fallen to return to their former level. This is a basic concrete fact —there will be economic hardship and popular discontent in the coming years.

—A second basic fact for a strategy is the high degree of unionization of the workers of Uruguay. Even if all unions do not have a high degree of militancy—either because of their composition or because of their leaders—the mere fact that virtually all the basic services of the state, banking, industry, and commerce are organized constitutes by itself a highly positive fact without parallel in Latin America. The possibility of paralyzing the state services has created and can create very interesting conjunctures from the viewpoint of insurrection because— to give an example—it is not the same to attack a state at full strength as it is to attack one half-paralyzed by strikes.

—Another strategic factor to take into account, this one negative, is the geograpic factor. We do not have impregnable locations in Uruguay where we could install a guerrilla *foco* which could hold out, although we do have places in the countryside where access is difficult. To compensate, we have a big city with more than 300 square kilometers of buildings, which allows for the development of an urban struggle. This means that we cannot copy the strategy of those countries where geographic conditions permit installation of a *foco* in the mountains or woods with a chance of stabilizing itself. On the contrary, we must elaborate a strategy suitable to a reality different from that of most countries of Latin America.

—In addition, in any strategic survey, we must always take into account the forces of repression. Our armed forces, some 12,000 men sketchily equipped and trained, constitute one of the weakest organizations of repression in America.

—Another important strategic factor is our powerful neighbors and the United States, always potentially disposed to intervene against revolution on the continent.

—And finally, a fundamental strategic factor is the degree of preparation of the revolutionary armed group.

19. How do the present crisis and popular discontent enter into the strategy?

In the objective and subjective conditions for the Revolution. It is fundamental that the majority of the population, although not in favor of throwing themselves into an insurrection, at least not be prepared to kill for a regime which holds them down. This, among other things, reduces the strategic calculations regarding the forces of the enemy, in all practicality, to its organized armed forces, and raises the possibility of a favorable climate for the first stages of revolutionary government.

0. And as regards the forces of repression?

They should be evaluated by taking into account their level of combat preparation, their means, and their distribution in the country. In the interior there is one military unit (200 men) about every 10,000 square kilometers, and a police commissariat about every 1,000 square kilometers. The armed forces have to cover all the objectives that might be attacked by an insurrectionary movement with 12,000 military person-

nel and 22,000 police, of whom half of the former and 6,000 of the latter
are concentrated in the capital. Of the police, only about 1,000 have
been trained and equipped for truly military action.

*21. Can the possibility of foreign intervention be a reason for postpon-
ing all armed struggle in Uruguay?*

If that were so, Cuba would not have carried out its revolution 90 miles
from the United States; nor would there be guerrillas in Bolivia, a
country which borders on Brazil and Argentina, as does ours. Foreign
intervention can constitute an immediate military reverse but also a
political advantage which in time will become a military advantage.
Imagine the city of Montevideo occupied by foreign troops, with the
resulting outrage to nationalist feeling and harassment of the population, and imagine that force being confronted by an armed revolutionary group within the city . . . You can get a perfect idea of what
the so greatly feared foreign intervention means politically and militarily.

Besides, in any case, our strategy is contained within the continental
strategy of creating many Vietnams, and the interventionists will have
a lot of work on many, scattered fronts.

*22. How does the high level of unionization figure in a revolutionary
strategy?*

The trade unions, even with their present limitations, have committed
and can involve the majority of the working population in a direct
struggle against the government, a sort of situation which the government has often resolved by calling out the armed forces. Through the
existence of an armed revolutionary group capable of raising the class
struggle to a higher stage, we can conduct the struggle under better
conditions, with a large part of the population behind us and with
the basic services of the State deteriorating.

23. Is our geography completely adverse to a struggle in the countr
side?

That is not strictly so. We do not have impregnable spots like other
countries, but there are accidents of nature which allow temporary
refuge to an armed group. The latifundio is a great ally. In latifundio
areas, that is to say, in two-thirds of the country, the population density is less than 0.6 inhabitants per square kilometer, which facilitates

the clandestine movement of an armed contingent; compare that with the over-all average of Cuba, more than twenty inhabitants per square kilometer, and even with the regions of small farms in our country, like Canelones and the south of San José, with the same average density.

At the same time, the livestock-breeding latifundio solves the tricky logistical problem of food supplies that in other places requires a supply line, which can be achieved only with great complicity on the part of the population.

In addition, the frightful living conditions of the rural wage earners, some already organized into unions, have created a spontaneous rebel sector which can be very useful in the rural struggle. If our countryside cannot be used to shelter a permanent *foco,* at least it can serve to disperse the forces of repression.

24. And for the urban struggle, do the conditions exist?
Montevideo is a city sufficiently large and polarized by social struggles to give cover to a vast active commando contingent. It constitutes a far better framework than that which other revolutionary movements have had for the urban struggle. To be sure, any organization which hopes to last in the urban struggle should patiently construct its material bases and the vast support network which an armed contingent needs to operate or subsist in the city.

25. How does the fact of the existence of a prepared armed group figure in strategic planning?
If there is not a reasonably prepared group, the revolutionary conjunctures are simply wasted or not taken advantage of for the revolution. Things like the *Bogotazo*[3] happen.

The armed group goes about creating or helping to create the subjective conditions for the revolution from the very moment at which it begins to prepare itself, but especially after it begins to act.

26. What will be, then, the general strategic lines for the present moment?
To form an armed force with the greatest possible speed, with the capacity to take advantage of any propitious conjuncture created by the

[3] The *Bogotazo* was a spontaneous urban riot in Bogotá, Colombia in 1948. Triggered by the assassination of populist Jorge Gaitán, it led to a civil war called, simply, "La Violencia."

crisis or other factors. To create an awareness in the population, through actions of the armed group or other means, that without revolution there will be no change. To strengthen the trade unions and to radicalize their struggles and link them with the revolutionary movement.

To link up with the other revolutionary movements of Latin America, for continental action.

27. Is this a blueprint of your organization excusively?
No, it is one for all authentically revolutionary organizations and for all the individuals who really desire a revolution.

28. Do you consider all these tasks to be equally revolutionary?
Yes. Some believe that we are doing a revloutionary task only when we are training to fight or when we go into action, but all the tasks which help the strategic plan are equally important for the revolution.

29. Can you give me an illustrative example?
Whoever runs an errand to acquire equipment necessary for a base of operations, whoever obtains money, whoever lends his automobile for mobilization, whoever lends his house is running as much risk, and sometimes more, than the member of the action group. It must be realized that the majority of the revolutionaries have spent most of their time on these small practical things without which there is no revolution.

30. Does that mean that a strategic possibility can open up with our daily effort?
Yes. Our strategy for revolution depends partly on the conditions which we may be able to create through our efforts aimed at the seizure of power and partly on not losing sight of the conditions which reality presents to us.

Pando Operation
by María Esther Gilio

Recounted here is the Tupamaro occupation of the town of Pando on October 8, 1969, in commemoration of the death of Che Guevara two years earlier. The occupation signalled an intensification of the struggle within Uruguay and provided the model for similar actions by Argentine guerrillas. In military terms, the action was the first involving a coordinated combat effort by some 50 guerrillas.

At ten o'clock in the morning, Antonio and I mounted the bus. It was almost empty, but we still preferred the long seat at the back. Antonio had bought a morning paper but didn't open it; he looked at the headlines on the front page, folded it in fourths, and put it in his pocket. We were both silent, intent on the transit vocation of examining each and every one who got on the bus. An old man dressed in *chacarero*[1] clothing, two fat women loaded down with packages, a mother and three children, high school students with books under their arms, scholars. . . . As we passed Maronas, a young couple got on and sat down opposite us. I looked at them as I had looked at each of the others who got on. She had on wool slacks, dark glasses, a red silk scarf on her head, and a plaid knapsack with a thermos sticking out of it; he, in gray pants and a suede jacket, had his right arm across her shoulders while, with the left, he held some fishing rods wrapped in a blue canvas bag. He looked out. The day was radiant: resplendent the green of the countryside and the yellow acacias covered with late flowers . . . . To sit down under a willow tree and wait unhurriedly until the fish bite . . . . how far away all of that was, as if it belonged to another world, despite the sun shining there as always, despite the couple with their thermos and fishing rods. I turned to Antonio to tell him something about the strange sensation of belonging to another planet. But Antonio had his eyes glued on the blue bag the boy had

María Esther Gilio, an Uruguayan lawyer, won the 1970 Testimonial Prize of the Casa de las Americas competition for her book *La Guerrilla Tupamara*. This excerpt is a chapter from the book which appeared in *Tricontinental* (North American edition, Berkeley, California), no. 2, pp. 4–21. She was detained, and possibly killed, by the junta in Chile after the September 1973 coup.

[1] Owner or tenant of a *chacra* or small individual plot.

between his legs. I followed the direction of his gaze. At the bottom of the sack, the butt of a long gun was outlined against the cloth. We looked at each other again and smiled.

How many more of us are there? How many more? This one with the checked shirt waiting in the corridor . . . . this lanky one with a pensive air who had seated himself beside us . . . . Young, pale, well-dressed, glancing at his watch from time to time. Those two girls chattering endlessly in a front seat . . . .

The bus had slowed down as it smoothly turned right. Antonio and I simultaneously turned to the window. The funeral cortege was already there and was beginning to pass us. Ahead, the hearse piled with wreaths; behind, six black *remises*[2] bearing a few mourners. In the first one, a silent couple; he dressed in dark blue, smoking; she supporting her head in her right hand and drying her eyes with a handkerchief from time to time. I felt myself beginning to laugh and pressed Antonio's arm. With a nervous gesture, he indicated the rest of the bus. A respectful silence had settled over the passengers. The men looked at each other, some of the women made the sign of the cross. The young man on the other side, removed from everything, continued looking far away, deep in who-knows-what serious thoughts. But for one second our glances crossed, and suddenly and violently I was certain he was one of ours. I turned back toward the window and did not look at him again.

Days later, in the papers, I recognized his sad eyes, his dark straight hair, his fine features. He was Jorge Salerno,[3] whom a few hours later they would assassinate during the evacuation of Pando.

—Very well, as I am going to tell you . . . . it was impossible to suspect. The person who came to request the service looked so . . . .
—Distinguished?
—Exactly, distinguished. He seemed to be a young man from a well-to-do family.
—Because of his clothes . . . .
—Because of everything . . . . his clothes, his manners . . . . He

---

[2] Automobile for hire for a funeral procession.
[3] Young Tupamaro fighter, shot by the police, after having been disarmed and wounded, during Operation Pando.

explained to me that it was for an uncle who had died in Buenos Aires, and it seemed natural to me.

—It was very natural. Why wouldn't he have an uncle who died in Buenos Aires?

—Exactly. . . . anybody can, I mean to say. . . . I don't have any uncles, but if I had. . . .

—What explanation did he give for wanting to bring him here?

—He said that now that the estate was settled, this was the moment to comply with the will of the deceased.

—Yes, but why did the deceased want this?

—It seems that the man was from Soca[4] and wanted to rest in the earth where he had spent his infancy.

—This is what the boy said?

—Exactly. "He lived in Buenos Aires for 60 years, but he was always homesick for this land." This is what he said. Then they who were the heirs were going to fulfill his will.

—They talked about the type of service they wanted . . . . prices, all this . . . .

—Yes, the funeral coach they wanted to be good but not ostentatious. I immediately suggested the American. It seemed to me to be ideal in this case. It is substantial but without being extravagant, and completely closed as they wished.

—Did it seem ideal to him?

—Exactly.

—He told you so?

—Yes, he said: "The car that uncle would have hired."

—Then they spoke about the *remises*. . . .

—Yes, exactly six. Although there would only be 12 or 14 leaving from here, they needed the six cars because they had to pick up other members of the family in Empalme Olmos.

—And with all this . . . . did they give you the name of the deceased?

—Of course! The name was one of the best. Even if they had made it up . . . .

—Well. . . . actually they did. . . .

[4] Neighboring town to Pando, in the department of Canelones.

—Yes, yes, of course. . . . I mean to say. . . . it was very well thought up.

—It was?

—Antúnez Burgueño. . . ! Doesn't it sound familiar?

—No.

—The Antúnez own half of Pando and half of Soca.

—Ah. . . . it was really a snow job. It was a good name. . . . And what did the whole thing come to?

—Twenty-one thousand pesos that they paid like gentlemen.

—Like gentlemen. . . .

—Yes. I have to be honest, and I don't know what you will think, but we don't have any complaints.

—At no moment, then, did you suspect anything?

—There was just one thing that seemed to us a little. . . . extravagant. . . . that the urn with the remains would be brought by them personally. It is always the funeral service that takes care of the customs transfers and all this. . . . In this case, they would bring the urn to the place.

—What was the urn made of?

—Of lead.

—And they would have placed the bones in it. . . .

—Bones? I say arms. But who would have thought of that if they were the best of people? That's hindsight. You should have seen how the niece cried that morning, October 8, when we left. . . . She brought a bunch of flowers and cried. . . . so did the other one. They both cried. After all. . . . it is very natural in such cases. . . . people cry.

—Of course.

All at once I realized he had given up analyzing our immediate surroundings and was immersed in the theme that had monopolized my thinking for several days "What are you thinking about?" Antonio asked me.

—What you imagine. The same thing you're thinking. What did you tell your wife when you left today?

—I told her I had to go to Aiguia on business for the old man.

—And the old man?

—I told the old man not to say anything, that I had a date with a woman.

—And your boss?

—That I had a problem with my teeth and would be out all morning.

—You think you'll be back at three?

—If all goes as it should. . . . why not? . . . sometimes I think that being clandestine like you is a solution.

—Well. . . . maybe—I said it and was silent.

For seven months I haven't seen my wife; for two years I haven't caressed my daughter. I often hear that "they" have been to the house, that they searched everything and asked a thousand questions. And a hundred times I have imagined the little face of María Esther, her big dark eyes, her braids like parentheses around both sides of her face. . . . and her "no" said in a very careful voice. "No, sir, he wasn't here. No, sir, I didn't see him; I never see my papa."

I looked at the horizon, the sun continued in splendor, the couple in the front were getting ready to get off. Almost mechanically I thought: "Kilometer 29; they are going to enter Pando by an oblique road." I tapped the pistol, made a second knot in my shoe laces, and began to review, perhaps for the hundredth time, all the details of the task I had ahead.

Seated under a tree at the edge of the adjoining road that leads into the point of kilometer 29 on route 8, Diego, Gerardo, and Ismael waited for the two comrades they were to meet around 12 noon.

As always before an important action, Diego was composing interminable complicated melodies that none of us knew. "But tell me," said Ismael, "don't you know anything by Gardel?" Diego smiled. "I promise you that for the next time I will learn 'The day you love me.' "

Gerardo looked at his watch. It was two minutes to twelve. "What time do you have?" said Diego checking his watch for the fourth time that morning. "The hour that Ana and Julio should be arriving," said Gerardo at the same time that he closed his jacket zipper. Ismael registered the gesture and stood up, felt the pistol and the two grenades through his jacket, pulled out and put back the white handkerchief he was to wear on his left arm during the action and raised both hands in greeting: Ana and Julio were slowly approaching along the road. Ana with her plaid knapsack, Julio with his sack for fishing rods. "Good, let's go," said Gerardo, and felt a violent contraction grabbing at his stomach.

Without speaking, they started down the road. Diego and Gerardo ahead, Ana and Julio thirty meters behind, Ismael between the two groups stopping from time to time to imitate with a whistle, the song of a bird.

Ismael was the newest of the five. He had come to Cerro Largo six months before looking for work. At that time all his political culture was reduced to a healthy lack of confidence in the politics and the politicians he had known from his infancy. It was a good beginning. Today, after four months in the organization, he was a first-rank cadre. Tireless in his work, always serene and with a quality which, if it is not included in the manual of what makes a good guerrilla, was nevertheless appreciated by all the comrades: cheerfulness and good humor.

It was 12:15 when they entered the first streets of Pando. There was more than a half hour to waste. Without losing sight of each other, they began to walk without any fixed course. Gerardo began to think—although he knew the calculation was absurd—that out of each ten persons that went by, one was of the party. He said so to Diego. Diego let out a guffaw. "Your know what that's called? Delusions of grandeur. Pando has 60,000 inhabitants, and there will be about 50 of us when we take it. . . . If you do a little arithmetic. . . ." Gerardo insisted. This idea of "one in ten" always soothed him. And so, even though he realized it was irrational, he insisted. "But I am talking about the street, about the people walking in the street at this minute." "Look," said Diego, pointing to a fat blond who, valise in hand, seemed to have stopped, dazzled, in front of a shoe store window. "Look, be happy, this might be one of your ten." "She really could be," Gerardo thought and went back to checking the time. Eight minutes to go. "Come on," he said, and once more felt that old familiar cramp in the stomach. "Christ, I'm sure that if I could come to the actions with something in my belly my stomach wouldn't bother me like this every time I think," he said. "Bullets and sausages with fried potatoes never go well to-gether," said Diego. "Bowels empty, stomach empty, and a clear card with blood type and RH in the pocket is the sign of every obedient guerrilla who is going to enter action. Don't complain. Let's go."

Before turning the corner, Gerardo looked back. The blond with the valise had abandoned the store window and appeared to be moving toward the avenue at a rapid pace.

—I went with the chauffeur in the Catalina.

—It wasn't an American funeral coach?

—At the last moment we sent a Catalina.

—Leading the funeral procession. . . .

—Certainly. Don't tell me you've never seen a funeral. . . .

—Yes, I've seen funerals. Was it a slow trip as is appropriate?

—No. We went at road speed—that is to say, about 50 miles an hour.

—The mourners, at first, quite grief-stricken. . . .

—Yes, yes, the women cried, and the men were very serious and wore the proper clothes, dark clothes. . . .

—The urn with the remains was in the Catalina. . . .

—Yes, well, remains. . . .

—That's true. . . . with the arms, you say.

—That's right. . . . although to be honest, I did not see the arms.

—Yes, of course. . . . You had no reason to see them.

—No, no, no. . . . at no time.

—They themselves placed the urn in the funeral coach?

—No, but they watched attentively while the employees loaded it.

—And you continued the same. . . . without suspecting. . . .

—Quite the contrary, they impressed me favorably, it seemed to me that this man, the deceased, must have been a very respected person. . . . a dearly loved person. Understand? Because of the family atti-tude. Later this was confirmed.

—How was it confirmed?

—Yes, one of the nephews who was riding in the funeral coach with me and the chauffeur, told us that he was an extraordinary per-son. . . . very benevolent and so forth. . . .

—How long did it take to get to Empalme Olmos?

—A little over an hour. When we arrived the other relatives were already waiting for us on the highway, six or seven.

—Did they bring flowers?

—There they didn't bring flowers. Unless they had put them in their purses. . . . there wasn't one that didn't have a purse in hand.

—You are thinking that there were guns in the purses?

—It's logical! Guns and whatever else. . . . leaflets. . . .

—Leaflets?

—Lots of leaflets. . . . In Pando we really threw leaflets.

—Everybody? You threw them too?

—We were handcuffed, you understand. . . . but since we went through so many changes with them, at the end one hardly knows what to say.

—It's natural, very natural to get mixed up. They took Pando with leaflets then?

—For me, yes.

—What happened after Empalme Olmos?

—That is where the Uncle Pascual affair occurred. They began to say that Uncle Pascual was at kilometer 40 and they had to go pick him up there.

—And you?

—Us, nothing. . . . we went.

—And when they reached kilometer 40?

—There was a Volkswagen bus, a Kombi, waiting. A man got out and I thought: "This one is no uncle." He seemed very young for an uncle, you understand?

—And of course he wasn't either.

—How could he be. . . . They made the six chauffeurs and me get out.

—At gunpoint?

—Just by hand. They searched us thoroughly and put on us those handcuffs they make themselves, you know them?

—I've never seen them.

—How strange! There are always pictures of them in the newspapers. They are homemade of wire. . . . Well, they talked among themselves, they said they couldn't put us in the funeral coach because we didn't fit or something. They put us in the bus and after we were all in, we turned around toward Pando ten kilometers back.

—And the *remises* and everything?

—It seems that the funeral coach would go first to the Pando cemetery where they would leave the flowers, that is what I heard them say. Meanwhile, we in the Kombi would be driving around because it was early and it was necessary to waste time.

—Early for what?

—For the assault!

—Ah, and how were you seated in the bus?

—In the front, the driver and two others. In the back, the six chauffeurs, me, and three of them.

—Did they talk?

—Naturally.

—What did they talk about?

—A little about everything.

—About what they were going to do in Pando?

—No. . . .

—Politics?

—A little. . . . you know that their custom is always to explain.

—Explain what?

—But you are a journalist and you don't read the newspapers? They explain why they do this and the other and how they think they will improve things and so forth. They always explain everything.

—That is to say, they were not nervous. . . . because it's their thing to give explanations. . . .

—But of course!

—And you?

—You mean were we nervous?

—Yes.

—You are going to get nervous talking with three boys who could be the sons of one of you. . . . We were calm!

Fifteen minutes before the hour, Antonio and I and the other two who made up the commando were posted around the bus station, 80 meters from our objective and awaiting the determined moment. I looked at the watch. It was ten minutes to one. Half of Pando would be eating at this hour. With a quick glance, I saw that the comrades were ready. Next to one column, Antonio, with the newsaper he had bought before setting out, was feigning reading. A few meters away from Antonio, almost at the edge of the park, Guillermo was explaining to Nato, with an enthusiasm that would have moved stones, how Spence[5] had missed a goal in the last quarter. I smiled inwardly. In the eyes of any observer who happened by, Nato was hypnotized by Guillermo's explanations. I knew he didn't have the slightest idea what he was saying; that his eyes and his entire attention were concentrated on a point behind Guillermo, 80 meters behind.

I pulled out the pack, rolled a cigarette, and began to smoke slowly. I felt very calm. For three days, we had watched the movements of the firemen's barracks we had as our objective, and the four of us agreed that, if the seizure of the commissary which was to take place one or two minutes prior to that of the barracks did not become complicated, the job with the firemen was going to be easy. I looked at my watch again, six minutes to go. Two *remises,* black and imposing, with their velvet curtains half drawn, turned the corner and moved slowly toward the banking zone. Seconds later, the third passed. A little later, a fourth quickly went around the Plaza. On the corner of the commissary, the "weeper" was already at his post. Slender, tall, grave, dressed in funeral garb, he was the model weeper. No one would have thought he had ever done anything in this life except take care of funerals. I imagined the pistol resting on his right side, then, just as when I was a child and invented pleasant stories, I imagined that he was raising both arms and yelling: "Pando is ours, comrades."

A fifth *remise* approached and followed at a distance. I knew the driver. I lowered my head, drew a deep breath, and looked at the hour again. Within 30 seconds, the commando in charge of the commissary was to start action.

One o'clock sharp. We saw the comrades enter the commissary door and very slowly we began to cross.

"It was approximately 1:00 when a man and a woman appeared at the commissary asking for the person in charge. I said he wasn't there

[5] A famous soccer player on the Peñarol team.

and went inside to investigate. When I returned, they pointed a gun at me and told me to put up my hands. I laughed because I thought it was a joke. But I saw that there were several Air Force uniforms, one with a machine gun, and I heard one of them say: "Raise your hands, you're covered." They made me go to the back patio where I found other officials in the same situation. They had taken the eyeglasses of one of the sergeants from him; he said he couldn't see anything, to which they answered that there was no need to see anything there, that the less he saw the better off he was, but they gave him back his glasses, putting them in his pocket.

"From the patio where I was, I saw Sergeant Olivera leave with his revolver, prepared to confront them. Three people fired at him. Standing at a distance, he tried to resist, but they threatened to throw grenades at him. Olivera surrendered; he was hurt in one arm. They fastened our hands in copper shackles and all ten of us were taken inside the jail, where they lined us up with our faces to the wall. The one in command said: "Bring the package carefully." As if it was a bomb, they placed it in the middle of the cell. But they took it out immediately and put a woman in charge of us, saying that at the slightest movement she should shoot. She answered that there was no problem. At that moment, they brought into the cell the chief commissar Cabrera accompanied by the assistant Floro Caraballa. Like the rest of us, they placed them in handcuffs facing the wall. The one who brought the commissar said, pointing at his neck: "Do you remember when you searched my house?" Someone said that it wasn't Cabrera and that he was mixing him up with the former commissar, at which the other drew back his gun and said: "Keep quiet, fat one, just don't make any problem and nothing will happen to you." The girl stayed watching us a few minutes and then closed the door from the outside but without padlocking it, then went away saying that we must not move for ten minutes, that there was a guard waiting upstairs. Everything was quiet.

"When we were able to leave with the aid of some neighbors, we wanted to go after the culprits but we were aware that we were without arms and we had to begin by begging in the neighborhood. We ran toward the Republic[6] but they had already gone. From all sides you

[6] Bank of the Republic, a state institution.

could hear the echo of shots. Taking inventory of what was missing, we could see that a dozen guns were missing, four sabres, two police truncheons, five caps, three officer's hats, three jackets, and four pistols."

We saw the comrades enter the commissary and very slowly we began to cross over. Eighty meters separated us from our objective. It would take us a minute to reach it. If all went well, this minute would be almost enough for the commissary to be occupied.

The bus stop was full of people. We advanced more or less together. We had gone about 30 meters when we heard the sound of several shots. For a tenth of a second we stopped and looked at each other. Something was wrong in the commissary. The glass from a window fell in splinters into the street. The fireman on guard at the door of the barracks raised his head in surprise and threatened to enter to investigate, but then stopped. He threw a glance at the window and with a gesture that said "it's not important" went back to his post. Without stopping, I glanced quickly toward the bus station but wasn't able to tell whether the shots had been heard. We reached the barracks gate, rapidly disarmed the guard, and put him inside. Now we had all the weapons in hand and on our arms the handkerchief that would prevent confusion. Antonio stayed to watch the gate, and the rest of us quickly ran inside. We found the patio deserted and entered the dormitories. Five or six men were there taking siesta. When they saw us enter, armed, they were paralyzed, more out of surprise than fear I think. Without wasting a minute, we searched them and pushed them out toward the patio, forcing them to stand facing the wall. I heard Guillermo say to them: "We are Tupamaros, we are seizing Pando and nothing will happen to you. We will only keep you a little while." Meanwhile, I had run toward a bathroom. A giant of a man was urinating, with his back to the door. "Hands up," I yelled. He gave a little smile and went on with what he was doing. I repeated the order, at the same time sticking the gun in his ribs. At that point he began to understand and without turning around slowly raised his hands. I made him go out on the patio and, like the others, stand with his face to the wall. We were in control.

But again there was the problem of the commissary from which we heard shots once more. Something was going wrong. We quickly got together and decided that two should run over and help them. But from the patio in back, where the barracks and the commissary joined, a comrade announced: "Quiet, I said, everything is under control."

Everything was under control there, quiet and under control. The problem now was in the street where the people, alerted by the shots, alarmed, had gone to look for any roaming policemen in the area.

Guillermo and I, who a minute earlier had been ready to go over to the commissary, now went out toward the gate. Two armed policemen were approaching, running down the center of the street. We advanced toward the paved street, protecting ourselves behind a column. The police halted and motioned for us to come closer. We, in turn, invited them to approach us. If it had not been for the fact that the hands which made the gestures held guns, all would have appeared to be a game. But they and we knew we were not playing. The people in the street, on the other hand, didn't seem to know it because, from all sides, in front and behind, they surrounded us. People, people, and more people. . . . curious, unconcerned, unaware that at any minute death could be touched off.

An incongruous voice broke the silence that suddenly seemed to have descended over the group: "It's the Tupamaros, it's the Tupamaros. They are seizing Pando."

I saw the disconcerted look on the faces of the police, their slow withdrawal and disappearance behind the doors of a financial firm. But this was not the end of the problem. Increasingly numerous groups of people, anxious not to miss anything, assembled on the sidewalks, the street, the balconies. In the distance, the sound of shots could be heard. In a few minutes, the actions would be over and the most diffi-cult task of all would begin: the withdrawal. We needed streets that were free, not filled with curious spectators who would impede our exit. We yelled at them to go away, but they withdrew two steps and re-mained there. We threatened them with violence, arms in hand; their faces change all the time, but give way to others who surround us, and then they come back again. Afterwards, we learned it was this way all over Pando. People, cordial or annoyed, impatient or sympathetic, had always been around, indifferent to the arms the comrades carried, getting into the middle of things, wanting to see, protesting or approving, asking. . . . at times collaborating. . . .

"It was 1:05 when the couple entered and said they wanted to make a call. I showed them the phone booth. Immediately several men from Intelligence and Liaison came in and showed a card I didn't even look at because I didn't have my glasses on and I can't see anything without glasses. The one who seemed more important ordered all the employees into a room in the back while they proceeded to search for a bomb which, according to them, would be in the machine shop. When I was the only one left, a policeman came running in yelling for a telephone and saying that the commissary had been attacked by the Tupamaros. The one who seemed to be in charge told him that they were also Tupamaros and that he should surrender his gun, and the policeman obeyed. We all went into the back room and they placed us with our faces to the wall except for one employee who, because she was pregnant, was authorized to sit down. Once we were there, one of them told us they were members of the MLN, that we should remain calm and nothing would happen to us. Several of the employees became very nervous and started to shout. The woman who had first entered asking for the telephone, dressed in a leather jacket, opened her bag, pulled out a machine gun and said that if we didn't keep quiet for a while she was going to have to use another method. After five or six minutes, they announced they would leave but that we were prohibited from leaving for ten more minutes. Our door had not been padlocked, only the one into the machine and work shop. When the time specified was up, we left to advise the commissar, and we understood that all of Pando had been seized."

At ten to one we were all in the Pando plaza already, prepared for the assault. Ana and Julio seated on a bench: a happy vacationing couple. Ismael and Diego walking around talking. Gerardo, with a fake air of distraction, gazing at the treetops while fingering for the tenth time this morning his pistol, which now had the safety catch off and a bullet in the chamber. As was his custom, he could now think of the immediate action without his stomach twisting in pain. As always in these last few minutes, he felt a little hungry and the total, indestructible security that everything would come out right. He drew a mint out of his pocket and began to chew on it. Eating a candy before an operation was no violation of the rules, he thought, and laughed at the idiocy of the idea. He didn't know why, at these moments, he always had idiotic ideas. He gave a quick glance toward the left side of the plaza and noted that the black *remise* was still there. Ahead, the four comrades that completed the commando, wearing the grave air of the funeral cortege. At a few seconds after one, the white banner that was to indicate the starting moment was supposed to wave across the avenue on a motorcycle. One o'clock had scarcely passed when, from the left, there was the violent sound of a motor and, flying in the air, the awaited flag passed like a small cloud.

Those who were in the plaza stood up and began to walk toward the Bank of Pando. The black *remise* started its motor and waited a few seconds. Everyone had to enter the bank at the same time. While Ana, Julio, and the others were walking along the sidewalk, the *remise* slowly passed them. Through the door that opened onto A street, those in the *remise* entered. Through the one at right angles to this and opening onto B street, those approaching by foot entered. The *remise* remained in front of the bank. Four men got out and began to cross the street. A passerby saw them and felt that something strange was taking place. Perhaps the machine gun that Gabriel was carrying under his overcoat betrayed them; perhaps it was simply the expressions on their faces. The man knew that they were not innocent clients and tried to turn back, cross, and give the alarm for sure. He was rapidly surrounded and forced to enter the bank. A pistol that nobody saw but that he felt jabbed into his ribs immobilized him for a few seconds. Meanwhile, Gabriel hurried ahead with one jump, mounted the counter, machine gun in hand, and announced that they were members of the MLN, that they were making an expropriation. "Keep quiet and face the wall," he said. Then each of them began his task.

Diego and Ismael went to the vault, preceded by the manager. The vault was open. It wasn't even necessary to say, "open sesame"; it freely offered its 8 million pesos. All that had to be done was put it into the bags. In a minute and a half it had been transferred.

Meanwhile, the clients began to enter and, at Gerardo's insistence, raised their hands and faced the wall. A woman came running in, stopped in the door and screamed: "They are attacking the Republic!" Then she saw Julio who, from a half-meter away, poked her with his gun. "Really, here too?" she said laughing. Julio also laughed while nodding his head affirmatively.

Ana began to distribute leaflets. Some, despite the fact that they had their hands up, managed to read them. Ana, who was perhaps encouraged by the gesture, began to explain why they were doing this and what they intended in the short and long run.

The quiet air of absurd normalcy presented by the arms, the flyers, the bags with their millions, was suddenly ended by the sound of a siren. For several seconds everything was paralyzed. Ana stopped speaking. Ismael lifted the bag and embraced it as if it were a child. Diego halted, holding the bag, a worried expression on his face. Gerardo and Julio raised their guns a little higher and surveyed the surroundings with a sharp gaze. "Calm," said Gabriel at the same time that he got down from the counter. "It's nothing; it's the Republic alarm."

The gears began to move again. Ana continued speaking as she moved back toward the door and distributed the final leaflets. Diego began his march again. Later he would explain to Ismael that the siren had not frightened him but that he felt an irrational disgust for strident sounds, that they paralyzed him as if he had banged his nose against a wall. They prepared everything for the departure. Outside the door, Jorge talked with an old lady in a fancy hat and a long gray scarf. She had a paper in her hand and was waving it under Jorge's nose, as he openly exhibited a Colt rifle. "But I have to collect my pension; it came out in the paper that today they would pay us."

"Yes, madame," Jorge was bellowing in her ear, "but it can't be today, the bank was seized by the Tupamaros. Enter, it's dangerous out here." "Do you think they'll pay me tomorrow?" "I'm sure they will, but now get inside," he told her again at the top of his voice. But she didn't move. "Will the Tupamaros pay me tomorrow?" Jorge took her by both shoulders and shoved her inside. She still said: "I don't know why you make me go inside if they aren't going to pay me today."

Ismael, doubled over with laughter, had rested the bag on the floor. "OK, let's go," said Gerardo, making a gesture with his pistol. Hand on his arm, Jorge stopped him. A policeman had stationed himself behind the *remise* and was pointing toward the door of the bank, guard ing the exit. Julio, who was in the best position, began to fire. The bullets hit the car but did not touch the policeman, who remained in his place. "Murder," said Gerardo, "it's 1:10 and they're all waiting for us." Diego, his face blazing, his eyes like hot coals, snatched the machine gun from Gabriel's hands and pointed it. Ismael and Ana grabbed him at the same time. "Calm down," said Ana, "don't forget that we brought it to threaten, not to use." "In extreme situations it has to be used, right?" said Diego in the low, hoarse voice that Ana now knew. "The situation is not yet extreme," said Gabriel, at the same time that he glued himself to the wall; a bullet had grazed his overcoat. Gabriel pulled his pistol out of his pocket and also began to shoot.

Four minutes of a rough exchange of shots ended with the policeman wounded on the ground. Everyone ran toward the car, which was as full of holes as a sieve. The policeman who was lying on the sidewalk saw us coming. "Don't kill me," he said, "don't kill me." "And why would we kill you, imbecile, son of a thousand devils?" said Gerardo, pushing him hard. Julio sat down at the wheel. Eight faces taut with anxiety focused their gazes on the hand that turned the key in the motor and pressed the starter button. A tremble shook the old *remise* and the hoarse, well-known, dear rumble emerged from the motor. A unanimous cry welcomed it. Ana threw the last leaflets out of the open window and for a few seconds they floated around the car. Then they fell.

The policeman got up, dragging his leg, crossed the street, reloaded his gun and fired. He fired several times until he hit the wheels.

With two flat tires, describing an "s," we reached the cemetery. When the others saw us coming, they started their cars. Those arriving had to fire into the air to stop them. They abandoned the useless car and distributed themselves in the others as they could.

Gerardo, one of the few members of this commando who later was saved from death or prison, would explain to a comrade days later: "That is where we lost our unity as a group. We distributed ourselves in different cars, we didn't know anyone. We didn't know who were officers and who were soldiers. No one knew whom to obey. This problem hurt us later when we fell into the net of Toledo Chico." [7]

[7] Toledo Chico is a ranching zone in the area between Montevideo and Canelones.

"It was one o'clock. Some seven or eight armed persons entered the bank. One of them mounted the counter.

"They said they were Tupamaros, that we should keep quiet because they were workers like us. In a few minutes they took all the money out of the cash box. They called the manager and the chief by their names. They asked the manager for the keys to his car and for the weapon he was carrying. Then they sent us, hands up, into the back where there was a sort of deposit with an exit to the outside, with no key. When they left, they announced that they had taken the commissary and the Republic Bank. The assault lasted three minutes."

—So the six chauffeurs and you . . . ? What was your job?

—I was in charge of the funeral procession. I don't know whether you know. . . . but our business always sends someone in general charge.

—I didn't know . . . . Then they put the seven of you in the Kombi. . . .

—Yes, and they began to drive around because it was early for the assault.

—Which of the assaults?

—Ours was the Republic Bank.

—But you didn't see anything of the assault. . . .

—What did you want us to see? They didn't let us see anything. Before they got out, they recommended that we keep quiet.

—Who recommended?

—One of them, one who was called Pedro . . . . from his voice, very young.

—Why from his voice? Didn't you see him?

—We had to look down so as not to see their faces.

—And how did the assault go?

—The assault was fantastic . . . . In a few minutes they got 40,000,-000 pesos. There was just one problem with a girl. . . . She accidentally fired and hit a comrade in the stomach . . . . They had to take him to a hospital . . . . Immediately . . . . To operate on him.

—A hospital there in Pando?

—No! What do you mean in Pando! One of these hospitals they have hidden around here . . . . who knows where.

—Except for this difficulty. . . . everything was fine . . . ?

—Yes, very well; it seems that inside the bank one of them mounted the counter and gave a speech.

—You knew about that later, from the newspapers . . . .

—No. . . . we learned about it when the boys that had come with us returned . . . . because they made fun of the one who gave the speech . . . . they said he should dedicate himself to becoming a deputy and that if the bankers hadn't had their arms in the air they surely would have applauded him.

—And he, what did he say?

—Nothing, he laughed.

—They were very calm then . . . .

—Just like you and me.

—Did you take the injured one?

—No. . . . The millions went with us! They threw the money in with us . . . 40,000,000 . . . imagine! The other car must have taken the wounded one.

—What other?

—There were two cars at the assault. The Kombi with us and some of them in it, and a *remise* that would hold I don't know how many others.

—Where were you when the alarm at Republic began to sound?

—Almost at the door of the bank. . . . leaving at that moment.

—And?

—It started a scandal of all the demons, you could hear the horns, the gunshots.

—And they?

—As if nothing was going on. We from the funeral parlor got a little nervous. . . . but they weren't at all. Throwing leaflets, honking the horns like crazy, because the people were walking around in the middle of the street and wouldn't let them pass. It was like a stream. They were yelling: "Long live the revolution!" One of the chauffeurs who could see out says that there were boys with white armbands directing traffic.

—Tupamaros?

—And who would they be, boy scouts? Everybody walking around with a white armband on that day in Pando was a Tupamaro.

—You made the trip back to Montevideo with them?

—No, a little while after we left the cemetery, since the cars were very full, we had to get out.

—With your handcuffs on?

—First they took the handcuffs off, then they thanked us. . . .

—What did they thank you for?

—I don't know. . . . they said "Many thanks for everything."

The caravan started on its way. A wind of happiness swept over them like a wave, irresistible.

With rumpled hair, bright rosy faces as if they had just participated in a sports competition, laughing and talking at the same time, seated in the funeral coaches, they were an unforgettable picture that fits no known category.

Telling absurd or funny stories as if they were drunk, they covered the first kilometers.

Only the leaders of the group seemed to escape the general craziness. It was easy to find them. All eight of them were quiet, concentrated, wary, isolated from this drunken victory that enveloped the others.

Gerardo, silent, seated beside the chauffeur in one of the *remises*, tried to control his stomach which now, yes, was contracting without letup. He had dug his nails into the palms of his hands and, with his right foot tense, was accelerating into space. All his attention was concentrated on the speed which was not and could not, without grave risk, go over 60 kilometers per hour. He had a premonition that something would go wrong. He turned to his comrade on his right, a young light-haired and almost imperturbable young man who had been chattering, singing, and laughing, since the moment they had left, and said to him: "You know, I have a feeling that the police already have us surrounded." The other stopped talking and laughing and looked at him as if he were crazy. Then, wrinkling his forehead, he looked all around carefully. A patrol came slowly up the road. The police touched their caps in a sign of respect. Gerardo breathed a sigh of relief. He had been an idiot to communicate an unhappy and for the moment useless intuition to someone who up until two seconds ago was so euphoric. "I'm sure I'm wrong," he said smiling and, with an evident effort, calmed the other while he thought: "He is still very green, he can't have been a militant for more than a year." The light-haired man did not smile. He took the white armband off his sleeve, folded it carefully, put in his back pocket, and with a grave expression turned to look at Gerardo. Gerardo knew what this look meant and hastened to excuse himself: "Forgive me," he said. "I have been in the organization for four years," said the boy. "Forgive me, forgive me," Gerardo said again. "You look like you're 20 years old." "I'm 24."

Eusebio, in the Kombi, was also silent and serious. A patrol, the third in two kilometers, was just passing them. The last two with great speed and in the opposite direction from them. "They have known about it for a while, but they think we're still in the outskirts of Pando," he thought. At that moment Antonio turned around and pointed to the patrol that had just passed. "What do you think?" said Eusebio. "That now they know, but that they are quite confused. They think we are still in Pando." "Yes," said Eusebio.

"Six minutes is what we need, exactly six," says Diego in another of the *remises*. "Let's suppose the police have known about it for 20 minutes. They are still giving orders and making decisions. When all that gets under way, they won't find any of us."

He was wrong: two minutes later, just before Cassarino near the outskirts of Montevideo, the patrol police saw them coming and got behind an auto to shoot at them. But they didn't do it. That funeral cortege headed by uniformed chauffeurs and police seated in some of the *remises* confused them.

From then on, a heavy, profound silence fell over the caravan. They were now certain. The police were alert and on the move. Avoiding a confrontation could be a matter of minutes.

Quickly, they entered Montevideo. On the road from Andaluz and Camino de las Castañas, in a solitary area, still suburban but very close to transit lines, the caravan divided into three groups which took different directions. Near there, at specified points, two of the groups handed over their arms and the clandestine militants to legal cars. The nonclandestine militants left on foot, one by one, to look for a bus or taxi.

Antonio covered 500 meters, reached an avenue, took a bus, sat down, opened the paper he had bought in the morning and began to read, this time for real. At 2:40 he got out in front of his office. He bought a sandwich on the corner, ate it in a hurry, and went in. The owner asked him about his tooth. "It's OK now, thanks," Antonio said rubbing his left hand over his face at the same time he signed the check-in book. Before three, he was to receive a call from Pedro confirming that everything was going all right. At ten to three the telephone rang.

"Antonio?" "Yes." "Everything's fine, there are still three cartons of books missing that should be arriving now. As soon as they're here, I'll let you know." "That's fine, thanks." He sat down at the adding machine and began to work. A half hour later a friend in the office came running in from the street. "Did you see the latest about the Tupamaros?" "No," said Antonio with an innocent face. And he hoped with all his heart that the other one would say something about Pando. The other said: "They're shooting it out with the police in Toledo Chico."

Days later, Gerardo, one of the few who escaped the Toledo encirclement, informed a group of comrades:

"We were going along the road as planned, two *remises* and the Kombi. We were without arms or clandestine comrades since they had already been handed over to the legal car. We were very close to the point where we would abandon our vehicles and go the rest of the way on foot, separately, unarmed, looking for some ordinary transportation. Ahead was the other *remise,* which Roberto was driving, still loaded; it was to meet its legal car nearby, less than a kilometer away. Behind us was the Kombi which had just handed over its cargo—money and arms—to Tito's little bus, which followed behind us waiting until it came to the crossroad which would permit it to enter the city along a series of almost parallel roads. We were only two kilometers away, two minutes in time, from the spot where we would abandon these accursed solitary suburbs with their ranches and wastelands, and enter the zone where we could effectively lose ourselves, when, around a sharp curve that prevented us from seeing what was on the other side, the confrontation occurred. First one patrol and immediately after it, a second blocked the road, We saw that it was useless to fight. Only six of us had arms and what we saw around us had the appearance of the inevitable. We would have liked to turn around and go back but the road, very twisting and with ravines on both sides, made any kind of operation impossible. Only the little truck that was last in the caravan could accomplish that maneuver. Alerted, it quickly turned around and was lost in the country roads not covered by the net.

"We decided to leave the vehicles and disperse. Try to lose ourselves among the ranches. We scarcely knew each other. Almost no one knew who anyone was. Matters were determined in a disorderly fashion. The commandos who were dispersed after the cars broke down in Pando weakened our group. We didn't know what possibilities each had, who was an officer and who was a soldier, whom we were to obey. We abandoned the cars and went off as best we could in twos or threes toward the flat country fields, without any geographical interruption as a protection and with scarcely any ranches.

"*Chanchas*,[8] army trucks, patrols, and two helicopters that flew so low they practically grazed our heads, amplifiers, shots, and orders yelled over loudspeakers filled the 30 or 40 hectares in which we had been trapped. We were all certain, without saying anything, that they were going to massacre us. I hated the sun that made the trap in which we were caught a resplendent scene in which not a leaf moved without being detected. From the air came the screeching voices pointing out movements, ordering the maneuvers. Behind the windows of the houses enclosed in the net, one could see worried faces, their eyes wide with surprise and dread. The police, like a blind beast, made no distinction. Any human being that walked within their closed trap was subjected to beating, kicks, and blows in the police cars. The persecution had a single characteristic: hysteria. If there was almost no other testimony, the three dead comrades would be definitive proof. Apprehended without arms, they were killed when they surrendered, they fired at them indefinitely when they were already dead. After hitting one of them 30 times, they bashed his head in with the butts of their guns."

Popular mythology has it that Sendic was dressed like a *chacarero* and hidden by a family in the zone. Sendic, dressed as always, was driving the little truck which, when it quickly turned around, escaped like an eel through the holes in the net.

8 Popular nickname for the police wagons in which those arrested are transported.

The Tupamaros Attack a Garrison: A Step-by-Step Account by Julion Hernandez

Following the seizure of Pando, official policy became harsher, with torture assuming a more prominent place. The MLN also adopted a harder line featuring direct assaults on the police and military. The assault portrayed here, on the Navy Training Center in Montevideo, was the Tupamaros' first major attack on the armed forces.

Montevideo, Uruguay (LNS)—Fernando Garin takes off his helmet and puts it on again. It is 1:45 on the morning of May 29, 1970, and everything has been planned. Garin is an orderly of the guard, so the sentry standing at the entrance of the Uruguayan Navy Training Center pays no attention to this unimportant gesture.

The three men in the car which has just taken off down Washington Street toward the center know with certainty that the man who removed his helmet and put it on again is Fernando Garin, 23 years old, a native of the town of Juan Iacase, and son of one of the founders of the textile syndicate.

Next to the car rises the strongwall of the military center. A hundred meters away the traffic in Montevideo's seaside avenue is heavy in spite of the hour. On the roof of the entrance gate, there is another sentry. Around sixty persons—officers and sailors—sleep inside the old building.

Another guard stands in back, facing the street called Lindolfo Cuestas, and, in the surroundings of the garrison, 19 commandos belonging to the Tupamaros await a signal.

Now everything depends on the three revolutionaries who are in the car and, above all, on Fernando Garin's steady nerves.

When the car stops in front of the gate, the guards become worried. Two Tupamaros get out of the automobile. "We're from the police, we need to see the officer on duty," they command with an authoritarian voice.

The guard calls the orderly. Garin comes out frowning, pretending suspicion. He goes to one side and inspects the papers of the alleged police agents. He asks them to go in.

The text is from the Cuban news service *Prensa Latina,* reprinted in *The Black Panther* (New York), 21 August 1970, p. 10.

The scene is carefully watched by other members of the Tupamaros who are hiding in the darkness of the street a hundred meters away. Before crossing the entrance-gate one of the men looks rapidly above: On the roof, four meters above the ground, the sentry, now at ease, puts down his AR-15.

The garrison fortress is in a dock neighborhood on the corner of Washington and Guaraní Streets, only two blocks away from Buenos Aires Street. Twelve blocks away stands the Plaza de la Independencia and the Presidential Palace.

An enamored couple wanders down Washington Street. As they pass by the garrison's high grey wall, one of the newly arrived "policemen" halts them.

"Identification," he demands.

(Nervous hands, signs of weakness, the boy searches in his pockets, the girl in her purse.)

"We don't have any," they say in a low voice. "We're students from the Institute Vazquez Acevedo. We can prove it."

"We'll see," answers the policeman and orders them to go into the garrison.

Meanwhile, on the garrison roof, Garin walks up to the sentry and tells him he's come to substitute for him. There seems to be too much activity this morning, though, and the sentry feels that something is not working right; it can be observed in his indecision.

But Garin strikes the guard in the stomach with his Colt .45 and takes the rifle.

By now, the "policemen" and the two "students" have surrounded the sentry at the entrance gate. From above, Garin is pointing a rifle at him.

When Garin and the two Tupamaros disguised as policemen enter the military establishment, the corporal calls the officer on duty. He doesn't suspect anything and it doesn't occur to him to ring the alarm which would go off in the dormitories. The officer and the corporal are quickly overpowered and tied up.

Uruguayan sailors wear a special poncho which can easily be exchanged; two Tupamaros slip into the ponchos and take over the guard. From outside, the Navy Training Center looks just the same as on any other night.

Seventeen more Tupamaro commandos are let into the garrison courtyard. They take over the building in which 30 sailors are sleeping —and the infirmary, the dining room, the recruting office, the officers' rooms, the artillery section . . .

The startled sailors are lined up in the central patio, most of them still in underclothes. There is tension among the Tupamaros because the keys to the cells don't show up. Twenty minutes later the cells are opened and the sailors are locked up.

A truck enters through the entrance gate and parks in the middle of the patio. The commandos empty the arsenal and gather up the arms left in the dormitories. A total of 300 rifles, two .30 calibre machine guns, 60,000 bullets, 150 Colt .45 calibre pistols, several submachine guns, and six AR-15 rifles used by the Americans in Vietnam plus 75 powerful grenades also used in Indochina.

Just at this moment, two sailors belonging to the garrison arrive at the entrance, greet the disguised Tupamaros, and go on in. But the commandos have prepared for this kind of an emergency, and a special trap controls them as they enter.

At 3:30 A.M., the truck carrying the arsenal and the commandos pulls out of the garrison unnoticed, leaving six Tupamaros behind. All the telephone wires have been cut from the beginning. The garrison is completely quiet; only the traffic on the nearby avenue can be heard.

One of the remaining commandos quietly raises the Tupamaro flag, takes photographs of the jailed officers and sailors, of the flag, and of the revolutionary slogans written on the walls.

Garin leaves a letter explaining how he could no longer endure seeing the tortures inflicted on the workers of "Usinas y Telefonos del Estado" who were arrested during a strike.

At 4:15, the remaining Tupamaros depart from the garrison and drive out of the area in a number of cars left parked in the vicinity.

Quite some time passes before a group of Navy officers manage to open up their locks, and run to warn the Army Intelligence Service, located two blocks away.

Agents and Navy forces begin to mobilize, but only the Tupamaro flag remains in the morning of the 29th, when the president, the minister of defense, and high military chiefs begin an emergency meeting.

How the Tupamaros Attacked the Homes of Four Uruguayan Police Officials by Luis Martirena

Throughout 1970, the Tupamaros engaged in a campaign against the police apparatus. Street attacks for weapons, assassinations, and occupations of the type indicated here were all employed to neutralize the police as an instrument of repression. The campaign culminated with the kidnapping of Dan Mitrione and his subsequent execution. The cumulative damage to the police was sufficient to entail greater participation by the military in urban counterinsurgency.

Montevideo, July 12 (PL)—The Tupamaros National Liberation Movement yesterday carried out another vast operational plan of intimidation against the repressive agencies, by attacking the homes of four police officers.

The event came close on the heels of the disarming actions which were carried out last Saturday, in which a police agent was killed and three others wounded when they resisted the Tupamaros, one of whom (Néstor Peralta Larrosa) was seriously wounded and arrested.

The Tupamaros used at least eight vehicles—which were taken from their owners yesterday afternoon—to carry out the operation.

In all cases, the owners of the cars were overpowered and later accompanied for several hours by members of the revolutionary organization.

The taxi drivers whose vehicles were used were paid for the time during which the cars had been out of service. All the cars turned up where the Tupamaros had previously indicated they would appear.

The first attack occurred late in the afternoon, when three boys and a girl (ranging in age from 18 to 22) arrived at the home of Julio César Peirano Alarcón, an official of the Information and Intelligence Department. Present at the moment of the attack in addition to the above-mentioned police official were his wife and father-in-law. The attackers identified themselves as Tupamaros and, after overpowering the three and tying them up, searched the home thoroughly, taking a 22-calibre revolver, a pistol, and an album with pictures and personal documents of the political police agent. Then, for five or six minutes, the Tupamaros talked with Peirano Alarcón and his relatives, to whom they explained that their struggle is not "against the police but against the regime" and that, whether "in uniform or in plain clothes," they would be attacked by the organization.

The second attack was carried out at the home of Corporal Luis Alberto Boer of the Theft and Robbery Section, who has been working on investigations lately. The police officer wasn't at home; the only ones present were his wife and 15-year-old daughter. Three people, two men and a woman, arrived at the home and said that they were police officials with a message for Boer. His wife let them in. Then, after identifying themselves as Tupamaros, the members of the group searched the home and took a small revolver. Then another of the couple's daughters arrived home and started screaming on encountering this situation. She was quickly calmed by the young woman Tupamaro, who embraced her. The Tupamaros asked the mother if the girls had nervous or other health problems and told her, "This is a war, but there's no need to cry." They told Boer's wife that it would be better if her husband left the police force. They also left a mimeographed letter for the police officer.

The third visit of the afternoon was to the home of César Diez, aide to the Technical Police, who wasn't at home either. His wife noticed something strange in the way some of the people who called at her door acted and she didn't let them in but started screaming, so they left without entering.

The last attack was at the home of First Sergeant Luis Eduardo Batalla, who works in the Interpol and Docks Section of the Investigations Department. The four young attackers (three boys and a girl) passed themselves off as police officers to enter the house, then said, "Don't worry; we're Tupamaros." They searched the home, took .38-calibre bullets and pictures of the police official, and talked with Mrs. Batalla, since her husband wasn't home. According to today's reports in the right-wing press, she told the Tupamaros, "The old Tupamaros were good people who fought for the independence of their country, but all you do is steal and attack." According to the same reports, they replied, "Sometimes circumstances force us to rob. We fight against the regime, not the police." After tying her up loosely, they explained, "The police carry out attacks like this against us and other workers."

The Saturday attacks caused a great stir in police circles, as they have proved that the Tupamaros can strike at the rear guard of the repressive agencies.

Police Inspector Victor Castiglioni, of the Investigations Department (the successor of Héctor Moran Charquero, who was executed by the Tupamaros last May [sic])[1] threatened the relatives of imprisoned Tupamaros in a radio interview, saying, "They should recall that they too have wives and mothers." This was viewed in journalistic circles as going a bit too far.

Other police spokesmen expressed their concern over the fact that the Tupamaros knew the addresses and habits of even the lower-ranking police officers.

[1] See Chronology, April 13, 1970.

Interview with Urbano by Leopoldo Madruga

The Mitrione affair precipitated an apparent setback for the MLN. The arrest of nine important members nearly decapitated the Tupamaros, but did not in fact destroy them. The following interview was conducted in the aftermath of Mitrione's death, at a time when many observers had declared the end of the movement.

This calm man who is talking to me somewhere in bayonet-covered Montevideo is being sought by thousands of policemen, soldiers, and sailors, who are turning the city upside down looking for him.

With Raúl Sendic and other leaders of the Tupamaros in jail, this man, who goes by the name of Urbano, . . . became one of the top leaders in the National Liberation Movement of Uruguay.

Like the mythological animal which grew seven heads when one was cut off, the Tupamaros have an amazing recovery power, the ability to instantly fill the gaps in their invisible trench of struggle against the regime.

Urbano is a young but amazingly mature man. He talks in the same calm way he smokes his cigarettes, and the maté he sips grows colder as his interest in what he is thinking and saying increases.

He has a great responsibility on his shoulders: he speaks on behalf of a movement that, with an endless series of attacks, has shaken the system from top to bottom. And, if it is a case of talking about his Movement, its strategy and tactics, the men who make it up and their attitude toward the struggle, the reasons for and the results of their kidnappings, why they executed Mitrione, and their goal of making the revolution in Uruguay, he is willing to talk all night—which is just what we did.

What were the real and apparent aims of the Movement with the kidnappings of Mitrione, Dias Gomide, and Fly, and what were the results of the confrontation with the government on the matter?
Well, on the one hand, there is the action in itself, and, on other, the

Tricontinental Bulletin (Havana, Cuba), no. 57 (December 1970), pp. 2–17, and no. 58 (January 1971), pp. 3–15.

attitude—or, rather, the different attitudes—taken by the government in the course of the operation.

At first it involved a simple exchange, like those in other Latin American countries: a group of guerrillas captures a foreign diplomat and proposes an exchange of imprisoned revolutionaries for the captured diplomat. From then on, a series of things happened, and the situation, which at first was the same as the others, began to take on a different aspect.

What were those events? What was the change in the situation?
First, Mitrione and Dias Gomide were kidnapped. Gordon Jones got away from us. Foreign and domestic pressures began to be exerted immediately—from the "democratic sectors," the clergy, the intermediate strata of the population, etc.

Giambruno, director of the foreign policy department of the Foreign Ministry, who had displayed a flexible attitude, was rebuked by the Executive. Vice President Abdala began talking about pacification and amnesty. Up until then we hadn't said anything; the Tupamaros hadn't issued any communiqués.

With the crisis in the power structure going full force, with two visible trends in the government—those in favor of the exchange and the hardliners—the Movement issued a communiqué setting a time limit. This was to sharpen the contradictions in the government, which may even result in the downfall of Pacheco Areco. We increased the pressure with a third kidnapping: that of Fly.

We had thus reached the most favorable stage in the crisis from our point of view, and the release or amnesty of our comrades seemed near. The crisis in the government increased, and the downfall of Pacheco appeared imminent. This was when an important group of comrades was arrested, which served to bolster Pacheco's position: the capture of Sendic and the other comrades on Almería Street pushed the scales toward nonacceptance of the exchange proposals.

The situation is similar to that in which the capture of a chess piece results in a change of tactics by both sides. Using the kidnappings as an excuse, two sources of power are waging a direct confrontation: on the one hand, the dictatorship is strengthening its position and carrying the repression into the street, and, on the other, the National Liberation Movement, which bears the brunt of the repression, holds on to the diplomats and once again proposes continuing the struggle, just as it was doing before the kidnappings, but with the difference that now the struggle is being carried out with two prisoners in our hands, one of whom is under medical care and whose release we have proposed in exchange for the publication of a communiqué from the Movement.

Then the problem of the kidnappings must now be considered within the overall framework of the Movement's line of struggle against the regime?
Right. The line of the Movement is one of systematic harassment of the regime. The National Liberation Movement is carrying out constant attacks against the repressive forces which are the pillar of the regime. This doesn't necessarily mean that all attacks will always be aimed directly at them, because, on certain occasions, it may be advisable to attack in other ways—though always hitting, one way or another, at this fundamental support of the system.

We are weakening the offensive-repressive force of the regime, undermining the morale of the repressive forces. We are wearing them down. They believe that every blow they deal us will result in our annihilation, but the Movement counterattacks and quickly shows them how mistaken they really are.

We are, in short, applying the main law of urban—and, of course, rural—guerrilla warfare: continuity. As part of this line, it is possible to work out attacks which in one way or another are organized in a dialectical escalation against the system. That is, as the dictatorship steps up its repression and strikes more blows, the organized revolutionary forces respond with even more attacks.

Then the original concept of the kidnappings was already included in this line?
From the start. The kidnappings are part of an overall plan of harassment against the regime with the objective of obtaining the release of imprisoned comrades, and they are also—just like all the other attacks of our Movement—aimed at undermining the foundations of the system, wearing it down and overthrowing it, if our forces permit. This is what happened in the case of the captured diplomats. Pacheco

repeatedly proclaimed that he would not negotiate with us, that there would be no exchanges of imprisoned revolutionaries for captured diplomats here. But when we carried out the operation, we thought it would be possible with or without Pacheco: he would either have to change his position or resign, in which case the negotiations would be carried out with his successor.

These are the alternatives being discussed, but they don't explain a conduct or a line. They are variants, possibilities which may occur and in the face of which the Tupamaros must remain very alert to deal with any changes in the situation. We will act in a dialectical manner, in every instance.

You felt that a certain combination of forces would objectively strengthen the position of the Movement?
Right. We felt that, at a given stage in the crisis, Pacheco would be isolated and subject to the pressures exerted by the forces that had been hurt by his policy of taking over the educational system, closing the senior high schools, firing teachers, bringing on a crisis in the University and freezing the wages of the workers.

We also felt that pressure would be applied by the economic sectors which cannot obtain their objectives under the present, very unstable system and the political sectors which, in one way or another, want to bring a certain stability to the country on the basis of negotiations with the Tupamaros.

These are elements which must be taken into account, but, in the final analysis, they are alien to the steps and objectives of the Movement. At a given moment we may act with them, but all of them were taken into consideration—without, however, changing the line or methodology of the Movement in the slightest. We took them into account so that we would be able to deal with whichever of the two situations should develop. If the exchange took place, with or without Pacheco, we had our plans for continuing to develop our Movement toward its ultimate objective of taking power with the people.

If the situation should grow worse—if (as turned out to be the case) the U.S. and Brazilian Embassies and the government should decide to sacrifice the captured diplomats because they envisaged a possibility of destroying the Movement—well, we were ready for that alternative, too, and it would only be another step in the antagonism between the dictatorship and the armed forces of the people, found in the National Liberation Movement.

What, in your opinion, were the factors which led to Pacheco's stubborn intransigence in refusing to budge from his position, no matter what?

In the first place, I would like to explain that his position was not all that firm as it was made out to be. During the whole time that he was saying he wouldn't negotiate with us, Minister Fleitas—who, obviously, couldn't be acting without Pacheco's consent—was negotiating with our imprisoned leaders, proposing the release of the student prisoners and making the others subject to trial by ordinary courts in exchange for the release of the diplomats. There was another try at negotiations through Judge Díaz Romeu, who requested a 72-hour extension of the deadline for the execution of Mitrione from Sendic. This effort failed because of the refusal of Colonel Rivero, the Police Chief.

It seems that Pacheco's refusal to negotiate (we realize, of course, that Pacheco doesn't speak for himself; he speaks for others) was caused by the fact that they felt, as a result of the capture of a series of comrades, that there was a possibility of destroying the organization. I think that the negative reply and the sentencing of Mitrione (because Mitrione was sentenced by the government and the U.S. Embassy before he was sentenced by us) were part of a plan which had, as one of its objectives, that of putting the Movement out of action and eliminating it. Unfortunately for them, they made a serious mistake.

With Mitrione dead, the position of the United States is more clearly seen and confirms the fact that it sacrificed its own agent. What, in your opinion, are the reasons for its position?

It's a matter of values. It felt it was worth sacrificing Mitrione to get the repressive forces into the streets, because it believed we had been dealt a mortal blow and that a dead Mitrione for a destroyed National Liberation Movement was a fair exchange.

Could it also have been a matter of having to support Pacheco in orde not to give the Tupamaros the polictical victory of overthrowing a

President and to avoid the implications that such a solution to the kidnappings would have had all over Latin America?

Those are cards which the imperialists can play any way they want. Imperialism can squeeze Pacheco like an orange and then replace him with another orange. We are well aware of the Latin American implications of the problem, and I believe we are answering the main aspect of your question. The matter also has other implications: I believe that, through all this, we have achieved the ability to impose revolutionary armed struggle as a method to obtain change.

Some government spokesmen and newspapers have said that the Tupamaros have been dealt a "mortal blow" and that they will soon disappear from the political scene. What are the facts? How much have the blows you have been dealt hurt the Movement?

All revolutionary movements know that they may be dealt blows at any time and that they may be adversely affected and shaken, as has been the case with us now.

Fidel landed from the *Granma* with 82 men and was left with a dozen, and Che was unable to develop the guerrilla process in Bolivia. It was continued by Inti, and now Chato[1] is leading the struggle over there. We have received a blow, yes; but the structure of the organization and the organization-people relationship is so great at this stage—the roots of the organization have sunk so deeply into the people—that it is practically impossible to isolate the organization. That is, we will always be nourished by the life-blood of the people—who will provide us with houses to hide in and cadres with which to recover and increase the forces we now have available.

Is this also the case at the leadership level? A series of important leaders had been arrested before the kidnappings, and others have been arrested since then. Can the Movement replace them with a similar level of efficiency?

As Fidel has said, the people produce many Camilos.[2]

---

[1] The reference is to the Peredo brothers: Roberto ("Coco") died in Che's *foco;* Guido ("Inti") took command of the Bolivian ELN until his death in 1968; Osvaldo ("Chato") presently heads the organization.
[2] Camilo Cienfuegos, a hero of the Cuban Revolution, died in a plane crash in October 1959.

Why did the Movement sentence Mitrione to death and execute him? There are a series of factors involved, relating to the Movement, to Mitrione, and to those with whom negotiation was attempted. In the first place, Mitrione represented the presence of the CIA and the Agency for International Development, which sends advisers to the countries of Latin America to aid the repressive forces. He had educated the Uruguayan police in the art of mass repression and torture.

His record in Brazil was not a very good one. He is mentioned in the book *Who's Who in the CIA*[3] Mitrione was clearly an agent of the repressive forces of the United States.

He was tried by a revolutionary tribunal, and his crimes were serious enough to warrant his receiving the sentence he did. But this was not all that was involved—it was not even the most important of the factors involved, because otherwise we wouldn't have proposed his exchange. We were willing to negotiate for the release of our comrades. The U.S. Embassy, acting through Pacheco, decided to sacrifice Mitrione.

We gave them a deadline, sentenced him, and warned that, if our comrades were not released or a reply was not made to our negotiation proposals within that period, Mitrione would be executed.

In such a case, the decision made by the revolutionary movement should be carried out, especially in view of the existing factors. These are the reasons for his execution.

The carrying out of this sentence implies a responsibility of the Movement not only to its people but to the other revolutionary movements of Latin America as well. This is what you mentioned a moment ago. The kidnapping-exchange method must be carried to its logical consequences in order to save it as a tool. This was also taken into consideration.

---

[3] See Julius Mader's *Who's Who in the CIA: A Biographical Reference Work on 3000 Officers of the Civil and Military Branches of the Secret Services of the USA in 120 Countries* (Berlin: Julius Mader, 1968), p. 364. This work is fairly well known, but not outstanding in its accuracy. In the case of Dan Mitrione, the important question is not his relationship to the CIA (although he may have been an agent), but rather his role in the escalation of official terror in Uruguay. Was he, or was he not, instrumental in militarizing the police, institutionalizing torture, and forming death squads? There is considerable evidence that he was. See the dossier in *State of Siege*, New York: Ballantine, 1973. One need not be on the Agency payroll to be an agent of repression.

In taking a step of this kind we were thinking not only of our situation here but of the situation faced by all the other revolutionary movements in Latin America and what the kidnappings mean to them. Imperialism is fully aware of this, and this was one of the reasons for its "no" in the case of the Mitrione exchange.

I think that the measure you took—or, to a certain extent, were forced to take—resulted in a certain immediate unpopularity. The level of political development of the Uruguayan masses, together with the campaigns in the press, caused this reaction among the people. I may be mistaken, but I believe that this action has resulted—at least for the moment—in a negative reaction from the people, which did not happen in the case of the other attacks you have carried out, which were quickly understood by the masses. To what extent do you think this is so?

I would have to disagree with what you say about the people's level of political development. I don't think our people are highly developed in this regard, but neither are they underdeveloped.

No, no; what I mean is, to what extent does the existing level of political development of the people enable them to understand the reasons for the fact that a CIA agent, whether kidnapped or not, in a supposedly sovereign country, should receive the sentence you applied?

Yes, I see your point. I believe that in this country an action which results in death has great disadvantages. We are in the first stages of a revolutionary war.

But, returning to the problem of political development and its extent, you shouldn't confuse the voices that weren't heard with those that were given play in the newspapers after the death of Mitrione. The voices that were heard were those that were carrying out official instructions: those of the press, radio, etc. But there are many who understand in silence but are unable to express themselves. Take the Gallup Poll that was taken here following the death of Mitrione and that wasn't made public, because the number of people who opposed the execution, those who were in favor of it, and those who had no opinion were so evenly divided that it wasn't in the regime's interests to make the poll public, nor would it have added to the climate of opinion being whipped up by the press.

But, in reply to another part of your question, we should add that not all our actions are of a propaganda nature. By propaganda actions we mean those which display the popular image of the Movement. Our denunciation of the financial houses, profiteering, and ill-gotten gains is an example of this, to which you can add the seizure of radio stations and the distribution of leaflets.

But there are other actions which are very important in a revolutionary process which are not always understood immediately by the people. The execution of an informer, for example, may not be immediately understood by the people, because the informer may be unknown to them and the press may cover up the real reasons for his excution.

But this execution is very important for the war which is being waged against the regime. It is a warning to all informers that there is a dual power in this country: that of the repression and that of the Tupamaros. The death of a policeman who is defending interests which are not his own may not be understood by that sector of the population which has not yet defined its position with regard to the government and the MLN. But, with the passing of the days and months, their doubts will be cleared up, and they will understand the reasons for this action.

Regarding Dias Gomide and Fly, what explains the exchange proposal for one of them?
This was clearly explained in our last communiqué: we are willing to release one of the hostages, who is under medical care, in exchange for the widescale publication of a document in which we analyze the situation of the country and set forth our program and the reasons for our struggle.

And the proposal for a truce which you have made to the government?
It was made on the basis of the six points which are the aspirations of the people of Uruguay. Pacheco accuses us of being responsible for the violence in the country. We say that he is the one responsible, because he uses it to defend an unjust social order. If he doesn't accept our proposals, it will clear up a lot of things.

But, of greater importance than the exchange and the proposals and counterproposals, there is the struggle between the repressive forces of the regime and us, for they are determined to find the hostages without negotiating, whereas we are determined to negotiate while keeping them from finding the hostages. It is a struggle between them and us. They have unleashed an unprecedented offensive; we have shown that we can take it, even though we are suffering casualties in the process, and the struggle has entered a new stage.

What are the future plans of the Movement?
First, we will have to see how the government reacts to our proposals, but we really don't have much hope in this regard. The dictatorship has responded to the negotiation proposal with greater repression. The police and Army have taken to the streets. They have raided 25,000 homes and even hospitals and churches in just a few days. Comrades have been killed. Comrades who were imprisoned during the period of the suspension of Constitutional guarantees have been injected with Pentothal and tortured to obtain confessions, but, in spite of all the technical and the practical methods employed, they remain firm.

To this reply by the dictatorship to our proposal concerning the captured diplomats, we will respond with more armed struggle.

How is that to be carried out, and what are its aims?
We could head this topic with the watchword of the campaign we Tupamaros are now launching: "If there isn't a homeland for all, there won't be a homeland for anybody." At present, the actions the dictatorship is now undertaking are in furtherance and defense of an established order. That order means hundreds of workers fired, hundreds of teachers without a job, the government meddling in educational matters, the senior high school closed, and a steady worsening of poverty—the result of the drastic freezing of wages and a far-from-drastic freezing of the prices of staple goods.

This situation had been dragging on for a long time, but now it has worsened drastically—the situation in the rural areas; the situation of the agricultural peons, of the *cantegriles;* the city's poverty belt; the so-called rat towns in the countryside; the plight of the rural wage workers, etc. The government has unleashed all this repression in defense of this order. There are imprisoned workers in the Army garrisons and scores of political and revolutionary prisoners in the jails of Montevideo—that is the order defended by the regime.

That is the order that makes it possible for certain financial groups to promote a devaluation of the currency and, knowing about it in advance, make a killing with a single stroke. It is a paradise for the financiers and latifundists who are in power. It is in the defense of that order that the government is unleashing its repressive forces, so as to decapitate or crush the people's armed vanguard.

It is against that order that we reply. Against that order backed by the dictatorship's bayonets, we reply with a watchword, an immediate objective which we are advancing with our armed struggle. At this moment, the dictatorship can neither master nor rule the Uruguayan people. This is our watchword. We are launching armed struggle at all levels, through our regular commandos and through what is the Tupamaros' mass line; to carry armed struggle to the level of the masses.

The Movement understands this to be the only possible way for the masses to express their will, but to what extent do the masses understand that this is the road?

The masses are learning that whatever action on their part affects the regime always clashes with it in one way or another; that their struggle for wage increases invariably comes up against the regime's wage-freeze laws; that any attempts at demonstrating or holding assemblies aimed against the interests of the regime or the order the regime defends are repressed; and that any means for the expression of ideas that say something critical of the order defended by bayonets is muzzled, as has happened to so many newspapers.

The people, the workers, are learning that any action they may undertake always, inevitably, winds up in a confrontation with the regime and that the methods which, to some extent, the MLN is teaching them —the methods of direct, clandestine action—are the only means of effective expression and action, given the present state of affairs.

What is the immediate program of the MLN?

During this period our program consists of six points. The first one is the release of all imprisoned comrades. The second point calls for the unfreezing of wages. Next comes the lifting of all governmental interventions in the state's industrial and trade agencies and particularly in education, the lifting of the state of emergency measures and all laws applied in this connection, and the reinstatement of all workers who have lost their jobs.

Defending this program, we Tupamaros call on the people to fight the order of the dictatorship and claim the right of all to a homeland —this homeland of ours, which is now a homeland for the few but is denied to the many.

Aside from the political significance often implicit in some of the Tupamaros' actions, have the Tupamaros set themselves the specific task of carrying out work of political clarification, of spreading ideas and their line among the people of Uruguay?

We believe that we have already won the support of the mass of the people, or those sectors that we could have expectd to be able to count on. By the same token, in this struggle, the dictatorship has drawn closer to the other members of its class.

Between these two extremes, there is a mass we wish to win over to our side or, eventually, neutralize.

It is becoming increasingly more clear to that sector of the population that there is a duality of powers in this country. This duality of powers is going to continue for a long time, as we think the struggle will be a long one. But there is one thing that is crystal-clear to the man in the street—the kind of justice employed by the dictatorship, expressed in the raiding of homes, jailings, and torture, is one thing; and revolutionary justice, ranging from the execution of torturers who work for the regime to the raiding of the homes of those men who support the dictatorship, is another.

For example, take the judiciary. We knew that the courts bore down hard on our comrades and handled the agents of the dictatorship with kid gloves in such cases as the one at Cuchilla Alta, in which four of our comrades were declared guilty of homicide when the court knew that a police agent was guilty of the crime.

In another case, when a police agent killed a man after demanding that he produce his identification papers—and it just so happened that the man had nothing to do with our organization—the policeman was freed 48 hours after his arrest.

We detained Pereira Manelli, the judge who had handled the case, and, on interrogation, he admitted and later stated publicly that it was a fact that he had glossed over some cases and been unduly harsh in others. But the worst thing that came out was his statement concerning the notorious "malfeasance" case involving the embezzlement of a large sum of money in which Jorge Batlle, a government figure, was implicated, for he declared that, while it was assigned to his Court, it was decided by others higher up.

With respect to Pereira Manelli, the MLN took justice into its own hands.

If we have advanced this far and can count on a basic sector of the population that is definitely in favor of the National Liberation Movement, this is because the work that has been done with those people was not based solely on the actions the Movement carried out. Rather, parallel with those actions—though in the early days this was always considered a matter of secondary importance, and only now is it being given increasingly greater importance and attention—we have engaged in the tasks of educating and training the people, discussing materials, and spreading ideas.

In this respect, the limitations faced by an underground movement are most evident. For some time we had a clandestine radio station in operation. It appeared again recently, and it will surely return to the air again at any time.

The dissemination of printed material is being stepped up. As you know, this is a particularly dangerous kind of work. The mere fact that a person is caught with a document put out by our organization means indictment for "association to commit criminal acts" or "abetting association to commit criminal acts" and can result in a long jail sentence.

What organizational forms is the MLN planning to use for its work of influencing the people?

Here we can speak of a contradiction which we are trying to solve—especially in a period in which we are confronted with a struggle at all levels, armed struggle at all levels.

There is a big gap between the influence of the MLN and our development of the organization of that influence. There are many people who are ready to collaborate with us in various ways whom our organization cannot reach through its own structure. A call is being made for them to create what might be called Committees for the Support of the Tupamaros (CATs). Their structure and organization would be similar to the Movement's own, by cells, with small groups operating clandestinely and charged with the tasks of distributing the organization's materials and, eventually, conducting study groups on its objectives—and even, in such cases where the Committees display a sufficiently high degree of combativeness, planning some actions at the popular level.

Since we are on this subject, the Movement has shown proof of great efficiency not only in its actions but also in the defense of its organization. I believe the greatest proof of this is the unprecedented offensive launched by the government forces against the Movement and the poor results obtained. This presupposes a high level of organization in the Movement, which, in turn, must be known to the police, to a certain extent. That is why I don't believe it would be indiscreet to ask you to tell us of the internal organizational measures of the Movement which account for such a high degree of efficiency.

Yes, I can give you some general information on this. We could say that compartmentalization and discretion are, to the urban guerrilla, what the secret path is to the rural guerrilla. The system of not knowing any more than one should know, not commenting on more than what one should comment on, not knowing any places other than those needed to carry out one's own actions, and not knowing any names other than those which one must necessarily know—not even those of the comrades in one's own cell—and the use of noms de guerre instead of one's true name are a guarantee that, any time one of the cadres is captured, the damage to the Movement itself is slight or practically nil. Let us say that all these things constitute our protective shield.

Moreover, compartmentalization exists not only at the cell level but also at the column level. Each column has its own: action groups; logistics support; infrastructure; and MLN–people, MLN–trade union, MLN–student and MLN–Army relationship.

This structure allows for the simultaneous and autonomous operation of various columns. Should one of the columns be affected by the repression, its operative power may be impaired, but not that of the other columns. It may even be that more than one column is affected if the attack launched by the repression is as skillful as it is violent, but as long as one of these columns continues to exist, the organization will continue to exist and express itself.

We might say that, with this type of structure, the Movement is indestructible. Even when the organization is dealt a hard blow—as happened only recently, with the capture of an important group of comrades as a result of mass-scale raids never before seen in this country—this does not mean either the disappearance of the MLN or the end of MLN actions on the streets. To the contrary, even in the midst of these raids, the Movement can and has continued to act. In other words, those columns not affected by the repression retain their operational capacity and can continue the action—the essential continuity of action typical of the Tupamaros—while the other columns reorganize their cadres, headquarters, infrastructure and equipment.

The Tupamaros have carried out several types of action, ranging from sensational kidnappings and occupations of towns to the executions of torturers and the seizures of funds. I wish you would give us a little more information as to the purpose behind each type of action.
There are tactical actions, aimed at obtaining supplies; and there are propaganda actions and direct actions against the regime. The supply actions are carried out more or less continuously, and we might say that they include a constant search for funds and a series of other elements having a bearing on the logistical support of the Movement: plastic material for forged documents, dynamite, equipment for reloading shells, etc.—in short, everything that has a bearing on the logistical structure of the Movement.

Propaganda actions are those which by themselves define the Movement's objectives and conduct. These actions were the ones mainly carried out at the beginning. Even though they are part of the daily program, they are not being given priority at the moment.

The seizure of documents from a firm to show that there are a number of ministers linked to large firms or engaged in financial operations is an example of this type of propaganda action which, at the same time, defines the Movement's conduct. In other words, the Movement does not expropriate funds earmarked for the payment of workers' wages, but it will expropriate the gold that a family as financially powerful as the Mailhoses has continued to accumulate for so many years in the form of pounds sterling.

Actions against the regime are mainly aimed at undermining the foundations of the regime itself, particularly actions directed against the forces of repression. In other words, when we decide to raid the home of a political police agent, it's our way of showing them and the people that there are two powers in confrontation in the streets—that, just as our homes can be raided, so can those of the security agents.

The actions aimed at disarming policemen are of the same nature.

These actions are aimed not only at supplying ourselves with arms and ammunition. They also serve to undermine the morale of policemen who are discharging their duties as mercenaries and who, sooner or later, will ask themselves—in fact, they have already started asking these questions, and there are indications of the consequences that have followed—just who the devil they are defending with their uniform and their weapons, against whom they are fighting, and what order they are defending.

The Movement's history shows that the Tupamaros are everywhere. I would like to know what sector your militants come from, what they seek, and what they find in the Movement.

They seek—and find—a place in the struggle, no matter where they come from. They find an organization with armed struggle as its method and with clearly defined objectives. As far as their origin is concerned, the organization includes students and blue- and white-collar workers. The origin of the comrades who were captured can be taken as a reference point: they include a good number of agricultural workers, workers in metallurgy and in the textile industry, many of whom hold posts of leadership in their respective trade unions, and students—who constitute, as do all the other sectors of the radical middle class, an endless source of material for the MLN.

What role does the MLN give to the various social classes in the revolutionary struggle, and how does it operate in relation to the established organizations which represent those classes—for example, the trade unions?

The ideology of the Movement is not determined by its social makeup.

In other words, those who join the Movement, no matter what sector they come from, are in pursuit of specific methods. It doesn't matter whether they are peasants or blue- or white-collar workers.

In the course of a tactical period the participation of the students, the trade unions, and the peasants will eventually be of fundamental importance in creating a revolutionary situation. In this connection, everything they do—either temporary or continuous—with a view to the development of a methodology of the armed struggle at the grass-roots level will contribute to greater effectiveness.

However, when these methods are applied consistently, as part of a more or less long-term struggle, the brunt of the entire process is borne by the Movement's armed branch, which is constantly being reinforced with cadres that proceed from the workers' movement, the rural areas, the students' movement, and the Army. In other words, in periods of daily, persistent actions, while work is being done to create a revolutionary situation, the armed branch plays the leading role, while the aforementioned classes are engaged in learning the methodology of armed struggle and are gradually furnishing the armed vanguard with cadres that will contribute to its development.

In its early stages, what made the Movement decide on armed struggle, and why is this struggle limited, almost exclusively, to the urban zones? It may be useful to recall in this connection a series of opinions, derived from former experiences, as to the enormous risks an urban guerrilla unit must face. This, in turn, would lead us to comment on the originality of the Uruguayan urban guerrilla unit and its contribution to this type of struggle. My question, therefore, is multiple: Why did the Tupamaros choose armed struggle, why is this struggle of the urban type, and what are the characteristics that guarantee its successful operation?

I recall that Che once said that, in Latin America, the same objective conditions exist everywhere—the problem of the latifundia; the problem of imperialism distorting our respective economies; and, as a result of all this, the drama of hunger, poverty, and exploitation, objectively proved all over Latin America. These problems are quite sharply defined in some countries, while in others they are not so evident—the hand of imperialism being more or less disguised. However, Uruguay fits perfectly into this picture of objective conditions.

These conditions were not so evident during a certain period—principally during World War II and the postwar years, and also, to a certain extent, during the Korean war. Armies are large consumers of wool, and Uruguay is, fundamentally, a wool-producing country. Therefore, those were years of large incomes, of large amounts of foreign exchange that were squanderd. The foreign exchange came into the country, but it never reached the people. It went into the hands of the oligarchy.

These resources made possible, for a certain period of time, the enactment and implementation of a number of more or less progressive labor laws—for example, the establishment of the so-called Wage Councils, which consisted of commissions made up of blue- and white-collar workers plus one representative of the government whose job it was to study wage increases.

No solution whatever was found for the problem of unemployment, but it was possible to develop a number of mainly light industries—for example, a textile industry.

However, the entire process deteriorated quite rapidly. Uruguay's cattle production today, the number of head in the country at present, is the same as it was at the beginning of the century. Industry has not only stagnated but has even entered a stage of regression. The textile industry that flourished during the postwar period is systematically growing weaker.

Therefore, in those objective conditions—which, at a specific moment, might be considered to set Uruguay apart from the rest of Latin America—the process of the deterioration of its economy—foreseeable in a system such as ours—gradually included Uruguay in the rest of the Latin American scene.

Therefore, objective conditions in Uruguay are no longer different from those in the rest of Latin America. There is unemployment; there is a housing shortage; one-third of the country's arable lands are owned by 600 families; a policy of extensive cattle raising is being followed; and there are vast extensions of unproductive land, large estates with unproductive zones, while, right next door to them are poor settlements with a high child mortality rate due to malnutrition, diarrhea, and a lack of medical attention. In short, the same picture.

These are the objective conditions in Latin America that Che was talking about, and he added that, in Cuba, there had been some special objective conditions—Fidel and the 26th of July Movement. In other words, a Latin America with a vast explosive potential that had not as yet been touched off needed the presence of a subjective fuse to trigger the explosion. These objective conditions existed in Uruguay, and all that was necessary was to create the fuse that would open the way, a revolutionary path that would lead to a change in structures.

We chose the course of armed struggle because we thought it was the only effective way to dethrone those who are determined to remain in power with the backing of weapons once they find this power threatened by the classes they oppress.

In other words, if the present government of Uruguay were to find an answer to the workers' demands, there would be no reason for conflict. However, the government cannot find the answer—and won't even try to find it—because it is a government which serves the interests of the group of bankers headed by Peirano Facio and the group of latifundists who keep Bordaberry, a wealthy landowner, in the Ministry of Cattle Raising and Agriculture in order to make it possible for them to continue making enormous profits, with all of them providing fat dividends for the International Monetary Fund. This, plus the presence of imperialism—more or less disguised—creates a contradiction which makes it impossible, given its present structure, for the government to find an answer to the people's needs.

The people have begun to confront the regime by demanding wage increases, improvements, social laws, and so forth. Since these wage increases and improvements adversely affect the interests of the sectors represented by the government, the government refuses to make concessions. And, since the workers are not willing to resign themselves to this situation, we have the strikes and the workers' struggle for higher wages—which leads to the government's making use of its forces of repression.

If, when faced with the workers' demand for a wage increase or the students' demand for university autonomy, the government sends its troops out into the streets armed with riot guns, murders students and workers, fires workers, and fills the police station with them, what wouldn't this government—or any other similar government—do when the same forces, headed by a revolutionary vanguard try—as Guillén[4] says in his poem—to "put those on top at the bottom and those on the bottom at the top"?

The way of armed struggle is adopted when one is fully convinced that it is the way to overthrow those who hold on to power—that power that gives them all their profits, privileges, and pleasures at the cost of the efforts of others.

At this point, I would like to return to the second part of my question, that concerning the urban nature of the armed struggle.

I'll begin by saying that the decision to take the way of armed struggle was in no way dependent on the specific geographical characteristics of our country. It is a matter of concept. Otherwise, those countries lacking the geographical conditions favorable to rural guerrilla warfare, for example, would have to discard armed struggle in the process of a revolution.

There was a time when the urban guerrillas were looked upon as units to provide logistic support—communications, weapons, funds, etc. —for what should be the main nucleus: the rural guerrillas. This concept was discussed by the MLN on the basis of an analysis of our national situation—in which the possibilities for rural guerrilla warfare are practically nil, as we have neither vast jungles nor mountains—and some previous experiences, and we came to the conclusion that the development of urban struggle was possible, thanks to some very interesting, specific conditions.

We studied the French resistance to Nazi occupation; the Algerian struggle—which, even though it developed mainly in the mountains, had its counterpart in the cities—and an example which, as a result of its methodology, its being strictly limited to the urban areas, was extremely useful to the Movement: the struggle waged by the Jews against the English, reference to which is made in a booklet entitled *Rebellion in the Holy Land.*

4 Nicolás Guillén, Cuban poet.

On the basis of these facts, it was considered feasible to begin the experiment in Latin America, of a guerrilla force whose action would be centered in the cities instead of in the countryside.

Comparatively speaking, what are the advantages and disadvantages, as far as your organization is concerned, of urban and rural guerrilla warfare?

We believe that urban struggle has a number of advantages over rural struggle and that, in turn, the rural struggle also presents certain advantages over the urban struggle. However, the important thing, at this stage of the game, is the proof that the nucleus can come to life, survive, and develop within the city, and all this in keeping with its own laws. It is true that we are operating right in the mouth of the enemy, but it is also true that the enemy is gagging on us. We are faced with the inconvenience of having to lead a dual life, in which we carry on a public activity—whenever we are able to—yet, in reality, are somebody else altogether. But we have the advantage of having a series of indspensable resources at hand which rural guerrillas must engage in special operations to obtain: food, ammunition, weapons, and communications. The same thing applies with respect to the environment: our adaptation to it comes almost naturally.

Adaptation to the environment is another interesting factor. We, the urban guerrillas, move about in a city which we know like the palm of our hand, in which we look like everybody else, and where we go from one place to another with the same ease as do the other million people who live in it.

However, the rate of our losses, in relation to our experiences in Montevideo, shows a marked increase. Every week, every two weeks, every month, the number of comrades who are captured increases. Were it not for a very strong Tupamaros–people relationship, this might mean that the organization would be decimated.

However, the multiplication of the Movement is so great that it makes for an easy, rapid replacement of these losses.

Losses are relatively high in a city. For example, a person in hiding is identified by the police because his features were not disguised effectively enough; a house that serves as a base of operations begins to attract attention; a person in hiding is detected by the police, goes into a house, the house is raided, and he and other comrades are captured; or a comrade is captured with a document that belongs to the organization or an expropriated weapon on his person.

In other words, there are a number of mechanisms which, in a city, make it possible, beginning from a starting point, to unravel part of the skein. Hence, losses could be described as something inevitable, no matter what security measures are adopted in urban guerrilla warfare.

That is why the replacement of those who are captured, technological and political development and the training of military cadres are the burning issue. The loss of cadres and the loss of infrastructures are a necessary evil which the urban guerrilla force has to face.

I repeat, the replacement of those cadres, the replacement of the infrastructure, is the greatest problem.

Hasn't the organization, in view of the specific conditions that exist in Uruguay, thought of reversing the usual roles and developing some type of rural guerrilla unit that would serve as support or complement to the urban guerrilla action?

The tactical plan contemplated by the organization at present includes extending the war to the interior of the country. A series of actions that were planned recently, which included cutting off communications—tearing down telephone poles, etc.—have been carried out. Many of these actions will eventually be planned within the characteristics of the urban struggle. In other words, even though these actions will be carried out in the countryside, they will have characteristics not so much of rural guerrilla action but rather of a commando raid— that is, going out, completing the operation, and returning, if possible, to normal, everyday life.

The Uruguayan guerrillas have brought into play a number of resources of ingenuity and imagination that make them rather unique. Could you tell us how important these resources are to the Movement's operational effectiveness and name some cases where they have been particularly useful?

Yes, we believe that acute discernment and ingenuity play an important role in urban guerrilla warfare. Since the urban guerrilla always operates in enemy territory, always moves on enemy ground, since he must carry on his work near one of the repression's bases, he must, of necessity, depend on a series of resources which, given the circumstances, are of vital importance.

One example is his use of the same methods employed by the forces of repression.

In the case of the Banco Francés e Italiano, for example, one of our "mesengers" arrived at the bank, followed by comrades posing as members of the Intelligence Corps and police liaison men; they entered the bank when the door was opened to let in the "messenger" who customarily arrived at the bank at that time. Once inside the building, the group announced that the Tupamaros had placed a bomb on the premises, everybody was rounded up and then we told them who we were and that we intended to carry out an action.

That was the first stage of the operation. The second stage consisted of opening the vault. Three of the bank's officials had one key to the vault each. However, they were not in the bank at that moment. But there was a practically surefire way to bring them there. We found one of them, told him that the general manager had committed suicide and that there was chaos in his office, and asked him to please come with us. Then we visited the man who was supposed to have killed himself and told him the same story about the other one. The same procedure was employed with the third man. In this particular case, it was impossible to locate the third party, and, as a result, 380 million pesos remained safely ensconced in the vault, but we took with us a number of documents that proved that the bank was engaged in fraudulent operations and which practically determined the bank's closing.

The documents led to an investigation by the Department of Revenue. We were pretty unhappy about not having been able to get to the 380 million pesos so we tried a new raid, in which we were to pose as revenue agents who were to participate in the work of investigation.

These are examples of ingenuity, which are of the utmost importance in any type of urban action. Something quite similar happened in the taking of the Navy garrison.

Two comrades posing as security agents asked to see an official to clear up some incident. While someone went to find him, two soldiers walking along the side of the building were intercepted by one of our comrades impersonating an agent of the investigation department. The comrade demanded that they produce their identification papers, and a heated argument ensued in which the soldiers tried to justify their presence there even though they carried no identification. Needless to say, the two "soldiers" also belonged to our organization. At the right time, everybody went into action, the guards were subdued and the rest of the comrades who were to carry out the operation went into the building.

A similar procedure was employed for getting into the police headquarters in Pando. The action was carried out by two comrades who posed as army officers who were bringing in two captured Tupamaros.

Only a few days separated this action from the one at the El Mago supermarket, which took place the same day the government closed all the branch banks to keep the Movement from getting funds, and it had similar characteristics. Our comrades went into the supermarket posing as security agents looking for a Tupamaro who was working there. The supermarket's administration did a beautiful job of cooperating with us, rounding up all the employees to clear up the situation.

We have staged a number of raids this way.

Then there was a time when we got our weapons by raiding private collections. We used to forge search warrants, and one of our comrades dressed in a policeman's uniform would show the order and ask to be let in. This went on until the Minister of the Interior put an end to this wave of seizures from weapons collectors by announcing that weapons could only be seized provided an order signed by him was presented to the collector.

This, in turn, forced us to forge new orders, bearing his "signature" of course, so we could remove the weapons in question.

I may be getting away from the subject, but I'd like to know if many of the weapons you captured in the navy garrison action were recovered as a result of the latest wave of police raids.
Very, very few. Most of the weapons are still in our hands.

The Movement has paid its inevitable toll in martyrs. Those combatants, although highly admired, are little-known. Could you tell us about some of their characteristics; their way of life; their activities in the Movement, including the circumstances surrounding their deaths; and their present influence and meaning in the Movement?

Several of our comrades have been killed in the struggle. Many were murdered in Pando—students such as Ricardo Zabalza, Emilio Cultelli, and Jorge Salerno, the last a boy who wrote songs, played the guitar, and sang in songfests with our comrades; soldiers such as Mario Robaina and Father Olivera, who put aside his vestments to join the Movement; comrades who chose the way of struggle, leaving behind their homes and families—even their children—because they realized that their decision would reflect honor on them, their homes, their children, their families, on everything they held most dear. It is as Che said: the highest title to which a man can aspire is that of revolutionary.

Several comrades have died in combat, among them Nelson Flores, who covered his comrades' withdrawal to the very end. Others, like those who died in Pando, were murdered after they were captured, insulted, and beaten. And then there were others, such as Fernán Pucurull, killed in cold blood while unarmed.

The deaths of these comrades point up the risk involved in every action, raid, sortie, incursion, and contact. A risk that is in one's mind when one joins the Movement, but a risk that has also been described by Che when he said that death does not matter provided that the battle cry reaches some receptive ear and another hand is extended to take up the fallen weapons.

Tell me about the role of women in the Movement.

First of all, let me tell you that nothing makes men and women more equal than a .45-calibre pistol. One of the actions carried out with the highest spirit was that of getting the prisoners out of the women's prison. A series of photographs of the escapees, which appeared in the newspapers with a caption which read, "It's true: you can't make a revolution without them!" was placed on exhibit in one of the MLN headquarters.

There is a question that many people here—and in other countries, as well—ask themselves on seeing the revolutionary movement in Uruguay developing at greater speed than those in Brazil and Argentina, the two reactionary giants that border it.

The day may come when the people will take power in Uruguay while the other two movements are still in a stage more or less remote from power. How does the Movement view the situation that would arise in that case?

Entering into hypotheses is very much like skating on thin ice. However, the obvious thing in such a situation is that the vigor of the armed struggle should be maintained at all times. If we attack imperialism from all sides—as if it were a beast at bay—nipping at it from every angle, it won't be able to decide whom to face first. It's something akin to that of two, three, many Vietnams. Should the revolutionary process in Uruguay develop more rapidly than that in the neighboring countries and a situation arise whereby we succeed in taking power, we can certainly count on the possibility of an intervention by the United States, either directly or through the armies of the bordering countries. In that case, the struggle would be one of a national character against an invading army, and the conditions would be created for the very dialectics of the struggle to lead to a new Vietnam.

What you have just said leads me to another question. How does the Movement view the process of liberation in Latin America? There is some concrete evidence of this already—for example, Chato Peredo's expressions of gratitude for your help, which made it possible for him to reach the Bolivian jungles much sooner. Does this mean the beginning of an international strategy of the Latin American revolution proposed by the MLN?

It is quite evident that a revolutionary, internationalist spirit exists in Latin America, which has its roots in the struggle for our first independence. Today, it is a practical, concrete internationalism which is manifested tangibly. Our enemies are the same; our goals, methods, and weapons are the same.

How does the Uruguayan MLN interpret the victory scored by People's Unity—that is, by Salvador Allende—in the Chilean elections?

We look upon Salvador Allende's victory as a very positive thing. The process should be carefully studied with a view to the contributions it may provide as an event that appears to be particularly interesting with respect to the paths leading to power.

INTERVIEW WITH URBANO

However, as important as—or, rather, more important than—this study are the measures which, inevitably, the Government will have to adopt when it decides to put into practice the aims which imply changes of structure in Chile—which measures, in turn, will trigger off the reaction of the oligarchy and imperialism, which will then resort to the methods which they have traditionally employed whenever their interests have been threatened.

Sooner or later, the presence of the people in arms, vigilance and armed reply, and armed vigilance must constitute the elements that will guarantee the fulfillment of the program that the people of Chile, with Allende at the fore, have for their government.

And we find the statement by the Chilean MIR with respect to Allende's victory quite clear; the time has come to place men and weapons at the service of the program of the Chilean left.

Let's say the Tupamaros are in power. What do they intend to do with Uruguay?

The Movement's program is in no way different from those of other revolutionary movements which are now in power—as that of Cuba—or which aspire to power—as the several guerrilla movements in Latin America. The tasks to be tackled are clearly defined: the problem of latifundism, nationalization of the banks, the expulsion of imperialism, the achievement of a higher standard of living, education, health, housing, the restoration of man's full dignity, and the eradication of unemployment. These are the tasks that every revolutionary movement keeps in mind, awaiting the time when, once power is attained, the national program that will lead to those objectives can be put into practice.

The Tupamaros' Program for Revolutionary Government	The first specific statement by the MLN of its revolutionary program for social change. Many of these reforms were later included in the Broad Front's electoral campaign, critically supported by the Tupamaros, later in 1971.

The Tupamaros National Liberation Movement has reduced its revolutionary program to several essential points, which can only be put into practice by a revolutionary government that is inspired in this ideology.

The preparation of this program does not mean that we will not support another transitional program aimed at the same results, such as have been worked out by the CNT (Central Labor Organization) and other popular forces.

The MLN had prepared a brief, six-point platform that could have brought about a normalization, but it was rejected by the government. That program included the reinstatement of freedoms, unfreezing of wages, reinstatement of all employees and workers who were dismissed as a result of the security measures that have been taken, and freedom for political prisoners.

Our principal points for the stage of the country's reconstruction by a revolutionary government are:

Agrarian Reform

1. The large cattle ranches, plantations, and dairies are to be expropriated and turned over to the workers for administration.
2. Since the country's principal source of wealth is the countryside, farm production will be given a rapid boost through capital investments and mechanization.
3. All small farmers who work their own land will be respected. Farm workers such as tenant farmers who now have a precarious right to their land will be given an effective right to the land: the land will belong to those who work it.
4. The best of technical aid will be available to all rural producers, together with fertilizer, seeds, wire, and other materials necessary for better farming.

Granma Weekly (Havana, Cuba), 28 March 1971, p. 12.

Industry

1. The large factories are to be socialized and turned over to the workers for administration.
2. National industry is to be promoted and protected, especially those lines based on national raw materials (beef, wool, hides, oil-bearing plants, etc.), including all those that may have good prospects in the domestic or foreign markets.

Commerce

1. Exports and imports and foreign trade in general are to be run directly by the government.
2. All wholesale enterprises, the large supermarkets, warehouses, stores, meat markets, etc., are to be socialized and turned over to the workers for administration.

Credit

Both savings and loans will be centralized by the state, which is to guide investments toward productive sectors or desirable construction projects.

Urban Reform

1. The property of all landlords in excess of what they and their families need for dwelling purposes is to be expropriated, and the homeless are to be provided with housing.
2. All luxury mansions are also to be expropriated and used for cultural or other public purposes.
3. The building of sanitary housing for homeless families will be given priority in economic planning.

Planning

Production, commerce, credit and the economy in general are to be planned in detail in order to boost production, eliminate competition, and eradicate superfluous middleman operations and speculation.

Foreign Investments

All large factories, mercantile enterprises and banks that are completely or partially owned by foreign capital are to be expropriated, without compensation.

Wages

1. The living standard of all workers will be raised on the basis of a fair distribution of the nation's wealth and increasing productivity.
2. To the extent that increasing production permits, distribution will be on the basis of "To each according to his needs."

Education

1. The state will guarantee completely free education and provide all students with all the necessary study materials.
2. Education is to be oriented toward those specialties that have to do with highly technological production.
3. As in other fields of the nation's activities, the administration of the schools by those directly concerned will be promoted.

Public Health

The most modern means for providing medical attention are to be placed at the service of all the people, without preference for anyone. An example of this policy will be the expropriation of all private sanatoriums and all large pharmaceutical products laboratories.

Old Age and Disability

All persons who are not able to work because of physical disability are to receive state aid sufficient to cover all their needs.

Justice

1. The present codes, which were conceived with the idea of maintaining the private ownership principle of the capitalist system in general, are to be replaced by others that take essential human values into consideration.
2. Efforts will be made to rehabilitate criminals through training and work both before and after their release.
3. All sentences handed down by the bourgeois courts on persons who have committed so-called common crimes are to be reviewed, as are all acquittals granted to figures of the regime for crimes committed by them.
4. All persons who collaborate with the counterrevolution, such as those who have committed murders and other crimes in the service of the present regime or those who, taking advantage of the news media, have slandered or spread lies about the cause of the people,

will be punished by imprisonment, with sentences to be determined by the seriousness of the crime committed.

Armed Defense of the Revolution

Both the taking of power and the complete fulfillment of the objectives of the revolution can be guaranteed only by arming the people for their defense.

Montevideo, March 20, 1971

Tupamaros National Liberation Movement
Freedom or Death

Proclamation of Paysandú

Following the election of Juan María Bordaberry in November 1972, the Tupamaros ended their truce with a series of assaults in the vicinity of Paysandú. This proclamation explains their reasons for doing so. Militarily, the actions marked a move toward operations at the column level, involving hundreds of militants.

On the night of December 30, the Leandro Gómez column of the National Liberation Movement (Tupamaros) simultaneously occupied: the military airport of Paysandú, disarming its guard and taking three M-2 machine guns, ammunition, and three radio transmitters; the coastal radio beacon located three kilometers from the airport, expropriating two radio transmitters; a calcium quarry on the banks of the River Uruguay and its town, taking 40 kilos of Delfo gelatin explosives, 80 bomb cases, and powder, after disarming the police guard, from whom they took a battery radio transmitter; and the police station in the village of Constancia, 10 kilometers from Paysandú near the mountain ridge of Quebracho.

A hundred years ago others rose up in arms and fought here. A hundred years ago the same indomitable rebellion of the eastern man flared through these sierras. Then it was Timoteo Aparicio, former Lieutenant de Rivera, and Anacleto Medina,[1] who united their native lancer hosts and confronted the regular troops of the commanders who wanted to hand us over to the Brazilian empire.

A hundred years have passed. Little in this country has changed for the poor people. In the hamlets and *cantegriles* [belts of misery] the cold comes through the walls and the *guriserío* [the children] have to sleep embracing the dogs to keep warm. There are children who die of diarrhea in the garbage dumps or on the ranches. And those who survive the misery of the first years grow up with rickets, without knowing milk, sweets, fruit. They reach their youth with rotten teeth and delicate health, from poor nutrition and lack of medical care. Those who get to a hospital are given neither bed nor treatment and

Tricontinental Bulletin (Havana, Cuba), no. 73 (April 1972), pp. 38–41.

Heroes of the resistance against a Portuguese invasion begun in 1816 and resulting in occupation of the *Banda Oriental* (East Bank: Uruguay) until a treaty in 1828 ended the occupation and guaranteed Uruguayan independence.

often lack even cotton and bandages. There is little work. Neither in the city nor in the countryside are there jobs. And what is available is almost always badly paid. And worse, when the worker rebels and demands something more, the response is the stick, torture, jail, shooting.

For the rich of the country things haven't changed much either. They are the owners of the ranches, the cattle, the factories, the banks. They have comfortable homes, top physicians, vacation houses in the resorts; for them there is never any meat shortage. Their children grow up healthy, clean. They have good teachers, good doctors, and in their private hospitals there is never a lack of beds or correct treatment. They are the owners of the country. And they are in the government, occupying ministries, administrating what is theirs so that everything continues as it is, the rich rich and the poor poor.

It isn't always this way. Pacheco was a modest, second-rate journalist when he became president, and a short while later, an apartment costing 10 million pesos was built for his then wife.

These are the people who managed the elections so that the commissariat band would win. These are the ones who support the pro-Brazilian [Juan María] Bordaberry. Who caused more votes than voters to appear in the urns—and no one can tell whether even the dead voted in this election.

For them, Martín Fierro's refrain was written: "The law is like a knife, it doesn't cut the one that's using it." [2] When a rich man robs, speculates, swindles, the law doesn't touch him. If the scandal is very big, he takes a trip to Europe and nothing happens. But when a hungry *cantegril* dweller robs to get something to eat, then yes. First they beat him up and then let him rot in jail. And if this knave of the city becomes angry, then they assassinate him as they assassinated Chueco Maciel. A plantation owner can engage in troop contraband at will in behalf of the Brazilian meat packers. Leave the population without meat, leave the country without foreign exchange. This ranch owner can become minister at any moment. Or president. But for a man of the people who steals a sheep in Vichadero [a small, rural town] to feed his children who are dying of starvation, the price is three years in jail. That truth has not changed: their law does not offend them.

[2] From the epic nineteenth-century poem, *El Gaucho Martín Fierro*, by José Hernandez.

And when the people rebel against such injustice, the repression begins: the Metropolitan Guard, the police departments, the JUP [Uruguayan Youth Arise, a fascist group], the Squadron. Now they've also sent the army into the streets. In its new role, the army tortures, as in the case of the Ninth Cavalry, which put out its cigarettes on the chest of a 17-year-old student and walked on top of him, stepping on his testicles. And as evidence of their bestiality, in the same regiment, they foully violated a woman prisoner.

They have humiliated the eastern people. They have humiliated them with hunger and unemployment, with electoral swindle, with jail and exile, with torture and death.

But the eastern people, offended and humiliated, respond in the same way as those of long ago who arose in the hills (the sierra) against injustice. We are living in times such as those Aparicio Saravia described in his letter from Caraguaya: "This is the moment for action, which reigns above all sterile controversy and leads men into battle or into sacrifice."

That is why we end today the truce we unilaterally initiated before the elections. We have once more made clear our disposition to exhaust every possibility for bringing peace to the nation. It is also clear that this is the road that must be taken because the government neither permits nor desires any other out.

The responsibility for having unleashed this civil war then rests exclusively on their shoulders.

And in this war they are going to tremble, because the poor have nothing to lose in this battle except a very long hunger, and you, those who have always been rich, will sleep restlessly. Because we are going to enter your mansions, your kitchens, your strong boxes. You have slapped the people on both cheeks. There is nothing left. Now the humble rise up in arms; and be careful, there are many.

We are many. We are all. And we want our homeland.

There will be a homeland for all or there will be a homeland for no one.

Liberty or Death.

National Liberation Movement (Tupamaros)
Leandro Gómez column.

The Tupamaros: An Interview

This interview was conducted after the holocaust of April 14, 1972, between the time of the regime's offensive against the MLN and the coup of June 1973. The focus on the "emerging question of power" foreshadows the situation prevailing after the coup.

"Dawn never catches me where I spend the night." This slogan had been scrawled by a Tupamaro on the wall of the underground hideout where the interview with the National Liberation Movement took place. Next to the words was the now famous Tupamaro star. That night, Montevideo was particularly cold and overcast; a mist crept in over the wail of police sirens and military patrol cars constantly combing the Uruguayan capital. Just a few days earlier, the MLN had executed Colonel Artigas Alvarez, one of the most vicious engineers of the savage tortures recently intensified and "modernized" with the aid of American and Brazilian advisors. "Pigs die like pigs," a young woman had told me. Without warning, the Tupamaro whom I was to interview entered the room while I was asking another Tupamaro about a motto placed under the pictures of Uruguay's founding fathers Artigas and Aparicio Saravia:

There won't be a single tree left to give shade,
Nor a seed to sprout;
No wall will be left standing.
There will be a fatherland for all,
Or there won't be one for anyone.

As the maté was passed around the circle, the following interview took place.

PF *At the beginning of this year the MLN's executive committee stated that in 1972 the organization must become a real alternative for power in Uruguay. How does the MLN plan to apply this strategy*

This interview first appeared in *Punto Final* (Santiago, Chile), no. 165 (September 1972) and was reprinted by the Center for Information on Latin America (Montreal Canada), October 1972, pp. 2–6. The CILA translation used here is by Frank Terrugi who was murdered in September 1973 by the military junta in Chile.

to the present situation, considering what has happened since April 14th?

MLN The events of April 14th are symptomatic of a whole series of events in this country that clearly entail many changes in our original plans. We have always maintained that the Uruguayan revolutionary process would not progress linearly, but would in fact be vulnerable to sudden leaps as well as setbacks. We made this clear early in 1971 in our document No. 5. Due principally to government repression, our organization and our country have now been placed in a qualitatively different political position. We live in a state of war; not so much due to our own offensive, as to that of our enemies. This is no more than a tactical defeat. Day by day, the organization has been recovering its capacity to operate effectively. We have executed innumerable military torturers—which just in itself shows how much the characteristics of the struggle have changed.

When we spoke of ourselves as an alternative for power, we were referring basically to the need to move to another level of struggle—that of war. We shouldn't become demoralized just because we have lost a battle. It is not the first and it will not be the last. In 1966, 1969, and 1970,[1] our organization faced difficult and threatening situations, and some thought that our final hour had come. But from a political point of view, these situations in fact led to real advances, expressed in increased popular participation in a variety of forms which polarized the country into two clearly defined camps. Our people know that in the history of our organization there have been many tactical retreats which were gradually transformed into strategic advances.

Finally, it's important to emphasize how we have jumped from a situation of political equilibrium—where the existence of dual power was obvious—to a new level of struggle. This level is characteristically one of declared war of a united and armed people, in the spirit of Artigas, against the principal support of the bourgeois state and of foreign interests: the police and military Combined Forces. [The Combined Forces is a nationwide, centralized command network constructed with U.S. aid and advisors, such as Mitrione. Much of the

[1] See Chronology, December 22, 1966; October 8, 1969; August 7, 1970.

$700 million in AID funds which Uruguay received in 1971 went into this network.]

PF *What then, in the MLN's opinion, are the political perspectives for the future?*

MLN To characterize the present situation, we would say that we are now living in a prerevolutionary situation which could last months or years, but which will in any event continue to intensify. This is due to the present economic crisis, the increasing social unrest, and the continued integration of popular sectors into the revolutionary process. (In a Gallup poll taken in Montevideo in July, 20 percent of those asked admitted they were Tupamaro sympathizers.) We believe that one of the principal tasks today is to bring as many sectors of the population and as many popular organizations as possible into the struggle for liberation. The facts have demonstrated that no groups can be a priori excluded from this struggle. Therefore, the MLN considers that real revolutionary unity will come only in the course of the struggle. It's more positive to discuss and analyse the emerging question of power than to engage in theoretical digressions on methodology or on whether particular tactics were correct or not.

In our opinion, the facts exist right here in Uruguay today, and they are historically irreversible. Any valid interpretation of the situation leads to the same conclusion that only a people organized for and in the armed struggle will allow the complete destruction of the old so that we can begin to build a new, truly free country. During the present crisis, these premises present themselves immediately, especially since the rich—the privileged minority living off the sweat of the poor—are defending their interests with bullets and blood. Furthermore, they shield themselves behind the guns of those assassins who, forgetting their past, betray the best sentiments of the Uruguayan people. The powerful brutally repress any attempt to meet needs which threaten their interests in any way whatsoever.

In these circumstances, the correctness of the road we have chosen is clear as day. Therefore, our future perspective is one of greater contradictions and sharpened confrontations as our struggle moves to a higher level. It's the same old struggle between positions for and against national autonomy, between the Uruguayan people and those who have sold out to foreign interests.

PF *Some people say that the MLN has been destroyed by the recent offensive of the Combined Forces. What is the real situation?*

MLN From the most recent actions realized by the organization, it is easy to conclude that, if such statements have been made, they originate from:

1. the counterrevolutionary offensive of the Combined Forces; in this case, on the level of psychological warfare;
2. objective allies of the enemy;
3. those who confuse their expectations with reality; and
4. those defeatists who exist in any revolutionary process.

This last source probably involves the most serious distortion of the facts because it represents people who are not on the side of the enemy, but who nevertheless help convince people that they are helpless, that the seizure of power is a chimera thought up by so many adventurists. Today more than ever we must wage an incessant struggle against these incorrect ideas, which are characteristic of people looking for ways out and quick solutions; a common historical phenomenon.

If you are looking at the facts superficially and from the enemy's viewpoint, then there's no doubt that we've suffered serious reverses since April 14th. Two thousand brothers and sisters imprisoned, more than 20 killed, many of them murdered by torture; approximately 150 underground hideouts discovered; 500 weapons of all varieties confiscated—all testify to the seriousness of the blows we've received.

On April 14th, we had 370 *compañeros* forced underground because the enemy discovered they were members of the organization. Today our underground includes over 600. We answer with a question: if our organization had been destroyed, how could these *compañeros* survive in a militarily occupied city without being captured?

The Combined Forces' own dispatches show a "united and armed" people in the MLN: workers who have died in confrontation and on military bases; priests and young Christians; students and *pobladores* [squatters: people who live in *poblaciones*]; professionals and craftsmen, members of Congress as well as the unemployed; poor farm-workers and even a few landowners and industrialists. The only way the MLN has been and will be able to survive is with the continued popular support that we receive and that has meant, on a day-to-day basis, new fighters, new hideouts, and a structure and organizational dynamic suited to the new times.

Urban guerrilla warfare is governed by its own laws of development, and when you don't understand these correctly, you run the risk of falling into subjective, superficial, or one-sided evaluations. For us, the heart of the matter lies in understanding that urban guerrilla warfare is essentially a political war, and that its continued existence depends, therefore, on a correct line, adapted to concrete historical conditions and armed with an appropriate methodology. Armed action creates consciousness and forms of organization among the people that are totally opposed to traditional ones; as much in the area of political education as in the organization of certain sections of the population. For these reasons, our methodology as well as our organization correspond qualitatively to specific forms of struggle which cannot be reconciled in any way with the present society. The practice of ten years of struggle has demonstrated the viability of these forms and explains the dynamic of the people's participation at all levels. Without considering the specific context and norms characterizing this particular historical situation, it is impossible to draw accurate conclusions about the Tupamaros' present situation.

In sum, then, destroying the MLN today would involve the imprisonment and repression not only of known militants, but also of important sectors of the population which have rediscovered their history. And even then, we would reorganize, because, as Artigas said, "Uruguayans were born and will die free."

PF *The Congress as well as the Uruguayan and international press reported that there were negotiations and a truce between the army and the MLN in an attempt to avoid a confrontation by agreeing on a political solution. What is the real story?*
MLN There was in fact a truce, and negotiations did occur between the army and the MLN. This took place on the army's initiative, with concrete proposals to resolve the present political conflict. The deal

was brought to us by two captive *compañeros* temporarily released for this purpose. Under the terms of the truce, they were to suspend the tortures and their operations against us, and we the execution of torturers. With this agreed, our organization submitted the proposal to painstaking study on all levels. We found the terms unacceptable and made a counterproposal which called for the implementation of the points set out in the Broad Front's program, the only possible road to pacification. [The Broad Front is a coalition of Christian Democrats, Socialists, Communists, and Independents which supported the candidacy of General Liber Seregni in last November's presidential elections. Their program includes: agrarian reform, nationalization of banking and foreign commerce, freedom for all political prisoners, etc.] Our counterproposal was subsequently rejected and we ended the truce and resumed hostilities with the execution of Colonel Artigas Alvarez, head of Civil Defense and brother of Combined Forces Commander-in-Chief General Gregorio Alvarez. Those are the facts in brief.

PF *Why do you think the armed forces decided to negotiate when they held the offensive?*

MLN There are a number of reasons, but two basic ones stand out. First, the execution of important members of the repressive hierarchy created confusion and contradictions within the army, whose members were accustomed to its nonmilitarized *civilista* role in the society. These army personnel were now faced with the possibility of a death with no meaning beyond that of their complicity in a police apparatus that defended political and economic interests opposed to their own. The second reason, in our opinion, lies in the middle-class origins of most of the officers, who are also suffering the effects of the present crisis. In addition, they have begun to discover the corruption of the traditional politicians who have led the country to the worst economic situation in its history. Moreover, these military men have seen the nationalistic character of our struggle with all of its implications. Members from every branch of the military, from its officers to the lowest soldiers, are hunted or imprisoned for belonging to the MLN. Also, the repercussions of the Peruvian model of military government has the rank and file worried about the possible future for Uruguay.

PF *How have the traditional political groups reacted to these negotiations and to the growing rumors of preparations for a coup?*

MLN A representative of one of the major parties complained in Congress that "the army negotiates with the Tupamaros but won't speak to us." This expression accurately reflects the attitude of many men toward traditional politicians. Of late, there have been innumerable discussions, interviews, and tentative approaches between Bordaberry and the leaders of the Right: both Blancos and Colorados. The so-called opposition—the Blancos—continually negotiate for what they call "the survival of democratic institutions" against the demands the generals continually make in exchange for performing their repressive duties.

In our opinion, it is clear that our country's traditional democratic liberalism is dead. Not a single tenet of bourgeois law remains untouched. In the end, the congress as a state institution has been used to consolidate the legal dictatorship under the label of the "National Security Law." The efforts of the traditional politicians reflect nothing more than their attempts to keep from being pushed out of the principal power centers.

This is not a new phenomenon in Latin America; in order to survive, a disintegrating society must increasingly oppress the people. This role falls to the armed institutions. But there comes a time when the interests and attitudes toward the State's political leadership enter into contradiction, and the professional politicians are replaced by those with the real power. In the end, the machine kills its own inventor.

As to the second part of the question, a coup d'etat is not yet imminent, but the conditions are being created for the army's complete usurpation of power in the not too distant future. Of course, internal contradictions will continue to exist, because there are still *civilistas* in some high military commands. Besides, the army still lacks the political skill and training necessary to run the government.

PF *In its actions and documents, the MLN always stresses that it is a patriotic and authentically nationalistic revolutionary organization. What does this definition imply?*

MLN The Tupamaros define the nation as the people, and therefore to be nationalistic means to undertake the liberation of the people. This will only be possible through the complete destruction of the unjust society in which we live so that we can replace it with one in which all people can realize their full capabilities. That is, a society in which there is no exploitation and no injustice, and people themselves are the center of all social activity. Where the workers are the natural leaders of the entire society.

Furthermore, as nationalists, we identify ourselves with the best of our history, with those who raised the first banners of independence against the colonialists of their time. We resume the unfinished struggle initiated by Artigas and his gauchos, by the 33 Orientales, Leandro Gómez, and many others against the common enemy: the oligarchy and foreign domination. And, finally, we believe that Latin America is the great nation, the great homeland that will one day find itself on the road to its second and definitive independence.

Urban Guerrilla Organizations

MLN-Tupamaros	*Movimiento de Liberación Nacional*; National Liberation Movement

Named for José Gabriel Condorcanqui (Tupac Amaru), leader of Inca revolt against the Spanish in 1780–1781; founded in 1963, became an important political force by 1970; severely damaged in 1972.

Other Organizations

OPR-33	*Organización Populares Revolucionarios del 33*; Popular Organization of the 33

Named for the nineteenth-century Uruguayan national heroes; anarchist, labor-oriented offshoot of MLN.

FARO	*Fuerzas Armadas Revolucionarias Orientales*; Eastern (i.e., Uruguayan) Revolutionary Armed Forces

Founded by dissident members of MRO (*Movimiento Revolucionario Oriental*; Eastern Revolutionary Movement) in 1968; linked to MLN.

FER	*Frente Estudiantil Revolucionario*; Revolutionary Student Front

Formed in student struggles of 1968; apparently absorbed into MLN.

FRT	*Frente Revolucionario de Trabajadores*; Workers' Revolutionary Front

Labor-oriented splinter from MLN.

PCR/MIR	*Partido Comunista Revolucionario*; Revolutionary Communist Party/*Movimiento de la Izqui-*

erda Revolucionaria; Movement of the Revolutionary Left

MIR was the official Chinese Communist Party during the late 1960s, sectors of which went into the MLN; PCR, an apparently Maoist group, left the MLN after April 1972.

Grupos 22 de Diciembre

December 22 Groups

Named for the date of shooting of Carlos Flores, the first Tupamaro to die in combat; an offshoot of MLN in 1971.

Orán • • Tartagal

• Salta

• Tucumán

• Corrientes

• Córdoba

Santa Fe •

• Mendoza

Rosario •

• Martín García

Buenos Aires

Argentina

Uruguay

Atlantic Ocean

Rawson •
• Trelew

Argentina: Demographic Background

Population: 24 million (1970)
Size: 1,072,000 sq. miles
Gross National Product: $21 billion (1970)
Per Capita Income: $871 (1970)
Literacy: 91%
Exports: grain, beef, wool, hides
Life Expectancy: 67 years

4

**Urban Guerrilla
Warfare:
Argentina**

"We Argentines are leading exploited and oppressed lives and suffering from the brazen surrender of the country to imperialism by a handful of well-paid military men. We do not believe
in electoral farces, nor in promises of a 'Great
National Accord' or 'social peace,' implemented
with clubs, gases, and bullets. This is why we
call on all peoples to join the ERP and take up
arms for a just, free, and socialist Argentina
without exploiters or exploited."

Communiqué Number 6
People's Revolutionary Army
May 28, 1971

Introductory Essay

Urban guerrilla warfare in Argentina is an expression of both the
frustrations of the post-Perón experience and the contradictions
within Argentine society. The majority of Argentine urban guerrilla
organizations have been at least nominally Peronist, and their objective has been the return of Perón to power. Juan Domingo Perón's
uniqueness has been his ability to perceive the nation's social forces
correctly and to manipulate them more masterfully than his rivals.
Indeed, on the basis of policy made for a mere decade, Perón has become an Argentine political institution. After his overthrow in 1955,
no president, civilian or military, proved able to govern with any
degree of success. Perón's return in 1973 was a confirmation of this
fact and was the result of a political conjuncture forced, in large part,
by urban guerrilla warfare. As such, it constituted a victory for Peronist guerrillas and signalled the end of one phase of guerrilla warfare.
The objective of a social revolution through Peronism remains, and
here Perón's return brings a confrontation with the man, not the
myth. In a second phase of the struggle, non-Peronist urban guerrillas
seek both to expose the limitations of orthodox Peronism and to force

the next conjuncture, which will be the creation of a militant mass movement for a socialist Argentina.

The Peronist Experience

Juan Perón's unique effect on Argentine political life was first felt on October 17, 1945, when a massive demonstration by *descamisados* ("shirtless ones": workers) led to his release from imprisonment on the island of Martín García. As minister of war, minister of labor, and vice president in the military governments of Generals Pedro Ramírez and Edelmiro Farrell, Perón had slowly built a power base among the workers, until his frightened superiors decided to stop this accretion of power through imprisonment. They were too late, however, and, in a totally unprecedented confrontation, the factionalized military capitulated and labor freed its minister. Surprising as this event might have been, it was based on an astute analysis of the situation and considerable organizational effort by Perón and his charismatic mistress María Eva Duarte.

Perón's Argentina reflected a process of social and economic change which had begun in the late nineteenth century and was clearly evident by the 1940s: i.e., the shift from a rural, agricultural society to an urban, industrial nation. During the years 1935–1945 alone, the industrial work force, primarily centered in Buenos Aires Province, doubled to nearly one million, while industrial production increased by some 50 percent. This internal migration resulted in the proletarianization of the industrial centers of the littoral (Buenos Aires, Córdoba, Rosario). Nineteenth-century immigration, primarily European, had already created a middle class, which had found its political expression in the *Unión Cívica Radical* (ca. 1900–1930) and had wrested control of the government from the land-holding oligarchy. The new immigrants of the twentieth century were confronted with considerably less attractive prospects, however. Forced from the rural sector because of the low agricultural incomes which resulted from North American competition on the world market, the rural immigrants swelled the shanties ringing industrial centers. In this milieu, further depressed by declining living standards, inflation, and wage freezes, the unskilled urban migrant competed for industrial employment. Those who secured positions looked to labor unions to defend their interests. Unskilled workers in the newer unions tended to be organized by the Communist Party while those in skilled positions were generally socialist.

During the depression years, labor faced high unemployment and repression whenever its demands were militantly pressed. During the later 1930s and early 1940s, increased industrialization afforded greater employment security, but the trade unions failed to respond effectively to repression and internalized tensions. By 1942, the *Confederación General de Trabajadores* (CGT) had split into two wings; the socialist CGT 1 and the communist CGT 2, neither of which was successful in advancing workers' interests.

Workers were not alone in their dissatisfaction with the "Infamous Decade" of the 1930s. Political conflicts and polarization were exacerbated by rising national and international tensions. By 1940, serious political fissures were obvious within the nation's classes and institutions. President Ramón Castillo, who ruled through repression, corruption, and state of siege, contributed a great deal to the worsening situation. The Castillo years, especially after December 1941, reflected the contradictions of modern Argentina. Castillo continued to govern in the interests of the old land-owning oligarchy at a time when the country was assuming an urban character. The emerging industrial bourgeoisie found itself in opposition to the proagricultural policies of the regime, while Castillo's flagrant corruption alienated the middle class. A state of siege imposed after the Pearl Harbor incident and used to stifle opposition, combined with the suspicion that Castillo would, at the end of his term in 1943, pass presidential office to a crony, was too much.

It was in this atmosphere and with minimal opposition that a small clique of military officers seized political control of the country on June 4, 1943. The officers, who called themselves the GOU (*Grupo de Oficiales Unidos;* Group of United Officers), sought to reconstruct Argentina along corporatist lines and to establish an effective and forceful administration. Since its professionalization in the early 1900s by German missions, the Argentine military has come to equate its political interests with the national good, and its self-image of order and administrative competence has inescapably been translated, during periods of political chaos, into the arena of domestic politics. Indeed, no civilian president since the 1920s has managed to complete a term of elected office. The military itself, however, is no less influenced by political factionalism than the body politic in general. The GOU coup was implemented by a restive faction of junior officers opposed both to the direction of the civilian government and to the support given to that government by key senior officers.

Colonel Juan Domingo Perón was clearly the most perceptive member of the new GOU cabinet. In addition to his known talents (he was an expert skier and the outstanding fencer in the army), Perón also possessed an astute sense of Argentine sociopolitical forces at mid-century. This understanding had been cultivated by study at home and by a brief exposure to sociology and economics at Italian universities during his stint as observer with the Italian army in 1938–1939. Thus, it was no coincidence that Colonel Perón assumed the cabinet position of minister of labor, which, under his direction, was to become a base for unforeseen political power. Perón's strategy was to develop labor as a significant political force closely tied to his personal leadership. In this task, he succeeded beyond expectation and created a movement which has dominated recent Argentine history.

Perón's tactics for implementing his strategy included the cooptation of existing trade unions, the repression of leftist leadership, and the creation of new unions under his personal control. Perón sanctioned labor activities virtually unheard of in prior Argentine labor history: unionization, collective bargaining, strikes. As minister of labor, Perón officially represented the government in worker-employee arbitration, thereby developing an image of himself as an objective middleman in negotiations. At the same time, however, he worked to gain control over the actual unions themselves. Through an involved process of manipulation and intimidation, Perón gained control of the large but factionalized CGT. Similar efforts in other unions, both blue- and white-collar, resulted in a further accretion of power. In the urban meat-packing houses, Perón supported the workers led by Cipriano Reyes to the extent of turning the meat packers into his own personal labor shock-troops for his eventual confrontation with the antilabor forces in the cabinet. Perón also backed the formation of new unions, such as that of the sugar workers in northern Tucumán. Given the oligarchy's domination of the rural sector and the extent of its rural holdings, this unionization of the rural proletariat fundamentally challenged the provincial power structure.

Union ranks swelled from some 300,000 in 1943 to over 5 million by 1945 and labor's gains were many: real wages increased substantially; social security legislation, virtually nonexistent prior to 1944, was enacted; in 1945, a National Institute of Social Security was created for industrial, agricultural, and white-collar workers; the construction of low-cost housing projects began in 1943; and paid holidays and vacations were provided by a decree in 1945.

By 1945, Perón had established himself as patron of the emergent labor forces and strongman in the GOU government. In an attempt to curtail his ascendancy, a coup within the GOU succeeded in temporarily imprisoning him; but it was too late. The conspirators had misread the power of Perón's appeal to the masses and the organizational talents of Cipriano Reyes and Eva Duarte. The two began mobilizing workers immediately after Perón's imprisonment on October 9. The result was a direct confrontation between those who had imprisoned the influential vice president and the masses of workers who inundated Buenos Aires. Faced with internal quarrelling and an unprecedented display of civilian power, their self-confidence shaken, the military balked, then capitulated. On October 16, 1945, Perón was released and returned triumphantly to a mass demonstration in the capital and de facto control of the government. Then, relying on strong labor support, Perón orchestrated electoral legitimization of his position via a newly formed Labor Party. Victory in the presidential election of 1946 yielded de jure control of the government.

Perón's rule may be divided into two periods: the first, 1946–1952, was characterized by a series of administrative successes; the second, 1952–1955, by increasing difficulties, culminating in a military coup and Perón's exile. The successes of the 1940s were based on World War II and its effects on the Argentine economy. Beef and grain exports contributed to capital reserves which were then reinvested in the industrial sector. Establishment of the National Bank in 1944 and the Argentine Institute for the Promotion of Trade (IAPI) in 1946 furthered the prosperity of the early Perón years. During this period, the policy worked splendidly: national industries burgeoned, temporarily arresting the process of denationalization begun in the nineteenth century, and real wages rose over 30 percent between 1945 and 1949, expanding the domestic market.

Politically, Perón began to consolidate his position and to lay the foundations for the institution of *Peronismo* by setting forth the ideological concepts of the Third Position (in international affairs) and *Justicialismo* (in national affairs). Perón's political philosophy was, and remains, idiosyncratic: "Our Third Position is not a central position. It is an ideological position which is in the center, on the right, or on the left, according to specific circumstances." In foreign affairs, Perón's neutrality offended the United States, which wanted hemispheric support in its war with the Axis. Neutrality offered Argentine economic development a unique advantage in that Perón was able to play off Allies and Axis against each other, thereby securing for Argentina a measure of economic leverage and a favorable balance of trade. Nationally, the Third Position involved Perón's scheme to establish himself as the personal arbiter of Argentine life. Toward this end, universities were staffed with Peronist faculty while entrance requirements were lowered and fees abolished to allow greater access by the working class. Newspapers came under direct Peronist influence or were shut down, and individuals were jailed under the law of *desacato* (disrespect) if their behavior was deemed offensive to a government official.

Within the labor movement, *Personismo* came to mean increasing control over the leadership and direction of the assorted trade unions. Opposition to the Peronization of labor was dealt with in various ways, including the outright repression and imprisonment of dissident leaders, the creation of competing and parallel union structures, and the distribution of patronage to faithful leaders and followers. The CGT was converted into a Peronist organization; socialist and communist resistance to Peronism was smashed. Labor's goals were equated with those of Perón, and deviation was considered tantamont to treason. Thus, for example, Cipriano Reyes was to spend seven years in prison for resisting Peronization of the meat packers' union. The loyal were, however, well rewarded: minimum wage laws and a 40-hour week for urban labor; restriction of child labor; paid holidays and vacations; retirement pensions.

Additional benefits for the poor were dispensed through the Social Aid Foundation founded and directed by Eva Duarte Perón, now the president's wife. The Foundation served the paternalistic ends of the government by dispensing funds to those who were in need of such aid. Official philosophy presented this policy as social welfare and not charity, arguing that the recipients were the victims of the structural defects of Argentine society. The desired image is evidenced by the slogan "Perón delivers, Eva dignifies."

By 1950, Argentina began experiencing the vicissitudes of the world economy, and Perón, also facing internal problems, readjusted his goals with a second Five Year Plan. The 1949 world recession and the depletion of foreign exchange reserves (used for the nationalization of railroads, light and power utilities, telephone systems, etc.) contributed to a worsening balance of trade.[1] Meanwhile, oligarchic opposition to the drift of *Peronismo* was demonstrated by a decrease in agricultural production. Increased internal food consumption, accelerated by urban migration, and a series of droughts worsened the situation. The second Five Year Plan sought to redress the problem, but the adverse economic conditions made it impossible to satisfy everyone. Perón, true to his all-encompassing philosophy, now devalued the peso, stabilized wages, and readjusted prices to suit the agriculturally based oligarchy.

Conservative opposition, despite the new economic policies, continued. The Church, at first supportive of the government, began to criticize Perón. Peronization of the educational system, and a later decree ending religious instruction in schools, combined with pending reassessment of the relationship between Church and state, forced the Church's hand. Government scandals and Perón's acquisition of a 13-year-old mistress after Eva's death in 1952, outraged Catholic morality and alienated the moralistic middle classes. Perón responded through a series of decrees legitimizing "illigitimate" children (1953), legalizing divorce (1954), legalizing brothels, and eliminating religious holidays from the calendar.

[1] In 1948, for example, Perón squandered some $6 million of the nation's precious wartime reserves in purchasing the decrepit British-owned railroad system—one-third of the engines alone were nearly 40 years old and in abysmally poor repair.

Opposition also developed within the military, despite the fact that Perón had consciously effected reforms that improved the lot of enlisted men and had courted favor with officers: proclerical conservatives such as General Eduardo Lonardi chafed at Perón's feud with the Church; naval officers, primarily upper class, resented Perón's authoritarian style and the dominant position accorded the president's service, the army; and the whole officer corps disliked his interest in the proletariat. Numerous purges of officers in all services added to military disaffection. Nationalists noted the contradiction between Perón's highly touted economic nationalism and the realities of the second Five Year Plan, during which loans were secured from the United States Export-Import Bank and favorable concessions were granted to Armour and Company and Standard Oil.

Social tensions worsened throughout Perón's second term, and official repression only increased opposition. The beginning of the end came on September 16, 1955, when military garrisons revolted in the interior. Three days later, after a naval fleet under Admiral Isaac Rojas had positioned itself off Buenos Aires and threatened to shell the city, Juan Perón unceremoniously fled the country. Despite threats to arm the workers and fight until the end, Perón blanched at the prospects of civil war.

After the Fall: The Problem of Power

The military coup ushered in nearly twenty years of political chaos, during which neither military nor civilian governments were able to reconcile the social forces set in motion during the Perón years. The shadow of Peronism loomed over all of the nation's institutions—Congress, the courts, the universities, the unions, the military, and the Constitution. The series of post-Perón governments from Lonardi to Lanusse tried nearly everything—reconciliation, repression, cooptation, and cooperation—in a host of strategies for effective rule, but they all had the same result, failure. Finally, after an elaborate period of political maneuvering that was strongly influenced by severe internal violence and instability, the old dictator was recalled in June 1973.

General Eduardo Lonardi (September 1955–November 1955) set the tone for the immediate postcoup weeks with a "neither victors, nor vanquished," [2] speech in which he urged national reconciliation. Resentment of military hard-liners and the realities of *Peronismo* without Perón quickly demonstrated the inefficacy of such a policy. A military coup which came only eight weeks later and the subsequent administration of General Pedro Aramburu (December 1955–February 1958) underscored the point. Repression and not reconciliation was to be the hallmark of Aramburu's rule, as the General devoted his energies to the task of "de-Peronization." Aramburu dissolved Congress, purged the courts, and ruled by presidential decree. The problem of constitutionality was resolved by decreeing Perón's 1949 document void and decreeing an earlier 1853 version back into existence. The Peronist party was outlawed, Peronist officeholders were ousted, and some 300 Peronist business firms were "intervened" (i.e., occupied by government administrators). Economically, the government's "Prebisch Plan" (named after Raúl Prebisch, the Argentine economist) was biased toward business and particularly favorable to foreign enterprise. Wage controls and an end to Peronist economism provoked labor discontent and led to a general strike in November 1955. Aramburu's response was resolute: labor leaders were arrested, the strikers' pay was impounded, and the CGT was intervened. Military dissonance was dealt with no less harshly. An attempted coup by General Juan José Valle and other Peronists on June 9, 1956 was thwarted, and 27 officers, including Valle, were summarily executed.

A measure of Aramburu's perceived success was his decision to allow elections in 1958, an act which, ironically, demonstrated his failure. The Peronist party was banned, but a secret pact between Arturo Frondizi, the UCRI (*Unión Cívica Radical Intransigente;* Intransigent Radical Civic Union) candidate and Perón provided for the transfer of some two million votes to Frondizi, who won the election handily. Clearly, Aramburu's de-Peronization was a failure and the General more than a bit naive.

Civilian rule could not, in itself, arrest the serious socioeconomic downturn that had begun in the late 1940s. Inflation continued its spiral upward, the peso continued to decline steadily in value (from

[2] A phrase borrowed from a speech by the victorious caudillo Justo José Urquiza after he had defeated his rival Juan Manuel de Rosas at the Battle of Monte Caseros in 1852.

28 to the U.S. dollar in 1955 to 140 to the dollar in 1960), and the cost of living continued its steep climb (rising 400 percent in the period 1955–1960). Frondizi adhered to International Monetary Fund stabilization agreements and froze wages, thus worsening the position of workers, while offering foreign capitalists such preferential forms of treatment as the free repatriation of capital. Foreign industries utilized capital-intensive technology with negative effects on employment. This, combined with continuing urban migration, made for increased unemployment in the urban areas. Labor, already disenchanted by Frondizi's failure to honor election agreements to free jailed militants and meet union demands, was further alienated by the repression of strikes and the state of siege in 1962.

Aramburu's military faction, known as the *colorados*, hoodwinked by the 1958 election agreement, was even less pleased with the developments that followed. In exchange for the Peronist vote, Frondizi had promised legalization of the Peronist party. In 1962, the agreement was partly met, and Peronist candidates participated in provincial elections, winning in nine provinces including the important governorship of Buenos Aires (the military quickly forced Frondizi to intervene in five of the provinces to remove the elected Peronist candidates from office). This, the termination of CGT internment and its immediate return to Peronist control, and a neutral foreign policy, especially toward Cuba, incensed the reactionary and repressive *colorados*. On March 30, 1962, a *colorado* coup forestalled the scheduled presidential election.

For the next 17 months, a divided military, behind the caretaker Guido government, administered an equally divided country. Severe military conflicts were resolved through force of arms. In September 1962, the *azul* faction took over control from the *colorados*, and then consolidated their power after an unsuccessful *colorado* naval revolt seven months later. The *azules* sought a political formula based on civilian administration. Their problem was how to accomplish this without bringing to power Peronists, the spokesmen of the majority of the voting population, who were still unacceptable. A national front was the military's first proposed vehicle for resolving the lack of civilian consensus, but the major parties refused to participate. Next, a theoretically clever plan involving intricate proportional representation was tried and backfired.

The elections held in July 1963 only underscored national divisions —both civilian and military. Arturo Illia won the presidency with a meager 26 percent of the popular vote and then, quixotically, proceeded to alienate his few bases of support. Illia's three years in office were marked by a disregard for the very parties which had supported his candidacy, the alienation of powerful North American economic interests (provoked by a refusal to renew contracts), the repression of unions, and the circumscription of CGT autonomy. Within the military, the *azules* found that, despite their victory in the intraservice rivalry and their sponsorship of the 1963 elections, Illia proved pro*colorado* in sympathy. The government's neglect of the military's interest in undertaking a forceful hemispheric role, illustrated by the absence of Argentine troops from the invasion of the Dominican Republic in 1965, and its tolerance of communism at home further distressed the generals. As in 1963, forthcoming national elections forced the military's hand. Fearful of Peronist participation and its obvious outcome, officers again moved to preempt the inevitable. On June 28, 1966, President Illia was escorted from office, and a military junta under General Juan Carlos Onganía assumed power.

Exasperated with the complexities of civilian political maneuvering and haunted by the omnipresence of Peronism, Onganía devoted himself to the task of restructuring Argentine political life. His strategy seems to have involved an attempt to simplify political variables through direct confrontation and repression. Congress was dissolved, and political parties were outlawed and their property, including membership lists, confiscated. State and municipal officeholders— governors, mayors, members of the state and federal courts—were removed from office, and military officers took their places. Universities and unions were intervened and activists were imprisoned, exiled, or driven underground. Onganía, a devout Catholic, acted as a defender of Christianity and the moral and spiritual verities of Western Civilization. A National Security Council, composed of the president, five ministers of state, and the commander-in-chief of the three services formally administered Onganía's national regeneration.

An ever increasing number of Argentines did not share Onganía's vision and were driven to the conclusion that the general served not as paladin of a national revival, but as a pawn of multinational capital. The influx of foreign investment, which had begun during Perón's second Five Year Plan and increased in following administrations, accelerated rapidly during the Onganía period. This trend alienated the national bourgeoisie, which was ill-prepared to compete with the rich and powerful representatives of international capital. The middle classes also became increasingly disturbed at the disregard for constitutional rule and flagrant disrespect for legal amenities which characterized the military domination of national politics since Perón's fall.

The most serious and strident opposition to the Onganía regime, however, came from workers and revolutionaries. Perón's legacy to Argentine politics, an organized and militant trade union movement, could not easily be returned to the status quo ante Perón. Nevertheless, the unions were not politically monolithic and had become increasingly factionalized. After Perón's exit, unions were divided into three groupings: the Peronist "62 Organizations"; the Marxist "19"; and the noncommunist but anti-Peronist "32." The pressures of de-Peronization furthered polarization and factionalism: blue-collar workers were centered in the Peronist "62"; and after a series of shifts an independent white-collar group emerged. Continued conflict then led to a split between the militantly Peronist "62" under José Alonso and a more moderate, accommodationist sector under Augusto Vandor. The 1964 CGT *"Plan de Lucha"* (Plan of Struggle), involving a general strike and factory oppositions, definitively divided the "62" into pro-Alonso and pro-Vandor factions. In 1966, Vandor succeeded in displacing Alonso as secretary-general of the CGT, and Alonso bolted the CGT to form a rival "62 That Stand Up and Fight for Perón." This process reached its acme in 1968 with the formation of the "oppositionist" CGT of Raimundo Ongaro and the "participationist" Vandor-led CGT: the former hostile to and the latter cooperative with government policy.

Internal divisions within the trade unions did not impair the effectiveness of working-class resistance to military rule. The decade of the 1960s was a watershed in Argentine labor history. A wave of strikes and factory occupations, highlighted by a general strike in December 1966 which shut down some 80 percent of the nation's transport and industrial facilities, culminated in the so-called *Cordobazo* of May 1969. The *Cordobazo*, a general strike combined with a popular rebellion against the government in Córdoba, spread to other major centers of the industrial interior and demonstrated a new level in resistance to authoritarian rule. It also suggested events to come and was coincident with the start of urban guerrilla opposition to the military dictatorship.

Defeat in the Mountains

Guerrillas had appeared in rural Argentina briefly in the late 1950s and early 1960s. In 1959, an ill-fated guerrilla force, the Peronist Liberation Movement (*Movimiento Peronista de Liberación;* MPL) began operations in the mountains of northeast Tucumán Province. Popularly referred to as the "Uturuncos" (Quechua: "Tigermen"), after the nom de guerre of their commander, the 20 guerrillas had been influenced by the victory of the Cuban revolution. The unit, composed primarily of urbanites and students, lacked sufficient centralization of leadership, ideological homogeneity, and military discipline to be effective. After only a few weeks of combat, the force was surrounded and captured at its base camp.

Guerrilla activity again flared up in the northeast during mid-1963, but now the influence and composition was more Castroite. The People's Revolutionary Army (*Ejercito Guerrillero del Pueblo;* EGP), began operation in the mountainous countryside of Oran, Salta Province. The EGP, led by the Argentine journalist Jorge Masetti ("Commandante Segundo"), a former head of the Cuban news agency *Prensa Latina,* included three veterans of the Sierra Maestra as well as numerous *Peronistas*.[3] The organization was quickly infiltrated by police agents and, on March 4, 1964, was surrounded and defeated. Masetti fled to the woods where, it is assumed, he perished.

[3] Literature on the EGP is sparse: for the relationship with Che, allegedly personally involved ("Commandante Primero"?, or "Martin Fierro"?), see Ricardo Rojo, *My Friend Che* (New York: Dial Press, 1968), chapter 7; daily life in the *foco* is chronicled in the diary of the guerrilla "Hermes," reprinted in Luis Mercier Vega, ed., *Guerrillas in Latin America* (New York: Frederick A. Praeger, 1969). pp. 157–170.

A final attempt at a rural guerrilla *foco* in 1968 was quickly infiltrated by state security agents and then—while the embryonic unit was asleep in a training camp at Taco Ralo (Tucumán Province)—overwhelmed by a local police force. This group, the "October 17" detachment of the Peronist Armed Forces (*Fuerzas Armadas Peronistas;* FAP), had also been inspired by the continental strategy of Che Guevara and, like the Uturuncos and ERP, adhered to a curious mix of Peronist and Marxist ideologies. However, the FAP would not prove as ephemeral as previous rural organizations. Influenced by its failure in the countryside and by the surprising popular militancy of the *Cordobazo,* the FAP was reconstituted in the urban sector.

A confluence of factors, including the defeats of rural *focos* throughout Latin America, Che's death, the *Cordobazo,* the rise of urban guerrilla warfare in Brazil and Uruguay, and a realization of the urban nature of Argentine demography, suggested the obvious. The revolutionary strategy of the 1970s would necessarily be urban and involve a relationship with the working class.

Insurgency in the Cities

This new strategy made a dramatic entrance into the national consciousness with the execution of the accommodationist union leader Augusto Vandor on June 30, 1969. Vandor's execution by the National Revolutionary Army (ENR) thwarted a probable rapprochement between Onganía and the labor leader's sector of the CGT.[4] It also allowed for the subsequent gains within the union movement made by the intransigent Ongaro sector. Revolutionary justice was likewise visited on General Pedro Aramburu, the architect of de-Peronization. In "Communiqué #1," the Montoneros, an urban guerrilla organization formed in 1968, claimed credit for the kidnapping and trial of the ex-dictator. A second communiqué announced his death sentence and execution. To be fully understood, this act must be seen in its political context and not as a simple or random act of terrorism. Unpopular as he was for the severe repression of the immediate post-Perón years, Aramburu's execution would have in any case aroused considerable

---

[4] Vandor's relationship with the trade union movement and reasons for his execution are presented in "To the People of the Fatherland," an ENR communiqué of February 7, 1971 printed in *Cristianismo y Revolución,* April 1971, pp. 47–54.

sympathy. However, the Montoneros' action was more significant: it destroyed Aramburu's maneuvering toward a second seizure of power, a fact which was widely known but, until then, ineffectively opposed. The kidnapping and sentence illustrate the organization's tactic of a "military action . . . which implies a political stand in itself." [5] Successful in its own terms, the Aramburu incident was a significant act in a process of escalating labor demands and revolutionary violence against the regime, and as such it contributed to Onganía's downfall on June 18, 1970.

The military faction which displaced Onganía, headed by General Roberto Marcello Levingston, was no more successful in dealing with the country's social and economic problems or with the rising guerrilla and labor opposition to military domination. In 1970 alone, $200 million was spent on counterinsurgency matériel. Economically, a worsening of conditions continued: on the day before the Levingston coup, the peso had been devalued; during 1970 the rate of inflation was 20 percent and this same rate was projected for 1971. Beef exports dwindled as herds declined both quantitatively and qualitatively. And the cost of living increased 10 percent in the first two months of 1971 alone.

A serious and violent wave of strikes swept the country. On November 12, 1971, a general strike demanded a return to electoral democracy and civilian rule. Strikes and occupations of industrial plants in the interior, principally Córdoba, seriously threatened Levingston's position. Labor resistance crested with a strike at the Fiat factory in Córdoba. The strike, begun in the second week of March by the SITRAC and SITRAM unions, developed in the direction of factory occupations and a popular uprising in the city. By March 18, property damage had reached about $4 million, and the government was forced to declare a "state of emergency" and to call in troops to occupy the city.

Occasionally, workers and guerrillas united in resistance, as, for example, in the SITRAC/SITRAM occupations, which had been aided by militants from the People's Revolutionary Army (*Ejército Revolucionario del Pueblo;* ERP). Other guerrilla actions underscored their

[5] From a Montoneros statement printed in *Cristianismo y Revolución,* November–December 1970, p. 14.

support of the masses while demonstrating government inadequacies and revolutionary alternatives. Starting in 1970, there had been a rapid escalation in revolutionary attacks against the regime, and techniques were initiated which have been continued to the present. A variety of actions evolved, aimed at: acquiring organizational necessities; demonstrating a revolutionary alternative to government neglect; seizing and trying government figures or agents of foreign powers; and establishing dual power. These categories are not mutually exclusive, however, and each action must be understood in its specific context.

The cumulative effect of revolutionary insurgency and working-class militancy was too much for Levingston. A retired colonel's quip that "Levingston will fall the day he tries to take a serious initiative," was prophetic. Criticized for indecision and incompetence in meeting guerrilla insurgency, by now a daily occurrence on a national scale, Levingston moved decisively against strike- and riot-torn Córdoba. When General Alejandro Lanusse, the commander of Córdoba's Third Army Corps, refused to take the president's advice regarding increased repression, Levingston dismissed him. In the confrontation that followed, Lanusse, widely regarded as the strongman in the armed forces, ousted the hapless Levingston. Combined labor and revolutionary opposition had precipitated the collapse of the second military government in nine months and ushered into office a general noted, comparatively, as a moderate and a constitutionalist.[6]

The junta led by Lanusse faced a continuing process of revolutionary warfare, now coming primarily from five organizations. In addition to the Peronist Armed Forces and the Montoneros, the opposition now included the Trotskyist People's Revolutionary Army (*Ejército Revolucionario del Pueblo;* ERP), and the Marxist-Leninist Liberation Armed Forces (*Fuerzas Armadas de Liberación;* FAL) and Revolutionary Armed Forces (*Fuerzas Armadas Revolucionarias;* FAR). All three groups surfaced in early 1970 and continually escalated their assaults on the regime.

The FAR appeared at the time of the coup against Onganía and

[6] In an interview in 1971, Lanusse, who was jailed during the Perón era, noted his opposition to Perón's authoritarian rule rather than his social and economic policies. See *New York Times,* 7 April 1971, p. 43.

established its potential with the occupation of the town of Garín on July 30, 1970. The organization's roots, however, go back to Che Guevara's attempt to create a continental revolution, when the FAR was formed as the Argentine arm of the struggle. Che's defeat and the unexpected militancy of the *Cordobazo* in 1969 forced the group to reappraise its strategy and to turn toward urban insurgency. The FAR has orchestrated its actions in order to develop its organizational capability carefully in a period of increased recruitment as well as repression. The capture of four militants in Córdoba in early 1971 and the exposure of vital data which followed, temporarily arrested the FAR's development and dictated a return to an emphasis on actions of tactical importance. Ultimately, the FAR envisions a program of "people's army, people's war." Curiously, the organization calls itself Marxist-Leninist-Peronist: Marxism-Leninism is considered a "theoretical instrument" of social analysis and Peronism an expression of the experience of the Argentine masses. The FAR's gravitation toward Peronism appears more a function of political necessity than of internal ideology, however; and this drift may well represent tactical rather than strategic considerations.

Both the FAL and the ERP are politically less ambiguous. The FAL's origins go back to 1962 and the Frondizi administration, but the public became aware of the group's existence only much later, with the kidnapping of Paraguayan Consul Joaquin Waldemar Sánchez in March 1970. The FAL explicitly rejects Peronist optimism regarding reforms from above, and seeks to create "a different process where the people are really proponents of history." This process begins with integration of the urban poor, students, and workers into a revolutionary movement. Ultimately, the struggle is to proceed from urban guerrilla warfare to a combined urban-rural thrust, hopefully in combination with a continental upheaval in which a broad liberation front composed of national and domestic revolutionary organizations will unite in a socialist, anti-imperialist revolution. The *Cordobazo* revealed the limitations of spontaneity and the need of an armed vanguard to lead the struggle: the Liberation Armed Forces considers tself to be that vanguard, and the group moved into a very active role n 1970–1971. Relative quiescence in the last two years has led to peculation that the organization has merged, perhaps with the ERP.

The People's Revolutionary Army, or ERP, was formally established as the armed wing of the Workers' Revolutionary Party (*Partido Revolucionario de los Trabajadores;* PRT) at the party's Fifth Congress on July 28, 1970. Included in the eleven member executive committee of the PRT are representatives of the military committee, who form the leadership nucleus of the ERP. Although formal adherence to revolutionary warfare was decided upon in July 1970, ERP actions had begun months earlier, and Mario Roberto Santucho, ERP founder, had already been arrested for revolutionary activities and had then managed to escape police custody. Following a series of actions involving expropriations of arms and matériel, the ERP, in late 1970, initiated a spectacular series of "Hunger Commando" seizures and distributions of food and milk to the urban poor. Most of these actions were centered in the industrial interior—Córdoba, Rosario, Tucumán —where the organization felt the revolutionary struggle to be most developed. PRT cadres were involved in the resistance of sugar workers to unemployment in Tucumán in the late 1960s, and ERP guerrillas actively participated in the SITRAC/SITRAM occupations of Fiat plants in Córdoba during December 1971.

While their present strategy is marked by attempts at creating direct links between the urban guerrilla movement and the proletariat, the ERP looks to a future stage in which a rural front will be initiated. This will follow after a period of intensified urban warfare, increased recruitment and the consolidation of cadres, and actions designed to bring about the requisite objective conditions. Meanwhile, the PRT-ERP seeks a sharpening of contradictions within Argentine society and, through direct involvement in the struggle, a heightening of mass consciousness regarding the regime. Thus, the organization works with workers and the urban poor to demonstrate both the possibilities of a socialist alternative and the limitations of Peronist paternalism.

Lanusse's regime was transitional, leading to elections, civilian rule, and, ultimately, Perón's return from seventeen years of exile. This extremely complicated course of events was characterized by contradictory public statements and counterstatements and by byzantine maneuvering and countermaneuvering by all involved. It should be noted that none of the protagonistic forces in the struggle are monolithic.

The military is seriously divided on questions of constitutionality, national development, and foreign policy, and thus on the acceptability of Perón's return. Peronism has become a catchall for a host of personalities and ideologies capitalizing on the popular nostalgia for the populist experience. As such, the word is now bereft of precise meaning but strongly laden with emotional import. Internal contradictions and tensions within the Peronist grouping grew sharper as a return to power became increasingly probable.

The one certainty in this process has been the failure of the successive military governments to rule with popular support, political institutions, or a coherent economic policy. This absence has led to internal chaos and a reliance on military force as a substitute for an administrative program. In economic terms, the Lanusse years continued the pattern of previous military regimes: a rate of inflation over 50 percent per annum; capital outflow and a decrease of national reserves; rising wholesale and retail food prices; increasing military expenditures—up 75 percent between 1971 and 1973 alone. Resistance to these worsening conditions in the form of strikes, riots, and urban rebellions have led to greater hostility between civilians and the military. A 15 percent wage increase on May 1, 1972, while a national palliative, only resulted in the abrupt termination of negotiations for a prospective International Monetary Fund loan, the government's only prospective savior in the crisis.

Significant guerrilla actions through mid-1972 exploited local issues to demonstrate these inequities. Thus, for example, Stanley Sylvester, British consul and manager of Swift and Company, was kidnapped on May 23, 1971 in Rosario. Swift, under Sylvester, had fired 4,000 workers without recompense. The kidnapping publicized the plight of these citizens manipulated by a foreign hand and succeeded in forcing reforms by Swift. One week later, ERP demands were met: the workers were rehired, with compensation for lost wages; working conditions in the packinghouses were improved; and $50,000 in food was distributed in Rosario slums. The "Hunger Commando" had taken a new form.

An initially similar kidnapping ten months later resulted in the death of Oberdan Sallustro, head of Fiat-Argentina. Lanusse, fearing that capitulation would encourage repetition, forbade Fiat to meet the ERP demands (payment of $1 million to be distributed to Córdoba's poor) and himself refused to meet demands that included the release of 50 political prisoners and jailed SITRAC/SITRAM workers. This led to an impasse, which was only resolved when a government patrol stumbled on the ERP "people's prison." In the ensuing fracas, Sallustro was executed by the fleeing guerrillas.[7] While the international press was horrified by this "terrorism," Argentines remembered Sallustro's intransigence in the face of labor confrontations and the resultant bloody repression of the striking SITRAC/SITRAM workers. Moreover, Fiat, which was about to invest $90 million in Argentina, was incensed by this government which was willing to sacrifice the company's chief representatives and turned instead to the more favorable investment climate of Brazil. Again the guerrillas had managed to exploit an issue and publicly repudiate Lanusse's policy.

Contrary to government aims, the hard line adopted in the Sallustro affair did not lead to the abandonment of kidnapping as a guerrilla tactic. Quite the contrary, the host of abductions beginning in December 1972 and continuing into the present directly stems from governmental inability to protect executives against revolutionary will. Worse yet, even high military officials proved vulnerable: General Juan Carlos Sánchez, perhaps the most outspoken proponent of repression, was assassinated on the same day as Sallustro. Sánchez had gained the enmity of the working class in Rosario through his energetic and harsh strikebreaking. His direction of a vigorous counterinsurgency program led to the boast that he had eliminated 85 percent of the guerrillas. On April 10, 1972, a combined ERP-FAR tactical unit demonstrated the hollowness of that figure, leaving the General's bullet-ridden body and the slogan: "Sánchez, the 15 percent lives!"

Military revenge took the form of a massacre four months later at Trelew Airport. The airport had been occupied by guerrillas following an escape from nearby Rawson Prison. Owing to an unfortunate contingency, only half the group was able to board the plane that had been expropriated to take them to Chile. Military forces surrounded

---

[7] One of the guerrillas, official investigation would disclose, was José ("Joe") Baxter. Baxter's urban guerrilla experience is lengthy and legendary: he began as a militant in the ultra rightist Tacuara during the 1960s and, a decade later, had become a member of the Trotskyist ERP.

those who remained, who then surrendered and were placed in a local navy jail. One week later, the captured guerrillas were machine-gunned: sixteen were killed, three wounded. Early government reports of an attempted escape were soon discredited and official complicity confirmed. Perón, who has found guerrilla warfare "the natural escape of oppressed persons," sent flowers to the victims and joined the public clamor against official violence.

Lanusse was faced not only with external opposition but also with the usual military factionalism; and of late the most symptomatic division has been that between *peruanistas* and *brasileños*. The *peruanistas,* who sympathize with the developmental model currently followed by the reformist Peruvian military government, are the numerically stronger grouping and draw their greatest support from the air force and junior officers in the army. Ex-President Roberto Levingston is a leading figure in this camp. The *brasileños,* who sympathize with the Brazilian military dictatorship, find their support among senior army officers with ties to important financial interests. The *brasileños* are implacably anti-Peronist.

In 1971, overt opposition to Lanusse's position twice took the form of coup attempts. In May, the Peronist General Eduardo Labanca led an unsuccessful uprising; and later, in October, two *peruanista* army colonels, opposed to the possibility of civilian elections with Peronist participation, revolted. This attempt also failed, but other tensions remained. Generals Juan Carlos Sánchez and Alcides López Aufranc, both hard-line *brasileños,* opposed accommodation with Peronism, particularly in elections. Sánchez's assassination by the ERP in April 1972 removed him as a potential obstacle (he was plotting a coup at the time of his death). López Aufranc, in a twist, came out in favor of elections, albeit with the understanding that, after the civilians had failed to make good an impossible situation, the military could again seize power. He felt that elections would force the nation to deal with reality, thereby scotching Perón's myth and simplifying the political process. Lanusse's decision to allow elections should be seen in this context: a steadily worsening economic situation; continuing labor and popular resistance; and an escalated revolutionary attack on dictatorial rule.

"Cámpora to the Presidency, Perón to Power"

By 1971, the probability of elections was about the only clear issue emerging from the baroque and confusing political atmosphere, and the specific nature of the elections formed the subject of intense and vitriolic disputation by all involved for the next two years. The dominant voices within the military had resolved to end this period of political control in the hopes of a future resolution more to their satisfaction. The precise circumstances for such a retreat, however, remained a point of contention until the electoral denouement on March 11, 1973.

Perón's position remained, as ever, unclear save in his determination to return to power. Juan Perón, 77 years old in 1972, had lost none of his astuteness and wielded his myth to effect in a series of intricate moves leading toward a dignified and effective return from exile. It is here only necessary to note the more salient developments: first, Lanusse's "Great National Accord" aimed at Peronist electoral participation within the military's parameters (i.e., cooperation and cooptation in national unification through the adoption of an electoral form favorable to the military) was rejected; next, a well-timed but brief visit to Argentina on November 17, 1972 was turned to advantage by an independent meeting between Perón and 22 important labor and political leaders who supported his demands (e.g., the release of political prisoners); then, Héctor Cámpora, a proven loyalist, was chosen as Perón's presidential stand-in for the elections of March 1973; and finally, Cámpora's victory was followed by his resignation from the presidency and the announcement of new elections in which Perón would be a legal candidate.

In late 1972, the results of Perón's relentless drive toward power appeared inevitable. Military intelligence was most precise in predicting Cámpora's eventual victory (within three to five percentage points) despite repeated maneuvers aimed at sabotaging the situation. Further complicating these developments, and of greater moment, were the machinations of major and minor figures within the Peronist umbrella FREJULI (*Frente Justicialista de Liberación;* Peronist Liberation Front). As elections moved toward realization, cleavages within Peronism crystallized. Perón's absence had allowed the growth of an entire spectrum of political factions within his movement, which also suffers from an overabundance of bureaucratic hacks and nepotists within the party apparatus and the trade union leadership.

The right enjoys Perón's confidence and includes such personalities as Jorge Osinde, a former chief of security and an infamous torturer, José López Rega, once Perón's personal secretary, and union leaders like Rogelio Coria and José Rucci with their base in the Buenos Aires CGT. The left is centered in the Peronist Youth (e.g., ex-Secretary General Rodolfo Galimberti), the Peronist urban guerrillas (*formaciones especiales;* special formations), and the militant provincial trade unions. A scramble has ensued as these interests have sought to establish their positions firmly within a nebulous Peronism.

The tensions between the two camps have twice surfaced in the form of spectacular and violent shoot-outs at public ceremonies. The most publicized incident occured on the occasion of Perón's homecoming on June 20, 1973 at Ezeiza Airport. Hundreds of thousands of the faithful had gathered to welcome the leader home from exile when conservative unionists and thugs under Osinde's command fired upon Peronist Youths carrying banners emblazoned with the names and insignias of urban guerrilla organizations. In the melee that followed, some 30 persons were killed and 300 injured. Later, Osinde and Norma Kennedy were accused of torturing prisoners in a nearby hotel room. This incident had been prefaced by an earlier clash at a commemorative ceremony for the martyred J. J. Valle, leader of the 1956 Peronist revolt. Here, rival groups of right-wing unionists and Peronist guerrillas degenerated from Peronist versus socialist chants to a shoot-out which produced numerous casualties.

The Peronist election victory and its aftermath has occasioned a reassessment of the situation and consequent adjustments by the urban guerrillas. Strategy following the Trelew massacre had addressed itself to revolutionary justice and the approaching presidential election of March 1973. Revolutionary justice involved reprisals against military officers held directly responsible for Trelew and began with the assassination of Admiral Emilio R. Berisso, the ranking naval intelligence officer on December 28, 1972. A combined ERP-FAR-Montonero commando claimed responsibility for the action, the first in a series of assassinations and kidnappings of military officers. In addition to meting out vengeance for fallen comrades, these actions were also designed to put the government on the defensive and assure some bargaining power in the election period. The kidnapped officers were held as leverage for the release of political prisoners.

Most Peronist guerrillas publicly supported Héctor Cámpora's presidential candidacy with the proviso that revolutionary change follow the electoral victory. The Marxist left, most notably the ERP, warned of reactionary influences within the Peronist camp, cautioned against paternalism, and stressed the need for socialism at the grass roots level. Tensions within the ERP over the issue of support for Cámpora led to the fission of an ERP-22 de Agosto (ERP-22 August; named for the date of the Trelew massacre) faction. The ERP-22 de Agosto actively supported the FREJULI ticket headed by Cámpora while the main-line ERP maintained a critical neutrality toward the elections.

After Perón's bloody homecoming at Ezeiza Airport, the support of Peronist urban guerrillas and the neutrality expressed by the Marxist ERP and FAL shifted to opposition by the Marxists and critical support by the FAR and FAP. The position of the Montoneros, on the whole the most conservative of the Peronist special formations, is less clear. Recent Montonero statements are inconsistent; at times a socialist and critical antireformist position is argued, but other communiqués suggest—at least rhetorically—the influence of the more conservative sectors of Peronism.[8] The Ezeiza incident catalyzed political forces within the movement and may well have presaged forthcoming developments. Certainly a confrontation much more serious than that at Ezeiza is in the works. Paramilitary death squads have expanded operations since Cámpora's May 15 inauguration; existing death squads have executed over 50 leftists (including, for example, the FAR leader Juan Pable Mastre in 1971) during the last three years.

Juan Perón meanwhile continues to juggle his political equation to suit developing circumstances. Thus, in the wake of Ezeiza, Jorge Osinde was shuffled from head of the department of tourism to director of internal security and the leftist Esteban Righi was simultane-

[8] For a glimpse of these tendencies see Fernando Vaca Narvaja's comments in "The Argentine Guerrillas Speak," reprinted below, and the entries of May 24 and June 27, 1973 in the Chronology.

ously replaced as minister of the interior by the conservative (and non-Peronist) retired General Miguel Ángel Iníguez. Meanwhile, the conservative José Gelbard, spokesman for the national bourgeoisie, continues as minister of finance and the rightist José López Rega remains as minister of social welfare. Other important business and industrial figures surround Perón. The guerrillas have publicized these relationships as well as Perón's close personal contacts with Spanish and Italian industrialists; it seems that anti-imperialism, a constant Peronist theme, remains essentially anti-Yankee. Of even greater significance to the left was Cámpora's sudden resignation and the announcement of Perón's candidacy in a new presidential election. As his vice president, Perón chose his wife Isabel, a conservative ex-barmaid lacking in Eva's commitment to the poor, over the more liberal Cámpora. It seems that Cámpora's willingness to negotiate with the guerrillas and his subsequent inability to influence their maneuvering, contributed strongly to his removal. Perón has already shown his preference for a harder line.

Presently, only the ERP is pursuing a strategy of confrontation to expose the contradictions within Peronism and the movement's inherent limitations. Both the ERP[9] and the ERP-22 de Agosto[10] have announced an independent pursuit of a socialist revolution from below —tantamount to throwing down the glove to resurgent Peronism. After the election, but prior to Ezeiza, the ERP took a position of continued hostility toward the military and industrial sectors, while maintaining neutrality vis à vis Cámpora and Perón. Ezeiza prompted an analysis openly critical of Peronism: "we do not consider its bourgeois and bureaucratic leadership capable of carrying out the revolu-

[9] The ERP's position is presented in the communiqué "To the People: Why and Against Whom the ERP Will Continue Fighting," issued on May 30, 1973: "At the risk of being misunderstood by many of our compatriots . . . the present parliamentary government has neither the intentions, nor the capability—because of its methods and its composition—to lead the revolutionary struggle efficiently."
[10] The ERP-22 de Agosto analysis is spelled out in a communiqué of July 19, 1973: ". . . the leadership of the Peronist movement attempts to distort the historic contents of the popular triumph of 11 March, betraying the aspirations and wishes of the workers . . . the Ruccis, López Rega, Gelbard, Osinde, and company have no place in the popular movement . . . national reconstruction should be paid for by the rich, the persons responsible for the disaster, and not the poor, who are tired of working so that others might pocket the profits. The people want a revolution, and no maneuver will prevent them from achieving this aim."

tionary changes the nation requires. We respect, however, the people's hope in Peronism . . ." [11]

The Peronist guerrillas refused to lay down their arms despite Cámpora's demands that all clandestine organizations do so. All three major organizations—FAP, FAR, Montoneros—acknowledged the possibilities attendant to the election victory, but noted the need to develop the movement in terms of economic improvements, social reforms, the creation of popular militias, and the establishing of popular control over the military. As a joint communiqué cautioned: "We have won a battle with the election victory, but the war is not over."

For the military, ever faithful watchdogs of Argentine politics, the war is likewise not over. Unable to govern effectively in the eighteen years following Perón's departure, the armed forces at last bowed to popular will. The decision to allow free elections was shrewd, as political considerations must now consider Perón as man, not myth. It is symbolic that violence prevented Perón's return at Ezeiza and instead forced a contingency landing—at a nearby military airfield.

Large herds and bumper crops may well forestall economic difficulty in the coming year, obviating a perennial difficulty. If Perón is to persist as a political arbiter, however, he must move to restore a centrist equilibrium to his movement. Presently, considerable energy is concentrated in the political left, Peronist and non-Peronist, while much of Perón's support is derived from those who consider him the country's last bastion against communism. Thus, one might expect a forthcoming attempt to repress the most outspoken of Perón's critics, beginning with the ERP. Such a move would present a moment of truth within the more internally heterogeneous special formations. Urban guerrilla warfare will undoubtedly face its greatest test in the months to come. Meanwhile for the guerrillas, the choice remains: "la patria peronista," or, "la patria socialista."

Postscript

On September 23, 1973, Juan Domingo Perón was elected president with 62 percent of the vote, an event of immense importance since it means that henceforth Perón himself will define the policies of the Peronist government. No longer can he conveniently encourage muriad

[11] *Foreign Broadcast Information Service*, 24 July 1973, p. B5.

contradictory tendencies, repudiating failures and affirming advances. In terms of the left-right struggle within Peronism, the importance of which Perón has so consistently denied, the result will be a retreat from both the revolutionary rhetoric of the Lanusse period and the flirtation with the Left of the Cámpora period. Perón's policy has been articulated, and its main points of stability (the "social pact" between labor and national industry and a reliance on European investment) are hardly the social revolution the Peronist Left envisioned.

Organizationally, Perón has attempted to purge the movement and the government of leftist elements, pushing until mass resistance is encountered. Within days of assuming office, Perón, now clad in his reinstated lieutenant-general's uniform, declared war on the ERP and Marxism. The assassination of José Rucci on September 25, while probably not the work of the ERP, served to intensify Perón's campaign against the Left. The ERP, for its part, emerged from a period of intense internal struggle to pick up the gauntlet by stepping up its military action.

There was nothing new or unexpected in this open confrontation, as both Perón and the ERP had clearly indicated their respective paths before the election. On September 14, the ERP had assaulted an army sanitation post, killing a colonel, and it continued its campaign of kidnappings against industrialists. Meanwhile, Perón was reorganizing the *Justicialista* movement, shuffling those sympathetic to the Left (e.g., Galimberti, Abal Medina, Righi, and Cámpora) out of power. The result was to increase the pressure on the Peronist left—JP, unions, and guerrillas—which had hitherto been content to organize quietly while the contradictions within Peronism gradually forced a clarification of the issues. Indeed, the Peronist left found itself increasingly the target of right-wing attacks, and responded in kind.

While most of the left Peronist organizations still adhere to Perón personally, their position in the movement is weakening. Gradually, sections of the special formations are returning to action against the government. A striking example of this occurred on November 22, when the FAP assassinated Ford executive John Swint and two of his bodyguards, with no effort made at kidnapping. Perón's attempts at increased security for foreign businessmen were belied again two weeks later, when five bodyguards and military protection failed to prevent the ERP from taking Esso executive Victor Samuelson. During 1973, there were over 170 business kidnappings, leading to an exodus of 60 percent of all foreign businessmen.[12] On January 19, 1974, the ERP attacked the Azul garrison, killing one sentry, a colonel and his wife, and abducting another colonel, while losing two guerrillas. Stiffened repression then led to the resignation of eight leftist deputies and their expulsion from the movement. These events may indicate a general regrouping of left Peronist and guerrilla organizations outside the boundaries of official Peronism, as witnessed by the October 1973 merger of the Montoneros and the FAP.

[12] *Time*, 14 January 1974, p. 25.

Chronology

June 4, 1943	GOU military coup, led by General Pedro Ramírez and including Colonel Juan Perón, seizes power; Perón serves as minister of war, minister of labor, and then vice president.
October 17, 1945	Colonel Juan Perón, temporarily jailed by GOU officers, is brought to power by a massive demonstration of *descamisados* in Buenos Aires.
1946–1951	First Five Year Plan: period of economic prosperity and nationalism; expropriation of railroads, urban transport, light and power utilities, telephones; minimum wages, 40-hour week, paid holidays and vacations for workers; IAPI created to channel agricultural profits into industrial sector.
1952–1955	Second Five Year Plan: period of declining economic prosperity, beginning of denationalization (e.g., Standard Oil and Armour and Co. granted concessions); decrease in agricultural production, wage stabilization, price readjustments; rising Church opposition.
1955 September 19	Perón overthrown by military; General Eduardo Lonardi appointed provisional president.
November 13	General Pedro Aramburu assumes presidency.
November 14–17	Aramburu crushes revolutionary general strike by CGT (General Workers Confederation); unions promptly de-Peronized.
June 9, 1956	Peronist military revolt led by General Juan José Valle suppressed; Valle and 26 others executed.

| May 1, 1958 | Arturo Frondizi, elected president by UCRI (Intransigent Radical Civic Union) with Peronist backing, assumes office. |
| December 1959 | Uturunco guerrilla movement suppressed in Tucumán. |

1962

March	Frondizi allows Peronists to enter candidates in provincial elections; Peronists win in nine provinces; military forces Frondizi to "intervene" in five provinces to nullify Peronist victories.
March 30	Military coup by *colorado* faction ousts Frondizi and installs José M. Guido as civilian figurehead.
August 23	Felipe Vallese, militant Peronist Union leader kidnapped and executed by unknown group.
September	Military infighting between *azul* and *colorado* factions; *azules* triumph.

1963

April 3–6	*Colorado* naval revolt crushed.
October 12	Arturo Illia, president elect, takes office.
October 23	Tacuara guerrillas, led by José ("Joe") Baxter, assault Policlinico Bancario, Buenos Aires; 12,000,000 pesos expropriated.

1964

| March 4 | EGP, led by Jorge Masetti, defeated in mountains of Oran, Salta Province. |

1966

| June 28 | *Azul* military coup, led by General Juan Onganía deposes Illia; Onganía dissolves Congress, |

disbands political parties, packs Supreme Court, suppresses unions.

December 14   General strike: 80 percent of transportation, industry and commerce shut down.

1967

January 1   Argentine citizen Silvio Halperín Burnstein arrested in Montevideo, Uruguay, carrying a pistol, 100,000 pesos, and incriminating letters from Argentine leftists addressed to their Uruguayan counterparts.

March 1   CGT "Plan de Acción" general strike begins; Onganía decrees six major unions illegal and freezes their accounts; strike fizzles.

Police arrest two militants with Castroite literature and intelligence data in northern Santa Fe Province; the two are allegedly linked to a guerrilla training camp at Fortún Olmos, Santa Fe Province.

March 6   Guerrilla training camp at Fortún Olmos investigated by authorities; 100 students had allegedly received guerrilla training at the camp between November–December 1966.

May 8   Chief of Argentine Rural Guard reports Bolivian ELN guerrilla *foco* retreating toward Argentine border.

May 18   Police raid on apartment of Ramón Zavala yields weapons, ammunition, 60,000,000 pesos in counterfeit bonds, checks, and banknotes, 120 Paraguayan passports; subsequent arrests net five other militants with "vast underground links in Uruguay."

June 16   Six militants arrested in Córdoba; captured documents indicate formation of "terrorist cells" in urban zones, particularly Córdoba and Tucumán.

July 11	Troops sent to Bolivian border to thwart possible ingress of ELN led by Che Guevara.
July 21	Newspapers note unconfirmed reports of two guerrillas armed and dressed in battle fatigues in area of Tartagal, Salta Province.
July 24	Local airport at Tartagal, Salta, temporarily converted into military base; observation planes with photographic equipment scour region for guerrillas. U.S. military advisors present.
September 20, 1968	Police force captures FAP "October 17" detachment at Taco Ralo, Tucumán; 14 guerrillas arrested, 40 arrests follow throughout the country.

1969

May	Cordobazo: *Workers rebellion begins in Córdoba; 20 killed, including student Emilio Jauregui, as military occupies the city; revolt spreads to Rosario, Tucumán, Corrientes.*
June 26	FAR bombs nine "Minimax" (Rockefeller-owned) supermarkets shortly before Governor Nelson Rockefeller arrives in Buenos Aires.
June 30	ENR unit occupies Metallurgical Workers Union facility, tries Augusto Vandor for suborning workers' interests, and dynamites the building.
	President Onganía declares state of siege.

1970

January 3	FAP command occupies Villa Piolín in Buenos Aires, disarming guard and distributing toys to children.

February 1	FAP unit occupies Junior Officer section of Campo de Mayo garrison, Buenos Aires, taking arms.
March 17	Bombing of Misereo Plaza, Buenos Aires, by ERP.
March 24	Joaquin Waldemar Sánchez, Paraguayan consul, kidnapped by FAL command.
March 29	Waldemar Sánchez released.
April 5	Attack on Campo de Mayo military garrison by FAL commandos.
April 12	Felipe Vallese unit (FAP) occupies National Maritime Headquarters in Tigres; 15 machine guns, 4 rifles, and numerous pistols seized.
April 27	ERP unit attacks police station in Rosario.
May 22	FAP seizes 602 cases of dynamite in Buenos Aires.
May 29	Ex-President Pedro Aramburu kidnapped by J. J. Valle command (Montoneros).
June 1	*General Pedro Aramburu tried by revolutionary court for 271 crimes (including execution of J. J. Valle and 26 other Peronists); executed by Montoneros.*
June 2	President Onganía reinstitutes death penalty, banned since 1886, to combat guerrillas.
June 6	Horacio Wenceslao Orue, photographer, arrested as suspect in Aramburu affair.
June 8	Onganía deposed by military coup.
June 18	General Roberto Marcello Levingston sworn in as president in aftermath of coup.
	Two million pesos taken from Banco de la Provincia de Córdoba by FAL.

July 1	Town of La Calera occupied by 25 guerrillas from Eva Perón, Uturuncos, San Martín, and May 29th Montonero commandos; bank, telephone center, post office occupied; two guerrillas captured.
July 6	Perón endorses armed revolutionary action.
July 7	Emilio Masa (Montonero) killed.
July 9	Montoneros seize 28,000,000 pesos from Banco del Interior in Laguna Larga, Córdoba.
July 11	Mario Roberto Santucho, ERP founder, wounded by police but escapes from hospital.
July 21	Suspect in Aramburu slaying killed by police in Córdoba.
July 27	Radio Rivadavia seized by Eva Perón command (FAP).
July 30	FAR guerrillas occupy town of Garin; railroad and police station occupied, telephone lines cut, and money taken from banks.
August 8	FAL distributes truckload of poultry to poor in Córdoba.
August 24–27	PRT National Congress endorses armed line; ERP formally announces strategy of revolutionary warfare.
August 27	MRA team of twenty men seizes weapons and office equipment from police station in Córdoba.
August 28	José Alonso, secretary-general of Garment Workers Union, executed by guerrillas.
September 1	Occupation of Ramos Mejia branch of Banco de Galicia y Buenos Aires by Montoneros; 13,750,-000 pesos seized.
September 16	Twenty-three bombings carried out in Buenos Aires and Córdoba by FAP.

September 18	Chiquito Barrios commando (ERP) raids police station in Rosario, seizing arms and killing two policemen.
September 24	Expropriation of 510,000,000 pesos by FAL Juana Azurduy group from El Rosarino train in transit between Rosario and Buenos Aires.
September 29	FAP expropriates 14 million pesos from Banco Alemán Transatlantico in El Palomar.
September 30	FAL seizes 8,000 census forms from school in Buenos Aires.
	Bombing of Ministry of Social Welfare and Municipal Housing Commission by FAP as reprisal for evictions in Martín Guemes housing development.
October 2	ERP bombs seven public buildings in Rosario.
	ERP attacks police station in Buenos Aires.
	FAP raids Villa Guemes: two guards relieved of weapons and uniforms.
October 6	FAL seizes surgical equipment from Mayo Clinic in La Plata.
October 13	FAL rural unit occupies police post in El Timbo, Tucumán; arms and uniforms taken.
	Ricardo Masetti group (FAL) broadcasts proclamation over occupied Córdoba radio station.
October 15	October 8 unit (FAL) skyjacks airplane in Rosario and leaflets city.
October 16	Facundo Quiroga unit (FAP) distributes milk to slum dwellers in Buenos Aires.
October 21	FAR attacks Córdoba police station, destroying a number of vehicles with flamethrowers.

October 25	May 29th commando (ERP) seizes 700,000 pesos from ENTEL (State Telephone Company) offices in Córdoba.
October 28	Emilio Jauregui group (FAL) assaults three police guards at U.S. Embassy in Buenos Aires; weapons and uniforms taken.
November 2	Montoneros raid Córdoba Jockey Club; 7,000,-000 pesos taken.
November 9	Montonero team seizes 4,000,000 pesos from railroad station in Córdoba.
November 12	General strike as labor demands return to electoral democracy.
November 14	Oswaldo Sandoval (subcommissioner of political affairs in Buenos Aires) assassinated by FAL Alejandro Baldu commando.
November 15	MRA Maximo Mena and Felipe Vallese cells raid two Córdoba police stations, taking arms and ammunition.
	FAL executes police inspector due to testify in trial of Aramburu defendant.
November 16	ERP takes 22,000,000 pesos from Banco Comercial del Norte in Tucumán.
	May 29th unit of ERP occupies railroad station of Juarez Gelman (Córdoba Province).
November 18	Bank of Galicia in Gerli robbed of 30,000,000 pesos by FAR unit.
November 19	Montoneros take weapons and communication equipment from INTI (National Institute of Industrial Technology) guard station in Córdoba.
November 20	ERP takes 60 wigs from store in Rosario.
November 21	FAL burns three yachts docked at Punta Chica.

November 23	ERP expropriates 16,000,000 from Banco de la Nación.
November 24	ERP rescues wounded comrade from Tucumán hospital.
November 26	ERP team distributes 200,000 pesos to student groups at Tucumán "to aid in their struggles."
November 27	Homes of three U.S. military attachés in Martinez raided by FAP; documents, weapons, uniforms taken.
November 28	Comandos Descamisados occupy movie theater in La Matanza; leaflets distributed and Peronist newsreel shown.
November 30	ERP May 29th unit gives away 2,500 liters of milk in Córdoba slums.
	María Pacheco group (FAL) seizes 8,000,000 pesos in raid on French Hospital.
December 4	ERP distributes 220 cases of milk in Tucumán slums.
December 7	Meat truck in Córdoba seized by ERP; contents distributed to poor in Barrio Avallaneda.
December 14	Montoneros occupy civilian registry in Bella Vista and seize a variety of documents.
December 15	Banco Comercial de la Plata relieved of 10,000,-000 pesos by FAR; two policemen killed.
	Hilda Guerrero command (ERP) occupies LW3 Radio Station in Tucumán.
December 16	Three guerrillas found guilty of kidnapping and execution of Pedro Aramburu.
	Twenty guerrillas from Felipe Vallese unit (FAP) attack Rio Lujan police station in Escobar; one policeman killed, arms seized.

December 17	Documents taken from Caseros branch of Bureau of Motor Vehicles by FAL.
December 18	Spanish Consulate in Rosario raided by FAL; 300,000 pesos taken and building set afire.
December 20	Santa Fe police station occupied by ERP Cabral unit; arms and ammunition taken.
December 22	Fiat factory in Ferreyra, Córdoba, occupied by ERP; 1,000 workers given speech.
December 25	House of General Osiris Villegas (ambassador to Brazil) bombed by Montoneros.
December 28	MRA occupies offices of *Official Bulletin* in Córdoba and seizes equipment.
December 29	Chaco Peñaloza group (Montoneros) assaults president's house in Olivos, killing a guard.
	Bank of the Province of Córdoba attacked by FAR unit; FAR militant Raquel Liliana Gelin killed in shoot-out with police in Córdoba.
December 30	Montoneros seize 5,000,000 pesos from Córdoba post office.
1971	
January 2	ERP unit distributes milk and toys in Córdoba slum.
January 3	Guerrillas seize 14,300,000 pesos from the Banco de Credito Rural in the town of Transito, Córdoba.
January 5	Tejeda Pinto command (ERP) seizes mimeograph machine and typewriters from INTA (National Institute of Agricultural Technology) office in Salta.
	Montonero unit attacks marine post at Zárate, north of Buenos Aires.

January 12	Raquel Gelin unit (CARP) seizes uniform and weapon from a policeman in Rosario.
January 13	ERP unit expropriates a milk truck; contents distributed to slum dwellers in Santa Fe.
January 15	Raquel Gelin unit (FAL) expropriates numerous documents from Office of Vital Statistics, Ituzaingo, Buenos Aires Province.
January 15	Twenty-five hundred workers occupy Fiat Concord enterprise in Ferreyra, Córdoba.
January 17	Ángel Bengochea unit of ERP attacks police station in La Plata.
	ERP unit occupies the Cascallares Dam on the Reconquista River; weapon and uniform taken from policeman; guerrillas lecture.the workers.
January 19	ERP unit expropriates cattle truck in Rosario; cattle distributed in slums.
January 22	ERP expropriates meat truck in Tucumán; contents distributed to slum dwellers.
	Ten FAP commandos expropriate 6,000,000 pesos, one machine gun, and three .45-calibre pistols after occupying Banco de Galicia in Banfield; policeman who resists is killed.
	María Pacheco unit (ERP) seizes meat truck in Tucumán.
	ERP seizes uniform and weapons from policeman in Córdoba.
January 28	Raquel Gelin unit (CARP) expropriates 4,000,-000 pesos from flour mill in Rosario.
January 29	H. L. Diaz unit (GEL) expropriates 1,500,000 pesos from the Isla Maciel post office.

"Loyalty" unit (Montoneros) occupies Banco de Hurlingham in Villa Bosch; 14,000,000 pesos seized; policeman who resists is wounded.

General strike in Córdoba; seven bombs explode.

January 30   ERP unit seizes weapons and uniforms of three policemen traveling in a bus in Córdoba.

February 1   Nestor Martins unit (GEL) seizes 303,000 pesos and documents from Ministry of Agricultural Affairs in La Plata.

February 4   FAP guerrillas take documents from vehicle registration office in San Fernando.

Camilo Gonzalez unit (ERP) occupies police station in San Felipe, Tucumán; weapons and uniforms expropriated.

ERP unit seizes money and documents from legal library in Córdoba.

February 6   ERP Ángel Bengochea unit occupies sanatorium in San Isidro and expropriates medicines and medical equipment.

February 8   Adolfo Bello unit (ERP) occupies police station in La Florida, Rosario.

ERP unit takes weapons and uniform from policeman in Córdoba.

February 11   FAL unit expropriates 2,500,000 pesos from a notary's office in La Plata.

H. A. Diaz unit (GEL) expropriates money and government bonds from post office in La Tablada.

Eva Perón unit (Montoneros) bombs police station in Santa Fe.

February 12	Che Guevara and May 29th units of ERP execute largest theft in Argentine history, expropriating 121,000,000 pesos from armored truck of Bank of Province of Córdoba, in Yocsina, Córdoba.
February 14	ERP unit expropriates 34,000,000 pesos from Banco de la Provincia de Córdoba.
February 16	Strikes at Ika-Renault factory in Córdoba.
February 24	Che Guevara and May 29th units (ERP) distribute a water pump, water tank, overalls, tools, school supplies, slippers, blankets, medicines, milk, and ice boxes, in working-class sections of Córdoba; recipients given vouchers for goods.
	Felipe Vallese unit (GEL) expropriates 670,000 pesos from bus terminal in La Plata.
	ERP commandos donate 50,000 pesos to medical students' center in Rosario.
February 26	FAL unit expropriates 26,000,000 pesos from central post office in La Plata.
February 27	Raquel Gelin unit (ERP) donates 100 sheets of zinc to flood victims in Alto Verde quarter of Santa Fe; another ERP unit donates orthopedic leg to pensioned worker in Rosario.
February 28	ERP unit seizes truck loaded with 300 bags of sugar; contents distributed in slums of Córdoba.
March 1	Ángel Bengochea command (ERP) seizes milk truck in La Plata; contents distributed to poor.
	ERP distributes lambs in slums of Rosario.
March 4	Benjo Cruz command (FAL) expropriates 21,-600,000 pesos from La Plata racetrack.

	Strike by workers protesting wages and citizens protesting appointment of new governor in Córdoba; rioting ensues, 300 arrested.
March 9	ERP unit seizes milk truck in Tucumán and distributes contents.
	Oscar Corvalen command (ERP) occupies Tucumán Statistical Office; documents and equipment expropriated.
March 12	SITRAC and SITRAM Unions begin strike against Fiat in Córdoba.
March 15	*Strike in Córdoba; 50 vehicles burned and a number of foreign businesses destroyed; $4,000,-000 in damages estimated.*
March 16	Montoneros unit occupies municipal police offices in Tucumán; documents and equipment seized.
March 18	*Córdoba strike resumes and clashes with army continue; state of emergency decreed; Córdoba is declared a military zone and 3,500 troops occupy the city.*
March 23	President Roberto M. Levingston deposed by a military coup; three-man junta led by General Alejandro Agustín Lanusse assumes power.
March 25	FAR command seizes documents from Vital Statistics Office in Buenos Aires.
	Adolfo Bello command (ERP) seizes milk truck and distributes contents in Pueblo Nuevo, Rosario.
March 28	Felipe Vallese command (FAP) dynamites home of Pedro Gnavi, commander-in-chief of the navy.

ERP Ángel Cepeda command occupies television station in Córdoba; statement is broadcast and ERP emblem and protrait of Che Guevara are televised for one-half hour.

April 1   Political parties legalized for first time since 1966.

April 2   FAL unit occupies naval office in Córdoba; weapons seized from officer and office partially burned.

ERP command seizes meat truck and distributes contents in slums of Rosario.

April 3   Ángel Cepeda unit (FAL) expropriates X-ray machine from clinic in Buenos Aires.

April 4   FAR commandos occupy police station in Virreys, Buenos Aires Province, taking weapons and uniforms.

April 5   Peso devalued.

ERP Emilio Jauregui command donates 16 beds and mattresses to urban migrants in Buenos Aires.

April 12   Raquel Gelin command (MRA) expropriates 14,000,000 pesos from Banco del Interior, Córdoba.

April 13   Eight ERP members arrested in Rosario.

April 14   ERP Ángel Bengochea unit, in conjunction with Tupamaros, occupies home of Uruguayan naval attache; documents seized.

ERP bombs ENTEL (National Telecommunications Enterprise) building in support of striking telephone workers.

ERP units bomb a number of police commissariats in Rosario; police club is machine-gunned; actions are a reprisal for torture of ERP prisoners.

April 18	Three ERP commandos killed by police.
April 19	ERP guerrillas attack police commissariat and place bomb at home of police commissioner in Santa Fe.
April 20	ERP units support occupation of empty bulding by fourteen poor families in Córdoba; building is christened with name of Ángel Cepeda, a youth killed by police.
April 22	Ángel Bengochea command (ERP) occupies offices of Parke-Davis Laboratory in La Plata and expropriates equipment.
April 27	Luis Blanco and Adolfo Bello units (ERP) place eleven bombs in United States business offices in Rosario.
	ERP unit of fourteen guerrillas occupies Nelson meatpacking plant in Santa Fe; earlier, the unit had occupied the home of the president of the corporation, expropriating a number of weapons.
April 28	ERP commandos seize a milk truck in Tucumán; contents distributed to poor.
April 30	Evita and Che Guevara units (FAR), some 30 guerrillas, expropriate 200 weapons from army truck; army officer killed.
May 3	Peso devalued.
	ERP bombs three foreign businesses in Buenos Aires.
May 12	Peronist General Eduardo Rafael Labanca leads abortive coup.

May 15	Buenos Aires court voids charges of statutory rape filed against Juan Perón, in absentia, in 1958.
May 19	Three ERP members arrested in Córdoba.
May 23	*Stanley Sylvester, honorary British consul and manager of Swift de la Plata packing plant in Rosario, kidnapped by ERP; Sylvester had laid off 4,000 workers in late 1970.*
May 31	Sylvester released by Luis Blanco ERP command after $50,000 in food and clothing is distributed by Swift and Company to the poor.
June 1	Montoneros Eva Perón, Fernando Luis, Abal Medina, and Carlos Gustavo Ramus commands occupy San Geronimo, town 500 kilometers north of Buenos Aires; 26 heavy arms seized.
July 7	ERP holds first revolutionary press conference.
July 15	Juan Pablo Maestre, marketing executive for Gillette and FAR leader, killed by death squad.
September 7	*Cristianismo y Revolución,* important leftist magazine, closed down by government.
September 27	Forty-eight Third World priests beaten and arrested at demonstration against repression in Rosario.
October 8	Attempted military coup against Lanusse by Peronist faction; Colonels Florentine Diaz Losa and Carlos Alejandro Garcia object to Lanusse's overtures to Perón and the possibility of a presidential election.
November 8	Police raid alleged FAR-ERP safe house in Córdoba and seize office equipment, masks, weapons.

November 24	Army and police under General Juan Carlos Sánchez search 207 square block area for urban guerrillas in Córdoba.
December 13	FAR commandos dynamite police station outside Buenos Aires.

1972

January 1	Montonero unit attacks prefecture in attempted occupation of town of Zárate.
January 18	Tortugas Country Club attacked by Montonero unit.
January 26	Juan Pablo Maestre unit (FAR) seizes $6,000 in medical supplies from clinic in Rosario.
January 30	CGT begins 48-hour strike in nation's major cities to demand release of political prisoners and salary increases.
March 17	San Jorge Club (used by army officers for polo and horse racing) bombed by combined Montonero, FAR, and Descamisado guerrillas.
March 18	Conservative leader Roberto Mario Uzal killed while resisting Montonero kidnappers.
March 21	*Luis Pujales and Segundo Telesforo Gomez units (ERP) kidnap Oberdan Sallustro, General Manager of Fiat-Concord; freedom for jailed strikers, rehiring of workers laid off because of 1971 strike, release of 50 detained guerrillas, and publication of ERP communiqués demanded as ransom.*
March 24	President Lanusse rejects ERP conditions for Sallustro's release and states: "I will not negotiate with common delinquents."
April 7	General strike in Mendoza as citizens protest new electricity hike; three killed, more wounded,

	and 700 jailed during four days of violence; governor resigns in protest against army brutality in strike suppression.
April 8	Lanusse suspends application of new electricity increase.
April 10	*General Juan Carlos Sánchez, commander of Second Army Corps, assassinated by Segundo Telesforo Gomez (ERP) and Juan Pablo Maestre (FAR) units in Rosario.*
	Oberdan Sallustro executed after police discover people's prison; government had earlier prohibited payment of ransom; police jail four suspected kidnappers.
April 19	Eduardo Coppo and Manuel Negrin, members of the ERP unit involved in the Sallustro kidnapping, caught by police in San Javier, Tucumán Province.
April 28	ERP distributes candy and school supplies to school children in Buenos Aires.
July 26	Commemoration of twentieth anniversary of the death of Eva Perón; twenty buildings bombed, primarily in Buenos Aires, Tucumán, and Santa Fe.
August 15	*Twenty-five prisoners escape from Rawson Prison, Patagonia; prisoners flee to nearby Trelew Airport where one group commandeers plane to Chile while a second is captured by the military.*
	Carlos Capuano Martínez, a member of Montonero unit involved in Aramburu execution, is killed in a police shoot-out.
August 22	*Sixteen political prisoners are massacred by naval captors at Trelew; three others are seriously wounded.*

September 9	ERP seizes 500 kilograms of dynamite, detonators, and fuses from mine outside Córdoba.
November 14	Miguel Ángel Bustos, Montonero involved in the Aramburu affair, captured by police.
November 25	Juan Perón finds urban guerrilla warfare "a natural escape of oppressed peoples."
December 10	Ronald Grove, British director of Vestey Corporation, kidnapped by ERP.
December 12	Argentine security authorities claim that Mario Roberto Santucho and Enrique Haroldo Gorriaran Melo have entered the country from Chile.
December 14	Grove's employer pays $500,000 for the executive's freedom.
December 18	Tortugas Country Club, on outskirts of Buenos Aires, occupied and then razed by Montonero command.
December 26	Right-wing metalworkers leader Luis Guerrero wounded by guerrillas in attempted assassination.
December 27	Death penalty abolished.
December 28	Rear Admiral Emilio R. Berisso, intelligence officer, assassinated in reprisal for Trelew massacre by combined ERP-FAR-Montonero tactical unit.
December 29	Vincenzo Russo, ITT executive, kidnapped; released after ransom of nearly $1,000,000 is paid.

1973

January 4	Fifty high naval officers sentenced to death by guerrilla organizations affected by the Trelew massacre (ERP, FAR, Montoneros).

January 10	FAR attacks railroad station in La Plata; money seized.
January 11	ERP unit holds up train in western Rosario.
February 7	Norman Lee, Coca-Cola executive, kidnapped by FAL.
February 16	Naum Kakabowycz, businessman, kidnapped; ransom of $1,500,000 demanded.
February 21	Norman Lee released after ransom of around $1,000,000 is paid.
February 25	Gerardo Scalmazzi, banker, kidnapped in Rosario.
March 8	ERP-22 de Agosto kidnaps Héctor Ricardo Garcia, owner of *Crónica,* a Buenos Aires newspaper.
March 30	Navy "Libertad" building in Buenos Aires bombed.
April 2	Rear Admiral Francisco Alemán, retired chief of naval intelligence, kidnapped in Buenos Aires by ERP.
	Courthouse in San Isidro attacked by FAL; 511 weapons taken.
April 2	Kodak executive Anthony de Cruz kidnapped near Buenos Aires by FALN; later released after $1,500,000 ransom is paid.
	FAL communiqué states that it is not enough to win power at the polls, that power is achieved through revolutionary warfare; need for agrarian reform, nationalization of monopolies and banks, amnesty for political prisoners is stressed.
April 3	Montoneros demand publication of information on repression by *Capital,* a Rosario newspaper.

April 4	Intelligence officer, Colonel Héctor Alberto Iribarren, killed while resisting kidnap by Marino Pujadas and Susana Lesgard units (Montoneros) in Córdoba.
	Gerardo Scalmazzi released after $750,000 ransom paid.
April 7	Anthony de Cruz released after Kodak pays $1,500,000 ransom.
April 8	Víctor Brimicombe, British citizen and manager of Nobleza Tobacco Company, kidnapped on outskirts of Buenos Aires.
April 10	Industrialist Alberto Faena kidnapped by FAL.
	Aborted assault on 141st Engineers Battalion in Santiago del Estero leads to arrest of four ERP members.
April 21	Town of Ingeniero Maschwitz, north of Buenos Aires, occupied by 60 ERP commandos in three groups; post office, railroad, and police stations attacked; communications equipment, arms, and ammunition seized.
April 25	*National elections held; Héctor Cámpora, the Peronist candidate, is elected.*
April 26	Major Jacobo Nasif, National Gendarmerie official, kidnapped in Córdoba by ERP.
April 29	Rodolfo Galimberti, Peronist Youth leader, removed by Perón after publicly urging creation of Peronist Youth militias.
	Santiago Soldati, son of bank president, kidnapped in Buenos Aires; $1,500,000 asked for his release.

April 30	ERP executes Rear Admiral Hermes José Quijada, retired chairman of the Joint Chiefs of Staff, in Buenos Aires.
	In response to Quijada execution, the military declares "emergency regions" in Federal Capital and Provinces of Buenos Aires, Santa Fe, Córdoba, Mendoza, and Tucumán.
May 18	Enrique Fridman, manager of Lanin Company, kidnapped by FAR.
May 22	David Kloosterman, Secretary General of SMTA (Union of Mechanics and Related Automotive Transport Workers) assassinated by ERP-22 de Agosto group in Buenos Aires.
	Oscar Ricardo Castel, General Manager of Coca-Cola, kidnapped in Córdoba.
May 23	Aaron Beilinson, Babic Paving Company executive, kidnapped.
May 23	Ford Motor Company agrees to pay $1,000,000 to the ERP to prevent kidnapping of the president of Ford's Argentine subsidiary; the money is to be used to purchase powdered milk for children in slums, equipment for two childrens' hospitals, and 154 ambulances to be distributed in seven provinces.
May 24	FAR and Montoneros issue joint press communiqué stating loyalty to Perón and support of Cámpora; Cámpora urged to fulfill election promises and free political prisoners.
May 25	First group of political prisoners pardoned by Cámpora freed; 186 more to be released from Villa Devoto Prison, Buenos Aires, after Cámpora accedes to pressures from 60,000 protestors outside the prison.

	Sheraton Hotel where United States Secretary of State William Rogers is staying is stoned by hundreds of Peronist demonstrators.
May 26	Riot in Caseros Prison after prisoners hear of Villa Devoto release; sixteen prisoners released by presidential decree.
	One hundred fifty-three prisoners freed from Rawson Prison.
May 30	Central Security Command of *Justicialista* Movement threatens to kill ten leftists for each Peronist killed by guerrillas.
	ERP, in two communiqués, calls for a "struggle for the socialist revolution," and denounces the Cámpora government for its connections with foreign monopolies and representatives of the national bourgeoisie.
	Rolando Felipe Larraux, president of La Armonia Milk Enterprises, kidnapped; 20,000,000 pesos demanded for his release.
May 31	ERP demands $500,000 for release of John Thomson, English manager of Golov Lopez y Carva textile company.
June 1	ERP threatens action against executives of Otis Elevator Company unless $500,000 ransom is paid.
June 4	ERP-22 de Agosto publishes two communiqués in *Crónica,* stating that it broke with parent ERP on May 21, 1973, over the issue of Cámpora's candidacy, which the 22 August faction supported.
June 5	Supreme Justicialist Security Command in Rosario threatens to kill 21 leftists in its custody if

ERP does not release all its prisoners within two hours.

ERP frees Jacobo Nasif because of government release of political prisoners.

June 6   Charles Lockwood, executive with Roberts Finance Corporation, kidnapped in Buenos Aires suburb.

June 7   ERP releases Admiral Aleman after its demands, including the broadcast of an ERP communiqué, the publication of a letter, and the telecast of Aleman's interrogation, are met.

June 9   Shoot-out between rightist and leftist Peronists at a funeral service commemorating the anniversary of the execution of J. J. Valle and 26 other Peronists; one killed, five wounded.

June 13   Radical Civic Union leader Miguel Sullivan is kidnapped.

June 14   Death Squadron in Córdoba announces it is collecting a file on "extremists" and in event of a police killing will execute the first extremist found.

          ERP threatens reprisals if industrialist Juan Romero does not give $1,000,000 in medicine and medical equipment to hospitals; salary increase for Romero's workers is also demanded.

June 20   Assassination attempt against General Juan Manuel Abal Medina, Secretary General of National Justicialist Movement.

          Twenty killed and 200 injured in shoot-out initiated by CGT and other right-wing gunmen under orders of Perón's personal secretary Jorge Osinde, at Ezeiza Airport homecoming for Juan Perón.

June 21	Luis Giovanelli, manager of Ford factory, mortally wounded during a kidnap attempt.
June 23	John Thompson, president of Firestone of Argentine, kidnapped; $1,500,000 ransom demanded.
June 25	Luis Giovanelli, manager of Ford factory in Pacheco, dies of wounds inflicted during guerrilla kidnap attempt.
June 26	Córdoba: twelve persons kidnapped by guerrillas within a 24-hour period.
June 27	*La Prensa* publishes an ERP communiqué which claims that Perón has defrauded the people and that there will be no truce; Osinde and Rucci of CGT blamed for Ezeiza incident.
	FAP holds press conference in industrial sector of Buenos Aires; states that it will organize the working class from the bottom, "independent of bureaucrats and traitors," and that it will continue fighting against the oligarchy, torturers, and the armed forces; rejects Cámpora's demand that urban guerrillas lay down arms.
	ERP unit intercepts milk truck and distributes contents to poor in Buenos Aires; leaflets left stating that the struggle for "democracy and freedom" must be intensified.
	Montonero communiqué to "Public Opinion and Paramilitary Groups" says that the "time has come to give up the fighting and start the reconstruction the country needs"; ERP is warned to contact them for agreements and to surrender arms.

Peronist Armed Forces: Arms in Hand by Héctor Víctor Suarez

This interview, conducted in the heyday of FAP activity, traces the organization's evolution from rural to urban strategy. Importantly, it suggests an appreciation of the possibility of an electoral return of Perón and a redefined Peronism, at a future conjuncture to be prepared and precipitated by armed struggle.

Two men and a woman; a bitter-tasting maté which is passed around; and, outside, Buenos Aires, with the Federal Police going crazy looking for this organization, the Peronist Armed Forces (FAP), which have given a special "you-too-can-do-it" flavor to their activities. This morning they took 14 million pesos from the German Transatlantic Bank. They kidnapped the treasurer, disarmed a policeman, took the key from the administrator, and made off with the money. "It was a nice, clean operation, without a shot." They don't brag, but they are undoubtedly happy.

"Don't insist too much, because we aren't very theoretical," says one as he passes me the maté. "Neither am I." "What luck." But what can you do if it's your job to insist?

You call yourselves Peronists. What is your opinion of the Peronist movement?
We consider it to be a movement of national liberation. Starting in 1955, when power was lost, the Peronist movement in Argentina has tried to recapture it in one way or another. This explains the Resistance, the big strikes, the attempt at a coup d'etat by General Valle, and the link between trade union leaderships and the military.

And the pact with Frondizi?[1]
Yes, the pact with Frondizi was made because, under the circumstances, it offered our movement, a heterogeneous movement which had been banned, the best opportunity to engage in the electoral process and to negotiate for a program favorable to the General Confederation of Workers (CGT). It was a tactical decision taken by

[1] Arturo Frondizi, the UCRI (Intransigent Radical Civic Union) presidential candidate in 1958; elected through a pact in which some 2 million Peronist votes were cast for the UCRI.

Perón at the time, and we consider it was a correct one because it made it possible to oppose the most pro-Yankee, most oligarchical sectors of the country by means of a national, popular program which contained certain ideas of economic independence.

But if we accept that the Peronist movement is a movement for national liberation, then isn't it clear that nothing could be expected from Frondizi from the strategic point of view?
It was quite clear that, in view of the classes that supported it, Frondizism didn't have the necessary historical perspective for leading a process of national liberation. We are well aware of the fact that the national bourgeoisie can't produce a process of national liberation and carry it to its ultimate consequences. There is no direct possibility of this happening today.

And now how do you view all these tactics used by the movement?
They weren't completely in vain, but they certainly were inadequate. They weakened the labor movement, but, at the same time, they served as a great lesson.

When you speak of recapturing power, you don't mean a return to 1955, do you?
We spoke of recapturing power while referring to an experience of our people in which they, to some extent, shared power. The three principles of Peronism—social justice, economic independence, and political sovereignty—are the foundation for a policy of national liberation. And, for the most exploited sectors of the people and the ones with the least political education, this means a return to the 1945–1955 era. But the great majority of the people of Argentina understand that a repeat performance is impossible. A return to power would mean going beyond what was done then, with different methods and a different scope.

The experience which I mentioned has not been in vain; the people have learned their lessons: we are lucky to have a very capable labor movement which discusses all problems, and, having lived in the factories, we have participated in neighborhood meetings. We know that the political level of our workers is very high. It is a national movement, not limited to Buenos Aires alone. Anyone who thinks that, when we speak of the return of Perón or the return to power, the workers will think that this means a return to the policies of 1955 is ignorant of the political level attained by our people. Our people are aware of this. Everybody says, "Perón should have tamed all the gorillas." [2] It is a clear expression of the fact that the only way to continue with a process of this kind is to maintain and improve upon its achievements.

Can this be done under the capitalist system?
We don't think so. The only way to do this is by eliminating the capitalist structure entirely.

Then, in your opinion, national liberation is closely linked to social liberation?
Absolutely.

Do you believe that imperialism and the oligarchy understand this, that the return of Perón would be a revolutionary event in itself—that is, that at this stage of the game Perón can't be made part of the system?
We don't think he can, and we, ourselves, have confidence in Perón as a leader—confidence which is based not on psychological knowledge of Perón's subjective level, but rather on his past and the commitment he has made with the people. Even supposing he were in a position to negotiate, to give up all he has been proposing and play ball with the regime, he would be politically dead if he were to do so. This is why we believe that, because of his commitment with the masses, with the people, Perón can't be made part of the system.

In view of the fact that the ruling classes have less and less room for maneuvering, do you think they would accept a compromise with Peronism as a last resort?
They aren't just thinking about it—they're already trying to do just that. The great problem of imperialism and the oligarchy in this country is how to bring the Peronist movement into the system.

Yes, all this is very clear: the fiasco of the attempts of the ruling class to make Peronism a part of the system is perfectly evident. All this history of elections and coups which has been repeated over and over

[2] A derogatory term first applied to the military faction which ousted Perón in 1955 and now generalized to include all reactionary officers in Latin America.

again during the past 15 years is all based on the problem of Peronism. The new element in the picture which is decisive, in my opinion, given the present situation, is armed struggle—which is incompatible with the system in every way, regardless of the extent to which Perón would be willing to compromise. My question is that, in view of the fiasco of the integration attempts, and confronted with armed struggle, couldn't the power structure resort to bringing back Perón as a last-ditch attempt to halt armed struggle in the country, or the armed struggle of Peronist organizations?

We don't believe there are any real possibilities for a return of Perón. If he returned, he would have to do so as an election candidate, with a political perspective. He would have to return "when conditions were ripe." What does this mean? It isn't very clear. It seems that Perón is maneuvering to force a definition from the government. It's no accident that Paladino should return from his interview with Perón saying that he will return. This is to force a definition from the government.

But Paladino,[3] whom Perón named as political leader of the movement in Argentina, has returned to the country saying that conditions for Perón's return to the country are ripe (although he doesn't explain what these conditions may be) and that elections are the only way to end violence in the country. Doesn't this aid Levingston? Isn't this an objective contribution to the plans of the government, in contradiction to your line of armed struggle?

In our opinion, Perón's return is a concrete demand. Anybody who supports this demand is contributing to the process of national liberation. His return is linked to the three principles of the movement: political sovereignty, economic independence, and social justice. In our opinion, anyone who in any way expresses his support for this demand contributes to the process of national liberation. Our process of national liberation is many-sided; it isn't as organized as we would like it to be. That is why support for the basic demands of the movement, regardless of who expresses it, helps.

[3] Jorge Paladino was later, in mid-1972, dismissed by Perón for his accommodationist position toward the military.

In your opinion, how can the development of a process of national liberation be guaranteed in the country?
We feel that this movement for national liberation has no chance of victory if an army of the people isn't established with an armed political-military organization.

What are the factors which make a perspective of armed struggle possible for the country today?
The experience of the Peronist movement led us to seek new methods, methods with a perspective of victory, of a real chance to obtain power for the people. In view of all the experiences which have weakened the labor movement, the fruitless strikes, the compromises which failed, and the resistance which wasn't effective, we feel that things have to be viewed from a different angle and that we must organize and develop armed struggle.

Peronism has made several attempts at armed struggle. What conclusions did you draw from those events, and how were they different from the present armed struggle?
The Peronists were among the first to raise the issue of armed struggle in Argentina. The first attempt at armed struggle was that of the Uturuncos in 1959, the Peronist guerrilla camp which was captured in Plumerillo; then there was the attack on polyclinic bank of the nationalist sector; and then Taco Ralo. The 1955–1957 resistance was a very incipient form of armed struggle. More bombs were set off then than in the period of the anarchists. The people really stuck their necks out.

Does the tactical defeat, which you suffered in Tucumán, in Taco Ralo —which, I understand, marks the beginning of FAP—and the renewal of your activities in the cities in 1960 and 1970 mean that your strategy now excludes rural guerrilla warfare?
No. Taco Ralo was carried out under the direct influence of the Cuban Revolution, which had great repercussions in the ranks of Peronism, leading its vanguard to aim for guerrilla warfare.

This tactical defeat doesn't mean we reject rural guerrilla warfare in our country. We have large urban areas in Argentina and areas which are suitable for rural struggle from the political and geographical points of view. This means that the armed struggle now under way in the cities will spread to the countryside.

And the Córdoba uprising? Can it be considered a factor which helped unleash armed struggle in the country?
We can say that, starting in 1966, from the Onganía regime to the Córdoba uprising, there was a retreat and a lack of struggle by the working class of Argentina. The Córdoba uprising called the attention of the armed organizations to the presence of the people: that the people were neither tamed nor sleeping. The Córdoba uprising had a great influence, especially in some sectors, but the roots of the organizations were already established.

But it gave a push to many people, didn't it?
Yes, undoubtedly. Many people participated in it—not just in Córdoba, but in Rosario, Santa Fe, and Tucumán, as well—and they drew their own conclusions about its positive and negative aspects. They decided that this was not the way. Once the elation of the moment was over, the problem of method, which had to be that of a clandestine organization, had to be decided. It doesn't always have to be armed, but, to some extent, its forms are those of an armed organization.

How is this methodology absorbed?
Small cells of five or six members of a political sector are set up, and, little by little, they turn toward armed struggle. Four big organizations and two small ones are operating in Argentina today. They aren't responsible for everything that happens: you read that a bomb exploded here and a policeman was disarmed there, but this isn't always the work of an organization. Although many of these commandos may join one of the existing organizations, many are still operating independently and are a product of the Córdoba uprising.

What did the uprising mean to FAP?
It pointed up the need to speed up the process of organizational consolidation and, reviewing the events, the need for the armed organizations to give a perspective to the Córdoba uprising in order to take advantage of the mass political awakening which had taken place. We asked ourselves how something like that could have happened without the armed organizations being there with their methodology.

How do you view mass work now?

The foundation of our policy is the organization of people's war. Everything must lead to that. The links of people's war with the masses are very complex. We consider ourselves to be a part of that war, but by no means the elite. We believe that one of our basic tasks as a political-military organization is to respond to the need of the working class to get organized, and adopt different methods. Our job is to set up organizational forms that will guarantee links with the people and the continuity and compartmentalization of armed action as well as the existence of a viable relationship between the people and the organization. We believe this complex problem is on the way toward being solved, thanks to our work.

How?

By providing cadres with a political-military mentality for the process of struggle at the mass level and by trying to extend the methodology of the armed organizations on all levels of the masses' confrontation with the regime. We link political with military work, and they should always go together. Our people need methodology for struggle.

In view of your concern that armed actions be understood by the masses, you must have analyzed the actions of other revolutionary organizations as well as your own. In view of this, what is your opinion of the kidnapping and execution of Aramburu?

We support the position of revolutionary execution set forth by the Montoneros. We base ourselves on a specific concrete fact: what he signified for the movement, the nation, and the working class. However, we think the comrades from the Montoneros didn't take the possibilities of continuing a process unleashed at this level into account. He deserved what he got, but this is something with which to end— not start—a process. But, anyway, we support it, because Aramburu had done more than enough to be sentenced to death by the revolutionary movement.

And the Alonso case?

Well, that's a bit more complicated. In spite of the fact that he was clearly a tool of the regime, a functionary of imperialism, we believe that the struggle against the trade union bureaucracy is one which the labor movement of Argentina should wage on an antiboss, anti-imperialist basis. If the labor movement isn't strong enough to get rid of its own parasites, it won't be able to make a revolution. Once the process is under way and the traitors clearly identified, it will be necessary to get rid of them, but we don't think the level of the process was high enough to warrant the execution of Alonso.

Among the people, nobody really gave a damn about his death; Levingston shed more tears for him than any worker did.

What about your relations with the other armed organizations?
Our position has been a broad-minded one, publicly expressed. We were perhaps the first group to take the other organizations into account. When we captured the Tigre police station, we said that, from our Peronist trench, we were in solidarity with the Liberation Armed Forces (FAL), an organization with which we differed over the political interpretation of reality—even though we weren't exactly sure where we stood at the time. This resulted in closer relations.

We feel that relations between armed organizations should be based on absolute respect. There must be a political exchange on all levels. We have proposed and put into effect a policy stipulating that every detachment or commando group of every organization make a written criticism of the documents of the others.

What unites you with and what separates you from the other organizations? Is there any chance of setting up a liberation front through the unification of the different armed organizations now operating in the country?
The way we understand the present situation in the country, the only way to make the revolution here is to be a Peronist. But this doesn't mean we are in any way denying the value of other comrades who don't happen to agree with this thesis—far from it. They are honest comrades who are on the same operational level as we are.

In our opinion, the factors which separate us are not basic, whereas what unites us is: a common methodology, enemy, and final objective.

These are the three things which unite us. We do not recognize the need, at this stage, to set up an artificial organization. The front will come as the result of a process. Now we are trying to avoid competition among the revolutionary organizations and achieve the greatest possible political and technical exchange.

And, as for the same question on a continental level?
We believe that imperialism must be defeated on a Latin American level. All our nations are faced by the same enemy, and this affects the revolutionary organizations. Having the same enemy makes all revolutionary organizations in Latin America allies, and we believe in having as many political ties as possible with organizations in other countries.

This will surely result in concrete agreements at organizational levels. We take advantage of all opportunities to confer with organizations from other countries, hoping to reach agreement. Revolutionary fraternity means making no concessions and being frank with criticism.

Relations among the revolutionary organizations of Argentina are, fortunately, very good: there's no competition among us, and there is real concern about carrying out a policy of collaboration.

And the Cuban Revolution?
It has all our support and confidence.

Peronist Armed Forces: Letter to Police

The death of policemen is a routine occurrence in the guerrilla struggle. Here the FAP attempts to counter the regime's propaganda with an analysis of the relationship of the police to the repressive apparatus, toward the end of encouraging neutrality.

We had nothing against Corporal Vallejos, who was seriously wounded by our Eva Perón detachment last 27 July when we seized the Evita Perón LS5 radio station. Our objetcive was to have the voice of our beloved comrade reach the people and accompany it with a fighting message of hope to confront these times through which we are living. The corporal tried to oppose our comrade who was attempting to get him to surrender, and the latter had to shoot him.

Our FAP comrades also had nothing against Corporal Sulling. But the corporal did not heed orders to keep quiet and attempted a useless resistance.

The purpose of this letter is to have you meditate on these events, because they will not be the last of this sort in the times of revolution in which our country is living.

We have nothing against any one of you as a person. Our enemy consists of the forces of repression as an organization and an instrument of the oligarchy, and we confront them as such, prepared to attack them whenever necessary.

The course of action against the people taken by the police during the past few years of military and antipatriotic government is not a matter of chance. This is attested to by the innumerable cases of violent repression, the illegal entries and searches, the murder of innocent victims and revolutionary militants, and the cases of vandalism in the slums, all of which have you as their perpetrators.

You have been the ones who have carried out this arbitrary and savage policy that the Argentine people are undergoing. You are the instrument that tortures, imprisons, kills in the defense of the interests of the rich and the rulers of the country. These are not your inter-

Cristianismo y Revolución (Buenos Aires), November–December 1970, pp. 53–58, as translated in Joint Publications Research Service, Translations on Latin America, no. 447, pp. 4–6.

ests, because you come from the people as we do. Like ourselves, you know about poverty, the lack of housing, the impossibility of sending our children to school or the university.

This is why the death of Corporal Sulling or the wounds of Corporal Vallejos are useless. They fell defending interests that were not theirs.

Policeman: We ask you today:

How do you benefit from the multimillionaire transactions that daily enrich the coffers of the oligarchs or businessmen, those who, at best, live in the houses or are owners of the banks that you guard.

Did any of them come to the funeral of your comrades?

Are they going to help your wife and children when they are left alone?

Did you ever ask yourself what all this about "defending order" and "defending the country" means when your family is dying of hunger and you earn just enough to keep on shooting?

Have you ever asked yourself why they hate you in the neighborhood, street, or housing development?

There is still time for you to ask for whom you are fighting, whom you are defending, why and for whom you risk your life daily, for whom you are serving as cannon fodder?

As you well know, the Peronist Armed Forces is not the only revolutionary organization that exists. Here today, in our country, there are many of us who are actively fighting.

Those of us in FAP never fire on an unarmed man, but neither will we leave unpunished any of the crimes that the regime carries out through you, their tool of execution, their cannon fodder.

Bear in mind that each operation we undertake is carefully planned and studied down to the smallest detail. When we undertake to carry it out, we come with superior firepower and complete knowledge of the terrain. Our weapons are carried with the chamber loaded and the safety catch off, and in the face of any attempt at resistance, there is no possible alternative. It is either you or we.

Bear in mind that with each action we take one more step in our fight for a just nation, free and sovereign, in which many of you lived when Perón was in power, and that we shall not retreat from anyone or anything.

Consider whether it is worthwhile to risk your life for the privileges of others, selling yourself for a miserable wage to the government in office and staining yourselves with the blood of the people for a raise.

We Argentine revolutionaries who are fighting and giving our lives for the cause of the people, who are fighting as well for your children, so that they will not serve as hangmen for the oligarchs, invite you to reconsider and join the cause of liberty and justice.

Keep it well in mind in the meantime that none of your crimes will remain unpunished and that revolutionary justice does not forget.

No matter what happens, no matter what it costs, we shall overcome!!

Peronist Armed Forces (FAP)

| Statement by Base Peronists | Argentine urban guerrillas have had particularly close ties with the more militant sectors of the labor movement, a fact that is illustrated by this statement issued by Peronist workers during the occupation of the Fiat factory in March 1971. |

Comrades:

The Peronists on a base level at Fiat Concord believe that this step we have taken today, for which a long process of provocation on the part of the ownership has laid the ground, should be clearly analyzed by all of us.

1. The seizure of the plant is also a measure of struggle which reflects high combativeness, an act of recovering what is ours, what has been built with our sweat and sacrifice. With each occupation we advance a little toward what will be the culmination of this struggle: the total recovery of what has been expropriated from us by the oligarchy and the imperialists—our labor, the means of labor, and its fruits.

2. The occupation of the plant should serve to consolidate our base organization, to strengthen us on the lower level, and to clarify our thinking in fraternal discussion among comrades. We have already stated earlier that a trade union with a class and revolutionary leadership has its limits; the owners and the government cannot allow it to exist because of the example it sets for the rest of the workers' class. Therefore, we must prepare ourselves to endure repression, so that our strength and clear thinking can continue in clandestineness, and for this it is essential to have a political organization at the base.

The first step is clearly to reveal the identity of the pimps who play the game of these bloodsucking gringos, the stubborn lackeys of the whites, the servile guard corps which directly defends these Yankee usurpers.

3. We must bear clearly in mind that this struggle is a long one, that no battle is the final one. Our struggle is not to win crumbs, but for

Cristianismo y Revolución (Buenos Aires), April 1971, pp. 8, 9, as translated in Joint Publication Research Service, Translations on Latin America, no. 517, pp. 28–30.

final liberation through the seizure of power by the workers' class and the exploited people in order to bring about a free, just, and sovereign fatherland, an Argentina with neither oppressors nor oppressed, in other words, a national and socialist revolution. General Lanusse, as a spokesman of the dominant classes, has already declared war on us, and we cannot allow ourselves to be crushed, to be outraged, remaining with our heads bowed. We must set forth our form of struggle for ourselves, which naturally does not mean confrontation before we have sufficient strength. We must strike where and when it hurts, where the enemy is weak, and little by little, along with the armed vanguards such as the Montoneros, the FAP, the ERP, the FAL, and the MRA, we will proceed to exhaust the regime, destroying this system on all sides. We must never lower our guard. If Lanusse has declared the imperialist and capitalist war on us, we declare revolutionary war. We shall use all of our potential as a people, from all the posts of struggle, and shall even make use of gaiety and dancing, which is the only way of triumphing over the brutal force used against us.

For this reason, the seizure represents a point, a step forward; it is one of the forms of the struggle of the people and the workers' class to recover power.

Fiat has set its example in combating the treasonable trade union leadership, those who lower their heads before the power of our enemies and sell out, those who have never trusted and do not now trust the forces of unity and class solidarity. We, as Base Peronist comrades, will never cease to outdo ourselves against the owners, the bureaucracy, oppression, and imperialism. Our place is not at the negotiation table. It continues to be, as it has been to date, in the streets, in the plant, in the mills, in the struggle for the organization of the workers' class and a consistent revolutionary leadership in order to achieve a better, new society, with neither hangmen nor exploiters, and if now we must burn the plant with the Yankees inside, we will do so. The will of 2,500 suffices to continue the struggle.

Organization from below for the liberation of the fatherland!
Revolution or death!
Free or dead, but never slaves!
Let those who must, fall, let it cost what it must!
Base Peronism!

The Revolutionary Armed Forces: With Che's Weapons by Héctor Víctor Suarez

An FAR leader recounts here the organization's shift from rural to urban struggle after Che's death in 1967. Interesting is the discussion of the FAR's curious blend of Marxism-Leninism-Peronism and the sense of optimism expressed with regard to the continental prospects for the revolutionary left, soon to be dimmed by the Bolivian coup of August 1971, the April 1972 setback for the Tupamaros, and the 1973 Chilean coup.

In the streets they are known as "The Garín Group," because of their having taken control of the town of that name—which has a population of 30,000—in an operation carried out with clocklike precision. In clandestine circles, they are called "Che's men," because they were preparing to join the guerrillas in Bolivia. They themselves, after considering various names, decided to fight under a name that is already making history: the Revolutionary Armed Forces (FAR).

Here's a tip for the Federal Police: It's going to be a tough job discovering that this well-dressed, slim, calm young man now talking with me about his organization in one of the thousand tea shops in Buenos Aires is the nationwide leader of the FAR.

"Yes, we began as a group that meant to join Che's guerrillas. We learned about the project shortly before it was launched, and we were getting ready to join. At the time, ours was a small group made up of people from the traditional left, a few Peronists and many new elements without a political background. We all knew one another—we were all friends and comrades in political struggle united by a single idea: to serve in Che Guevara's column in any way we could. We hadn't thought about adopting an independent political line. Logically, everything that had to do with the integral development of the organization was left up to Che.

"But Che was killed. Therefore, we had to change our way of thinking—we couldn't leave anything for others to do for us any more, but had to make an effort to start out as an organization ready to use all the different variants called for by revolutionary struggle.

Granma Weekly (Havana, Cuba), 17 January 1971, p. 9.

"Aware of the fact that, of course, we weren't the only ones, we decided that—in the first phase—the most advisable, wisest thing was for us to develop as a group, consolidating an organization with a certain degree of solidity and homogeneity, an organization which could, in addition, engage in actions. After this, we'd launch our opening policy.

"Then, from the time Che was killed up through the middle of 1969, there followed a transitional period for Argentina and for us, a year in which our work was mainly aimed at achieving organizational consolidation and defining our strategy.

"Though we had proceeded from the premise of a rural guerrilla unit, we never underestimated urban struggle. However, at that time, we didn't attach as much importance to it as we do now. We always kept it in mind, but we hadn't succeeded in organizing it adequately within our strategy. It was only last year that we incorporated urban struggle as a basic element of our strategy and started acting accordingly.

"Logically, our previous strategy was reflected in everything we did: our plans for military training were mainly aimed at preparing for waging rural guerrilla warfare, our cadre-training projects were aimed at the preservation of cadres—that is, we trained them and kept them out of danger with a view to a higher form of struggle, rural guerrilla fighting—and our plans for securing resources were put off until the time should be ripe for setting up a guerrilla unit. Everything was like that.

"We thus continued gaining experience, and well, what with the national reality, we completed our strategic plans—which, seen in retrospect, we consider to have been partial, incomplete, and insufficient.

"We had already started and were in the midst of discussing the importance of armed struggle when the Córdoba uprising took place. This shook us, as it did everyone else, and had the effect of waking us up, and, to a certain extent, it confirmed all those things.

"At that point, we began a whole new stage. We tried to define ourselves, but we always had the characteristic—which we may have gotten from the Tupamaros—that we really didn't write very much. We always said that we put things into practice before we made up theories about them.

"We're now making an effort to even up this situation. After making an organizational review, we came to the conclusion that structuring an organization of this type presupposed a simultaneous development —or as simultaneous as possible—of various areas of work.

"According to our terminology, these are what we call our basic principles in the construction of our organization: 1. What we refer to as continuity and operational progress; 2. strategic clarification; 3. technical training (in other words, military training); and 4. organizational technique—that is, everything that has to do with the organization's infrastructure in connection with both insuring the growth of the organization and recruiting personnel.

"Our history is one of alternate stages in these matters. We've had stages in which priority was given to technical training, but this resulted in less progress in other aspects. We have just begun to give due importance to those matters which are strictly strategic and political —although, naturally, we always discuss what is to be done beforehand.

"There was a time when we thought we had gotten enough technical experience, when we thought we had reached a fair degree of operational efficiency. We launched a series of operations—nobody knows we were responsible for them, as we hadn't appeared as an organization at the time—and were able to verify that our people did a good job, displaying good combativeness, and that we had the ability to plan and carry out complex operations and make what could be called our 'first public appearance.' It was imperative that we make a good showing.

"This was how the idea of taking Garín came up. This was no harebrained action, for, as we have said before, we had already carried out other operations calling for the mobilization of a good number of people, and we had quite a lot of experience in these matters.

"We had always admired the taking of Pando by the Tupamaros. In fact, such was our admiration for this feat that, while discussing our plans for the operation, we decided to call it 'Pandito'—even though, naturally, we eventually gave it another name.

"We wanted and we want to develop actions which combine different aspects, but always including expropriations, as, in our opinion, they are basic to organizational development and serve as a demonstration of efficiency, clearly revealing the effectiveness of a method of struggle.

"Political factors were not the most important ones at Garín. It was captured primarily for military reasons—although, if it would have had a negative political effect, we wouldn't have carried out the operation. Garín is near an area where important industrial development is under way: a Ford plant is near the area, as is an important paint factory, the Alba. All this development has come following the opening of the Pan American Highway as far as Garín, about 27 miles from Buenos Aires.

"After studying the place, we came to the conclusion that the spot was ideal. We set up an observation plan. We already had an idea of the action, but we wanted to see if it was really practicable. All the comrades who were sent to check out the area were asked to give their frank opinion. Nobody was forced to support the idea, but we told them that, if possible, it would be carried out—and carried out well. All the comrades thought the operation would be possible: everyone was in agreement on this.

"And it was done, and we really think it turned out quite well. We took over the town—which has a population of 30,000—for 50 minutes; we captured the police station, bank, telephone office (the lines were cut), and a radiotelephone device in a private home. We controlled the train station, which has independent communication, even though we didn't actually capture it, because it wasn't necessary; the two main accesses were controlled, and traffic was detoured. Nobody was allowed to leave, but people were allowed to enter after having passed through our checkpoint. (We made a policeman who came up in a car get out, and we kept him prisoner until the operation was concluded.) We seized three and a half million pesos, along with weapons, police uniforms, and many other things of value.

"In our opinion, the action impressed the people because of the synchronization and technical resources involved. It really shook up the repressive forces as well as public opinion.

"Now, starting from this point, we realize that we are going to enter an era in which we will have to deal with a great problem, a problem which confronts all organizations which have reached a certain level of development: the organization's links with the masses. We consider this to be a serious problem—not in terms of the links with the masses, which we consider will in some way be established through the actions themselves, but in terms of how the masses join the struggle (the famous problem of the transmission belts). We think that it is necessary to do political-military work in order to obtain mass participation.

"Now you ask how we view the Peronist problem in this context. We feel it plays a decisive role in the revolutionary struggle in Argentina. We are holding serious discussions on the problem of Peronism, and we have very cordial relations with the comrades from the Peronist Armed Forces.

"We don't agree with any political classification that draws lines between us, saying 'you come from the left, and the comrades of the Peronist Armed Forces, from that movement.' The fact that some of our members belonged to other leftist organizations doesn't stop us from understanding that Peronism was the highest level of revolutionary experience ever attained in this country—on a mass level, of course.

"We feel that Peronism is the political expression of the great majority of the working class, and a revolutionary policy should be based on that fact. We don't think that it is a movement which is no longer relevant or valid, that it is out of date. On the contrary, we think it is extremely valid, and important revolutionary forces such as the Peronist Armed Forces exist in it. As such, we believe we must start from that point and work to develop the most revolutionary aspects of Peronism.

"Should we join the Peronist movement? Well, this is a question that's still being thrashed out by our national leadership, and I can't speak on behalf of the FAR, because it has a national structure and its national leadership has this whole question of Peronism under discussion at present. I think we've made great progress in this matter, but I, for one, still don't know if we'll become part of the Peronist movement or not. In our last talks with the comrades from the Peronist Armed Forces, they told us they considered themselves to be part of the Peronist movement—which, they feel, is a movement for national liberation. We're not convinced of this, but, I repeat, these opinions I'm throwing out are not the official views of the FAR.

"As far as our being Marxist-Leninists goes, I'd say that we consider ourselves to be Marxist-Leninists in the sense that we use it as a method for studying reality—but not as a political straitjacket.

"Armed struggle in Argentina is still young, and relations between the different organizations are not yet consolidated enough. There have been many attempts to achieve unity among the revolutionary political groups, but the difference is that those attempts were made at a negotiating table, whereas these are the result of practice and action in which we have participated together with the other organizations.

"Our relations with the comrades of the Peronist Armed Forces are the best. We also have close ties with the comrades from the Liberation Armed Forces, but, for some as yet undetermined reason, we aren't as close to the others.

"Our opinion on the Latin American scene is the same. We were confronted with a choice between a national and a continental strategy. In Che's time, it was clear. We also talked this problem over when Inti[1] returned to the mountains, and we held discussions with the National Liberation Army. We didn't agree with the continental strategy proposed by the Bolivian comrades, which consisted—at least this is how we understood it—of considering the Bolivian guerrillas as the vanguard of the revolutionary struggle in this part of the continent—which would be under a single leadership, to which all the national organizations would have to contribute—and waiting until this nucleus of the people's army was established before having its branches spread to the other countries.

"In our opinion, this was putting the cart before the horse. There's no doubt as to the continental nature of the struggle, for it's very clear that in Latin America there are more things—starting with our common enemy—that unite than separate us.

"We have the same goals and use the same methods; we have the same history; only a few things separate us, but there are national characteristics which cannot be swept away by decree.

[1] Guido ("Inti") Peredo commanded the Bolivian ELN from the time of the defeat of Che's *foco* until his own death in 1968.

"We discussed this problem of national characteristics with revolutionary comrades from other countries, and the more orthodox advocates of the guerrilla nucleus theory didn't agree with our point of view. They thought we were using the argument of the special characteristics of Argentina as an excuse for saying that there were no possibilities for revolutionary struggle here, whereas this is not at all the case; we feel that Argentina has some special characteristics which favor—not oppose—revolutionary struggle. This is especially so because of its working class, which is neither inexperienced nor unorganized; it has a lot of experience in struggle and a high level of trade union organization—which, though not sufficient, is much greater than what other countries have. Our working class has been responsible for important events, and its level of awareness is considerable.

"Now we have entered the period of armed struggle. National and international lessons have been learned in Argentina, and there is no doubt that any person or organization with a revolutionary perspective has to give serious consideration to armed struggle.

"This has been clear ever since 1962, when Peronist candidate Andrés Framini won the governorship of Buenos Aires but was not allowed to take office. This made it clear that the electoral road was closed.

"Before that, the problem could be debated—but not after this concrete demonstration. The high point was the overthrow of Illia, the famous Argentine 'Revolution.' Onganía swept everything away—Constitution, University, everything. Onganía has that to his credit—he is a great enemy, because, with a regime like that, what alternative is there but armed struggle?

"Today I read the statements of Paladino and Balbín[2] in the press. They go through incredible contortions to avoid saying that it's necessary to take up arms. Today even the members of the People's Radical Party (UCR) would be forced to say that armed struggle is needed. Paladino continues appealing to the 'good sense' of the government, but how long can this go on?

"The Córdoba uprising and everything else that happened in Argentina from May to September 1969—not just in Córdoba, but in

[2] Ricardo Balbín: perennial presidential or vice presidential candidate of the Radical Civic Union or one of its factions.

Rosario, Tucumán, Corrientes, and many other places—woke a lot of people up.

"During that period, we were holding discussions with the people who had invented the theory of the Europeanization of Argentina, of the aristocratization of the working class. After the Córdoba uprising, we were left with nobody to talk to! They were never heard from again! They spoke of the passivity of the working class in that period, and we replied that this passive attitude contained a positive element: their resistance to integration by the regime. Córdoba showed that this passive attitude was only skin deep.

"The conviction that the electoral road is closed has spread deep enough among the working class to make it receptive to an armed alternative. I don't mean to say they are absolutely clear on this—if they were, the masses would be making the revolution already—but there is a considerable degree of receptivity to armed struggle.

"We have always acted in keeping with Che's idea of the need for change and the possibility of change. Today the masses are demanding change—and not just any change, but a change with guidance. It is no accident that the people, the Peronists, rejoiced over Allende's victory in Chile, because the people have antioligarchical feelings and anti-imperialist feelings which it is impossible to ignore. I don't mean they're clear about socialism and communism, because that is something else again.

"Argentina is sitting on a powder keg, and the southern tip of South America is a volcano about to erupt: Uruguay, Bolivia, and now Chile. This is no longer the time for retreat; the time has come for an advance in this area—a more organized advance with the lessons that have been learned. We are very optimistic about the future of the struggle in Argentina."

Questions to a Militant of the PRT-ERP by James Petras

By the time of this interview, in June 1971, the ERP had emerged as the most dynamic of the Argentine urban guerrilla organizations. In this interview, an ERP leader discusses the origins and development of the movement and the role of its political wing, the Revolutionary Workers' Party.

What are the origins of the PRT-ERP?

In the early 1960s a number of groups fused together—Fidelistas, sugar workers from the North of Argentina and a Trotskyist group led by Moreno.[1] In 1968 and 1969, a number of groups—including Moreno —split off as we oriented our cadres toward armed struggle. We rejected the rural guerrilla strategy: the war is where the masses are and Argentina is mostly urban. It is false to dichotomize between the city and the country. We formed the PRT as a party of cadres; the ERP is the army of the masses. In 1970, we decided to form this army as an anti-imperialist group. We have drawn on the experiences of Vietnam in forming an army of the people; an insurrection in the Russian style is not possible. Our process is a prolonged war. The insurrection in the Dominican Republic and the *Cordobazo* show that spontaneous insurrections are not capable of winning.

What is the relation between the Party (PRT) *and the Army* (ERP)?

The Party contains the best cadres of the working class. The Army, based on the great combativeness of the masses, is an intermediate organization which links the masses to the Party. The Army is only one of many organizations that link the Party to the masses. The Army is necessary because of the prolonged nature of the struggle. The Party directs the ERP. The PRT always has a majority in the leadership of the ERP. As of now there are no differences in the membership and politics of the PRT-ERP.

New Left Review, January–February 1972, pp. 51–55. Reprinted with the permission of *New Left Review.*

1 Manuel Moreno was the person most associated with the antiguerrilla line in the PRT. He split before the 1970 conference that endorsed armed struggle, and has since become a leading spokesperson for his position in the Fourth (Trotskyist) International. In 1973, he and some other dissidents joined to form the *Partido Socialista Argentino,* which is now the official Trotskyist party in Argentina and is quite anti-ERP and antiguerrilla.

What events shaped the development of the PRT-ERP?
Onganía's dictatorship put an end to legal struggle, the trade unions
were intervened. The PRT had some influence in the trade union
movement and led some of the mobilizations of the sugar workers in
Tucumán. The *Tucumanos* asked for arms—we were not prepared at
the time. The guerrillas are a result of pressure of the masses; to give a
violent response to a military dictatorship.

What is the tactical orientation of the PRT-ERP?
We are based in industrial centers of the interior: Córdoba, Rosario,
Tucumán, because the conflict between the working class is more intense and the level of class consciousness is higher than in Buenos Aires,
which is most underdeveloped politically.

How is the PRT-ERP *evolving?*
Few old leaders remain. Many new cadres have been incorporated.
Many contacts with the masses. We have a crisis of growth. More people want to join than can be absorbed. We want to avoid populist
deviations, adventurist militarism. We want control of the military
cadre. In one year, we have tripled our membership.

What events have helped your growth?
The second *Cordobazo* (March 1971) was a qualitative leap. It was
organized and not spontaneous. People took over the *barrios* and put
up barricades. We disarmed the police, contributed to the defense of
the *barrios,* and distributed food from supermarkets.

*Some "leftist" groups have criticized your food distribution activity as
paternalistic.*
It is not paternalistic: we recruit cadres. In each *barrio* there are
comités de resistencia; there are neighborhood committees to distribute
food. The distribution of food is well received in the *barrios.* Workers
and taxi drivers cooperate. When we stop a meat truck now, we don't
have to pull out a gun—we tell the driver who we are and he only
asks "What *barrio* this week?"

How do you explain the growth of the ERP?
The ERP grows as the class struggle grows. It offers the masses an op-
tion—an alternative to Peronism. Our armed action receives publicity
from the bourgeois press. The dictatorship closes legal channels. Our
violence is linked to the masses—that causes us to grow. The so-called

insurrectional groups are politically and militarily incapable of opposing the government. The other left groups are in disintegration. There are three alternatives to the dictatorship: the bourgeois "Hour of the People" (a coalition of Peronist, Radical, and Liberal electoral parties); the reformist "Encounter of the Argentines," directed by the Communist Party; and the guerrilla alternative—the ERP. The left will choose one of these alternatives. The ERP is inserted in the working class—it orients the war toward working-class struggle.

What type of problems have you faced?
Lack of political material; decline in theoretical work, lack of analysis. However, these weaknesses are not due to a militarist approach. Since February 1971, we have begun to raise the quality of our political work. At first we were not lined up with the trade unions. Then we began to work in Fiat and other industries—now we are with the working class. With students we are discussing how to work with intermediary groups.

What are the politics of the PRT-ERP?
The ERP is a national liberation organization that struggles for the people. The PRT is based on the working class and fights for socialism. There is a difference in emphasis.

How do you view the guerrilla action within the revolutionary struggle?
The action of the guerrilla is linked to the masses; we participated in the barricade fighting in the *Cordobazo*. The political struggle reaches its highest point in arms. The guerrilla struggle is thus political. There are two types of activity: organized action, linked *indirectly* to the masses by its content—bank assaults; action linked to the masses through participation in their struggles—the case of Sylvester. This latter is more effective and squares with the level of mass awareness. Action against the police is not our line. Torturers are something else. . . . Military action is not the only form of struggle; there is trade union action; the struggle is multiple—it depends on the masses.

How do you conceive the revolution in Argentina?
Argentina is capitalist and semicolonial. The bourgeoisie is a junior partner of U.S. imperialism—there is no "national" bourgeoisie to promote independent capitalist development; the fight is for socialism.

The bourgeoisie cannot lead the revolution—only the working class can make the revolution. The Revolution must be worker and popular (*obrero y popular*)—"popular" means that it embraces petit bourgeois employees and students. There can be no "intermediary stage" and no participation of the bourgeoisie—the anti-imperialist struggle must be under working-class leadership. For our prolonged war, an army is needed, located not in rural areas, as in China, but in the cities, especially those of the interior. The insurrection will occur at the end of the process, with the disintegration of the army. The struggle will build up from small to big battles and be made up of thousands of conflicts and clashes.

What is the political situation today in Argentina?
Polarization is becoming acute. Peronism as an ideology is losing prestige, the workers in Córdoba are abandoning the Peronist leaders. The electoral agreements between the "Hour of the People" and Lanusse are means of avoiding *Cordobazos* and preventing the people from joining the guerrillas.

How do you view the trade union struggle in Argentina?
The trade union movement is mainly Peronist—it has evolved from state sponsorship (under Perón) to resistance directed by the bureaucrats. The trade unions have a limited role in the struggle of the masses —they are not an instrument of revolution, but reach the broadest mass of workers. The Party is the instrument of revolution. The PRT is only the embryo of the Revolutionary Party. Against the trade union bureaucracy, we support the formation of rank and file committees (*comités de base*). We hope that the Fiat unions become the basis for a new national labor union. We have political, not organizational links with the revolutionary class unions (*sindicatos clasistas*).

How do you view the Peronist movement?
It is an alliance of three classes: the bourgeoisie, the petite bourgeoisie and the working class. Ideologically, its politics are national-capitalist. The Peronist guerrillas, FAR, FAP, and Montoneros, are the popular sectors of the movement. The political apparatus is petit bourgeois. As the class struggle intensifies, Peronism will divide. Perón is a centrist: between the bourgeois and proletarian sectors of the movement. The revolution in Argentina will be made with Peronist workers, but

the leadership will not be Peronist but Socialist. The mass of workers will get rid of the bourgeois Peronists. We do not have a sectarian position toward Perón: the PRT carries on an ideological struggle with Peronism; the ERP does not engage in ideological debates with Peronists—some are in the ERP.

How do you view the other guerrilla groups (the FAR, FAP, FAL, and Montoneros)?
Despite ideological differences, we maintain fraternal relations. We are all embryos of any army of the people. When we liberated political prisoners we freed four ERP members and one Montonera.

What political ideas have influenced the PRT-ERP?
The PRT is primarily influenced by Marx and Lenin. Trotsky's works on Permanent Revolution and the Soviet Bureaucracy have also been influential; and we defend his political role in the Russian Revolution. Also Mao and Giap's work on the idea of a party-army. From Che, two basic lessons: first, all objective conditions need not be given to begin armed struggle; second, there is a need to create the New Man in the course of the struggle for socialism.

Is guerrilla struggle compatible with Leninism?
We base ourselves on Lenin's theory of the Party; armed struggles are compatible with the Leninist party. What is central is the construction of the party of the working class directed by Leninists. Lenin's criticism was directed against terrorism—action dissociated from the masses. We work to make the masses conscious, to mark a road for the masses. The guerrillas do not distract the masses—they show a method of struggle that raises consciousness more effectively than does distributing leaflets. The guerrillas are not a substitute, but a stimulator of the masses. The working class feels that the guerrillas support its actions.

How do you evaluate the revolutionary experiences in Russia, China, and Cuba?
In the Soviet Union, the revolution occurred in a backward country—these conditions produced Stalinism. In China, you have a workers' party with a peasant base that is in the process of continuous change. Cuba is the best product of revolution; in content it is closer to socialist man.

How do you evaluate the new experiences in Peru, Chile, and Bolivia?
Each is different. In Peru you have a nationalist bourgeois government
which is very lucid—more so than the bourgeoisie. But you cannot end
imperialism while the bourgeois heads the revolution. The Peruvian
experience influences some Argentinian military officers but not the
Argentinian people.

In Bolivia you have a Bonapartist regime in special conditions.[2] The
Bolivian working class is the most conscious in Latin America. What
they lack is a Party. The trade unions are combative and antibourgeois,
but they are no substitute for a Party. The Bonapartist regime is
shaky—the class struggle will lead to civil war. Regarding Chile, we
maintain fraternal relations and support the position of the MIR.

How do you view the position of the United States in Latin America?
The United States has pushed Brazilian development and tried to
push Argentinian—but has failed. The United States exercises hegemony in twenty countries and denationalizes industries. We do not
discount U.S. military intervention directly or through the Argentinian
or Brazilian armies. Defeat and internal problems are forcing the
United States out of Vietnam, in order to strengthen its position in
Latin America. The United States will intervene—it will not allow
a revolution in Argentina.

How do you view the revolutionary process in Latin America?
Two or three Vietnams . . . acute crisis in general, of which the
bourgeois reformists cannot take advantage . . . socialist revolution
is on the agenda . . . imperialism is taking a tactical retreat . . . in
some countries there are guerrillas, in others, movements of masses,
as in Bolivia and Chile . . . the confrontation will take place against
imperialism and the national bourgeoisie, which is counterrevolutionary. The situation is complex: the routes to revolution are different
in different countries. Revolution is in the Southern Cone [of S.
America—J.P.]. Between 1960 and 1967, Venezuela and Colombia
were in the vanguard—now the vanguard is the working class of the
Southern Cone. Uruguay and the Tupamaros, Argentina and the ERP,
the Chilean government and the MIR, Bolivia and the Popular As-

2 This answer was, of course, made before the counterrevolutionary coup in Bolivia
of September 1971.

sembly, are the key countries for leadership in the revolutionary struggle.

How do you view the possibilities of the United States and the national bourgeoisie imposing a Brazilian-type system in Argentina?

In Argentina, the bourgeoisie has no viable programme. To impose a Brazilian-type solution in Argentina will lead to a civil war. The Brazilian experience is possible in Argentina only after defeat in a civil war.

The Argentine Guerrillas Speak

This interview is with five survivors of the Trelew massacre of August 22, 1972, in which sixteen urban guerrillas were murdered by the regime. Interviewed are: Mario Roberto Santucho (ERP); Fernando Vaca Narvaja (Montoneros); Marcos Osatinsky (FAR); Roberto Jorge Quieto (FAR); and Domingo Menna (ERP).

In the cold afternoon of what would be the most disturbed Argentine winter in recent years, seven men were squeezed into an automobile traveling down a dusty highway in Patagonia. One of them wore an army officer's uniform. It was August 15th.

While this rich land that stretches from the subtropics to the frozen seas of the extreme south of America continues ensnared in the comings and goings of the supposed process of "institutionalization," a fistful of men and women violently shook the gloomy structure of the military dictatorship that holds power.

Twenty-five militants of three armed revolutionary groups acting jointly for the first time, escaped that day from Rawson Prison, located in Argentina and considered to be a maximum security prison.

The guerrillas—who with the collaboration of a small support group had escaped from the penal institution by overcoming the guard—captured the airport in the nearby city of Trelew moments later.

Along with four comrades from auxiliary command number six of the Rawson war prisoners—as they define themselves—in military uniforms taken from their jailers, they took over an Austral Airlines plane and reached Chile.

Unable to board the same plane because of last-minute difficulties, nineteen of the revolutionaries who escaped from Rawson were left behind. After maintaining the airport under their control for five hours, they surrendered to the repressive forces, which had promised to respect their lives. One week later, in savage revenge, the recaptured guerrillas were coldly shot in Trelew air-naval base by order of the Joint Commands of the Armed Forces. Sixteen of them were added

Tricontinental Bulletin (Havana, Cuba), no. 80 (November 1972), pp. 34–48.

to the already long list of victims of the tyranny, among them four women. Only three, thought to be dead, were miraculously saved.

The other ten protagonists of the tough blow against the regime of General Alejandro Lanusse received political asylum in Chile and made the trip to Havana. They are Mario Roberto Santucho, Domingo Menna, Enrique Gorriarán, Alejandro Ferreyra, and Víctor Fernández Palmeiro, of the People's Revolutionary Army; Fernando Vaca Narvaja, of the Montoneros organization, and Marcos Osatinsky, Roberto Jorge Quieto, Ana Dora Wiesen, and Carlos Goldenberg, of the Revolutionary Armed Forces.

Crisis with No Exit

Santucho:[1] In 1966, in the face of the rise of the mass movement, the military party intervened directly, with the Onganía attack and the establishment of a dictatorship with a fascist retinue. It used civil war methods to stop the mass movement, which had succeeded momentarily due to an energetic resistance to the military dictatorship in its first months; and it detoured to a certain extent the path that the broad mass struggle would take through its application of the "famous" plan for the modernization of the capitalist structure of Argentina.

Capitalism in Argentina is living in a structural crisis and must be modernized because it has a very uneven development. In order to achieve a growth in gross production, a capitalization of fundamental sectors of industry, and the expansion of certain branches of production that are essential in a capitalist country today—as well as a rhythm of production that provides some stability—the "modernization" plan was developed. It was based on an accumulation to be extracted from the superexploitation of the working class and the people.

At the same time that the exploitation of the working class sharpened, there also occurred the expropriation of sectors of the small and middle bourgeoisie that still had some resources.

Despite the fact that the militarists achieved some immediate success with the repression, they did not advance economically and soon,

---

[1] Mario Roberto Santucho is a public accountant, the secretary-general of the Revolutionary Workers' Party (PRT), founded June 28, 1970, and a member of the Executive of the People's Revolutionary Army (ERP). He began his revolutionary life while he was studying at the university. His wife, Ana María Villarreal, was assassinated at the air and naval base of Trelew.

in a couple of years, found themselves faced with a redoubled mass resistance, which, in these years of repression, has gathered strength and hatred and is preparing for a confrontation with the repression, with the understanding that the methods of struggle today have to change.

An ideological revolutionary process is taking place, a raising of consciousness that began to express itself in the big mobilizations of 1969, such as the Córdoba action. This was a new type of mass struggle, headed by the students and working class, which extended to big cities like Rosario and Tucumán as well as Córdoba and a dozen other smaller cities where the entire population took to the streets.

The army intervened, trying to silence the popular protest; violent confrontations took place in the streets, resulting in dozens of dead, and from these experiences the armed organizations that now exist sprang or became stronger.

The vanguard has affirmed the belief that the repression led by the military party must be answered in part with the uprising and mobilization of all the people, and in part with the establishment of functioning guerrilla units, which is the most efficient method of harassing and striking the enemy and of developing in homogenous form a process of revolutionary war.

Thus, in the years 1969 and 1970, the military dictatorship found that it had not succeeded in solving any of the economic problems and that, in addition, the reaction of the masses prevented it from testing any coherent plan of stabilization. Faced with the impossibility of detaining popular mobilizations and the strengthening of guerrilla units, the bourgeoisie now tried to deceive and confuse with its plan of "institutionalization" and its Great National Accord (GAN).

Vaca Narvaja:[2] The possibility of a "Brazilian" solution exists in Argentina, but at the present level it is clear that there will be no easy exits for the bourgeoisie and imperialism. This is because the social situation in Brazil is different from ours, although the objective, the structure, and the action of both dictatorships are the same in the end.

[2] Fernando Vaca Narvaja is 24 years old, and a member of the Montoneros. He joined the revolutionary struggle through the student movement, and in 1968 was a member of the workers' sector, as a political cadre. After April 1970, he went into the underground struggle. His wife Susana Lesgart, 23 years old, was one of the victims of the Trelew massacre.

We do not forget that the so-called Argentine revolution included in its projection ten to fifteen years under Onganía. It was unable to succeed because of the advance of the people's struggles, because of that qualitative change that took place in the actions of the masses with the rise and the strengthening of armed detachments which continue placing obstacles and barriers in the path of the enemy's political projects.

A "Brazilian" regime would surprise no one at this time, nor would a populist exit. But neither of the two roads offer perspectives for a military dictatorship that can't even provide certain immediate solutions to popular demands. The level of consciousness of the Argentine masses prevents the regime's projects from being concretized.

The bourgeoisie is surprised and frightened by the development of a revolutionary process it is unable to halt. Its fear is evidenced in its reactions. The Trelew massacre indicates this.

Osatinsky:[3] For them, Brazil is an example of the "stability" that the big monopolies need, but it is evident that in Argentina there are no possibilities for achieving it. This is because while there may be partial defeats, the Argentine people, the working class, have learned a great deal and have political answers, framed within the development of the revolutionary war.

Confronting the Army

Santucho: The Argentine army—and by that we mean all the armed forces—is one of the most homogenous in Latin America today. There isn't a single current within it that, even in a distorted way, can reflect mass aspirations.

All the tendencies that exist within the army are reactionary. There are no honorable sectors nor any more or less organized sectors sensitive in any degree to the mass struggle and able to contribute to the advance of the people's camp. This does not exclude the fact that there are officers who, individually, are of this persuasion and that a certain permeability exists among the lower officers.

What must be pointed out is that, if the army is homogenous as far as its leadership cadres are concerned, its Achilles heel is obligatory

3 Marcos Osatinsky is 38 years old. He was employed in a private enterprise. A member of the FAR from its founding, his revolutionary activities began in 1951. He participated in all the FAR's revolutionary actions.

military service. Its soldiers are of the people, workers, peasants, students.

Our task, the center of revolutionary activity against the enemy force, is to influence these sectors politically and win them over. Principally the soldiers, without leaving aside the officers, the young officers. But we can place no hope that currents or tendencies among the officers (and even less among the colonels) can contribute to our struggle.

Osatinsky: The base of this policy is the development of the revolutionary war. And only on the basis of armed confrontation with the Armed Forces (there are signs, minimum experiences that indicate this) is it probable that these isolated elements which are evident within the army today are going to take a positive attitude with respect to our political-military line.

Vaca Narvaja: Only in a few exceptional cases—as also and especially occurred in Brazil—can it happen that, within the bosom of the army, some officer arises and assumes the interest of the working class and the revolutionary camp.

But politically, we characterize the Argentine army as a military party, because it has very homogenous characteristics that differentiate it from other Latin American armies, except that of Brazil, which is a direct representative of the bourgeoisie and imperialism.

Nevertheless, the army is subject to the same interbourgeois contradictions as the rest of the ruling class, and suffers them in its own bosom. This is evident in the development of the whole Argentine process, in the various-colored *golpes* [coups]—one more gorilla-like, the other more populist and with special characteristics, but never abandoning the capitalist structures.

Because of this, we are aware that the best policy is to develop the revolutionary war; confront the army, strike at it, provoke contradictions within the military aspect of its structure, tied to the obligatory military service which, as comrade Santucho said, does not allow it to develop its effectiveness.

So that when we say that our labor is to wipe out this army, we don't mean that we are going to kill the very last of the 250,000 troops it has, but rather that, within this policy of armed confrontation, there is also the political confrontation, the sharpening of contradictions.

The Argentine army has one peculiarity: its concept of institution. This, finally, is its essence, its own life as an army, which apart from class interests, regroups its ranks against any eventuality.

Thus, except in extraordinary cases, we don't grant it any possibility of joining the revolutionary camp. Its position is clearly defined: to confront the people and repress popular demonstrations through its antiguerrilla methods.

Quieto:[4] From 1956 on, the Argentine army has been characterized by its efforts at political indoctrination, exemplified by the training of officers in the military schools of the Panama Canal Zone and in the United States, by the sending of missions to Vietnam, as it did last year, and by the selecting of certain American-oriented professors and programs for military colleges and the Higher War School.

From the Germanophile tradition that the Argentine army had at its beginning, it has moved to Yankophile influence at its end. And beyond this, it is completed with the "institution" of the highest grade in the ranks of the Armed Forces, namely that of being president or vice president of a company, as in the United States.

In the directories of foreign companies in Argentina, one finds the names of high officers of the armed forces. Bureaucrats, ministers, presidents, commanders-in-chief are there. That is, they are all employed by these monopolies.

As an organized or important sector, we know of no existing group of progressive military. We think there may be some officers who sympathize with the Peruvian phenomenon, but Argentina does not have a socioeconomic structure that makes possible events and situations such as those in Peru. And these officers have no strength or organizational force within the Argentine armed forces.

One Single People's Army

Vaca Narvaja: Our strategic objective is to attain a socialist government in Argentina. To do this, we must form a people's army that represents the interests of the working class, the only vanguard that can lead our revolutionary process.

If our organization speaks of a "national" socialism, it is very clear—

[4] Roberto Jorge Quieto is a 34-year-old lawyer and leader of the Revolutionary Armed Forces (FAR). He has been a member of FAR since 1967, and of the student movement since 1967. He participated in the seizure of Garin in 1970.

as are the other organizations—that socialism is one. Our duty is to expel the reformist currents within the Peronist movement and constitute a solid, clear vanguard, with a defined strategy of power. We are agreed on objectives and strategy with the other revolutionary organizations that are currently developing in Argentina.

Quieto: In the course of the struggle, we will see, as we have up to now, the unification of both armed and nonarmed organizations around the proposal of revolutionary war. In this way there will be developed one sole organization that carries forward both the armed and the nonarmed struggle.

We want all the revolutionary forces to unite because we have common objectives and a common enemy to defeat. But everyone knows that this task of unification is not simple, that it presents difficulties because of long-range visions and interpretations of reality and the different methods utilized to transfer this reality.

However, the process of dispersion of revolutionary forces is now being reversed; and we have in the past few years begun to advance along the road of unification, which is proposed not as something to be resolved immediately but rather as an objective to be achieved.

Various organizations have already incorporated into their slogans the text, "For the unity of armed organizations." As a consequence, specific organizational measures that contribute to achieving this objective are being established. In some cases, they have advanced considerably, in others less so, but we are moving in this direction. From it will come a single people's army.

Osatinsky: The revolution our country needs has to be socialist and nationalist, it must liberate the country from its economic dependence on imperialism, from its monopolistic dependence, and must break with the capitalist structure.

Santucho: We are aware of the responsibility of revolutionaries in this critical situation, and that is why we have inscribed as a fundamental point in our program the unity of the armed organizations and the necessity of joining the people's sectors, which embrace a very broad spectrum in Argentina.

This unity must revolve around the proletariat, but it includes other very important sectors, principally of the urban bourgeoisie and of the poor peasantry, which have special political expressions.

The PRT and the ERP are open to important sectors of Peronism, to the Communist Party of Argentina (PCA), to the National Encounter of Argentines (which is a group headed by the PCA), and to other people's sectors. The aim must be to unite all the popular forces in the process of revolutionary war.

It is necessary to continue the dedicated development of urban guerrilla movements, to open rural fronts and incorporate into the working-class and people's struggles, in a massive form, more organized types of revolutionary violence.

But it is also necessary to include in this overall process the struggle for democratic rights. That is, it is necessary to embrace, in a coordinated manner, armed and nonarmed forms of struggle. For the broadest development of the revolutionary struggle in Argentina, the key point is the effectiveness of the armed organizations, of the workers' vanguard, of the student vanguard, and of the most dynamic sectors of the working class and the Argentine people.

At this time, we have exceptional opportunities such as we have never before had in all the recent history of the Argentine people's struggle. It is imperative that we take advantage of them.

Menna:[5] The three organizations are very clear that GAN, which Lanusse and his clique seek to use, is a farce. It is an accord between bourgeois sectors to deceive the masses one time more and to brake the advance of the revolutionary process. This is GAN's real objective.

To carry it out, the dictatorship uses two methods. On the one hand, it tries to create alliances with bourgeois groups, naturally with the guarantee of the monopolies, those who grant a certain "legality"; on the other hand, it engages in ferocious selective repression against the revolutionary sectors, especially the guerrilla organizations, and the mass organizations linked to armed groups in some way.

Very clear and recent examples of this latter approach are the massacre at Trelew, the assault by the army on the office of the Justice Party where three of our companions were being honored before their burial, and the seizure of the magazine *Primera Plana*.

Quieto: It is certain, according to the interpretation of FAR and

---

5 Domingo Menna is 25 years old, a medical student, and a member of the Executive Committee of the PRT and the ERP. He began his revolutionary struggle at the end of 1965 as student leader at the University of Córdoba.

the Montoneros, that one of the pillars of this so-called institution-alization or GAN was to achieve Peronist participation in these elections because this is a very important political phenomenon in Argentina, but to do so on a conditioned basis.

That is, they pursued the objective that Peronism should approve the electoral process by participating positively, neither abstaining nor casting blank ballots as on other occasions, but on the basis of an accord with the armed forces which would include candidates and programs.

At no time did the dictatorship promise or concretize the possibility of an authentically democratic electoral process that would respect the will of the majority of the Argentine people. For that reason, it is necessary to emphasize that the Peronist armed organizations do not reject out of hand the possibility of participating in the electoral process; we do not automatically decree revolutionary abstention from the elections.

What we always demand is that the elections be held without proscriptions of any kind and that the regime release all political and trade union prisoners; moreover, as Peronists, we propose both a specific program of government measures and Perón's candidacy for president.

But it happens that this is not a clean electoral process, as we said before. It is proscriptive, conditional, and definitely a farce, a maneuver to keep the Argentine people subjected and exploited.

Santucho: GAN emerged as a new form of bourgeois unity to deceive the masses, distract them, confuse them, prevent the development of the revolutionary war which endangers capitalism.

The bourgeois parties, together with the military, offer a new perspective, an exit that can be electoral. This exit is first of all directed against the guerrilla movement, seeks to isolate it, separate it from the mass movement.

It can be inferred from the declarations of López Aufranc,[6] for example, that it is necessary to separate the just demands of the people from subversion. Or those of Uriburu, the governor whom ex-President Levingston ordered to Córdoba [a prelude to the fall of the gov-

[6] The reference is to General Alcides López Aufranc, known for his hard line against the guerrillas.

ernment], that the communist viper sheltered in the bosom of the masses had to be wiped out. This is GAN's objective.

We consider that any type of concession, far from stabilizing capitalism, will be nothing more than a new base for mobilization of the masses in the legal and semilegal area. For this reason, we are not concerned with this bourgeois maneuver since whatever the way out may be for the present group—an increase in repression or a populist opening that tries to deceive the masses—we revolutionaries have answers.

What we must not do is to play the enemy's game. He wants us to appear to be centering the axis of our struggle on the rejection of elections. But this is not our policy.

We are prepared to utilize the legal concessions that the enemy finds himself forced to make, and to do this we are preparing and organizing ourselves in new forms that have been incorporated into mass work. Our perspective is the broadening of the front of revolutionary groupings, the organization of broader sectors of the people, aware that in the long or the short run a generalization of armed struggle and violent mass mobilization will be proposed.

One Great Homeland

Vaca Narvaja: The Argentine liberation process is only going to take place within the Latin American framework; the experience that is now being developed in Cuba and other Latin American countries, the experience of Che and even of the guerrillas in Salta, now serve to make Argentines understand that the framework within which the process of liberation unfolds in other Latin American countries is essentially the same as in ours.

Menna: Our principal effort, which is to fulfill our own revolutionary process, is in no way opposed to our internationalist convictions, but rather the opposite is true.

Osatinsky: We have seen in practical experience, both in Chile where we had to land after seizing the plane, as well as here, that the solidarity and proletarian internationalism that arose was the principal factor in our reaching Cuba.

To a great extent, the Tupamaros have helped us break with certain rigid concepts as far as the breadth of political-military action is concerned. They have helped us both with their example and with their struggle. For us, they are the inventors of the people's prison, and this has become one of the many tasks of our comrades.

We are inspired by the message and example of Che who, as Fidel Castro said, is the highest exponent of Latin American revolutionaries.

Ours is a national and simultaneously a Latin American process. We must give our efforts to its development. We do not know what the future will be. But we have a long historic tradition, that of the Army of the Andes, of San Martín, O'Higgins, Bolívar. There is no contradiction between national struggles and the struggle of all Latin America.

Quieto: We consider Latin America to be a continental unit with not only a common geography, but a common history as well, the same language, the same enemy, and similar characteristics with respect to the type of exploitation the people have to suffer.

On the road of struggle, the approximation of the revolutionary movements of different Latin American countries will increase constantly. Nevertheless, we believe that each country, or at least ours, has its own characteristics and that at this moment and for some time ahead, our revolutionary process will have to be contained within what is Argentina as a country.

Our immediate objective is to effect the change, to take power in Argentina. This is our present political proposal, although of course we see how necessary and desirable it is that this revolutionary process advance in all of Latin America.

Santucho: The Latin American revolution is one process, as Che Guevara understood. For this reason, our ultimate goal must be to unify all Latin American revolutionary organizations.

Urban Guerrilla Organizations

ERP   *Ejército Revolucionario del Pueblo;* People's Revolutionary Army
Formally organized as an armed branch of the PRT (*Partido Revolucionario de los Trabajadores;* Workers Revolutionary Party) on June 28, 1970 at the party's Fifth Congress, but had informally initiated armed actions earlier; the Trotskyist main-line PRT-ERP maintains an intransigent position toward Peronism and thus the ERP "22 de Agosto" faction split off on May 21, 1973 over the issue of support for the Cámpora presidential candidacy; the most active of the urban guerrilla groups since its inception.

FAL   *Fuerzas Armadas de Liberación;* Liberation Armed Forces
Early Marxist-Leninist organization; formed in 1962, but remained quiescent until early 1970; still urban-based, FAL's long-range strategy points toward combined urban-rural fronts within the context of a continental upheaval.

FAR   *Fuerzas Armadas Revolucionarias;* Revolutionary Armed Forces
Originated in efforts to internationalize Che Guevara's 1967 Bolivian *foco;* failed to integrate with the Bolivian movement and submerged until the Garín seizure in 1970; currently regards itself as Marxist-Leninist-Peronist with an emphasis on the latter.

FAP   *Fuerzas Armadas Peronistas;* Peronist Armed Forces
Originally formed as a rural guerrilla *foco,* but was reconstituted in the urban sector after the defeat of the "October 17" detachment at Taco

Ralo in 1968; the largest of the Peronist organizations, with close ties to the Montoneros; the FAP's strategic objective is a Peronist renaissance.

Montoneros — Organized in 1968 by Christian, Peronist, and ex-rightist elements; emerged publicly with the kidnap, trial, and execution of ex-president Pedro Aramburu; has recently gravitated toward the left wing of Peronism, as witnessed by a merger with the FAR in October 1973.

Other Organizations

MRA — *Movimiento Revolucionario Argentino;* Argentine Revolutionary Movement

APL — *Acción Peronista de Liberación;* Peronist Liberation Action

MRP — *Movimiento Revolucionario del Pueblo;* People's Revolutionary Movement

ENR — *Ejército Revolucionario Nacional;* National Revolutionary Army

GEL — *Guerrilla del Ejército Libertador;* Liberation Army Guerrilla

EGP — *Ejército Guerrillero del Pueblo;* People's Guerrilla Army

CARP — *Comando de Acción Revolucionaria Popular;* Revolutionary Popular Action Command

Comandos Descamisados — Shirtless Commandos

Bibliography

Alexander, Robert   *The Communist Party of Venezuela*. Palo Alto: Hoover
                           Institution, 1969.

Alexander, Robert   *The Perón Era*. New York: Columbia University Press,
                           1951.

American Committee   *Terror in Brazil: A Dossier*. New York: American Com-
for Information on   mittee for Information on Brazil, April 1970.
Brazil

Arraes, Miguel   *Brazil: The People and the Power*. Translated by Lance-
                           lot Sheppard. Harmondsworth, England: Pelican, 1972.

Barnet, Richard   *Intervention and Revolution: The United States in the
                           Third World*. New York: World, 1968.

Bayo, Alberto   *150 Questions to a Guerrilla*. Boulder, Colorado: Panther
                           Publications, 1963.

Béjar, Héctor   *Peru 1965: Notes on a Guerrilla Experience*. Translated
                           by William Rose. New York: Monthly Review, 1970.

Blackburn, Robin, ed.   *Strategy for Revolution: Essays on Latin America by
                           Régis Debray*. New York: Monthly Review, 1970.

Blanco, Hugo   *Land or Death*. New York: Pathfinder, 1972.

Blanksten, George   *Perón's Argentina*. Chicago: University of Chicago Press,
                           1953.

Caso, Antonio   *Los Subversivos*. Havana: Casa de las Americas, 1973.

Committee of Re-   *Brazil: Who Pulls the Strings?* Chicago: Committee of
turned Volunteers,   Returned Volunteers, 1973.
eds.

Costa, Omar   *Los Tupamaros*. México, D.F.: Colección Ancho Mundo,
                           1971.

Costa-Gavras and   *State of Siege*. Screenplay translated by Brooke Leveque;
Franco Solinas   documents translated by Raymond Rosenthal. New
                           York: Ballantine, 1973.

Daniels, Ed	"From Mercantilism to Imperialism: The Argentine Case," Part 2. *North American Congress on Latin America,* October 1970, pp. 1–12.
Debray, Régis	*Revolution in the Revolution?* Translated by Bobbye Ortiz. New York: Grove Press, 1967.
Della Cava, Ralph	"Torture in Brazil." *Commonweal,* 24 April 1970, pp. 135–141.
Dueñas Ruiz, Oscar and Mirna Rugnon de Dueñas	*Tupamaros, libertad o muerte.* Bogotá, Colombia: Ediciones Mundo Andino, 1971.
Finch, H. M. J.	"Three Perspectives on the Crisis in Uruguay." *Journal of Latin American Studies,* vol. 3, part 2 (November 1971), pp. 173–190.
Fortuny, José M.	"Guatemala: The Political Situation and Revolutionary Politics." *World Marxist Review,* February 1967, pp. 57–58.
Gadea, Hilda	*Ernesto: A Memoir of Che Guevara.* Garden City, New York: Doubleday, 1972.
Galeano, Eduardo	"Brazil and Uruguay: Euphoria and Agony." *Monthly Review,* February 1972, pp. 25–43.
Galeano, Eduardo	"The De-Nationalization of Brazilian Industry." *Monthly Review,* December 1969, pp. 11–30.
Galeano, Eduardo	*Guatemala: Occupied Country.* Translated by Cedric Belfrage. New York: *Monthly Review,* 1969.
Galeano, Eduardo	"The New Frontiers." *Monthly Review,* December 1968, pp. 19–29.
Gall, Norman	"Santo Domingo: The Politics of Terror." *New York Review of Books,* 22 July 1971, pp. 15–19.
Gall, Norman	"Slaughter in Guatemala," *New York Review of Books,* 20 May 1971, pp. 13–17.
Gilio, María Esther	*The Tupamaro Guerrillas.* Translated by Anne Edmondson. New York: Saturday Review Press, 1972.
Gott, Richard	*Guerrilla Movements in Latin America.* Garden City, New York: Doubleday, 1971.

BIBLIOGRAPHY   408

Guevara, Che	*Guerrilla Warfare.* Translated by J. P. Morray. New York: Vintage, 1961.
Guevara, Che	"Instructions for Cadres Assigned to Urban Work," *Tricontinental Bulletin,* no. 8 (September–October 1968), pp. 94–96.
Guevara, Che	*Reminiscences of the Cuban Revolutionary War.* Translated by Victoria Ortiz. New York: Monthly Review, 1968.
Guillén, Abraham	*Philosophy of the Urban Guerrilla.* Translated and edited by Donald C. Hodges. New York: William Morrow, 1973.
Gutiérrez, Carlos María	*The Dominican Republic: Rebellion and Repression.* New York: Monthly Review, 1972.
Horowitz, David	*The Free World Colossus.* Rev. ed. New York: Hill and Wang, 1971.
Horowitz, Irving Louis, ed.	*The Rise and Fall of Project Camelot.* Cambridge, Mass.: M.I.T. Press, 1967.
Huberman, Leo and Paul Sweezy, eds.	*Régis Debray and the Latin American Revolution.* New York: Monthly Review, 1968.
Ianni, Octavio	*Crisis in Brazil.* Translated by Phyllis B. Eveleth. New York: Columbia University Press, 1970.
Imaz, José Luis de	*Los Que Mandan.* Translated by Carlos A. Astiz. Albany, New York: State University of New York Press, 1970.
James, Daniel, ed.	*The Complete Bolivian Diary of Che Guevara and Other Captured Documents.* New York: Stein and Day, 1969.
Johnson, Kenneth	*Argentina's Mosaic of Discord, 1966–1968.* Washington, D.C.: Institute for Comparative Study of Political Systems, 1969.
Kadt, Emanuel de	*Catholic Radicals in Brazil.* London and New York: Oxford University Press, 1970.
Klare, Michael	*War Without End: America's Planning for the Next Vietnams.* New York: Alfred Knopf, 1972.
Lartéguy, Jean	*The Guerrillas.* Translated by Stanley Hochman. New York: New American Library, 1970.

Mader, Julius	*Who's Who in the CIA: A Biographical Reference Work on 3000 Officers of the Civil and Military Branches of the Secret Services of the USA in 120 Countries.* Berlin: Julius Mader, 1968.
Marighella, Carlos	*For the Liberation of Brazil.* Translated by John Butt and Rosemary Sheed. Harmondsworth, England: Penguin, 1971.
Marighella, Carlos	*Teoría y Acción Revolucionaria.* Cuernavaca, Mexico: Editorial Diogenes, 1971.
Marini, Mauro	"Brazilian Subimperialism." *Monthly Review,* February 1972, pp. 14–24.
Martínez Anzorena, G.	*Los Tupamaros.* Mendoza, Argentina: Editorial la Tecla, n.d.
Martz, John	*Acción Democrática.* Princeton: Princeton University Press, 1966.
Mayans, Ernesto, ed.	*Tupamaros, antología documental.* Cuernavaca, México: Centro Intercultural de Documentación, 1971.
Mercader, Antonio and Jorge de Vera	*Tupamaros: Estrategia y Acción.* Montevideo: Editorial Alfa, 1971.
Mercier Vega, Luis, ed.	*Guerrillas in Latin America.* New York: Frederick A. Praeger, 1969.
Moraes, Clodomir	"Peasant Leagues in Brazil." In *Agrarian Problems and Peasant Movements in Latin America,* edited by Rodolfo Stavenhagen, pp. 453–501. New York: Anchor, 1970.
Moreno, José	*Barrios in Arms: Revolution in Santo Domingo.* Pittsburgh: University of Pittsburgh Press, 1970.
Morales, Emilio	*Uturunco y las Guerrillas en la Argentina.* Montevideo: Editorial SEPE, 1964.
Moreira Alves, Marcio	*A Grain of Mustard Seed: The Awakening of the Brazilian Revolution.* Garden City, New York: Doubleday, 1973.
Movimiento de Liberación Nacional	*Actas Tupamaras.* Buenos Aires: Schapire, 1971.

Nuñez, Carlos	*Los Tupamaros: Vanguardia Armada en el Uruguay.* Montevideo: Ediciones Provincias Unidas, 1969.
Page, Joseph	*The Revolution that Never Was.* New York: Grossman, 1972.
Pendle, George	*Argentina.* 3rd ed. London and New York: Oxford University Press, 1965.
Pendle, George	*Uruguay.* 3rd ed. London and New York: Oxford University Press, 1963.
Petras, Betty and James Petras	"Ballots into Bullets: Epitaph for a Peaceful Revolution." *Ramparts,* November 1973, p. 21.
Potash, Robert	*The Army and Politics in Argentina, 1928–1945.* Palo Alto: Stanford University Press, 1969.
Quartim, João	*Dictatorship and Armed Struggle in Brazil.* Translated by David Fernbach. London: New Left Review, 1971.
Quartim, João	"Régis Debray and the Brazilian Revolution." *New Left Review,* January–February 1970, pp. 61–82.
Ransom, David	"The Berkeley Mafia and the Indonesian Massacre." *Ramparts,* October 1970, p. 24.
Reno, Philip	*The Ordeal of British Guiana.* New York: Monthly Review, 1964.
Roett, Riordan, ed.	*Brazil in the 1960's.* Nashville: Vanderbilt University Press, 1972.
Rojo, Ricardo	*My Friend Che.* Translated by Julian Casart. New York: Dial Press, 1968.
Rotcage, Lionel	"Going for a Ride with Brazil's Guerrilleros." *Atlas,* August 1970, pp. 51–53.
Scheer, Robert, ed.	*The Diary of Che Guevara.* New York: Bantam, 1968.
Schilling, Paulo	"Brazil: The Accelerated Sell Out." *Tricontinental,* no. 11 (March–April 1969), pp. 47–78.
Schneider, Ronald	*The Political System of Brazil: Emergence of a "Modernizing" Authoritarian Regime, 1964–1970.* New York: Columbia University Press, 1971.

Scobie, James

Argentina: A City and a Nation. London and New York: Oxford University Press, 1964.

Siekman, Philip

"When Executives Turned Revolutionaries." *Fortune*, September 1964, p. 147.

Skidmore, Thomas

Politics in Brazil. London and New York: Oxford University Press, 1967.

Snow, Peter

Political Forces in Argentina. Boston: Allyn and Bacon, 1971.

Solar, Daniel del

"Allende's Death: A Pentagon Checkmate." *New Times*, 3 October 1973, pp. 1–2.

Stepan, Alfred

The Military in Politics: Changing Patterns in Brazil. Princeton: Princeton University Press, 1971.

St. George, Andrew

"How the U.S. Got Che." *True*, April 1969, p. 29.

St. George, Andrew

"Watergate: The Cold War Comes Home." *Harpers*, November 1973, pp. 68–82.

Suárez, Carlos and Rubén Anaya Sarmiento

Los Tupamaros. México, D.F.: Editorial Extemporaneos, 1971.

Tavares, Flavio

"Pau de Arara," la Violencia Militar en el Brasil. México, D.F.: Siglo Veintiuno, 1972.

Taylor, Philip, Jr.

Government and Politics of Uruguay. New Orleans: Tulane Studies in Political Science, vol. 7, 1960.

United States Senate, Committee on Foreign Relations, Subcommittee on American Republic Affairs

Survey of the Alliance for Progress. April 29, 1969.

United States Senate, Committee on Foreign Relations, Subcommittee on Western Hemispheric Affairs

United States Policies and Programs in Brazil, May 4, 5, 11, 1971.

Weid, Jean Marc von der

Brazil: 1964 to Present. Montreal, Canada: Editions Latin America, 1972.

| Wolf, Eric and Joseph Jorgenson | "Anthropology on the Warpath in Thailand." *New York Review of Books,* 19 November 1970, pp. 26–35. |

Films

Introduction	*End of a Revolution?* (Brian Moses, 1970: Bolivia)
	FALN (Dawn Films, 1965: Venezuela)
	Fuera Yankee (1965: Dominican Republic)
	Girón (1972: Cuba)
	Golpeando en la Selva (Santiago Alvarez, 1970: Colombia)
	Hasta la Victoria Siempre (Santiago Alvarez, 1965: Bolivia)
	Historia de Una Batalla (Manuel Gómez, 1961: Cuba)
	Manuela (Humberto Solás, 1966: Cuba)
	Who Invited Us? (Alan Levin, 1970: Latin America)

Brazil	*Brazil: No Time for Tears* (Pedro Chaskel and Luis Alberto Sanz, 1971)
	Oz Fuzis (Ruy Guerra, 1963)
	Vidas Sêcas (Nelson Pereira dos Santos, 1963)

Uruguay	*El Problema de la Carne* (Mario Handler, 1968)
	State of Siege (Constantine Costa-Gavras, 1973)
	Tupamaros (Jan Lindqvist and MLN, 1972)

Argentina	*Alliance for Progress* (Julio Ludvena, 1972)
	La Hora de los Hornos (Fernando Solanas and Octavio Getino, 1968)
	La Paz (Anonymous, 1971)
	The Traitor (Grupo Cine de la Base, 1973)

Periodicals

The following publications were particularly useful in tracing recent developments in Latin America: *Brazilian Information Bulletin* (Berkeley), *Center for Information on Latin America* (Montreal), *Cristianismo y Revolución** (Buenos Aires), *The Economist* (London), *Economist Intelligence Unit* (London), *Foreign Broadcast Information Service* (Washington, D.C.), *Granma* (Havana), *Latin America* (London), *Marcha** (Montevideo), *Monthly Review* (New York), *New Left Review* (London), *New York Times,* *North American Congress on Latin America* (Berkeley and New York), *Punto Final** (Santiago), *Ramparts* (Berkeley), *Translations on Latin America* (Washington, D.C.), *Tricontinental* (Havana).

* No longer in publication.

Index